Multi–Core Computer Vision and Image Processing for Intelligent Applications

Mohan S.
Al Yamamah University, Saudi Arabia

Vani V.
Al Yamamah University, Saudi Arabia

A volume in the Advances in Computational Intelligence and Robotics (ACIR) Book Series

www.igi-global.com

Published in the United States of America by
  IGI Global
  Information Science Reference (an imprint of IGI Global)
  701 E. Chocolate Avenue
  Hershey PA 17033
  Tel: 717-533-8845
  Fax: 717-533-8661
  E-mail: cust@igi-global.com
  Web site: http://www.igi-global.com

Library of Congress Cataloging-in-Publication Data

Names: Mohan S (Computer scientist), editor. | Vani V (Vani Vasudevan), 1978-
  editor.
Title: Multi-core computer vision and image processing for intelligent
  applications / Mohan S and Vani V, editors.
Other titles: Multicore computer vision and image processing for intelligent
  applications
Description: Hershey, PA : Information Science Reference, [2017] | Series:
  Advances in computational intelligence and robotics | Includes
  bibliographical references and index.
Identifiers: LCCN 2016029355| ISBN 9781522508892 (hardcover) | ISBN
  9781522508908 (ebook)
Subjects: LCSH: Computer vision. | Multiprocessors.
Classification: LCC TA1634 .M86 2017 | DDC 006.3/7--dc23 LC record available at https://lccn.
loc.gov/2016029355

This book is published in the IGI Global book series Advances in Computational Intelligence and Robotics (ACIR) (ISSN: 2327-0411; eISSN: 2327-042X)

British Cataloguing in Publication Data
A Cataloguing in Publication record for this book is available from the British Library.

Advances in Computational Intelligence and Robotics (ACIR) Book Series

ISSN: 2327-0411
EISSN: 2327-042X

MISSION

While intelligence is traditionally a term applied to humans and human cognition, technology has progressed in such a way to allow for the development of intelligent systems able to simulate many human traits. With this new era of simulated and artificial intelligence, much research is needed in order to continue to advance the field and also to evaluate the ethical and societal concerns of the existence of artificial life and machine learning.

The **Advances in Computational Intelligence and Robotics (ACIR) Book Series** encourages scholarly discourse on all topics pertaining to evolutionary computing, artificial life, computational intelligence, machine learning, and robotics. ACIR presents the latest research being conducted on diverse topics in intelligence technologies with the goal of advancing knowledge and applications in this rapidly evolving field.

COVERAGE

- Agent technologies
- Natural Language Processing
- Algorithmic Learning
- Machine Learning
- Neural Networks
- Computational Intelligence
- Automated Reasoning
- Pattern Recognition
- Intelligent control
- Adaptive and Complex Systems

IGI Global is currently accepting manuscripts for publication within this series. To submit a proposal for a volume in this series, please contact our Acquisition Editors at Acquisitions@igi-global.com or visit: http://www.igi-global.com/publish/.

Titles in this Series

For a list of additional titles in this series, please visit: www.igi-global.com

Pattern Recognition and Classification in Time Series Data
Eva Volna (University of Ostrava, Czech Republic) Martin Kotyrba (University of Ostrava, Czech Republic) and Michal Janosek (University of Ostrava, Czech Republic)
Information Science Reference • copyright 2017 • 282pp • H/C (ISBN: 9781522505655) • US $185.00 (our price)

Integrating Cognitive Architectures into Virtual Character Design
Jeremy Owen Turner (Simon Fraser University, Canada) Michael Nixon (Simon Fraser University, Canada) Ulysses Bernardet (Simon Fraser University, Canada) and Steve DiPaola (Simon Fraser University, Canada)
Information Science Reference • copyright 2016 • 346pp • H/C (ISBN: 9781522504542) • US $185.00 (our price)

Handbook of Research on Natural Computing for Optimization Problems
Jyotsna Kumar Mandal (University of Kalyani, India) Somnath Mukhopadhyay (Calcutta Business School, India) and Tandra Pal (National Institute of Technology Durgapur, India)
Information Science Reference • copyright 2016 • 1015pp • H/C (ISBN: 9781522500582) • US $465.00 (our price)

Applied Artificial Higher Order Neural Networks for Control and Recognition
Ming Zhang (Christopher Newport University, USA)
Information Science Reference • copyright 2016 • 511pp • H/C (ISBN: 9781522500636) • US $215.00 (our price)

Handbook of Research on Generalized and Hybrid Set Structures and Applications for Soft Computing
Sunil Jacob John (National Institute of Technology Calicut, India)
Information Science Reference • copyright 2016 • 607pp • H/C (ISBN: 9781466697980) • US $375.00 (our price)

Handbook of Research on Modern Optimization Algorithms and Applications in Engineering and Economics
Pandian Vasant (Universiti Teknologi Petronas, Malaysia) Gerhard-Wilhelm Weber (Middle East Technical University, Turkey) and Vo Ngoc Dieu (Ho Chi Minh City University of Technology, Vietnam)
Engineering Science Reference • copyright 2016 • 960pp • H/C (ISBN: 9781466696440) • US $325.00 (our price)

www.igi-global.com

701 E. Chocolate Ave., Hershey, PA 17033
Order online at www.igi-global.com or call 717-533-8845 x100
To place a standing order for titles released in this series,
contact: cust@igi-global.com
Mon-Fri 8:00 am - 5:00 pm (est) or fax 24 hours a day 717-533-8661

Editorial Advisory Board

Table of Contents

Preface.. xv

Chapter 1
FPGA-Based Re-Configurable Architecture for Window-Based Image
Processing 1
> *Kamarujjaman Sk, Government College of Engineering and Ceramic
>   Technology, India*
> *Manali Mukherjee, Government College of Engineering and Ceramic
>   Technology, India*
> *Mausumi Maitra, Government College of Engineering and Ceramic
>   Technology, India*

Chapter 2
Mobile Platform Challenges in Interactive Computer Vision............................ 47
> *Miguel Bordallo López, University of Oulu, Finland*

Chapter 3
Fish Tracking with Computer Vision Techniques: An Application to Vertical
Slot Fishways 74
> *Alvaro Rodriguez, University of Umeå, Sweden*
> *Angel Jose Rico-Diaz, University of A Coruña, Spain*
> *Juan R. Rabuñal, University of A Coruña, Spain*
> *Marcos Gestal, University of A Coruña, Spain*

Chapter 4
Computer Vision Based Classification on Commercial Videos 105
> *B. Rebecca Jeya Vadhanam, SRM University, India*
> *Mohan S., Al Yamamah University, Saudi Arabia*
> *V. Sugumaran, VIT University Chennai, India*
> *Vani V., Al Yamamah University, Saudi Arabia*
> *V. V. Ramalingam, SRM University, India*

Chapter 5
Creating Sound Glyph Database for Video Subtitling......................................137
  Chitralekha Ganapati Bhat, TCS Innovation Labs, India
  Sunil Kumar Kopparapu, TCS Innovation Labs, India

Chapter 6
Parallel Computing in Face Image Retrieval: Practical Approach to the Real-
World Image Search...156
  Eugene Borovikov, National Library of Medicine, USA
  Szilárd Vajda, National Library of Medicine, USA
  Girish Lingappa, National Library of Medicine, USA
  Michael C Bonifant, National Library of Medicine, USA

Chapter 7
Fish Monitoring, Sizing, and Detection Using Stereovision, Laser
Technology, and Computer Vision...191
  Angel Jose Rico-Diaz, University of A Coruña, Spain
  Alvaro Rodriguez, University of Umeå, Sweden
  Jeronimo Puertas, University of A Coruña, Spain
  Maria Bermudez, University of A Coruña, Spain

Chapter 8
Controlling Prosthetic Limb Movements Using EEG Signals...........................212
  V. V. Ramalingam, SRM University, India
  Mohan S., Al Yamamah University, Saudi Arabia
  V. Sugumaran, VIT University, India
  Vani V., Al Yamamah University, Saudi Arabia
  B. Rebecca Jeya Vadhanam, SRM University, India

Chapter 9
A Technical Assessment on License Plate Detection System............................236
  Jeena Rita K. S., SCMS School of Engineering and Technology, India
  Bini Omman, SCMS School of Engineering and Technology, India

Compilation of References 261

About the Contributors 286

Index..291

Detailed Table of Contents

Preface.. xv

Chapter 1
FPGA-Based Re-Configurable Architecture for Window-Based Image
Processing 1

*Kamarujjaman Sk, Government College of Engineering and Ceramic
Technology, India*

*Manali Mukherjee, Government College of Engineering and Ceramic
Technology, India*

*Mausumi Maitra, Government College of Engineering and Ceramic
Technology, India*

In this proposed book chapter, a simple but efficient presentation of Median Filter, Switching Median Filter, Adaptive Median Filter and Decision-Based Adaptive Filtering Method and their hardware architecture for FPGA is described for removal of up to 99% impulse noise from Digital Images. For hardware architecture, simulation is done using Xilinx ISE 14.5 software of XILINX. For implementation, these approaches utilize Genesys VIRTEX V FPGA device of XC5VLX50T device family. In this approach, we proposed an efficient design for suppression of impulse noise from digital images corrupted by up to 99% impulse noise using decision based adaptive filtering method as well as preserve the details of image. The method works in two different stages – noise detection using switching technique and finally noise suppression and restoration. Experimental results show that our method perform better in terms of PSNR below 80% noise density but above 80% noise density it is almost comparable with the latest methods.

Chapter 2
Mobile Platform Challenges in Interactive Computer Vision............................47
   Miguel Bordallo López, University of Oulu, Finland

Computer vision can be used to increase the interactivity of existing and new camera-based applications. It can be used to build novel interaction methods and user interfaces. The computing and sensing needs of this kind of applications require a careful balance between quality and performance, a practical trade-off. This chapter shows the importance of using all the available resources to hide application latency and maximize computational throughput. The experience gained during the developing of interactive applications is utilized to characterize the constraints imposed by the mobile environment, discussing the most important design goals: high performance and low power consumption. In addition, this chapter discusses the use of heterogeneous computing via asymmetric multiprocessing to improve the throughput and energy efficiency of interactive vision-based applications.

Chapter 3
Fish Tracking with Computer Vision Techniques: An Application to Vertical
Slot Fishways 74
   Alvaro Rodriguez, University of Umeå, Sweden
   Angel Jose Rico-Diaz, University of A Coruña, Spain
   Juan R. Rabuñal, University of A Coruña, Spain
   Marcos Gestal, University of A Coruña, Spain

Vertical slot fishways are hydraulic structures which allow the upstream migration of fish through obstructions in rivers. Their design depends on the interplay between hydraulic and biological variables to match the requirements of the fish species for which they are intended. However, current mechanisms to study fish behavior in fishway models are impractical or unduly affect the animal behavior. In this chapter, we propose a new procedure for measuring fish behavior in fishways using Computer Vision (CV) techniques to analyze images obtained from the assays by means of a camera system designed for fishway integration. It is expected that this technique will provide detailed information about the fish behavior and will help to improve fish passage devices. A series of assays have been performed in order to validate this new approach in a full-scale fishway model and with living fishes. We have obtained very promising results that allow reconstructing correctly the movements of the fish within the fishway without disturbing fish.

Chapter 4

Computer Vision Based Classification on Commercial Videos 105

B. Rebecca Jeya Vadhanam, SRM University, India
Mohan S., Al Yamamah University, Saudi Arabia
V. Sugumaran, VIT University Chennai, India
Vani V., Al Yamamah University, Saudi Arabia
V. V. Ramalingam, SRM University, India

Computer vision is a study which concerned with the automatic mining, analysis, perception and extracting the essential information from a single frame or image and a sequence of frames. It focuses the development of automatic visual perception system to reconstruct and interpret a three-dimensional scene from two-dimensional images through the properties of the structures existing in the scene. The scene understanding is a great challenging task for the contemporary computer vision system. Hence, the present study mainly emerged for acquiring the essential information, processing, analysing and understanding the visual content from the advertisement videos and the general program video. It enables the user to retrieve the product based advertisement content, efficient browsing for their desired shows; you tube search strategy of the videos with advertisement content or without advertisement content and the final goal of the present study is to design the electronic embedded systems focuses on technology integration with a domestic utility concept. The demand for a solution is gaining momentum which will enable the viewers to skip the advertisements and move automatically to another channel. It is achieved, when the extracted frames of advertisements(ADD) and nonadvertisements videos (NADD) consisting of more visual information is classified. In this present work, there are two techniques have been attempted namely, Block Intensity Comparison Code technique (BICC) and Key frame rate (KFR) technique.In BICC technique, the descriptive feature is derived through the block intensity comparison technique and applied on various block sizes of the frame. The promising block size 8x8 has been chosen for the experimental study. The best performing features were selected through the decision tree C4.5 algorithm, and these features were taken as the input for various decision tree algorithms, namely J48, J48graft, LMT tree, Random Tree, Best first tree, REP tree to classify the video genre. An extensive investigation has made on the random tree classifier which produced better predictive performance than the other algorithms. The training and the optimization of random tree model with their essential parametric measures are reported. Based on the overall study, the random tree with Block Intensity Comparison Code (BICC) feature was found as the most preferred classification algorithm that achieved the best classification accuracy of 99.48%. Thus, the preference of the most proper key frame rate feature set is crucial to the quality of the classification and retrieval system of the study.

Chapter 5
Creating Sound Glyph Database for Video Subtitling 137
    Chitralekha Ganapati Bhat, TCS Innovation Labs, India
    Sunil Kumar Kopparapu, TCS Innovation Labs, India

Accessibility of speech information in videos is a huge challenge for the hearing impaired, making a visual representation such as text subtitling essential. Unavailability of a good Automatic Speech Recognition (ASR) engine, makes automatic generation of text subtitles for resource deficient languages such as Indian languages, extremely difficult. Techniques to build such an ASR using audio and corresponding transcription in the form of broadcast news or audio books have been proposed; however, these techniques require transcriptions corresponding to the audio in editable text format, which are unavailable for resource deficient languages. In this chapter, a novel technique of building a sound-glyph database for a resource deficient language has been described. The sound-glyph database can be used effectively to subtitle videos in the same language script. Considering large volumes of data that need to be processed, we propose a parallel processing method in a multiresolution setup, harnessing the multi-core capacity of present day computers.

Chapter 6
Parallel Computing in Face Image Retrieval: Practical Approach to the Real-World Image Search 156
    Eugene Borovikov, National Library of Medicine, USA
    Szilárd Vajda, National Library of Medicine, USA
    Girish Lingappa, National Library of Medicine, USA
    Michael C Bonifant, National Library of Medicine, USA

Modern digital photo collections contain vast multitudes of high-resolution color images, many containing faces, which are desirable to retrieve visually. This poses a problem for effective image browsing and calls for efficient Content Based Image Retrieval (CBIR) capabilities ensuring near-instantaneous visual query turn-around. This in turn necessitates parallelization of many existing image processing and information retrieval algorithms that can no longer satisfy the modern user demands, when executed sequentially. Hence a practical approach to Face Image Retrieval (FIR) is presented. It utilizes multi-core processing architectures to implement its major modules (e.g. face detection and matching) efficiently without sacrificing the image retrieval accuracy. The integration of FIR into a web-based family reunification system demonstrates the practicality of the proposed method. Several accuracy and speed evaluations on real-word data are presented and possible CBIR extensions are discussed.

Chapter 7

Fish Monitoring, Sizing, and Detection Using Stereovision, Laser
Technology, and Computer Vision... 191
Angel Jose Rico-Diaz, University of A Coruña, Spain
Alvaro Rodriguez, University of Umeå, Sweden
Jeronimo Puertas, University of A Coruña, Spain
Maria Bermudez, University of A Coruña, Spain

Stereovision and laser techniques allow for getting knowledge about fish, mostly when they are combined with computer vision. This kind of techniques avoid to use traditional procedures such as direct observation, which are impractical or can affect the fish behavior, in task such as aquarium and fish farm management or fishway, like vertical slot fishway, evaluation. This chapter describes in a first stage, the use stereovision join with computer vision to fish monitoring and measure size of fishes. In the second part, using laser technology and computer vision to fish detection, especially in slot fishways. Vertical slot fishways are structures that are placed in rivers to allow fish to avoid obstacles such as dams, hydroelectric plants. Then, it shows a results section and finally authors' conclusions.

Chapter 8

Controlling Prosthetic Limb Movements Using EEG Signals........................... 212
V. V. Ramalingam, SRM University, India
Mohan S., Al Yamamah University, Saudi Arabia
V. Sugumaran, VIT University, India
Vani V., Al Yamamah University, Saudi Arabia
B. Rebecca Jeya Vadhanam, SRM University, India

The EEG (electroencephalogram) signals have potential applications in modern medical sciences and technology. In the human brain, there are trillions of neurons, which are receptive cells. These cells play a vital role in transmitting messages between brain and other parts of the body. The motor activities, mental thoughts, memories, and dreams are occurring only by the neurons in the human brain. This study is mainly focused to replace the natural arms with an artificial arm with movements. There is a huge demand for the replacement of the damaged arms of the human beings. Many people meet with accidents and lose their hands. Some persons lose their limbs in the manufacturing industry during the working hours. For some people there is a deficiency in growth of fingers and limbs. In any case, the loss of human limb is a major issue that intensely limits the everyday capabilities and interaction of the persons. Hence, an attempt is made to find a solution for artificial limb with movements. There can be two types of signals that are of direct use for the above purpose: EMG and EEG. EMG (electromyogram) signals are available in the muscles and they contain a large amount of information for the purpose of limb movements. However, there are many instances where the subject loses most part of the limb. In such cases the EMG signals that are available near the affected area (shoulder, upper arm) may not be of great use. Moreover, EMG signals are secondary signals, whereas EEG signals are primary signals. The EEG signal originates from brain activities. The characteristics remain almost same irrespective of the extent of amputation. It gives a feeling that EEG signal is better candidate for controlling movements of artificial limbs. It is not fully true because of the fact that the EEG signals are product of some thought process; this complicates the decoding process of EEG signals. Now, the challenges are to decode effectively the information buried inside the EEG signals. This study is a humble attempt to do the same for the purpose of controlling the prosthetic arm. From the acquired EEG signals, statistical and histogram features were extracted with each of the feature set, a detailed study was carried out to find the best possible features. Hence, the effect of a number of features was studied using decision tree. The selected features were classified using C4.5 decision tree algorithm, best first decision tree algorithm, Naïve Bayes algorithm, Bayes net algorithm, K star algorithm and ripple down rule learner algorithm. The results of statistical and histogram features are discussed and conclusions of the study are presented. Among the six classifiers, C4.5 decision tree with histogram features produced maximum classification accuracy (85.18%). More specifically, C4.5 decision tree model performs better with histogram features compared to statistical features and it is suggested as a good 'feature-classifier' pair for the prosthetic limb movement system. Finally, the possibilities of multicore implementation of the proposed algorithms are discussed in brief.

Chapter 9
A Technical Assessment on License Plate Detection System............................236
    Jeena Rita K. S., SCMS School of Engineering and Technology, India
    Bini Omman, SCMS School of Engineering and Technology, India

Identifying the region of interest from an image is an important task in the field of computer vision. This process is referred as Object Detection. Locating the object can be done by extracting the features from the image and the features depend on the application. Image retrieval and surveillance are two important applications of Object Detection. Surveillance is an active research topic in computer vision that tries to detect, recognize and track objects over images. An interesting application of it is License Plate Recognition module in Intelligent Transportation System. The speedy developments in economic and social life bring on for a large increase in the number of vehicles in the city. This makes the traffic management difficult. It has great impact on human life as it aims to increase the transportation safety through innovative technologies. An important function that need for majority of ITS application is to identify the vehicle using LPR. This chapter presents assessment on different methods in detecting the license plate and discusses a case study on it.

Compilation of References 261

About the Contributors 286

Index 291

Preface

AN OVERVIEW OF THE BOOK

In recent years, computing over multicore processors have been showing significant importance as it gives the parallel architecture for implementation of traditional algorithms. The computer vision and image processing algorithms have a wide scope for parrallel programming and hence implementation of the same in multicore would reveal new results and avenues.

Multicore is a platform involving distributed or parallel computing in a single computer. Early parallel programming was possible by clustering many computers or building a special purpose machine. It was expensive in terms of money and infrastructure. The main challenges in building such systems were maintenance and hardware upgradation to adapt to change in computing infrastructure. With the advancement in fabricating more number of cores in single processor, avenues for such parallel computing have been opened up where the parallel computing could be carried out in a very cost effective infrastructure. This means the parallel programming is available to any common programmers. One of the computing intensive domains in computer science is the Digital Imaging and Computer Vision as it involves redundant processing at the pixel level of digital images, videos and graphics. Conventional imaging algorithms are sequential in nature. With the parallel computing possibilities, the image processing algorithms could potentially reduce computational complexities. By implementing those algorithms in multicore computing platform, the same can be analyzed and justified. Hence there could be a huge room for improving the performance of imaging, video and vision algorithms which could lead to development of cost effective devices like intelligent video surveillance cameras. The applications of such developments could vary from simple imaging device to mission critical satellite and medical imaging.

This book looks to discuss and address the difficulties and challenges that the multicore version of computer vision and image processing algorithms need to be addressed. The editors will seek chapters that address different aspects of multicore adaptation of imaging and vision algorithms, ranging from image enhancement, segmentation, registration, to intelligent decision making using video surveillance applications, 3D virtual world construction, and augmented and virtual reality applications at the high level vision computing.

This comprehensive and timely publication aims to be an essential reference source, building on the available literature in the field of computer vision, Image processing and graphics using multicore computing while providing for further research opportunities in this dynamic field. It is hoped that this text will provide the resources necessary for young researchers, scholars, students and teachers to explore much more in this emerging field of computer science.

TARGET AUDIENCE

Policy makers, academicians, researchers, advanced-level students, technology developers, and government officials will find this text useful in furthering their research exposure to pertinent topics in electronic government and assisting in furthering their own research efforts in this field.

ABOUT THE CHAPTERS

The proposed publication focus on the computer vision algorithms, particluarly the computing intensive algorithms which has potential for parrallel implementation. Recent developments and their implementation of such algorithms on multicore computing will be published in the proposed book. Authors present their latest development of the graphics, vision and image processing algorithms using multicore processors.

In Chapter 1, which is on "FPGA-Based Re-Configurable Architecture for Window-Based Image Processing," a simple but efficient presentation of Median Filter, Switching Median Filter, Adaptive Median Filter and Decision-Based Adaptive Filtering Method and their hardware architecture for FPGA is described for removal of up to 99% impulse noise from Digital Images. For hardware architecture, simulation is done using Xilinx ISE 14.5 software of XILINX. For implementation, these approaches utilize Genesys VIRTEX V FPGA device of XC5VLX50T device family. In this approach, we proposed an efficient design for suppression of impulse noise from digital images corrupted by up to 99% impulse noise using decision based adaptive filtering method as well as preserve the details of image. The method works in two different stages – noise detection using switching technique and finally noise suppression and restoration. Experimental results show that our method perform better in terms of PSNR below 80% noise density but above 80% noise density it is almost comparable with the latest methods.

Chapter 2, on "Mobile Platform Challenges in Interactive Computer Vision Applications," shows the importance of using all the available resources to hide application latency and maximize computational throughput. The experience gained during the developing of interactive applications is utilized to characterize the constraints imposed by the mobile environment, discussing the most important design goals: high performance and low power consumption. In addition, this chapter discusses the use of heterogeneous computing via asymmetric multiprocessing to improve the throughput and energy efficiency of interactive vision-based applications.

Chapter 3, titled "Fish Tracking with Computer Vision Techniques: An Application to Vertical Slot Fishways," proposes a new procedure for measuring fish behavior in fishways using Computer Vision (CV) techniques to analyze images obtained from the assays by means of a camera system designed for fishway integration. It is expected that this technique will provide detailed information about the fish behavior and will help to improve fish passage devices. A series of assays have been performed in order to validate this new approach in a full-scale fishway model and with living fishes. We have obtained very promising results that allow reconstructing correctly the movements of the fish within the fishway without disturbing fish.

In Chapter 4, which is on "Computer Vision Based Classification on Commercial Videos," there are two techniques attempted namely, BICC and (KFR) technique for classifying videos as advertisements and Non-advertisements. The best performing features were selected through the decision tree C4.5 algorithm, and these features were taken as the input for various decision tree algorithms, namely J48, J48graft, LMT tree, Random Tree, Best first tree, REP tree to classify the video genre. Based on the overall study, the random tree with Block Intensity Comparison Code (BICC) feature was found as the most preferred classification algorithm that achieved the best classification accuracy of 99.48%.

Chapter 5, discusses a topic on "Creating Sound Glyph Database for Video Subtitling." This chapter discusses about accessibility of speech information in videos. It is a huge challenge for the hearing impaired, making a visual representation such as text subtitling essential. Unavailability of a good Automatic Speech Recognition (ASR) engine, makes automatic generation of text subtitles for resource deficient languages such as Indian languages, extremely difficult. Techniques to build such an ASR using audio and corresponding transcription in the form of broadcast news or audio books have been proposed; however these techniques require transcriptions corresponding to the audio in editable text format, which are unavailable for resource deficient languages. In this chapter, a novel technique of building a sound-glyph database for a resource deficient language has been described. The sound-glyph database can be used effectively to subtitle videos in the same language script. Considering large volumes of data that need to be processed, we propose a parallel processing method in a multiresolution setup, harnessing the multi-core capacity of present day computers.

In Chapter 6, a novel method on "Parallel Computing in Face Image Retrieval: Practical Approach to the Real-World Image Search" has been proposed. It utilizes multi-core processing architectures to implement its major modules (e.g. face detection and matching) efficiently without sacrificing the image retrieval accuracy. The integration of FIR into a web-based family reunification system demonstrates the practicality of the proposed method. Several accuracy and speed evaluations on real-word data are presented and possible CBIR extensions are discussed

Chapter 7 discussed about "Fish Monitoring, Sizing, and Detection Using Stereovision, Laser Technology, and Computer Vision." This chapter describes in a first stage, the use stereovision join with computer vision to fish monitoring and measure size of fishes. In the second part, using laser technology and computer vision to fish detection, especially in slot fishways. Vertical slot fishways are structures that are placed in rivers to allow fish to avoid obstacles such as dams, hydroelectric plants. Then, it shows a results section and finally authors' conclusions

Chapter 8, titled "Controlling Prosthetic Limb Movements Using EEG Signals," proposes methods to classify the acquired EEG signals of limb, statistical and histogram features extracted with each of the feature set, to find the best possible features. The effect of a number of features was studied using decision tree. The selected features were classified using C4.5 decision tree algorithm, best first decision tree algorithm, Naïve Bayes algorithm, Bayes net algorithm, K star algorithm and ripple down rule learner algorithm. The results of statistical and histogram features are discussed and conclusions of the study are presented. Among the six classifiers, C4.5 decision tree with histogram features produced maximum classification accuracy (85.18%). More specifically, C4.5 decision tree model performs better with histogram features compared to statistical features and it is suggested as a good 'feature-classifier' pair for the prosthetic limb movement system. Finally, the possibilities of multicore implementation of the proposed algorithms are discussed in brief.

Chapter 9, "A Technical Assessment on License Plate Detection System," presents assessment on different methods in detecting the license plate and discusses a case study on it. Identifying the region of interest from an image is an important task in the field of computer vision. This process is referred as Object Detection. Locating the object can be done by extracting the features from the image and the features depend on the application. Image retrieval and surveillance are two important applications of Object Detection. Surveillance is an active research topic in computer vision that tries to detect, recognize and track objects over images. An interesting application of it is License Plate Recognition module in Intelligent Transportation System. The speedy developments in economic and social life bring on for a large increase in the number of vehicles in the city. This makes the traffic management difficult. It has great impact on human life as it aims to increase the transportation safety through innovative technologies. An important function that need for majority of ITS application is to identify the vehicle using LPR.

CONCLUSION

It is very much sure that the proposed topics of this book are futuristic in terms of computational resources. As the computing architecture is advancing day by day in terms of parallelizing the processing capacities by introducing more cores in the single processor, the state of the art computer vision applications need to be relooked in order to optimize the computational time. The chapters in this book are believed to give an insight into such methods and the possibilities of considering them for more optimization. Though some of the chapters only proposed at a theoretical level of parallelism using multicore computing, there is a tremendous scope for the potential researchers and authors to pursue further implementations and analysis on these proposed methods.

Mohan S.
Al Yamamah University, Saudi Arabia

Vani V.
Al Yamamah University, Saudi Arabia

Chapter 1
FPGA–Based Re– Configurable Architecture for Window–Based Image Processing

Kamarujjaman Sk
Government College of Engineering and Ceramic Technology, India

Manali Mukherjee
Government College of Engineering and Ceramic Technology, India

Mausumi Maitra
Government College of Engineering and Ceramic Technology, India

ABSTRACT

In this proposed book chapter, a simple but efficient presentation of Median Filter, Switching Median Filter, Adaptive Median Filter and Decision-Based Adaptive Filtering Method and their hardware architecture for FPGA is described for removal of up to 99% impulse noise from Digital Images. For hardware architecture, simulation is done using Xilinx ISE 14.5 software of XILINX. For implementation, these approaches utilize Genesys VIRTEX V FPGA device of XC5VLX50T device family. In this approach, we proposed an efficient design for suppression of impulse noise from digital images corrupted by up to 99% impulse noise using decision based adaptive filtering method as well as preserve the details of image. The method works in two different stages – noise detection using switching technique and finally noise suppression and restoration. Experimental results show that our method perform better in terms of PSNR below 80% noise density but above 80% noise density it is almost comparable with the latest methods.

DOI: 10.4018/978-1-5225-0889-2.ch001

1. INTRODUCTION

Now a day, in image processing, Filtering is a basic need because of different kinds of noise invoke into an image. Noise is any kind of unwanted signal. For our design the authors consider the impulse noise which is also known as classical salt and pepper noise for gray-scale image. Impulse noise exists in many practical applications and can be generated by various sources, including many man-made phenomena such as unprotected switches, industrial machines, and car ignition systems. Images are often corrupted by impulse noise due to a noisy sensor or channel transmission errors. Impulse noise can appear because of a random bit error on a communication channel. The most common method used for impulse noise suppression for gray-scale and colour images is the median filter. In the area of image processing two important applications are needed that is noise filtering and image enhancement (Gonzalez & Woods, 2009). Many types of noises including impulse noises are the normal sources of image corruption which are the subset of digital signals (Gonzalez & Woods, 2009). Noise filtering aim is to eliminate noise by affecting lesser on the original images (Andreadisand & Louverdis, 2004). Very high contrast to the surrounding of impulse noise comprises a set of random pixels (Petrou & Bosdogianni, 2000; Wang & Lin, 1997). Some common causes for impulse noise are transmission of image in noisy channel, camera sensors containing malfunctioned pixels, or faulty memory locations in hardware (Chan, Ho, & Nikolova, 2005). Filters are chosen according to their noise pattern in the field of image processing. Comparing with linear filters, nonlinear filters give better results in case of order statistics filters. A proposal was made for correlation between a number of nonlinear filters and vectors by using various distance measurement (Arce et. al., 1986, Pitas et. al., 1990 and Hodgson et. al., 1985). Analysis and comparisons of different filtering algorithms are already discussed in quite a few literatures and number of different improved algorithms are put forwarded (Chang, 1995: Ng et. al., 2006). The computational complexity for filtering applications wants an amount of huge data for presenting image information in a digital way. Comparing with software implementation, hardware implementation can result better speed with the help of pipelining and parallelism technique. Semi-custom hardware device i.e., Field programmable gate arrays (FPGAs) achieve advantage over Application specific integrated circuits (ASIC) and Digital signal processors (DSPs). Reconfigurable nature of FPGAs consisting with pipeline and parallelism technique make it efficient to reduce the complexity of algorithms and simplify the debugging and verification. In this report, the algorithms of median and switching median filter are proposed in the means of software as well as hardware implementation for removal of impulse noise considering salt and pepper noise from gray scale images. Utilization of median filter and switching median filter is done in such a way that experimental results show their improved performances. The proposed algorithms are capable for 8-bit gray scale image processing and as image neighbourhood, 3x3 and 5x5 moving window are chosen which are also expandable as the design needs. The hardware implementations are done on FPGAs which associate with flexibility, high performance and low cost (Pratt, 1991). The software implementation for proposed algorithms is done on MATLAB (v 2012a). The software design, compilation and simulation are associated with that. The hardware structure is designed and simulated using System Generator of Xilinx ISE (14.5) developed by XILINX. The system level simulations are done on Matlab and System Generator and RTL level simulations are done on Isim Simulator. The proposed designs are realized on Genesys Virtex V FPGA Board of XC5VLX50T device family. These two designs can be implemented for real time imaging applications where ultimate importance is fast processing (Dougherty & Laplante, 1995). This paper is organized with some stages. At first stage, a brief overview of median and switching median filter is provided, in next stage the algorithms are provided, after that the architectures with their functional stages are presented in detail. In the next stage performances of software and hardware implementation are provided following the timing, area and power analysis. In the last stage conclusions are discussed in detail. Now, the discussions are based on a new technique for removing high density impulse noise from a corrupted image without changing the image details. Removal of impulse noise from highly corrupted images is important for different kind of imaging applications i.e. image segmentation, edge detection and image compression (Nooshyar, 2013). In signal processing noise suppression and detection of thin details are not easy. Now a days, impulse noise is divided into two parts depending on their noise value, i) Fixed valued (0 or 255) and ii) Random valued (Between 0 & 255) impulse noise. Filters are chosen according to their noise pattern in the field of image processing. Comparing with linear filters, nonlinear filters give better results in case of order statistics filters. Depending on the de-noising capability and simplicity median filter was used to restore noisy image (Huang, 1979). But thin lines, edges and details are not preserved when noise level is higher (>50%) (Nodes, T. A. and Gallagher Jr., N. C. 1984). To improve image details different kinds of median based filters have been proposed in different time. These are the weighted median based filter (Ko & Lee, 1991), adaptive window based median filter (Gonzalez, et. al. 2004)., decision based adaptive filter (Kasparis, Tzannes, & Chen, 1992), switching median filter (Sun & Neuvo, 1994), mean based rank order filter (Abreu, Lightstone, Mitra, & Arakawa, 1996), weighted adaptive median filter (Lin, 2007) etc. These filters detect the noisy pixels and alter them instead of altering all pixels with median value. Some of these filters work well for various conditions but the problem stood still for higher noise density (above 80%). Because of these details, preserving is still a very important issue. This problem is arising due to threshold calculation. There is some problem related to threshold because some median based filters determine their threshold depending on their assumptions (Sultana, 2013). It is very difficult to obtain the magnitude of impulse noise in noisy cases and impulse strength is not very high with respect to the fine changes of the signal (Arakawa, 1996). Some fuzzy based median and adaptive filters are designed (Thirilogasundari, et. al. 2012; Nair, 2012) to solve the above mentioned issue. Recently, Sultana et. al. (2013) proposed a fully adaptive fuzzy based median filter over standard median filter, Nooshyar et. al. (2013) designed a decision based adaptive weighted and trimmed median filter (Nooshyar, 2013) for removing the noise of higher density. To remove high density impulse noise, linear mean-median filter (Utaminingrum, 2013) and iterative adaptive fuzzy filter based on alpha trimmed (Ahmed, 2013) is proposed recently.

2. RELATED WORK AND MOTIVATION

Now a day, in image processing, Filtering is a basic need because of different kinds of noise invoke into an image. Noise is any kind of unwanted signal. For our design the authors consider the impulse noise which is also known as classical salt and pepper noise for gray scale image. Impulse noise exists in many practical applications and can be generated by various sources, including many man-made phenomena such as unprotected switches, industrial machines, and car ignition systems. Images are often corrupted by impulse noise due to a noisy sensor or channel transmission errors. Impulse noise can appear because of a random bit error on a communication channel. The most common method used for impulse noise suppression for gray-scale and color images is the median filter. Many more median based filtering designs are implemented by different person in different time and venue. Some of them are depicted bellow which is followed to implement the proposed median based filters.

Zhnget, S. et. al. (2002) implemented a new concept over normal median filter. They divided pixels into two sets, "noise-free pixel", these pixel values are copied directly to the output image and "noise-pixel", and these pixels are then filtered by a median filter. They got better result than normal median filter.

Andreadis and, I. and Louverdis, G. (2004) designed Adaptive Median Filter for real time noise removal. In this paper, a new intelligent hardware module suitable for the computation of an adaptive median filter was presented for the first time. The function of the proposed circuit is to detect the existence of impulse noise in an image neighborhood and apply the operator of the median filter only when it is necessary. Typical clock frequency is 65 MHz.

Chan, Ho, and Nikolova (2005) designed a median based noise detection algorithm which preserve details of the image. This paper proposed a two-phase scheme for removing salt-and-pepper impulse noise. In the first phase, an adaptive median filter is used to identify pixels which are likely to be contaminated by noise. In the second phase, the image is restored using a specialized regularization method that applies only to those selected noise candidates. Their scheme can remove salt-and-pepper-noise with a noise level as high as 90%.

Luo (2005) proposed a simple switching median filter based on fuzzy impulse detection technique. The method finds the two peaks from the histogram to approximate two intensity values that present the impulse noise. They divided central pixels into three different sets, which are "noise-free pixels", "noise-pixels", and "possibly noise pixels". For the "possible noise-pixels", the median value is first determined, and then this value is recombined with the intensity of the image, using a weighting value that is calculated based on a fuzzy membership function.

Luo (2006) presents a new efficient algorithm for the removal of impulse noise from corrupted images while preserving image details. The algorithm is based on the alpha-trimmed mean, which is a special case of the order-statistics filter. Once a noisy pixel is identified, its value is replaced by a linear combination of its original value and the median of its local window. Extensive computer simulations indicate that their algorithm provides a significant improvement over many other existing techniques.

Srinivasan and Ebenezer (2007) implemented a new decision-based algorithm for restoration of images that are highly corrupted by impulse noise. The algorithm shows significantly better image quality than a standard median filter, adaptive median filters, a threshold decomposition filter, cascade, and recursive nonlinear filters. The method, unlike other nonlinear filters, removes only corrupted pixel by the median value or by its neighboring pixel value. This method removes the noise effectively even at noise level as high as 90% and preserves the edges without any loss up to 80% of noise level.

Ibrahim et. al. (2008) presented a new hybrid adaptive median algorithm for highly corrupted images. This method comprises two stages. The first stage is to detect the impulse noise in the image. In this stage, based on only the intensity values, the pixels are roughly divided into two classes, which are "noise-free pixel" and "noise pixel". Then, the second stage is to eliminate the impulse noise from the image. In this stage, only the "noise-pixels" are processed. The "noise-free pixels" are copied directly to the output image. The method adaptively changes the size of the median filter based on the number of the "noise-free pixels" in the neighborhood. For the filtering, only "noise-free pixels" are considered for the finding of the median value.

Hu et. al., (2009) designed hardware architecture of Median filter and Multi-level median filter. They implement it on FPGA, which can preserve image features and thin lines. This paper also gives account to the FPGA implementation of the complete structure of a general filter including the filtering window generating module and the row-column counting module. These architectures are fully pipelined to improve the through put.

Munoz et. al. (2011) implemented the adaptive median filter in two different ways, Adaptive filters are used in a wide range of applications such as echo cancellation, noise cancellation, system identification, and prediction. It's hardware implementation becomes essential in many cases where real-time execution is needed. However, impulsive noise affects the proper operation of the filter and the adaptation process. This noise is one of the most damaging types of signal distortion, not always considered when implementing algorithms, particularly in specific hardware platforms. Field programmable gate arrays (FPGAs) are used widely for real-time applications where timing requirements are strict. Nowadays, two main design processes can be followed for embedded system design, namely, a hardware description language (e.g., VHDL) and a high-level synthesis design tool. This paper proposes the FPGA implementation of an adaptive algorithm that is robust to impulsive noise using these two approaches. Final comparison results are provided in order to test accuracy, performance, and logic occupation.

Salvadaret, R. et. al., (2013) designed an evolvable hardware system, fully contained in an FPGA, which is capable of autonomously generating digital processing circuits, implemented on an array of processing elements. Candidate circuits are generated by an embedded evolutionary algorithm and implemented by means of dynamic partial reconfiguration, enabling evaluation in the final hardware. The evolved filters yield better quality than classic linear and nonlinear filters using mean absolute error as standard comparison metric. Results do not only show better circuit adaptation to different noise types and intensities, but also a non-degrading filtering behaviour. This means they may be run iteratively to enhance filtering quality. These properties are even kept for high noise levels (40%). The system as a whole is a step toward fully autonomous, adaptive systems.

Possa, Mahammoudi, and Valderrama (2013) presents a new flexible parameterizable architecture for image and video processing with reduced latency and memory requirements, supporting a variable input resolution. They present the proposed architecture implementation on an FPGA-based platform and its analogous optimized implementation on a GPU-based architecture for comparison. A performance analysis of the FPGA and the GPU implementations, and an extra CPU reference implementation, shows the competitive throughput of the proposed architecture even at a much lower clock frequency than those of the GPU and the CPU. Also, the results show a clear advantage of the proposed architecture in terms of power consumption and maintain a reliable performance with noisy images, low latency and memory requirements.

Pande and Chen (2013). shown that digital camera identification can be accomplished based on sensor pattern noise which is unique to a device and serves as a distinct identification fingerprint. They proposed hardware architecture for source identification in networked cameras. The algorithms, an orthogonal forward and inverse Discrete Wavelet Transform (DWT) and Minimum Mean Square Error (MMSE) based Estimation have been optimized for 2D frame sequences in terms of area and throughput performance. They exploit parallelism, pipelining and hardware reuse techniques to minimize hardware resource utilization and increase the achievable throughput of the design.

Turcza and Duplaga (2013) presented the design of a hardware-efficient, low-power image processing system for next-generation wireless endoscopy. The novel hardware-efficient architecture designed for the presented system enables on-the-fly compression of the acquired image. Instant compression, together with elimination of the necessity of retransmitting erroneously received data by their prior FEC encoding, significantly reduces the size of the required memory in comparison to previous systems. The presented system was prototyped in a single, low-power, 65-nm field programmable gate arrays (FPGA) chip. Its power consumption is low and comparable to other application-specific-integrated-circuits-based systems, despite FPGA-based implementation.

Baha and Touzene (2013) proposed the adaptation and optimization of the well-known Disparity Space Image (DSI) on a single FPGA (Field programmable gate Arrays) that is designed for high efficiency when realized in hardware.

Sun and Neuvo (1994) implement a switching scheme for median filtering which is suitable to be a pre-filter before edge detection or data compression is presented to remove impulse noises in digital images with small signal distortion. The switching procedure is based on the local measurements of impulse noise.

Wang and Zhang (1999) proposed new progressive switching median (PSM) filter to restore images corrupted by salt–pepper impulse noise. The algorithm is developed by the following two main points: 1) switching scheme—an impulse detection algorithm is used before filtering, thus only a proportion of all the pixels will be filtered and 2) progressive methods—both the impulse detection and the noise filtering procedures are progressively applied through several iterations.

Chen et. al. (1999) proposed a novel nonlinear tri-state median (TSM) filter, for preserving image details while effectively suppressing impulse noise. They incorporate the standard median (SM) filter and the center weighted median (CWM) filter into a noise detection framework to determine whether a pixel is corrupted, before applying filtering unconditionally.

Abreu et. al. (1996) represented a new framework for removing impulse noise from images is presented in which the nature of the filtering operation is conditioned on a state variable defined as the output of a classifier that operates on the differences between the input pixel and the remaining rank-ordered pixels in a sliding window. As part of this framework, several algorithms are examined, each of which is applicable to fixed and random-valued impulse noise models. First, a simple two-state approach is described in which the algorithm switches between the output of an identity filter and a rank-ordered mean (ROM) filter. The technique achieves an excellent tradeoff between noise suppression and detail preservation with little increase in computational complexity over the simple median filter. For a small additional cost in memory, this simple strategy is easily generalized into a multistate approach using weighted combinations of the identity and ROM filter in which the weighting coefficients can be optimized using image training data. The method is shown to be extremely robust with respect to the training data and the percentage of impulse noise.

Eng and Ma (2001) proposed a novel switching-based median filter with incorporation of fuzzy-set concept, called the noise adaptive soft-switching median (NASM) filter, to achieve much improved filtering performance in terms of effectiveness in removing impulse noise while preserving signal details and robustness in combating noise density variations. This filter consists of two stages i) Asoft-switching noise-detection scheme was developed to classify each pixel to be uncorrupted pixel, isolated impulse noise, non-isolated impulse noise or image object's edge pixel. ii) "No filtering" standard median (SM) filter or their developed fuzzy weighted median (FWM) filter will then be employed according to the respective characteristic type identified.

Nooshyar and Momeny (2013) proposed a novel technique for detecting and removing of impulse noise, while the significant information of image, such as edges and texture, are remind untouched. Algorithm uses the weighted window with variable sizes and applies median filtering on them.

Huang, Yang, and Tang (1979) presented a fast algorithm for two-dimensional median filtering. It is based on storing and updating the gray level histogram of the picture elements in the window. The algorithm is much faster than conventional sorting methods for a window size of m X n, the computer time required is O(n).

Ko and Lee (1991) followed center weighted median (CWM) filter, which is a weighted median filter giving more weight only to the central value of each window, is studied. This filter can preserve image details while suppressing additive white and/or impulsive-type noise. The statistical properties of the CWM filter are analyzed. It is shown that the CWM filter can outperform the median filter. In an attempt to improve the performance of CWM filters, an adaptive CWM (ACWM) filter having a space varying central weight is proposed. It is shown that the ACWM filter is an excellent detail preserving smoother that can suppress signal-dependent noise as well as signal-independent noise.

Lin (2007) proposed a new adaptive center weighted median (ACWM) filter for improving the performance of median-based filters, preserving image details while effectively suppressing impulsive noise. The proposed filter is an adaptive CWM filter with an adjustable central weight obtained by partitioning the observation vector space. To obtain the optimal weight for each block, the efficient scalar quantization

(SQ) method is used to partition the observation vector space. The center weight within each block is obtained by using a learning approach based on the least mean square (LMS) algorithm. The proposed new filter also provides excellent robustness at various percentages of impulsive noise.

A new decision-based algorithm is proposed for restoration of images that are highly corrupted by impulse noise by Srinivasan and Ebenezer (2007). The algorithm shows significantly better image quality than a standard median filter (SMF), adaptive median filters (AMF), a threshold decomposition filter (TDF), cascade, and recursive nonlinear filters. The proposed method, unlike other nonlinear filters, removes only corrupted pixel by the median value or by its neighboring pixel value. As a result of this, the proposed method removes the noise effectively even at noise level as high as 90% and preserves the edges without any loss up to 80% of noise level.

Sultana, Uddin, and Sabrina (2013) proposed a new adaptive fuzzy median filter is presented to provide optimum detail preservation along with very high density noise removal. Firstly, they used a triangular fuzzy membership function to determine the level of corruption at each pixel that consequently ensures the replacement of noisy pixels according to the extent of corruption. Secondly, they exploited fully adaptive and automatically adjustable threshold value to provide ease of computation.

Thirilogasundari, Babu, and Janet (2012) concentrated on the removal of impulse noise which mainly occurs due to the transmission medium imperfections, transmission system errors, and faulty memory units. The proposed method is based on switching median filter. It consists of two stages namely detection stage and filtering stage. In the detection stage neighbourhood mapping based algorithm is used to detect the corrupted pixels. In the filtering stage, the corrupted pixels are filtered by using fuzzy membership function. The uncorrupted pixels are retained as such. The proposed method is compared with many existing algorithms. The proposed algorithm can restore images which are highly corrupted up to 90% noise density.

Own and Huang (2013) proposed a novel filter method, a neighboring selection method based on the fuzzy median filter to improve the existing filter so that more image details can be preserved while effectively suppressing impulse noise. The proposed filter mechanism is composed of a new efficient noise eliminator based on the ideal of image rotation and LVQ network.

Saeidi, Anzabi, and Khalegi (2009) proposed a novel spatiotemporal fuzzy based algorithm for noise filtering of image sequences. Proposed algorithm uses adaptive weights based on a triangular membership functions. In this algorithm median filter is used to suppress noise. Indeed, assigned weights to noisy pixels are very adaptive so that they will make use of correlation of pixels. On the other hand, the motion estimation methods are erroneous and in highdensity noise they may degrade the filter performance. Therefore, our proposed fuzzy algorithm doesn't need any estimation of motion trajectory.

Nair and Raju (2012) proposed a new efficient fuzzy-based decision algorithm (FBDA) for the restoration of images that are corrupted with high density of impulse noises. FBDA is a fuzzy-based switching median filter in which the filtering is applied only to corrupted pixels in the image while the uncorrupted pixels are left unchanged. The proposed algorithm computes the difference measure for each pixel based on the central pixel (corrupted pixel) in a selected window and then calculates the membership value for each pixel based on the highest difference. The algorithm then eliminates those pixels from the window with very high and very low membership values, which might represent the impulse noises. Median filter is then applied to the remaining pixels in the window to get the restored value for the current pixel position.

Utaminingrum, Uchimura, and Koutaki (2013) presented Linear Mean-Median (LMM) filter that used to reduce impulse noise. LMM filter is a combination between Mean and Median filter. Wherein, linear value is acquired from the linearity between mean and median value. Mean and Median filter are only applied for free-noise pixel on the 3×3 windows that has been sorted from the smallest to the largest value. The mean value is obtained from the average value of all free-noise pixels without including the median pixel position. Meanwhile, median pixel is the middle position of the pixel that has been sorted. LMM uses nine sample pixels to determine a pixel for replacement a corrupted pixel. Our filter also provides the impulse noise prediction systems that serve as a facilitator to give information about noise content. If the noise is greater than 30%, the performance of LMM filter needs to be improved by an adaptive rank order mean filters.

Ahmed and Das (2013) proposed a novel adaptive, iterative, fuzzy filter for denoising images corrupted by impulse noise. It operates in two stages - detection of noisy pixels with an adaptive fuzzy detector followed by de-noising using a weighted mean filter on the "good" pixels in the filter window. The filter is also shown to be robust to very high levels of noise, retrieving meaningful detail at noise levels as high as 97%.

3. MEDIAN BASED FILTERING ALGORITHMS

Images are often corrupted by impulse noise when they are recorded by noisy sensors or sent over noisy transmission channels. Many impulse noise removal techniques have been developed to suppress impulse noise while preserving image details (Gonzalez & Woods, 2009). The median filter, the most popular kind of nonlinear filter, has been extensively used for the removal of impulse noise due to its simplicity. However, the median filter tends to blur fine details and lines in many cases. To avoid damage to good pixels, decision-based median filters realized by threshold operations have been introduced in some recently published works (Zhnget et. al. 2002; Baha et. al. 2013). In general, the decision-based filtering procedure consists of the following two steps: an impulse detector that classifies the input pixels as either noise or noise free, and a noise reduction filter that modifies only those pixels that are classified as noise-corrupted. In general, the main issue concerning the design of the decision-based median filter focuses on how to extract features from the local information and establish the decision rule, in such a way to distinguish noise-free pixels from contaminated ones as precisely as possible. In addition, to achieve high noise reduction with fine detail preservation, it is also crucial to apply the optimal threshold value to the local signal statistics.

3.1 Effects of Impulse Noise

Image noise is random (not present in the object imaged) variation of brightness or color information in images, and is usually an aspect of electronic noise. It can be produced by the sensor and circuitry of a scanner or digital camera. Image noise can also originate in film grain and in the unavoidable shot noise of an ideal photon detector. Image noise is an undesirable by-product of image capture that adds spurious and extraneous information. Fat-tail distributed or "impulsive" noise is sometimes called salt-and-pepper noise or spike noise in specifically for gray image. An image containing salt-and-pepper noise will have dark pixels in bright regions and bright pixels in dark regions. This type of noise can be caused by analog-to-digital converter errors, bit errors in transmission, etc. It can be mostly eliminated by using dark frame subtraction and interpolating around dark/bright pixels.

3.1.1 Impulse Noise Model

Before introducing the proposed MTS filter, some notation must be defined first. Let the filter window $w(k)$ (or a sliding window) sized $2n + 1$ cover the image X from left to right, top to bottom in a raster scan fashion.

$$w(k) = (x_{-n}(k), \ldots, x_{-1}(k), x_0(k), x_1(k), \ldots, x_n(k)) \tag{1}$$

where $x_0(k)$ (or $x(k)$) is the original central vector-valued pixel at location k. In this work, the authors consider a 3×3 filter window $w(k)$ centered around $x_0(k)$

$$w(k) = (x_{-4}(k), \ldots, x_{-1}(k), x_0(k), x_1(k), \ldots, x_4(k)) \tag{2}$$

Impulse noise can appear because of a random bit error on a communication channel. In this work, the source images are corrupted only by salt-pepper impulse noise, which means a noisy pixel has a high value due to positive impulse noise, or has a low value due to a negative impulse noise.

3.2 Theoretical Aspects of Median Filter

One of the nonlinear filters is median filter. Median filtering has proved an effective way to satisfy the dual requirements of removing impulse noise while preserving rapid signal changes (Baha & Touzene, 2013; Huang, Yaw, and Tang, 1980). The rank order filter is a particularly common algorithm in image processing systems. Impulse noise can appear because of a random bit error on a communication channel. This kind of noise is known as classical salt & pepper noise for gray scale image. A classic general purpose Median filter is based on a sorting approach over the entire window elements to find the median value. Median filters operate by replacing a given sample in a signal by the median of the signal values in a window around the sample. A block diagram of median filter is depicted in Figure 1.

Suppose I is an input image and p is any point at I. For calculation of median value of p ($\in$ I) neighbour pixels are needed. Neighbourhood pixels can find by designing a window W, considering p as origin.

If the total number of elements (n) in W is odd then n=2m+1, where m is positive integer. $I(p_1)$ $I(p_2)$,........, $I(p_n)$ represents the gray scale value of n points p_1,p_2,......, p_n respectively. This values are sorted in ascending order to form the order set { I_1,I_2,....., I_n} such that $I_1 \le I_2 \le$ .... $\le I_n$. Then,

Median=I_{m+1}|(m+1)th value of set {I_1,I_2,........, I_n}.

To demonstrate, using a window size of three with one entry immediately preceding and following each entry, a median filter will be applied to the following simple 1D signal:x = [2 80 6 3] So, the median filtered output signal y will be:

Figure 1. Block diagram of median filter

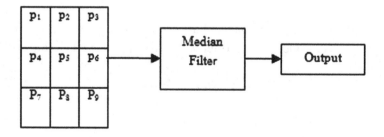

y[1] = Median[0 2 80] = 2
y[2] = Median[2 80 6] = Median[2 6 80] = 6
y[3] = Median[80 6 3] = Median[3 6 80] = 6
y[4] = Median[6 3 0] = Median[3 3 6] = 3
i.e. y = [2 6 6 3].

Note that, in the example above, because there is no entry preceding the first value, the first value is Zero (Gonzalez & Woods, 2009), as with the last value, to obtain enough entries to fill the window. This is one way of handling missing window entries at the boundaries of the signal, but there are other schemes that have different properties that might be preferred in particular circumstances.

Median filtering follows this basic prescription. The median filter is normally used to reduce noise in an image, somewhat like the mean filter. However, it often does a better job than the mean filter of preserving useful detail in the image. This class of filter belongs to the class of edge preserving smoothing filters which are non-linear filters. This means that for two images $A(x)$ and $B(x)$:

$$Median[A(x)+B(x)] \neq Median [A(x)]+Median[B(x)] \tag{3}$$

These filters smooth the data while keeping the small and sharp details. The median is just the middle value of all the values of the pixels in the neighbourhood. Note that this is not the same as the average (or mean); instead, the median has half the values in the neighbourhood larger and half smaller. The median is a stronger

Figure 2. Example of median filter

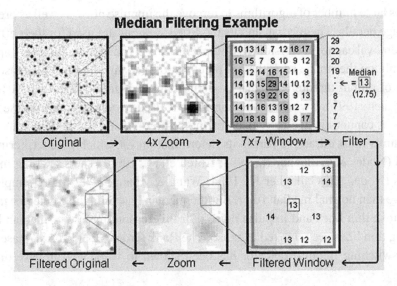

Figure 3. Median value calculation

123	125	126	130	140
122	124	126	127	135
118	120	150	125	134
119	115	119	123	133
111	116	110	120	130

Neighbourhood values:

115, 119, 120, 123, 124, 125, 126, 127, 150

Median value: 124

"central indicator" than the average. In particular, the median is hardly affected by a small number of discrepant values among the pixels in the neighbourhood. Consequently, median filtering is very effective at removing various kinds of noise. Figure 2 illustrates an example of median filtering.

Like the mean filter, the median filter considers each pixel in the image in turn and looks at its nearby neighbours to decide whether or not it is representative of its surroundings. Instead of simply replacing the pixel value with the mean of neighbouring pixel values, it replaces it with the median of those values. The median is calculated by first sort the pixel values from the surrounding neighbourhood into numerical order and then replace the processing pixel value with the median value. Figure 3 illustrates an example of median value calculation from a window.

3.3 Theoretical Aspects of Switching Median Filter

There is large number of algorithms to remove the impulse noise as well as preserve the image details. The median and its modified versions are used for their efficient noise removal capability (Astola & Campbell, 1989). The median filters are applied uniformly on the image such that all pixels tend to change and for this reason the feature of output or filtered image is often going to blur and distorted (Astola & Kuosmanen, 1997). Switching median filter is used to remove the impulse noise because it cannot change or replace the noise–free pixel with median value. The algorithm's most attractive part is its determination for which pixels filtering are needed (Nodes & Gallagher Jr., 1984; Abreu et. al., 1996). The switching median filter is (Nodes *& Gallagher Jr., 1984; Wang & Zhang, 1999) more simple and effective than normal median filter. But the median based impulse detector fails to distinguish thin lines and impulse noise. For this reason, in case of median based filtering thin lines are removed as noise. The Rank Order Mean (ROM)-based and a soft-switching impulse detector has been shown to work well in case of high impulse noise but high cost of increasing computational complexity (Chen et. al., 1999; Abreu et. al., 1996). Our switching median filter is based on some assumptions, these are i) a noise free image consists locally smooth areas, ii) a noise pixel takes the higher as well as smaller gray value than its neighbours.

Let $I_{i,j}$ and $B_{i,j}$ represents the pixel value (i,j) of corrupted and filtered image respectively. The median, $m_{i,j}$ for $I_{i,j}$ is calculated as

$$m_{ij} = \text{median}\{I_{i-p,j-p}, \dots, I_{ij}, \dots, I_{i+j,j+p}, \dots\} \tag{4}$$

where, $p = \text{floor}(S_{max}/2)$ and $S_{max} = $ Size of the window.

Whether $I_{i,j}$ is impulse or not is determined by a simple threshold. The authors use two level of threshold value T1 and T2, where T1 is lower limit and T2 is upper limit. $I_{i,j}$ is noise-free pixel if $T1 < I_{i,j} < T2$ otherwise noisy pixel. Then the output image,

$$B_{i,j} = \begin{cases} I_{i,j}, \text{if } T1 < I_{i,j} < T2 \\ m_{i,j}, Otherwise \end{cases} \tag{5}$$

The proposed switching median filter (SMF) in Figure 4 can be utilized for impulse noise suppression for gray scale images. Its function is to detect the existence of impulse noise in the image and apply the corresponding median filter only when necessary. The noise detection for the case of positive (negative) noise is as follows:

1. For a neighbourhood window (W) that is located at point p of the image I, the value of central pixel is compared to predefined threshold (T1,T2). The threshold T is a main factor in performance of impulse noise detection. The central pixel is considered to be 'noise free' when its value between T1 & T2, Otherwise 'noisy pixel'.

2. When the central pixel is considered to be noise it is substituted by the median value of the neighbourhood, I_{m+1}. Incasae of noise free pixel, the value of the central pixel is directly copied to the output. This procedure is repeated for the next window.

Figure 4. Block diagram of SMF

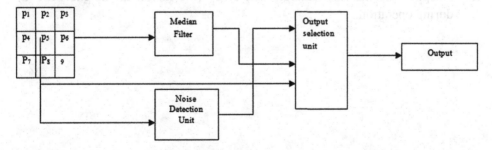

This technique is proficient in eliminating high densities of impulse noise as well as preserving the edges and fine details. However, the computational complexity involved in restoring the images is quite high. In this method, a corrupted pixel is replaced by the average value of already processed neighboring pixels inside the filter window. Although this filter suppresses impulse noise satisfactorily, it is found to exhibit inadequate performance in terms of preserving edges and fine details due to the aver-aging process involved in filtering.

3.4 Theoretical Aspects of Adaptive Median Filter

The application of median filter has been investigated. As an advanced method compared with standard median filtering, the Adaptive Median Filter performs spatial processing to preserve detail and smooth non-impulsive noise. A prime benefit to this adaptive approach to median filtering is that repeated applications of this Adaptive Median (Luo, 2005) Filter do not erode away edges or other small structure in the image. Therefore, the adaptive median filtering has been applied widely as an advanced method compared with standard median filtering. The Adaptive Median Filter performs spatial processing to determine which pixels in an image have been affected by impulse noise. The Adaptive Median Filter classifies pixels as noise by comparing each pixel in the image to its surrounding neighbour pixels (Gonzalez & Woods, 2009). The size of the neighbourhood is adjustable, as well as the threshold for the comparison. A pixel that is different from a majority of its neighbours, as well as being not structurally aligned with those pixels to which it is similar, is labelled as impulse noise. These noise pixels are then replaced by the median pixel value of the pixels in the neighbourhood that have passed the noise labelling test. Architecture of AMF is depicted in Figure 13.

Purpose

1. Remove impulse noise
2. Smoothing of other noise
3. Reduce distortion, like excessive thinning or thickening of object boundaries
4. Adaptive median filter changes size of S_{xy} (the size of the neighbourhood) during operation.

Notation

Z_{min} = minimum gray level value in S_{xy}
Z_{max} = maximum gray level value in S_{xy}
Z_{med} = median of gray levels in S_{xy}
Z_{xy} = gray level at coordinates (x, y)
S_{max} = maximum allowed size of S_{xy}

Algorithm

Level A

```
A1 = Z    - Z
       med    min
A2 = Z   -Z
       med  max
If A1 > 0 AND A2 < 0,
Go to level B
Else
Increase the window size
If window size <S    ,
                 max
Repeat level A
Else
OutputZ
        xy
```

Level B

```
B1 = Z   - Z
       xy    min
B2 = Z   - Z
       xy    max
If B1 > 0 AND B2 < 0,
OutputZ
        xy
Else
OutputZ   .
        med
```

The standard median filter does not perform well comparison shown in Figure 5 when impulse noise is

1. Greater than 0.2, while the adaptive median filter can better handle these noises.
2. The adaptive median filter preserves detail and smooth non-impulsive noise, while the standard median filter does not.

Figure 5. Performance comparison of median, switching median and adaptive median filter

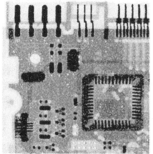

a) Image corrupted by impulse noise
with a probability of 0.1

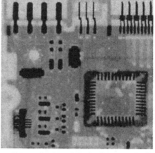

b) Result of median filter

c) Result of switching median filter

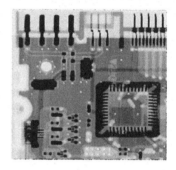

d) Result of adaptive median filter

3.5 Theoretical Aspects of Decision-Based Adaptive Filtering Method

We proposed a decision based adaptive filter to remove impulse noise which preserve the image details. The proposed algorithm detects the presence of noise in input images and removes the noise based on some predefined conditions. The authors take I as input image of size M×N corrupted by impulse noise and I(x,y) is the grayscale value of $(x,y)^{th}$ pixel. Assuming that the central pixel to be processed is situated at $(x,y)^{th}$ coordinate of the input image I and its intensity values before and after filtering are I(x,y) and Y(x,y) respectively. Our algorithm basically consists of two main parts which are elaborated below in details.

3.5.1 Noise Detection

To reduce the execution time, the authors take the switching concept to detect the impulse noise. Each pixel in I i.e. I(x,y) is compared with two predefined thresholds. I(x,y) is said to be noise free if I(x,y) lies between these two threshold values, otherwise I(x,y) is considered as noisy pixels.

Step 1: *Noise_free_pixel*= {I(x,y), if 0<I(x,y) <255 | x ∈ [1,M] & y ∈ [1,N]} and
Step 2: *Noisy_pixel*={I(x,y), if 0≥I(x,y) or I(x,y) ≥255 | x ∈ [1,M] & y ∈ [1,N]}.

3.5.2 Noise Suppression and Restoration

In noise detection phase, If I(x,y) is detected as impulse noise then depending on the condition a 3x3 or 5x5 window is designed. To detect the edge and thin line of input image the authors consider the adaptive concept with some decision. At first a 3x3 window (W_{3x3}) is created which is centered at I(x,y). Let mn, md and mx are the minimum, median and maximum value of W_{3x3}. If mn<md<mx and mn>0 and mx<255, then I(x,y) is altered with md otherwise design a 5×5 window (W_{5x5}) and check the above condition if count≥3 for 0<W_{5x5}<255, otherwise I(x,y) is altered with last processing value (LPV). The formulations and details steps of the algorithm are as follows:

W_{3x3}={(x-1:x+1,y-1:y+1) | x ∈ [2,P-1] & y ∈ [2,Q-1]}, where (P x Q) is the size
     of the I after zero padding.
W_{5x5}= {(x-2:x+2,y-2:y+2) | x ∈ [3,P-2] & y ∈ [3,Q-2]}, where (P x Q) is the size
     of the I after zero padding.
mn=min{W_{3x3} or 0<W_{5x5}<255},
md=median{W_{3x3} or 0<W_{5x5}<255},
mx=max{W_{3x3} or 0<W_{5x5}<255} and
count= number of element of [0<W_{5x5}<255].

The output of the proposed algorithm from the above steps and decision based adaptive filtering concepts are

Step 3: Y(x,y)= { I(x,y), if 0<I(x,y) <255 | x ∈ [1,M] & y ∈ [1,N]} else
Step 4: Y(x,y)={md, if mn<md<mx | mn, md & mx ∈ W_{3x3}} else
Step 5: Y(x,y))={md, if mn<md<mx | mn, md & mx ∈ [0<W_{5x5}<255] & count≥3}
     else
Step 6: Y(x,y))={md, if mn<md<mx | mn, md & mx ∈ W_{5x5}} else
Step 7: Y(x,y)={LPV, if exist(LPV)} else
Step 8: Y(x,y)=md
Step 9: LPV={Y(x,1), if y==N}else
Step 10: LPV=Y(x,y).

In the given algorithm, the authors can see that the noise free pixels are being unaltered and noisy pixels are altered by decision based median or LPV value to suppress the high density impulse noise.

4. HARDWARE ARCHITECTURE

The proposed architectures are based on a sequence of pipeline stages in order to reduce computational time. Parallel processing has been employed for further acceleration of the process. A 3x3 or 5x5 pixel image neighbourhood can be used for computation of the filter output. The design of the median filter consists of two basic operational units, the window creation unit and the median computation unit.

4.1 Implementation of Architectures

The proposed median filter and switching median filter structures are designed, compiled and simulated using Xilinx ISE (v. 14.5) software of XILINX Inc. For flexibility and advantageous characteristics of FPGA, the hardware implementation has been done into it. FPGA enables us for modification of the logic function of system by simply reconfiguring the device. Hardware implemented in other logic technologies cannot be changed once implemented in a system. Therefore, consisting of convenience and ease-of-use advantages, FPGAs are now a mainstream logic technology and provide a way of obtaining high performance on digital system design (Pande & Chen, 2013). at an economical price. The FPGA used for the proposed design is the Genesys Virtex5 board of the XC5VLX50T device family. The XC5VLX50T -2ff1136 device provides 120x30 CLB array, 28,800 number of 6-input LUTs, 28,800 number of slice registers, 28,800 number used as logic, 7,200 number of occupied slices, 480 kb maximum distributed RAM, 240 Kb shift registers and 28,800 number of Flip-flops is suitable for different kind of memory functions and large number of complex logic functions.

4.1.1 Median Filter

The design of the median filter consists of two basic operational units, the window creation unit and the median computation unit (Zhnget et. al., 2002; Luo, 2006). The input data of the system are the grayscale values of the pixels of the image neighbourhood. The image input data is imported serially into the first stage. In this way total number of input pins are 9 (8 inputs for the input image data and one is for clock signal). The output data of the system are the resultant grayscale values

Figure 6. Window creation unit

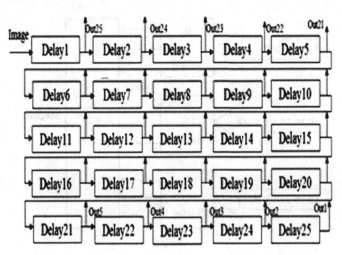

computed for the selected operation (eight output pins). The hardware structure of median filter and the computation procedure are illustrated in below figures. In the following subsections the design and functional characteristics of the two previously mentioned units are described in detail.

4.1.1.1 Window Creation Unit

The pixel values of the input image, denoted as "Input [7:0]", are imported into this unit serially. In order to obtain the n x n window, a set of dual port Delay Blocks are used to generate the row of the window. For generation of this window, n number of delay blocks are needed in which the first block takes zero latency and the other takes latency one. A 5x5 window creation unit is depicted in Figure 6.

These delay blocks are used to delay each input pixel by one clock period. By this way the authors can generate every filtering window at the rate of n pixel clock and the pixels in the filtering window are sent to the median computation unit in a parallel mode.

4.1.1.2 Median Computation

In this stage, the median value of the image neighbourhood is computed in order to substitute central pixel value. For 5x5 window, hardware implementation of median computation unit is depicted in Figure 7 and 8. In the Figure 7, the input data of median computation unit is the output of the filtering window creation unit, described by S. Zhang et. al. in 2002.In Figure 8, from stage 2, the authors can get the maximum and minimum output value. From stage 3, the authors can get the median.

Figure 7. Median computation unit

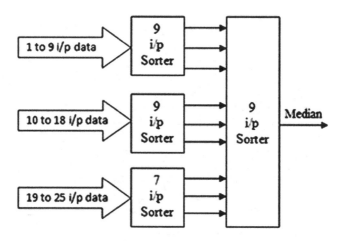

Figure 8. Internal structure of 9 input sorter

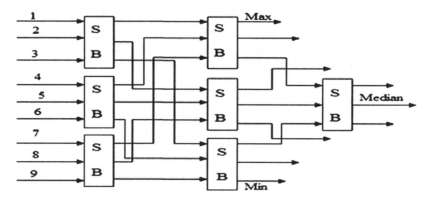

The median computation unit consists of 3 stages of comparing circuits. Each stage comprises three tri input comparators (SB) shown in Figure 9, whose outputs are organized in descending order. The maximum value of each comparator is put together as a group and that is the same with the median value and the minimum value of each comparator. The median computation stage consists of 3 stages of comparing blocks. Each stage comprises of tri input comparators (SB) in Figure 9. The maximum value of each comparator is put together as a group and that is the same with the median value and the minimum value of each comparator. From stage 3 the authors can get the median output value.

Figure 9. Internal diagram of sorter block (SB)

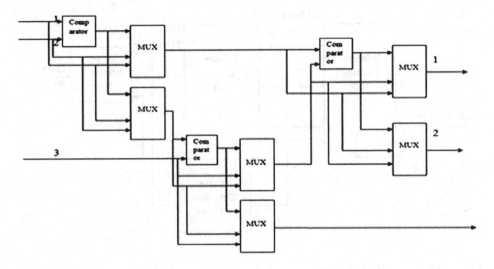

4.1.2 Switching Median Filter

The proposed architectures are based on a sequence of pipeline stages in order to reduce computational time. Parallel processing has been employed for further acceleration of the process (Srinivasan & Ebenezer, 2007). A 3x3 or 5x5 pixel image neighbourhood can be selected for computation of the filter output. The design of the switching median filter consists of four basic operational unit., the window creation unit, impulse noise detection unit, the median computation unit and output selection unit. The input data of the system are the gray scale values of the pixels of the image neighbourhood. The image input data is imported serially into the first stage. In this way total number of input pins are 9 (8 inputs for the input image data and one is for clock signal). The output data of the system are the resultant gray scale values computed for the selected operation (eight output pins). The hardware structure of switching median filter and the computation procedure are illustrated in Figure 10. In the following subsections the design and functional characteristics of the two previously mentioned units are described in detail.

4.1.2.1 Window Creation Unit
The pixel values of the input image, denoted as "Input [7:0]", are imported into this unit serially. In order to obtain the n x n window, a set of dual port Delay Blocks are used to generate the row of the window. For generation of this window, n number of delay blocks are needed in which the first block takes zero latency and the other takes latency one. A 5x5 window creation unit is depicted in Figure 6. These delay

Figure 10. Hardware design of switching median filter

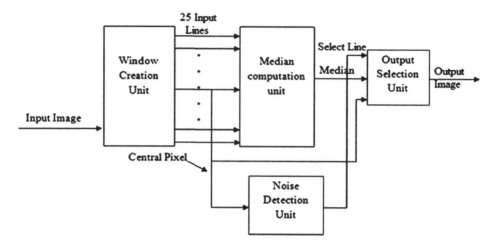

Figure 11. Noise detection unit

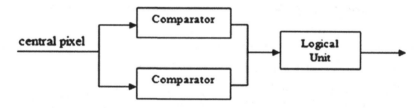

blocks are used to delay each input pixel by one clock period. By this way the authors can generate every filtering window at the rate of n pixel clock and the pixels in the filtering window are sent to the median computation unit in a parallel mode.

4.1.2.2 Noise Detection Unit

The aim of noise detection unit is to detect the noise pixel with the help of threshold value (Luo, 2005; Hu et. al., 2009). Each central pixel should be compared with predefined threshold values (T1 & T2) shown in Figure 11.

The noise detection unit is designed with two comparator blocks and one logic block. The output of the logical unit is the input of the output selection unit for output selection. The central pixel is considered to be noise free when its value between T1 & T2, otherwise it is considered as noisy pixel.

4.1.2.3 Median Computation Unit

In this stage, the median value of the image neighbourhood is computed only when it is necessary in order to substitute central pixel value. For 5x5 windows, hardware

Figure 12. Output selection unit

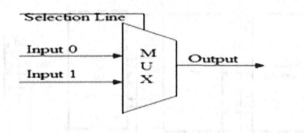

implementation of median computation unit is as previously depicted in Figure 7 and 8. Median computation unit is same for median filter and switching median filter.

4.1.2.4 Output Selection Unit

The final stage of the design is the output selection unit is shown in Figure 12. In this stage, the output value for the performed operation is selected depending on the output of noise detection unit.

Depending on the result of comparison between central pixel and threshold values, the central pixel is considered to be corrupted by noise or not. For the case of impulse noise, if the central pixel value is not between T1 and T2, then the central pixel is impulse noise and has to be eliminated. For this reason, the output of the noise detection unit is used as selection signal of a multiplexer whose inputs are the central pixel and the corresponding median value for the image neighbourhood. The output of multiplexer, denoted as "OUT [7:0]" is the output of this stage and the final output of the circuit of the switching median filter.

4.1.3 Adaptive Median Filter

The proposed architecture is based on a sequence of pipeline stages in order to reduce computational time same as MF and SMF. Parallel processing has been employed for further acceleration of the process (Luo, 2005). A 3x3 or 5x5 pixel image neighbourhood can be selected for computation of the filtered output. The design of the Adaptive median filter (AMF) consists of four basic operational units, i) the window creation unit, ii) impulse noise detection unit, iii) the adaptive median computation unit and iv) output selection unit. The input data of the system are the gray scale values of the pixels of the image neighbourhood window. The image input data is imported serially into the first stage. In this way total number of input pins are 9 (8 inputs for the input image data and one is for clock signal). The output data of the system are the resultant gray scale values computed for the selected operation (eight output pins). The hardware structure of AMF of window size 5x5 and

Figure 13. Hardware design of adaptive median filter

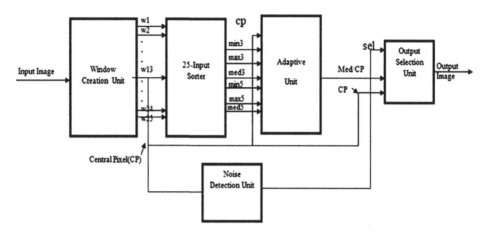

the computation procedure are illustrated in Figure 13. In the following subsections the design and functional characteristics of the two previously mentioned units are described in detail.

4.1.3.1 Window Creation Unit

The pixel values of the input image, denoted as "Input [7:0]", are imported into this unit serially. In order to obtain the n x n window, a set of dual port Delay Blocks are used to generate the row of the window. For generation of this window, n number of delay blocks are needed in which the first block takes zero latency and the other takes latency one. A 5x5 window creation unit is depicted in Figure 6. These delay blocks are used to delay each input pixel by one clock period. By this way the authors can generate every filtering window at the rate of n pixel clock and the pixels in the filtering window are sent to the median computation unit in a parallel mode.

4.1.3.2 Noise Detection Unit

The aim of noise detection unit is to detect the noise pixel with the help of threshold value. Each central pixel should be compared with predefined threshold values (T1 & T2) shown in Figure 11. The noise detection unit is designed with two comparator blocks and one logic block. The output of the logical unit is the input of the output selection unit for output selection. The central pixel is considered to be noise free when its value between T1 & T2, otherwise it is considered as noisy pixel.

4.1.3.3 Adaptive Median Value Computation Unit

The main part of AMF is the adaptive median value computation unit shown in Figure 14. The authors designed this stage with the help of three 9-input sorter block,

Figure 14. Adaptive median value computation unit

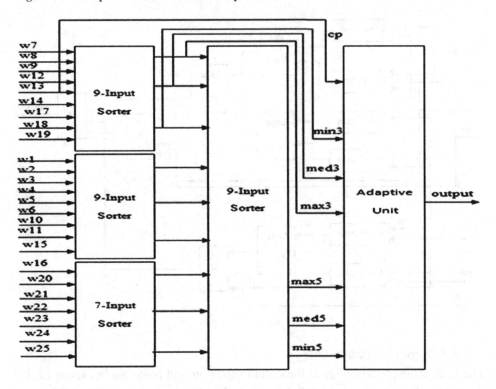

one 7-input sorter block and one adaptive unit. The 9-input sorter blocks are shown in previously depicted Figure 8. The incoming window (5x5) is divided into three parts the windowing elements w7, w8, w9, w12, w13, w14, w17, w18 and w19 are the input of 1st sorter block and remain elements are divided into two sets one with nine elements and another with 7 elements. The output of 1st sorter block is the output of a 3x3 window; its origin is the origin of the 5x5 window. All the max, min and meds are the input of the fourth 9-input sorter which generate the output of 5x5 window. Next the all min, max, med and cp of window size 3x3 and 5x5 are the input of Adaptive unit shown in Figure 15which create the adaptive median value as output. The adaptive unit is designed with six comparator blocks, four logic blocks and three multiplexer blocks. In this unit, depending on the impulse noise characters it selects the median value of window 3x3 or window 5x5 or the central pixel value. Detail is shown in Figure 15.

Figure 15. Adaptive unit

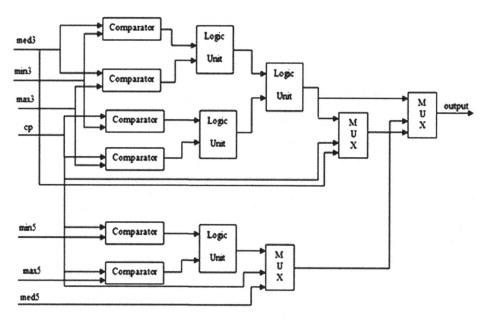

4.1.3.4 Output Selection Unit

The final stage of the design is the output selection unit is shown in Figure 12. In this stage, the output value for the performed operation is selected depending on the output of noise detection unit.

Depending on the result of comparison between central pixel and threshold values, the central pixel is considered to be corrupted by noise or not. For the case of impulse noise, if the central pixel value is not between T1 and T2, then the central pixel is impulse noise and has to be eliminated. For this reason, the output of the noise detection unit is used as selection signal of a multiplexer whose inputs are the central pixel and the corresponding median value for the image neighbourhood. The output of multiplexer denoted as "OUT [7:0]" is the output of this stage and the final output of the circuit of the switching median filter.

4.1.4 Decision-Based Adaptive Filtering Method

The proposed architecture is designed in pipeline manner to minimize computational time. Parallel processing has also been introduced to accelerate the design. A 3x3 or 5x5 pixel image neighborhood can be selected for computation of the filter output. The design of the DBAM filter consists of three different operational stages which are described in the following paragraphs. The hardware structure of DBAM filter

Figure 16. Hardware design of DBAM filter

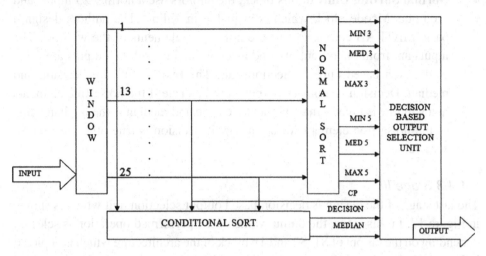

and the computation procedure are illustrated in Figure 16. In the following subsections the design and functional characteristics of previously mentioned stages are described in detail.

4.1.4.1 Stage I
The pixel values of the input image are imported into this module serially to design a moving window. In order to obtain the n x n window, a set of Delay Blocks are used to generate the row of the window. For generation of this window, (n x n) numbers of delay blocks are required with latency one. A 5x5 window creation module is depicted in Figure 6.

4.1.4.2 Stage II
- **Normal Sorting Unit:** In this stage, computation of minimum, median and maximum values of windows (3x3 and 5x5) are done from image neighborhood. For 5x5 window, hardware implementation of median computation module is depicted in Figure 7 and 8. In the Figure 7, the input data of normal sort module is the output of the filtering window creation module. In Figure 8, from stage 2, the authors can get the maximum and minimum output value. From stage 4, the authors can get the median value. The normal sort module consists of 4 stages of comparing blocks. Each stage comprises of tri input comparators (SB) in Figure 6, whose outputs are organized in descending order. The maximum value of each comparator is put together as a group and that is the same with the median value and the minimum value of each comparator. From stage 4 the authors get the median output value.

- • **Normal Sorting Unit:** In this block, the authors use a normal 25 inputs and 2 outputs Mcode block which is available in Xilinx. The authors design a basic MATLAB coding to sort the noise free elements of the window. The inputs are from the output of window creation unit and the outputs are input of decision based output selection unit. The two outputs are decision and median. Decision is a binary output, which is true if the noise free elements in a window is greater than 3 otherwise false and median is the median value of the noise free elements of a window if decision is true otherwise return zero value.

4.1.4.3 Stage III

The last stage of the design is decision based output selection unit which is shown in Figure 17. In this stage, the output value of the performed operation is selected depending on the output of S1, S2 and Th block of the architecture which is depicted in Figure 17. The internal structure of S1 and S2 block is shown in Figure 18 and the Th block is illustrated in Figure 11.

Figure 17. Diagram of decision based output selection

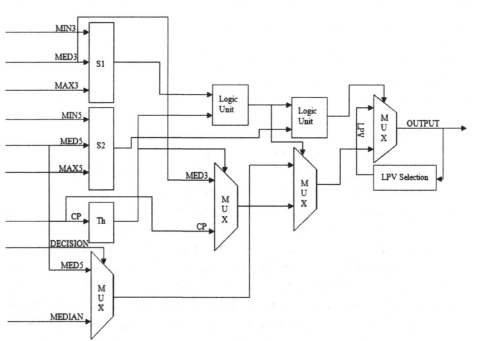

Figure 18. Diagram of S1 and S2 Block

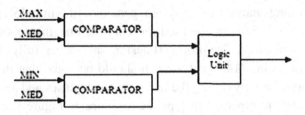

- **The Module:** The aim of noise Th module is to detect the noisy pixel with the help of threshold value. Each central pixel should be compared with pre-defined threshold values (T1 & T2) shown in Figure 11. The central pixel is considered to be noise free when its value between T1 & T2, otherwise it is considered as noisy pixel.
- **Adaptive Module:** The decision based output selection unit itself is an adaptive module, which is the most important part of the design. The aim of this module is to implement the decision based adaptive algorithm. The output of this module is median value of 3 x 3 neighbor window or 5 x 5 neighbor window or central pixel or median value of noise free pixels in the window or last processing value (LPV) depending on the adaptive condition. This module is depicted in Figure 18.

5. IMPLEMENTATION ISSUES OF HARDWARE ARCHITECTURE

The proposed median filter and switching median filter structures are designed, compiled and simulated using Xilinx ISE (v. 14.5) software of XILINX Inc. For flexibility and advantageous characteristics of FPGA, the hardware implementation has been done into it. FPGA enables us for modification of the logic function of system by simply reconfiguring the device. Hardware implemented in other logic technologies cannot be changed once implemented in a system. Therefore, consisting of convenience and ease-of-use advantages, FPGAs are now a mainstream logic technology and provide a way of obtaining high performance on digital system design (Pande & Chen, 2013). at an economical price. The FPGA used for the proposed design is the Genesys Virtex5 board of the XC5VLX50T device family. The XC5VLX50T -2ff1136 device provides 120x30 CLB array, 28,800 number of 6-input LUTs, 28,800 number of slice registers, 28,800 number used as logic, 7,200 number of occupied slices, 480 kb maximum distributed RAM, 240 Kb shift registers and 28,800 number of Flip-flops is suitable for different kind of memory functions and large number of complex logic functions.

The typical maximum operating clock frequency of the proposed designs is estimated by the timing analyzer using system generator of Xilinx ISE software. The presented hardware designs can be used for real time imaging applications where fast processing is required. The proposed designs are successfully simulated with Isim simulator of Xilinx (14.5) software. It should be noted that the image input values are imported serially during the first nine clock pulses and generated output timings are decided in respect of its pipeline structure. In Figure 19 and Figure 20, the routed logic block design view of the XC5VLX50T-2ff1136 device used to for the implementation of the median filter and switching median filter respectively, extracted by the FPGA editor of Genesys Virtex5 board, are illustrated. These views show the interiors of the chip used, including the individual logic cells within each routed logic block design.

By making only a small number of changes, the system can be modified to accommodate windows for larger sizes in simple way. In a more specific way it could be said that, in the first unit, window size increases following a square law and in the second unit, if the last input stage is i and number of SB in $(i-1)^{th}$ input stage is n then the number of SB is required in ith stage is n+(2*i+1)., whereas no changes are required in the last two units of switching median filter.

6. RESULTS AND ITS ANALYSIS

6.1 Median, Switching and Adaptive Median Filter

In Figure 21 (a), the original uncorrupted image "Lena" is depicted, in Figure 21 (b), the original image is degraded by 3% impulse noise (salt & pepper noise). In Figure 21(c) and 21(d), the resultant images of the application of median and switching median filter for a 3x3 pixel window are shown respectively. The resultant images of the application of median filter and switching median filter for a 5x5 pixel window are presented in Figure 21(e) and Figure 21(f) and finally, the results for 3x3 and 5x5 window for AMF are shown in Figure 21(g) and 21(h) respectively.

In Figure 22 (a), 23(a) and 24(a), the original uncorrupted "Peppers", "Baboon" and "Lena" image is depicted respectively, in Figure 22 (b), 23(b) and 24(b), the original image is degraded by 5% impulse noise (salt & pepper noise). In Figure 22(c), 22(d) & 23(c), 23(d)& 24(c), 24(d) shows the result for median filter for "Peppers", "Baboon" and "Lena" image for window 3x3 and 5x5 respectively. In Figure 22(e), 22(f) & 23(e), 23(f) & 24(e), 24(f) shows the result for SMF for "Peppers", "Baboon" and "Lena" image for window 3x3 and 5x5 respectively. In Figure 22(g), 22(h) & 23(g), 23(h) & 24(g), 24(h) shows the result for AMF for "Peppers", "Baboon" and "Lena" image for window 3x3 and 5x5 respectively.

Figure 19. The routed logic block design view for median filter (5x5) of the XC5V-LX50T-2ff1136 device

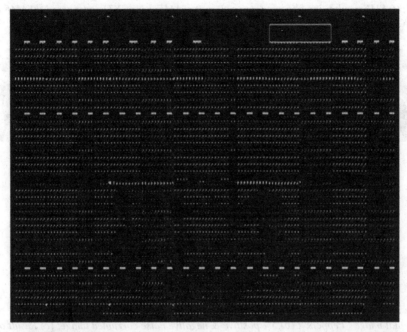

Figure 20. The routed logic block design view for switching median filter (5x5) of the XC5VLX50T-2ff1136 device

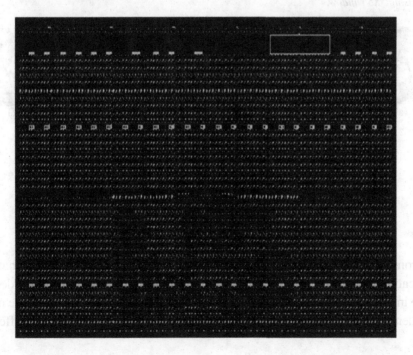

Figure 21. Impulse noise suppression using software based method
(a) Original image "Lena"; (b) 3% positive & negative noise corrupted image; (c) Result of median filter using 3X3 window; (d) SMF result using 3X3 window; (e) Result of median filter using 5X5 window; (f) SMF result using 5X5 window; (g) Result of AMF using 3X3 window; and (h) AMF result using 5X5 window.

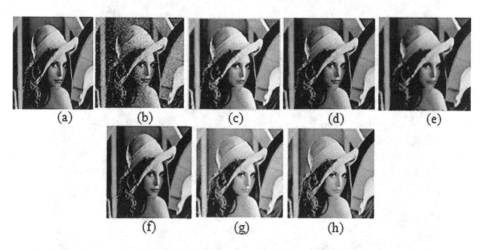

Figure 22. Impulse noise suppression
(a) Original image "Peppers"; (b) 5% positive & negative noise corrupted image; (c) Result of median filter using 3X3 window; (d) SMF result using 3X3 window; (e) Result of median filter using 5X5 window; (f) SMF result using 5X5 window; (g) Result of AMF using 3X3 window; and (h) AMF result using 5X5 window.

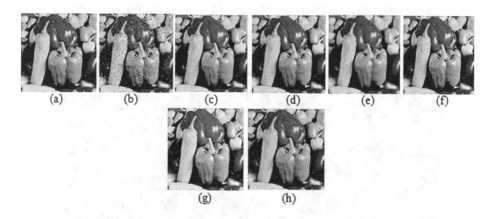

From Figure 21, Figure 22, Figure 23 and Figure 24, it can be noticed that the application of Adaptive median filter (AMF) preserves much better edges and details of the images in comparison to the median type filters. Different performance measurements can be used for calculation of these results. By explanation the different

Figure 23. Impulse noise suppression
(a) Original image "Baboon"; (b) 5% positive & negative noise corrupted image; (c) Result of median filter using 3X3 window; (d) SMF result using 3X3 window; (e) Result of median filter using 5X5 window; (f) SMF result using 5X5 window; (g) Result of AMF using 3X3 window; and (h) AMF result using 5X5 window.

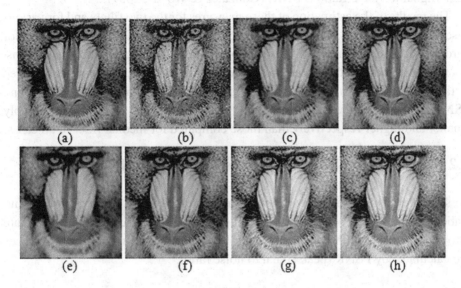

Figure 24. Impulse noise suppression
(a) Original image "Lena"; (b) 5% positive & negative noise corrupted image; (c) Result of median filter using 3X3 window; (d) SMF result using 3X3 window; (e) Result of median filter using 5X5 window; (f) SMF result using 5X5 window; (g) Result of AMF using 3X3 window; and (h) AMF result using 5X5 window.

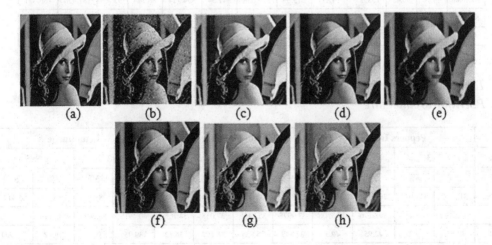

in the statistical distributions of the pixel values, all of the measurements provide some measure of closeness between two digital images, in (Andreadisand & Louverdis, 2004). The most widely used measures are Mean Square Error (MSE) and Peak Signal to Noise Ratio (PSNR) (Gonzalez & Woods, 2009).

The results of the estimation of these measures for the two filters and for various cases of impulse noise and window size are depicted in the Table 1 and Table 2 for hardware architecture and Table 3 and Table 4 for software based implementations. For the computation of these measures the resultant images of the filters are compared to the original uncorrupted image. From tables it can be noted that the MSE and PSNR computed for the application of the switching median filter are considerably smaller and higher respectively than those computed for median filter in all cases.

6.2 New Decision Based Adaptive Filtering Method

To simulate this proposed algorithm the authors used Lena, Pepper, Barbara and Baboon images of size 512×512 as test input image. Impulse noise is incorporate into the test images with a wide range from 0% to 99% and de-noising performances are calculated by PSNR (peak signal to noise ratio).

Table 1. Comparative results among proposed MF, SMF and AMF in terms of MSE for architecture

	Peppers Image				Baboon Image				Lena Image			
Size	3x3		5x5		3x3		5x5		3x3		5x5	
Noise	3%	5%	3%	5%	3%	5%	3%	5%	3%	5%	3%	5%
Median	44.98	50.45	135.069	147.71	213.09	219.638	347.54	354.724	86.794	92.32	181.436	186.771
SMF	3.874	7.037	7.101	11.913	10.311	16.92	12.802	21.705	6.367	9.737	10.045	12.57
AMF	3.92	7.693	*3.296*	*5.794*	10.547	16. 996	*9.861*	*15.938*	6.58	10.05	*6.934*	*10.537*

Table 2. Comparative results between proposed MF, SMF and AMF in terms of PSNRfor architecture

	Peppers Image				Baboon Image				Lena Image			
Size	3x3		5x5		3x3		5x5		3x3		5x5	
Noise	3%	5%	3%	5%	3%	5%	3%	5%	3%	5%	3%	5%
Median	31.6002	31.1022	26.8252	26.4367	24.8452	24.7137	22.7208	22.6319	28.7459	28.4778	25.5436	25.4177
SMF	42.2492	39.6569	39.6176	37.3706	37.9978	35.8468	37.058	34.7652	40.0915	38.2466	38.1113	37.1375
AMF	42.198	39.27	*42.95*	*40.5*	37.899	35.835	*38.192*	*36.12*	39.95	38.11	*39.72*	*37.904*

Table 3. Comparative results among proposed MF, SMF and AMF in terms of MSEfor software based method

Size	Peppers Image				Baboon Image				Lena Image			
	3x3		5x5		3x3		5x5		3x3		5x5	
Noise	3%	5%	3%	5%	3%	5%	3%	5%	3%	5%	3%	5%
Median	45.23	51.58	110.016	114.554	379.97	388.32	494.058	499.22	67.59	72.92	136.92	140.70
SMF	3.23	6.685	48.2	51.23	17.05	28.04	158.31	167.33	3.69	6.61	58.079	61.35
AMF	3.42	*5.94*	*10.02*	*13.29*	*16.84*	*27.99*	*70.4*	*77.71*	3.83	6.88	*16.84*	*19.71*

Table 4. Comparative results between proposed MF, SMF and AMF in terms of PSNRfor software based method

Size	Peppers Image				Baboon Image				Lena Image			
	3x3		5x5		3x3		5x5		3x3		5x5	
Noise	3%	5%	3%	5%	3%	5%	3%	5%	3%	5%	3%	5%
Median	31.576	31.006	27.716	27.54	22.333	22.29	21.19	21.15	29.83	29.50	26.77	26.65
SMF	43.03	39.88	31.3	31.035	35.814	33.653	26.136	25.89	42.46	39.93	30.49	30.25
AMF	42.79	*40.39*	*38.12*	*36.89*	*35.867*	*33.66*	*29.655*	*29.27*	42.299	39.755	*35.867*	*35.183*

$$PSNR = 10 \log_{10} \left(\frac{255 * 255}{MSE} \right) \qquad (6)$$

$$MSE = \frac{1}{R * C} \sum_{i=0}^{R-1} \sum_{j=0}^{C-1} \left[J(x,y) - I(x,y) \right] \qquad (7)$$

where MSE stands for mean square error, J stands for original image and I stand for output image and R×C is size of image.

The PSNR and CPU execution time in seconds are measured for our algorithm. The authors compare the proposed algorithm with some standard filter like normal median filter (MF), adaptive median filter (Gonzalez & Woods, 2009), conditional median filter (Kasparis, Tzannes, & Chen, 1992) and some latest filter such as fuzzy based decision algorithm (Nair 2012), decision based adaptive weighted and trimmed median filter (Nooshyar & Momeny, 2013), High Density Noise Removal based on Linear Mean-Median Filter (Utaminingrum, 2013), Adaptive Fuzzy Filter (Sultana, 2013) and Iterative Adaptive Fuzzy Filter using alpha-trimmed Mean (Ahmed, 2013).

Table 5. Comparison of PSNR of different filters for "LENA" image

Filters	Noise Density											
	5%	10%	20%	30%	40%	50%	60%	70%	80%	90%	95%	99%
FBDA (Nair, 2012)	–	–	–	35.0	33.5	32.1	30.8	29.6	28.0	25.6	20.9	–
DAWTMF (Nooshyar, 2013)	–	43.0	39.0	36.7	34.4	32.7	31.1	29.6	27.8	–	–	–
HDNRLMMF (Utaminingrum, 2013)	–	42.9	39.3	37.1	34.9	33.3	31.37	29.4	26.7	23.7	–	–
AFF (Sultana, 2013)	–	–	–	34.0	32.9	31.5	30.5	29.6	28.2	25.7	23.3	–
IAFFATM (Ahmed, 2013)	–	43.0	–	–	–	34.1	–	–	–	26.8	–	–
PA	51.4	47.4	42.7	39.7	37.1	34.7	32.5	29.6	27.3	23.5	21.4	16.6

Table 6. Comparison of TIME (SECONDS) of different filters for "LENA" image

Filters	Noise Density											
	5%	10%	20%	30%	40%	50%	60%	70%	80%	90%	95%	99%
HDNRLMMF (Utaminingrum, 2013)	–	1.12	1.14	1.17	1.23	1.30	1.36	1.41	1.45	1.50	–	–
FEDBA (Srinivasan, 2007)	–	36.26	36.29	36.30	36.15	36.40	36.32	36.10	36.42	36.25	–	–
AFF (Sultana, 2013)	14.01	14.01	14.01	14.01	14.01	14.01	14.01	14.01	14.01	14.01	–	–
IAFFATM (Ahmed, 2013)	–	–	4.61	–	–	39.59	–	–	109.98	–	–	–
PA	1.97	2.45	3.76	4.63	6.02	7.85	10.09	12.47	16.59	25.06	32.84	37.48

Table 7. Comparison of PSNR of different filters for "Peppers" image

Filters	Noise Density											
	5%	10%	20%	30%	40%	50%	60%	70%	80%	90%	95%	99%
DAWTMF (Nooshyar, 2013)	–	39.80	36.50	34.20	32.50	31.10	29.70	28.50	26.80	–	–	–
IAFFATM (Ahmed, 2013)	–	–	37.99	–	–	32.59	–	–	27.98	–	–	–
PA	52.0	47.77	42.92	39.89	37.34	34.71	32.56	30.56	27.55	25.20	22.45	16.79

Table 8. Comparison of TIME (SECONDS) of different filters for "Pepper" image

Filters	Noise Density											
	5%	10%	20%	30%	40%	50%	60%	70%	80%	90%	95%	99%
IAFFATM (Ahmed, 2013)	–	–	4.60	–	–	39.41	–	–	108.56	–	–	–
PA	1.70	2.27	3.38	4.77	5.96	7.75	10.54	12.54	16.15	26.15	32.46	41.25

The performance in terms of PSNR is depicted Table 5 and Table 7 and execution time is depicted in Table 6 and Table 8 respectively after simulating the Lena and Pepper images with different filters (see Figure 25 and Figure 26).

Figure 27 show the PSNR vs Noise density (5%- 95%) plot of PA and some of above said algorithms. The higher value of PSNR of proposed algorithm below 80% noise density and comparing PSNR above 80% and lower execution time (Sec.) shows that proposed algorithm is better in performance and throughput. Apart from the above performance boost up use of predefined threshold is another advantageous property of our algorithm over other advanced filtering algorithm. At first, the

Figure 25. Visual effect of Lena image corrupted by salt and pepper noise and filtered image as result

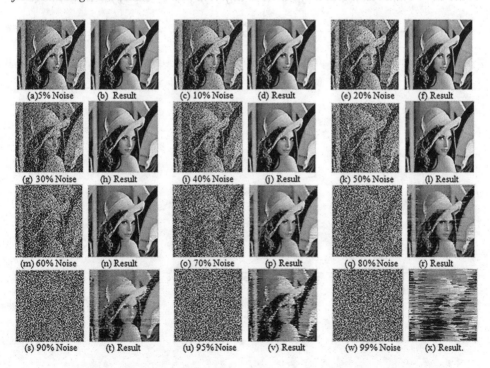

(a) 5% Noise   (b) Result   (c) 10% Noise   (d) Result   (e) 20% Noise   (f) Result

(g) 30% Noise   (h) Result   (i) 40% Noise   (j) Result   (k) 50% Noise   (l) Result

(m) 60% Noise   (n) Result   (o) 70% Noise   (p) Result   (q) 80% Noise   (r) Result

(s) 90% Noise   (t) Result   (u) 95% Noise   (v) Result   (w) 99% Noise   (x) Result.

Figure 26. Visual effect of Pepper image corrupted by salt and pepper noise and filtered image as result

Figure 27. Comparison graph of PSNR at different noise density for Lena image

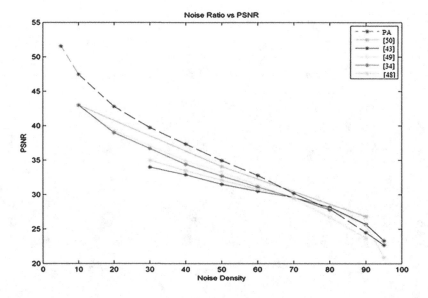

authors choose the adaptive window concept and predefined threshold rather than threshold measurement. Secondly, there is no need to measure threshold based on trial and error method as well as local mean for our proposed algorithm. Moreover, there is no window operation is needed for noise detection step and also window is designed only for noisy pixels. There is an ignorable disadvantage of proposed algorithm i.e. in higher density of noise, proposed algorithm gives little bit lower performance in terms of PSNR but the execution time is effective compare to other latest methods.

The computational time of our proposed algorithm for Lena and Pepper images is depicted in Table 6 and Table 8 respectively. Execution time (Sec.) is measured in Windows 7 environment, AMD processor (2.46 GHz) with 2GB RAM. The authors used Matlab (V. 2013a) for implementation and simulation of the proposed algorithm.

7. CONCLUSION

This chapter presents a new comparative architecture design of median filter, switching median filter and adaptive median filter which are capable of performing impulse noise suppression for 8 bit gray scale images using a 3x3 and 5x5 pixel neighbourhoods and an algorithm for removing the impulse noise using new decision based adaptive filtering method. The proposed design for SMF and AMF identifies the existence of impulse noise in the image neighbourhood and applies the corresponding median computation unit and adaptive median value computation unit respectively only when necessary but it is not true for median filter. Pixel values other than the two extreme ones can be considered as impulse noise, provided that they are significantly different from the central pixel value. Being compared with median filter, the switching median filter and adaptive median filter avoids the blurring of the image and preserves the detail information and edge integrity. Experimental results confirm the improved performance of adaptive median filter over switching median filter and switching median filter over median filter. These three systems are suitable for real time imaging applications. Moreover, the design of the three circuits can be easily modified to accommodate larger size windows requiring some small modifications in first two units. The proposed designs are successfully designed, compiled and simulated in FPGA. The device used for that circuit implementation is the XC5VLX50T-2ff1136 chip of Genesys Virtex5 board with 100MHz fixed oscillator and (up to) 400MHz programmable clock generator. The most significant features of modern image processing techniques are the robustness and image details i.e. edges, thin lines and small objects preservation. The authors proposed a decision based switching adaptive filter that gives the significant result for robustness and details preservation of the input image corrupted by high impulse noise. The Table 5 and Table 7 contains the quantitative measures in terms of PSNR which prove that our proposed filter is beneficial and the visualization of the filtered image is better than other filters at lower noise level and comparable even at higher impulse noise density up to 99%. Furthermore, the FPGA based architecture of the algorithm in Chapter 7 will be designed in future if there will be scope for real time image processing. The Table 6 contains the comparative execution time (in Second) which shows that the proposed algorithm is speeder than FEDBA (Srinivasan, 2007), AFF (Sultana, 2013) and IAFFATM (Ahmed, 2013) but slower than HDNRLMMF (Utaminingrum, 2013) for Lena image. The proposed method is tested and simulated for 8-bitgray-scale images corrupted with salt & pepper noise only. The method would be tested and simulated for different type of images and noises.

REFERENCES

Abreu, E., Lightstone, M., Mitra, S. K., & Arakawa, K. (1996). A New Efficient Approach For The Removal Of Impulse Noise From Highly Corrupted Images. *IEEE Transactions on Image Processing*, 5(6), 1012–1025. doi:10.1109/83.503916 PMID:18285188

Ahmed, F., & Das, S. (2013). Removal of High Density Salt-and-Pepper Noise in Images with an Iterative Adaptive Fuzzy Filter using alpha-trimmed Mean. *IEEE Transactions on Fuzzy Systems*, 22(5), 1352–1358. doi:10.1109/TFUZZ.2013.2286634

Andreadisand, I., & Louverdis, G. (2004). Real Time Adaptive Image Impulse Noise Suppression. *IEEE Transactions on Instrumentation and Measurement*, 53(3), 798–8064. doi:10.1109/TIM.2004.827306

Arakawa, K. (1996). Median Filter Based on Fuzzy Rules and Its Application to Image Restoration. *Fuzzy Sets and Systems*, 77(1), 3–13. doi:10.1016/0165-0114(95)00122-0

Arce, G. R., Gallagher, N. C., & Nodes, T. (1986). *Median filters: Theory and applications*. Advances in Computer Vision and Image Processing.

Astola, J. T., & Campbell, T. G. (1989). On Computation of the Running Median. *IEEE Transactions on Acoustics, Speech, and Signal Processing*, 37(4), 572–574. doi:10.1109/29.17539

Astola, J. T., & Kuosmanen, P. (1997). *Fundamentals of Nonlinear Digital Filtering*. New York: CRC.

Baha, N., & Touzene, H. (2013). FPGA Implementation for Stereo Matching Algorithm.*IEEE Science and Information Conference (SAI)*.

Chan, R. H., Ho, C. W., & Nikolova, M. (2005). Salt-and-Pepper Noise Removal by Median-Type Noise Detectors and Detail-Preserving Regularization. *IEEE Transactions on Image Processing*, *14*(10), 1479–1485. doi:10.1109/TIP.2005.852196 PMID:16238054

Chang, J. (1995). Modified 2D median filter for impulse noise suppression in a real-time system. *IEEE Transactions on Consumer Electronics*, *41*(1), 73–80. doi:10.1109/30.370312

Chen, T., Ma, K. K., & Chen, L. H. (1999). Tri-State Median Filter for Image Denoising. *IEEE Transactions on Image Processing*, *8*(12), 1834–1838. doi:10.1109/83.806630 PMID:18267461

Dougherty, E. R., & Laplante, P. (1995). *Introduction to Real-Time Imaging*. Bellingham, WA: SPIE.

Eng, H. L., & Ma, K. K. (2001). Noise Adaptive Soft-Switching Median Filter. *IEEE Transactions on Image Processing*, *10*(2), 242–251. doi:10.1109/83.902289 PMID:18249615

Gonzalez, R. C., & Woods, R. E. (2009). *Digital Image Processing* (3rd ed.). Prentice Hall.

Gonzalez, R. C., Woods, R. E., & Eddins, S. L. (2004). *Digital Image Processing Using MATLAB*. Prentice-Hall.

Hodgson, R. M., Bailey, D. G., Nhaylor, M. J., Ng, L. M., & Mc-Cneil, S. J. (1985). Properties, implementations and applications of rank filters. *Image and Vision Computing*, *3*(1), 3–14. doi:10.1016/0262-8856(85)90037-X

Hu, Y., & Ji, H. (2009). Research on Image Median Filtering Algorithm and Its FPGA Implementation.*IEEE Conference, Global Congress On Intelligent System*. doi:10.1109/GCIS.2009.130

Huang, T. S., Yang, G. J., & Tang, G. Y. (1979). Fast Two-Dimensional Median Filtering Algorithm. *IEEE Transactions on Acoustics, Speech, and Signal Processing*, *1*(1), 13–18. doi:10.1109/TASSP.1979.1163188

Huang, T. S., Yaw, G. J., & Tang, C. Y. (1980). A Fast Two Dimensional Median-Filtering Algorithm. *IEEE Transactions on Acoustics, Speech, and Signal Processing*, *28*, 415–421. doi:10.1109/TASSP.1980.1163426

Ibrahim, H., Kong, N. S. P., & Ng, T. F. (2008). Simple Adaptive Median Filter for the Removal of Impulse Noise from Highly Corrupted Images. *IEEE Transactions on Consumer Electronics*, *54*(4), 1920–1927. doi:10.1109/TCE.2008.4711254

Kasparis, T. N., Tzannes, S., & Chen, Q. (1992). Detail-Preserving Adaptive Conditional Filters. *Journal of Electronic Imaging*, *1*(4), 358–364. doi:10.1117/12.61062

Ko, S. J., & Lee, Y. H. (1991). Center Weighted Median Filters and Their Applications to Image Enhancement. *IEEE Transactions on Circuits and Systems*, *38*(9), 984–993. doi:10.1109/31.83870

Lin, T. C. (2007). A New Adaptive Center Weighted Median Filter for Suppressing Impulsive Noise in Images. *Information Sciences*, *177*(4), 1073–1087. doi:10.1016/j.ins.2006.07.030

Luo, W. (2005). Efficient Removal of Impulse Noise from Digital Images. *IEEE Transactions on Consumer Electronics*, *52*, 523–527.

Luo, W. (2006). An Efficient Detail-Preserving Approach for Removing Impulse Noise In Images. *IEEE Signal Processing Letters*, *13*(7), 413–416. doi:10.1109/LSP.2006.873144

Munoz, A. R., Mompean, M. B., Olivas, E. S., Scarante, C., & Martinez, J. F. G. (2011). FPGA Implementation of an Adaptive Filter Robust to Impulse Noise: Two Approaches. *IEEE Transactions on Industrial Electronics*, *58*(3), 860–870. doi:10.1109/TIE.2009.2023641

Nair, M. S., & Raju, G. (2012). A New Fuzzy-Based Decision Algorithm for High-Density Impulse Noise Removal. *Signal Image and Video Processing*, *6*(4), 579–595. doi:10.1007/s11760-010-0186-4

Ng, P. E., & Ma, K. K. (2006). A Switching Median Filter with Boundary Discriminative Noise Detection for Extremely Corrupted Images. *IEEE Transactions on Image Processing*, *15*(6), 1506–1516. doi:10.1109/TIP.2005.871129 PMID:16764275

Nodes, T. A., & Gallagher, N. C. Jr. (1984). The Output Distribution Of Median Type Filters. *IEEE Transactions on Communications*, *32*(5), 532–541. doi:10.1109/TCOM.1984.1096099

Nooshyar, M., & Momeny, M. (2013). Removal of High Density Impulse Noise Using A Novel Decision Based Adaptive Weighted and Trimmed Median Filter. *8th Iranian Conference on Machine Vision and Image Processing (MVIP)*. doi:10.1109/IranianMVIP.2013.6780016

Own, C. M., & Huang, C. S. (2013). On the Design of Neighboring Fuzzy Median Filter for Removal of Impulse Noises. *Intelligent Information and Database Systems*, *7802*, 99–107. doi:10.1007/978-3-642-36546-1_11

Pande, A., & Chen, S. (2013). Hardware Architecture for Video Authentication using Sensor Pattern Noise. *IEEE Transactions on Circuits and Systems*, *24*, 157–167.

Petrou, M., & Bosdogianni, P. (2000). *Image Processing: The Fundamental*. John Wiley & Sons Ltd.

Pitas, I., & Venestsanopoulos, A. N. (1990). Nonlinear Digital Filters: Principles and Applications. Boston, MA: Kluwer.

Possa, P. R., Mahammoudi, S., & Valderrama, C. (2013). AS Multi-Resolution FPGA-Based Architecture for Real-Time Edge and Corner Detection. *IEEE Transactions on Computers*, *63*(10), 2376–2388. doi:10.1109/TC.2013.130

Pratt, W. K. (1991). *Digital Image Processing*. New York: Wiley.

Saeidi, M., Anzabi, L. C., & Khalegi, M. (2009). Image Sequences Filtering using A New Fuzzy Algorithm Based on Triangular Membership Function. *International Journal of Signal Processing. Image Processing and Pattern Recognition*, *2*, 75–90.

Salvador, R., Otero, A., Mora, J., Torre, E. L., Riesgo, T., & Sekanina, L. (2013). Self-reconfigurable Evolvable Hardware system for Adaptive Image Processing. *IEEE Transactions on Computers*, *62*(8), 1481–1493. doi:10.1109/TC.2013.78

Srinivasan, K. S., & Ebenezer, D. (2007). A New Fast and Efficient Decision-Based Algorithm for Removal of High Density Impulse Noise. *IEEE Signal Processing Letters*, *14*(3), 189–192. doi:10.1109/LSP.2006.884018

Sultana, M., Uddin, M. S., & Sabrina, F. (2013). High Density Impulse Denoising by A Novel Adaptive Fuzzy Filter. *International Conference on Informatics, Electronics & Vision (ICIEV)*. doi:10.1109/ICIEV.2013.6572536

Sun, T., & Neuvo, Y. (1994). Detail-Preserving Median Based Filters in Image Processing. *Pattern Recognition Letters*, *15*(4), 341–347. doi:10.1016/0167-8655(94)90082-5

Thirilogasundari, V., babu, V. S., & Janet, S. A. (2012). Fuzzy Based Salt and Pepper Noise Removal Using Adaptive Switching Median Filter. *Procedia Engineering*, *38*, 2858–2865. doi:10.1016/j.proeng.2012.06.334

Turcza, P., & Duplaga, M. (2013). Hardware-Efficient Low-Power Image Processing System For Wireless Capsule Endoscopt. *IEEE Conference on Biomedical and Health Informatics*.

Utaminingrum, F., Uchimura, K., & Koutaki, G. (2013). High Density Noise Removal based on Linear Mean-Median Filter. *19th Korea-Japan Joint Workshop on Frontiers of Computer Vision*. doi:10.1109/FCV.2013.6485451

Wang, J. H., & Lin, L. (1997). Improved Median Filter using min-max algorithm for image processing. *Electronics Letters, 33*(16), 1362–1363. doi:10.1049/el:19970945

Wang, Z. and Zhang, D. (1999). Progressive switching median filter for the removal of impulse noise from highly corrupted images. *IEEE Trans. on Circuits Syst. II, 46*, 78-80.

Zhang, S., & Karim, M. A. (2002). A New Impulse Detector for Switching Median Filter. *IEEE Transactions on Signal Processing, 9*(11), 360–363. doi:10.1109/LSP.2002.805310

Chapter 2
Mobile Platform Challenges in Interactive Computer Vision

Miguel Bordallo López
University of Oulu, Finland

ABSTRACT

Computer vision can be used to increase the interactivity of existing and new camera-based applications. It can be used to build novel interaction methods and user interfaces. The computing and sensing needs of this kind of applications require a careful balance between quality and performance, a practical trade-off. This chapter shows the importance of using all the available resources to hide application latency and maximize computational throughput. The experience gained during the developing of interactive applications is utilized to characterize the constraints imposed by the mobile environment, discussing the most important design goals: high performance and low power consumption. In addition, this chapter discusses the use of heterogeneous computing via asymmetric multiprocessing to improve the throughput and energy efficiency of interactive vision-based applications.

In the twilight of Moore's Law, mainstream computers from 'desktops' to 'smartphones' are being permanently transformed into heterogeneous supercomputer clusters. Henceforth, a single compute-intensive application will need to harness different kinds of cores, in immense numbers, to get its job done. The free lunch is over. Now welcome to the hardware jungle. – Herb Sutter (2005)

DOI: 10.4018/978-1-5225-0889-2.ch002

1. INTRODUCTION

Computer vision can be used to increase the interactivity of existing and new camera-based applications. It can be used to build novel interaction methods and user interfaces. However, the computing and sensing needs of this kind of applications require a careful balance between quality and performance, a practical trade-off.

This chapter shows the importance of using all the available resources to hide application latency and maximize computational throughput. The experience gained during the developing of interactive applications is utilized to characterize the constraints imposed by the mobile environment, discussing the most important design goals: high performance and low power consumption. In addition, this chapter discusses the use of heterogeneous computing via asymmetric multiprocessing to improve the throughput and energy efficiency of interactive vision-based applications.

2. COMPUTATIONAL PERFORMANCE: LATENCY AND THROUGHPUT

To solve the problems they face, mobile vision-based applications become more complex, leading to tight requirements in order to efficiently address the computations they involve. Although this is also applicable in many other fields, computer vision algorithms are particularly constrained to the processing capabilities of the hardware platforms. In this context, there is a need to maximize the computational performance of such applications by adapting them to the particularities of mobile devices.

The first issue to encounter when optimizing or porting an interactive application to a mobile platform is how to define such computational performance. The speed of a system can be characterized by two terms; latency and throughput. Throughput is defined as the amount of work done per unit time. Latency is defined as the time between the start of a process and its completion. Although interrelated, a system can be designed to optimize one of both parameters, affecting the other (Grochowski et al. 2004). For example, pipelining an algorithm could increase its throughput, but actually increase the end-to-end latency.

The extensive amount of data processed by vision-based applications implies that the system implementation has a high throughput requirement, since many times it should be able to compute several millions of pixel in less than a second. However, interactive applications and user interfaces are in practice real-time systems that require a response in a limited amount of time. In this context, the implementation must assure a latency low enough to meet the requirements of interactivity. In practice, the designer needs to carefully balance both parameters in a practical trade-off.

2.1 Latency Considerations

The usability of camera-based user interfaces critically rests on their latency. Certain interactive applications such as web browsing can tolerate relatively long latencies (Abolfazli et al. 2013) that are unacceptable for others such as thin-client applications (Tolia et al. 2006). User interfaces are expected to have even faster response and spontaneous reflection to the arrival of new data. This becomes apparent with computer games in which action-to-display delays exceeding about 100-150 milliseconds are considered disturbing. The low-latency requirement applies even to simple key press-to-sound or display events (Dabrowski & Munson 2001).

Vision-based interactive applications employ a camera as an integral real-time application component. Consequently, in camera-based systems the sensor integration time will add to the latency, as well as the image analysis computing. When added to the presentation latency caused by the graphics overlaying and the display,

Figure 1. Latency diagrams for a vision-based application at 15 and 30fps. The latencies caused by the different parts of the system can be overlapped to increase throughput. The timing is constrained by the fixed latencies imposed by the hardware and the variable latency that depends on the processing.

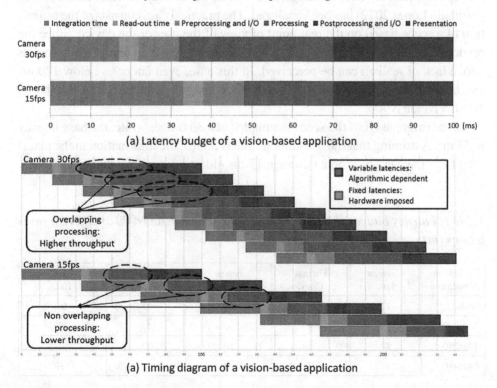

(a) Latency budget of a vision-based application

(a) Timing diagram of a vision-based application

it can be noted that the mobile hardware imposes a relatively long fixed latency that cannot be reduced by algorithmic tweaking. Therefore, the only possible way of reducing the end-to-end latency is to cut the computing times through algorithm or implementation optimization. Figure 1(a) shows the latency budget of a vision-based interactive application. It can be seen that at a lower framerate, the fixed latencies are longer, leaving a smaller time for processing.

In order to keep the throughput of the system as high as possible, the different latencies caused by the different parts of the system can be overlapped and executed at the same time. Figures 1(a) and 1(b) show the latency diagram of a vision-based application at 15and 30 fps.

At lower frame-rates, each frame can processed sequentially. However, it can be seen, that at higher frame-rates, keeping the highest throughput means that the processing of each frame must overlap with each other. This calls for the parallel or concurrent computation of different frames, which can be seen as an argument for multiple cores or processors.

2.1.1 *Virtual 3D Display Latency Analysis*

To provide an example of the latency measurement on a vision-based UI that requires a crisp response, the latency budget of a Virtual 3D display based in face tracking (Bordallo López 2012) has been analyzed. The practical case consists of the projection of a scene based on the real point of view of the user or the device. Since the rendering of the user interface is based on the camera position tens of milliseconds ago, a lack of realism can be perceived. In this case, even latencies below 100 ms can be disturbing. Table 1 depicts the latency budgets of the face-tracking based UI on a Nokia N900.

In the example UI, if the scene is sampled at a 30 frames/s rate, the base latency is 33 ms. Assuming that the integration time is 33 ms, the information in the pixels read from the camera is on an average 17 ms old using a rolling shutter approach.

Table 1. Latency budget of face tracking applications on an N900 at different resolutions (ms)

Tracking Resolution	Camera Lat.	Format Conv.	Image Analysis	GPU Rend.	Total Lat.
80x60	17	3	28	15	66
160x120	17	4	37	15	76
320x240	17	6	50	15	91
640x480	17	10	64	15	119

A typical touch screen has a presentation time that can be around 10 ms and the latency of the GPU rendering is about 15-20 ms. As the computing latencies need to be added, achieving the 100-150 ms range is challenging even with very fast computations. Again, the trade-off between resolution and the processing times that affect the latency can be observed.

2.1.2 A Latency Hiding Technique for Vision-Based UIs

The effect caused by high latencies of vision-based UIs can be partially mitigated by hiding them using the accurate knowledge of the system's timing. The processing latency of the vision algorithm can be estimated as the average of 1/Fps. Then, the total latency l_{tot} can be computed as the addition of the known camera latency l_{cam}, display latency l_{dis} and processing latency l_{proc}:

$$l_{tot} = l_{proc} + l_{cam} + l_{dis} \tag{1}$$

In order to hide the latencies that happen between the capturing and the displaying of the contents, it is possible to estimate the camera position at the moment of displaying. With the data obtained by the video analysis subsystem, and these latencies, a motion vector is constructed.

The motion vector mk consists of the position $x_k(x_k, y_k, z_k)$ velocities $(\dot{x}_k, \dot{y}_k, \dot{z}_k)$ and accelerations $(\ddot{x}_k, \ddot{y}_k, \ddot{z}_k)$ of the device at time instant k. It is defined as follows:

$$m_k = \left[x_k, y_k, z_k, \dot{x}_k, \dot{y}_k, \dot{z}_k, \ddot{x}_k, \ddot{y}_k, \ddot{z}_k \right]^T. \tag{2}$$

In the beginning, the elements of the state vector are set to zero. The time step between two successive images is set to l_{proc}. The motion vector is updated every frame:

$$\ddot{x}_k = \dot{x}_k - \dot{x}_{k-1} \tag{3}$$

$$\dot{x}_k = x_k - x_{k-1} + \ddot{x}_k * l_{tot} \tag{4}$$

Figure 2. The effect of latency hiding on a vision-based application. The prediction of the movement compensates the latencies.

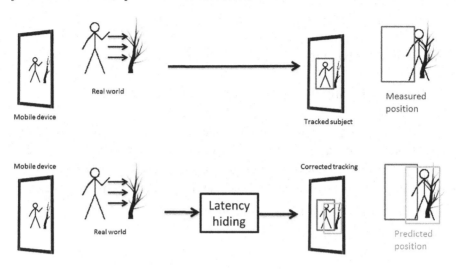

Finally, the predicted position that should be used for the re-projection is calculated based on the motion vector:

$$x_{predicted} = x_k + \dot{x}_k * l_{tot} \tag{5}$$

This technique reduces the user's perception of a lagged interface by reacting to the predicted current user's position instead of to the calculated one. Figure 2 depicts the effect of the estimated position. The predicted position is closer to the real position than the measured one. The drawback of this approach is that the accuracy of the model is hindered when the device is subject to sudden fast motion. However, in this case, the same device's fast motion makes the user less likely to perceive the possible errors that are quickly corrected when the device's motion speed is reduced.

2.2 Measuring Algorithmic Performance across Architectures

Modern computer performance is often described in MIPS (millions of instructions per second) or FLOPS (floating point operations per second). Since higher clock-rates can make a processor faster, a useful and widely applicable normalization consists of dividing the performance metric by the clock frequency, obtaining a measurement in MIPS/MHz. Not considering memory access bottlenecks, simple modern processors easily reach 1 MIPS/MHz while superscalar ones might achieve rates from 3 to 5. Multi-core and many-core processors can achieve even faster rates by distributing the tasks among all the cores, computing a large amount of data per second.

Vision algorithms operate with input data that mainly consists of images composed by pixels. Since the resolution of the input images often has a direct relation with the speed of the process, a good normalization strategy to measure the performance of certain architecture for a given algorithm consists of making the performance of the metric independent of the resolution. This allows the easy calculation of the maximum possible resolution of an algorithm constrained by latency needs.

The cycles-per-pixel (CPP) metric measures the number of clock cycles required to execute all the operations of an algorithm on each one of the pixels of the resulting image, normalizing the differences in frequency and, sometimes also by the number of identical cores (CPP per core). The metric, allows the comparison of several architectures despite of their different implementations.

3. ENERGY EFFICIENCY

Along with their small size and comparatively reduced computational power, the main constraint present in mobile devices is that they are, essentially, battery powered devices (Ferri et al. 2008). This implies that the application development trade-offs and challenges that need to be dealt with mobile devices are closely related not only to pure performance, but also to energy efficiency (Fabritius et al. 2003). In this thesis, energy-efficiency is defined as the capability of providing high computational power while presenting low average power dissipation (Balfour et al. 2008).

3.1 Characterizing Battery Life

The power offered by the battery is the main resource in mobile devices that requires an external source to be replenished (Miettinen & Nurminen 2010). Although current mobile devices integrate Lithium-ion batteries with moderate capacities between 1000 and 4000mAh, preserving battery life is still considered among the most important design constraints of highly interactive applications.

Consequently, energy efficiency is a key characteristic of a realizable interactive mobile application. Since battery-hungry applications can quickly deplete the available energy they can easily limit the usability of applications or even the device itself. In this context, the frequent need for battery recharging has become one of the most important usability issues of current mobile platforms (Heikkinen & Nurminen 2010) (Abolfazli et al. 2013) (Ferreira et al. 2011).

Although battery manufacturers are improving their technology to offer higher capacity batteries, still current battery cells are already very dense (Satyanarayanan 2005). The battery capacity growth per year can be estimated to be around 5 to 10%, clearly insufficient to catch up with the ever increasing application demands (Neuvo 2004). Alternative technologies to recharge the battery, such as harvesting from solar power or movement, are still far from offering a reliable solution in the immediate future (Pickard & Abbott 2012).

Since the battery life is a nonlinear function of the load current, small improvements in the energy efficiency of the applications can give high improvements in the operation times. Figure 3 shows the equivalent capacity of a 1320mAh Li-ON battery with different discharge times and power consumptions. The curves have been drawn assuming a Peukert coefficient of 1,1 (Peukert 1897; Doerffel & Sharkh 2006) and utilizing the nominative battery capacity measured at a 5h discharge rate (0.2C). It can be noted that with lower power consumptions, the perceived battery capacity increases dramatically.

These curves show the importance of reducing power consumption to maximize battery life. However, the availability of a fast application processor enables the straightforward implementation of novel camera-based applications, and even vision- based user interfaces. On the other hand, the versatility and easy programmability of the single processor solution have led to design decisions that compromise the battery life if high interactivity is needed. In an active-state, a fast application processor may consume more than 1200mW with memories, while the whole device can go up to more than 3W. This can push the life of typical mobile device's batteries below one hour, and increase its temperature to levels beyond the tolerable.

A possible solution has its roots in the employment of the processors at smaller loads or in the utilization of alternative processing devices that consume less power. The difference in power consumption of several mobile processors under different loads can be seen in Figure 4. The curve shows the measurements of the battery discharge times of a Nokia N9 phone under constant power consumption.

For applications with moderate loads, it can be seen that relatively small improvements in energy-efficiency, can push the power consumption out of the knee region, extending the battery life. Similar observations of the battery life and its knee region have been made by Silvén & Rintaluoma (2007) and can be found in the earlier work of Rakhmatov & Vrudhula (2003). Hence, an interactive applications design goal is to execute each part of the algorithm in the most suitable processor, trying to keep its load as low as possible.

Figure 3. 1320mAh Li-ON battery characterization curves. The real battery life depends on the power consumption and the time taken by the discharge.

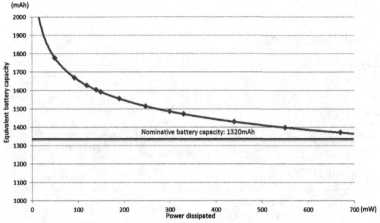

(a) Equivalent battery capacity and power consumption

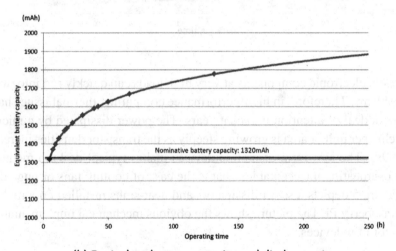

(b) Equivalent battery capacity and discharge time

3.2 Thermal Constraints

In the unlikely event of a sudden increase in battery capacities, an additional constraint is that the high-performance computing required by interactive mobile applications has to be performed in a small spatial volume. This requires the discharge of the heat into the environment. A mobile device utilizing all its resources can easily become too hot to handle.

Figure 4. Discharge time of a 1320mAh Li ON battery on an N900 phone. The shape of the discharge curve implies that small improvements in the applications' energy efficiency can achieve high improvements in the operation times.

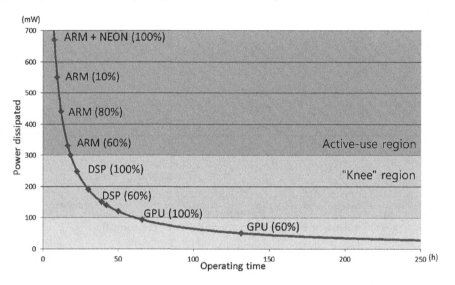

In addition, electronic components at very high loads can quickly run into over-heating problems. Therefore, in high-performance computing, thermal issues have gained a great deal of attention in recent years. The power dissipated by a micro-processor chip per unit of area is growing steeply as the transistor densities increase (Borkar 1999). The size form of mobile devices makes typical desktop methods to prevent overheating unacceptable. That is the case of cooling fans or huge dissipators. Figure 5 depicts a set of dissipators and heat-sinks installed on a mobile SoC, the Raspberry Pi. The picture shows the obvious mechanical implementation challenges for thin devices.

Figure 5. A set of dissipators and heat-sinks on an ARM-based SoC, the Raspberry Pi

3.3 Electrical Power Consumption

The combination of battery-life and thermal issues impose serious constrains in the power consumption of mobile devices. Power consumption on electrical circuits is composed of two main components: dynamic and static power consumption.

Dynamic power consumption, caused by the switches in the states of transistors, has a direct relation with the operating frequency. Dynamic power is used to dominate total power usage in CMOS circuits. However, in recent years, the semiconductor industry has kept the maximum operating frequencies steady, and has instead started making a big effort to increase the parallelism of most devices. Thus, multiprocessor solutions are becoming popular in high-performance mobile devices (Horowitz et al. 2005). The increase of symmetric parallelism through multi-core development has allowed the steady increase of performance while keeping dynamic consumption at a reasonable level.

On the other hand, static power consumption is independent of the system activity. Caused by the leakage currents in the silicon of the circuit, it only refers to the consumption of the system when all inputs are held, and are not changing their state. In recent years, the increase in the chip density and the thinner insulations between wires has made static power consumption very significant (Kim et al. 2003).

The number of transistors per processor has increased greatly with impacts in power and design complexity. This complexity has caused only a modest increase in application performance, as opposed to performance due to faster clock rates from technology scaling. Modern desktop chips, with a big form factor, have around 6-7 billion transistors. Current mobile chips with a smaller form factor can contain up to 2 billion. While desktop computers, equipped with fans and dissipators, can keep the processor in full load for long periods of time, in mobile devices this is a losing strategy. Since mobile application processors consume large amounts of power, the solution has been in reducing activity or turning off complete subsystems and parts of the chip in a process known as power throttling. This process is based on two classes of techniques: Voltage/frequency scaling and gating based. Both types of techniques incur on overhead with the extra circuitry and can only cut dynamic power. As a result, large areas of silicon remain inactive most of the time, in a phenomenon named dark silicon (Esmaeilzadeh et al. 2011).

Therefore, while the bigger cores provide for higher single thread performance, they also have reduced energy efficiency. With this in mind, it becomes apparent that for the current performance increase to hold, it will still be necessary to have a proportional scaling down of the transistors. The recent failure of Dennard's scaling (Dennard et al. 1974) suggests that the future reduction in power consumption might not be proportional to the reduction in transistor sizes. In this context, it can be predicted that newer architectures with novel approaches to energy efficiency are

Figure 6. Progress of processor technologies. From single-core to homogeneous multi-core and heterogeneous computing.

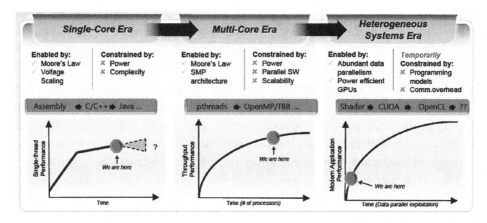

likely to appear, increasing the heterogeneity of future platforms (Esmaeilzadeh et al. 2012). Figure 6 depicts the increase in the heterogeneity of future platforms. The progress of processor technology moved from single-core, to multiple homogeneous cores and then to heterogeneous computing.

3.4 Measuring Energy-Efficiency

Since modern circuits have less power per transistor, as the number of transistors per chip grows, power efficiency has increased in importance. Therefore, it is advisable to know how much energy is required by certain applications when executed on a specific platform. However, predicting or estimating power for a certain algorithm running on a particular device is an extremely difficult task. Therefore, it is typical practice to measure the currents of the processor, translating them to power consumption values. In this context, several works have attempted to analyze the battery life of several mobile devices under different scenarios (Shye et al. 2009) (Carroll & Heiser 2010). An important notion arising from these kind of studies is that it can be established that it is sufficient to use the device's battery voltage sensors and knowledge about battery discharge behaviors to accurately estimate power consumption (Zhang et al. 2010) (Pathak et al. 2011).

The measurement of an application's power consumption is directly related to the energy-efficiency of the platform. Modern computer energy efficiency is often reported in performance per Watt, be it MIPS/W (millions of instructions per second per Watt) or FLOPS/W (floating-point operations per second per Watt). However, this is not a practical measurement metric (Akenine-Möller & Johnsson 2012), since its counter-intuitive nature does not allow the easy computation of aggregate statistics. To avoid these potential problems, a different metric that allows the comparison of different implementations across several platforms can be utilized. Analogously to the measurements of performance in the CPP metric, the Joules per pixel (JPP) metric measures the amount of energy consumed to execute all the operations of an algorithm on each one of the pixels of the resulting image.

4. ASYMMETRIC MULTIPROCESSING FOR VISION-BASED INTERACTIVITY

Vision-based applications require very high throughputs, and low latencies. A traditional solution has been to increase not only the clock frequency but also the complexity of the application processor to achieve a better ratio of operations per cycle. However, as discussed before, the energy-efficiency of the system decreases rapidly as the frequency is scaled. An industry solution has been the integration of different processors into the same chip or as independent subsystems. However, the strong heterogeneity of the computing devices and subsystems included on a mobile device, poses a significant challenge.

The exploitation of asymmetric processors is heavily dependent on the heterogeneity of the applications. Characterizing the application needs is not easily done in a simpler manner. While many types of applications can benefit from the speed of a large core or the efficiency of a small processor, the reality is that applications are usually composed of several tasks that could easily be matched to the most suitable platform.

Some application phases might have a large amount of instruction-level parallelism (ILP) where a VLIW architecture that issues many instructions per cycle can be exploited. Other application phases might require a processor that is able to process large amounts of data under the same operation and they are more suitable for processors that exploit the SIMD paradigm. Lastly, many applications require the repetition of a single complex operation that can be executed efficiently with a clever hardware design. In practice, this heterogeneity applied to mobile devices means that a mobile developer should be able to tackle different processors that have been incorporating varied parallelization strategies and optimization (Sutter 2005).

Even with careful partition of the tasks among the asymmetric cores, heterogeneous computing requires communication between them. An important design constraint in this kind of systems is the bandwidth of the memory access. While a certain amount of memory can be included in the specific processor, many times it is still required to access the memory in a separate component, and this will be limited by the communication bandwidth.

Fortunately, even with relatively infrequent switching among asymmetric cores, a performance and energy-efficiency increase of heterogeneous execution can be obtained (Kumar et al. 2005). When considering the inclusion of dedicated hardware accelerators, heterogeneous SoCs are likely to overcome homogeneous systems (Wolf 2004) in terms of performance. The average energy per instruction (EPI) of the system is also likely to be reduced, even by a factor of 4 to 6 fold (Grochowski et al. 2004).

4.1 Amdahl's Law and Asymmetric Multiprocessing

Parallelizing the computations of a given algorithm has a theoretical limit imposed by Amdahl's law (Amdahl 1967). This principle states that if certain computation has a fraction of the program that is inherently serial and cannot be parallelized, the speedup obtained by parallel computing is limited by a factor directly proportional to the time required by the sequential calculations.

As a counterpoint, Gustafson's laws point out that if the sequential part of an algorithm is fixed or grows slowly with the problem size, additional processing units can increase the problem size. In this case, the relative performance of the computation is not limited by the non-parallel part (Gustafson 1988).

Heterogeneous computing is able to tackle the implications of both statements by assigning each part of the processor (serial and parallel) to different processors that are specifically designed for each type of computations. Executing serial parts of the algorithm on a fast low-latency processor and parallel parts on many small cores can maximize the throughput while keeping the latency low. Applications based on asymmetric multiprocessing can then be designed for low latency. This implies high interactivity without compromising the general performance, directly related to the throughput. In addition, the efficiency of the specific processors also maximizes the ratio of performance to power consumption, increasing the total energy efficiency of the system.

4.2 Heterogeneous Computing and Software

The embedded nature of mobile devices implies that they are composed by carefully designed software and hardware, which should be able to work in close collaboration. The main challenge of exploiting heterogeneous computing lies in the lack of tools and models that allows the transparent usage of the asymmetric resources. Programming parallel applications requires awareness of the heterogeneity and a good understanding of the architecture.

A computing architecture can be seen as the interface between this software and hardware. Computing architectures essentially describe a computing system by specifying the relations between the parts that compose a device. In this context, the successful design and implementation of a mobile device with novel capabilities requires careful optimization across all interfaces.

Application developers are many times trained to assume that computational cores will provide similar performance independently of the task and that the addition of another core to the system will increase the performance similarly. The heterogeneous nature of mobile SoCs breaks the assumption, resulting in the unpredictability of the performance results.

In this context, a future area of interest is to focus on the development of interfaces that allow full access to the tool-chains, not hiding the complexity of the heterogeneity from the developers, but providing them with abstractions that allow the exploitation of the multiple cores to reduce the application latencies, while keeping the higher possible throughputs in an energy-efficient manner.

4.3 Concurrent Heterogeneous Implementation of Computer Vision Algorithms

As discussed before, the multiple heterogeneous processing cores present in current mobile SoCs offer the possibility of increasing the overall performance of the system by using asymmetric multiprocessing. A simple way of taking advantage of the heterogeneous cores consists of dividing the application into different tasks and offloading the CPU by executing them on the most suitable processor. A more efficient variant of this approach consists of pipelining the different tasks and executing them concurrently in different processors.

However, when a given algorithm is not easily divided but the involved data is, even the same task can be carefully partitioned and scheduled over the multiple heterogeneous cores, if a good knowledge of the performance of every core can be obtained (Leskelä et al. 2009). In a case of no data interdependency, the time t_d used by the speed-optimal workload distribution over two different processors can be expressed with the following equation:

$$t_d = \left(1 - \left(\left(t_{proc2} + t_{tran}\right) / \left(t_{cpu} + t_{proc2} + t_{tran}\right)\right)\right) \times \left(t_{proc2} + 2 * t_{ran}\right) \tag{6}$$

where t_{cpu} is the time measured using only the main processor, t_{proc2} is the time measured using only the secondary processor (e.g. mobile GPU or DSP) and t_{tran} is the time to transfer the data between processors, which in this case is considered to be CPU-bound.

Figure 7. Concurrent implementation speedups achieved depending on transmission and communication time and secondary processor speed

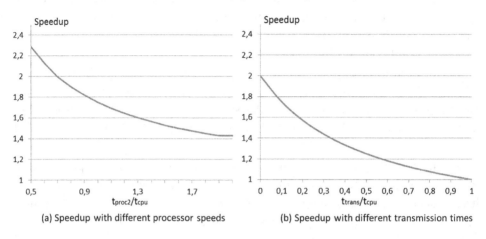

(a) Speedup with different processor speeds   (b) Speedup with different transmission times

In terms of power consumptions, if we define p_{cpu}, p_{proc2} and p_{tran} as the powers consumed by the corresponding actions, the total power drain p_d can be modeled as follows:

$$p_d = p_{cpu} + p_{proc2} \times \left(t_{proc2} / \left(t_{proc2} + t_{tran} \right) \right) + p_{tran} \times \left(t_{tran} / \left(t_{proc2} + t_{tran} \right) \right) \qquad (7)$$

and the total energy used can be obtained as:

$$E_d = p_d \times t_d \qquad (8)$$

Many computer vision operations can be easily partitioned by simply dividing the input image into sections that overlap several rows and/or columns. In this context, the processing of an image can be distributed on the heterogeneous cores by dividing the data proportionally to the inverse of the computing times while keeping the number of shared neighbors as small as possible. Figure 26 shows the impact of the speed of the secondary processor and transfer times in the algorithm speedup.

It can be seen in Figure 7(a) that even secondary processors slower than the CPU can result in an algorithm speedup if both are utilized concurrently. However, the speedups can be hindered by long transfer times, as can be seen in Figure 7(b).

5. MOBILE PLATFORM AS A SET OF HETEROGENEOUS COMPUTATIONAL DEVICES

Mobile communication devices are becoming attractive platforms for multimedia applications as their display and imaging capabilities are improving together with the computational resources. Many of the devices have increasingly been equipped with built-in cameras that allow the users to capture high resolution still images as well as lower resolution video frames.

With power efficiency and reduced space in mind, most mobile device manufacturers integrate several chips and subsystems on a System on Chip (SoC). Figure 8 depicts a simplified diagram of the top organization of an example OMAP3430 SoC from a mobile device.

Along with a general purpose processor (GPP), SoCs usually contain several domain- specific subsystems, such as DSPs or GPUs, packed in an application processor. As independent subsystems, they also include a set of dedicated processors that assist the computations needed by mixed-signal, camera sensors or radio functions. The SoC hardware is often shipped with a set of controlling software and APIs that handle the communication between processors, peripherals and interfaces.

5.1 Application Processors

A mobile application processor provides a self-contained operating environment that delivers all system capabilities needed to support a device's applications, including memory management, graphics processing and multimedia decoding. Mobile application processors may be independent of other specialized processors in the same mobile device, such as a phone's base-band, camera or processor.

Figure 8. A simplified diagram of an example mobile SoC, the OMAP3430 mobile SoC

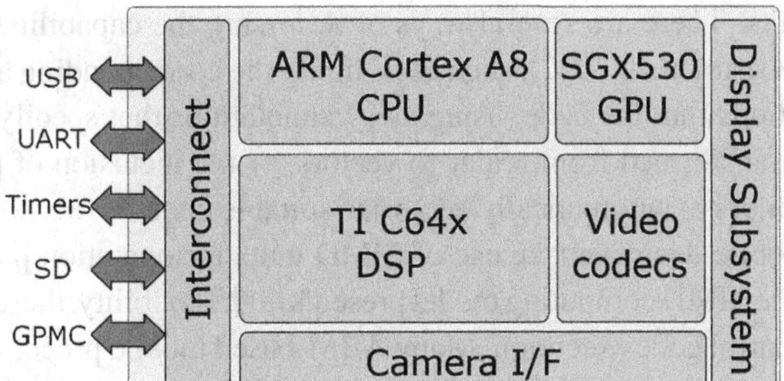

Mobile application processors are typically developed to consume less power and dissipate less heat than desktop computers, while using a smaller silicon size. To preserve battery life, mobile application processors can work with different power levels and clock frequencies (operating points) and it is usually possible to turn off several parts of the chip.

5.1.1 Single-Core General Purpose Processors

The most typical mobile general purpose processors are based on the ARM architecture, which describes a family of computer processors designed in accordance with a RISC CPU design. The ARM architecture includes a load/store architecture with restrictions to misaligned memory access and a uniform 16x32-bit register file. A fixed instruction width of 32-bits allows easy decoding and pipelining with a decreased code density. However, to improve compiled code-density, most ARM processors include Thumb, a 16-bit instruction subset. A VFP (Vector Floating Point) co-processor is included to provide for low-cost floating point computations, although later versions of the architecture have abandoned it in favor of more complete SIMD units. The particularities of ARM processors enable some code optimizations to achieve higher performance. General ARM optimization tips include, for example, the use of do-while loops and counter decrement.

5.1.2 NEON Co-Processors and SIMD Units

Despite the evolution of the industry, pure Single Instruction Single Data (SISD) microprocessors do not offer adequate performance for a large set of tasks. Many computationally intensive tasks require high performance computations that cannot be carried out efficiently by the mobile application processor alone. In this context, a wide range of accelerator modules have been included as specific arithmetic units or co-processors accessed through special sets of instructions. The inclusion of Single Instruction Multiple Data (SIMD) units is decisive for tasks such as video and image processing. SIMD processors have a unique control unit and multiple processing units. There are several ways of accessing the capabilities of modern SIMD units (Kristof et al. 2012), such as in-lining the corresponding assembly language instructions into the code, using array annotations that specify the sections that must be transformed from scalar to vectors, or the inclusion of pragmas that help the compilers to automatically vectorize suitable code.

Current mobile devices make use of SIMD units for operation parallelization. Even though the SIMD computing model presents high flexibility, these units rely on a CPU with control code execution. Many ARM-based mobile processors include a SIMD co-processor known as NEON that provides for signal processing acceleration.

NEON co-processors use combined 64- and 128-bit single instructions over multiple data, supporting up to 64-bit integer and 32-bit floating-point data types for a total of up to 16 concurrent operations at the same time. The NEON hardware shares the same floating-point registers with the VFP.

The exploitation of the NEON co-processor can be done in several ways. A compiler flag for automatic vectorization in NEON analyzes the code and vectorizes it where it is possible. A set of pragmas can be defined in the code to give information such as function pointers dependency, or minimum loop iterations, about suitable parallelizable code sections. Other ways of exploiting the NEON architecture are based on the programmer explicitly in-lining the appropriate assembly instructions on the source code or using the NEON intrinsics ARM extension.

The use of a NEON co-processor slightly increases the power consumption of the ARM-based SoCs. For example, Texas Instruments OMAP3530 Power Estimation Spreadsheet (Texas-Instruments 2011) depicts a power contribution of 120 mW for the use of a NEON co-processor at 600MHz, which means about a 20% increase in power consumption. If the performance gain is higher than such an increase, the utilization of a NEON unit implies a better performance over power.

5.1.3 Homogeneous Multi-Core Architectures

Most of the latest desktop computers include General Purpose Processors with several cores. In the majority of architectures, each one of the cores is usually identical and can include a SIMD unit. Identical or different tasks can be assigned to the cores by using several Application Programming Interfaces (APIs) such as Open MP (Kristof et al.2012). The multiple cores can share the data with several techniques such as shared caches or the implementation of message passing communication methods.

Multiple applications can exploit the multicore capabilities of vision-based applications. A straightforward approach consists of dividing several different and independent tasks among the total number of processors. This task parallelism is very easy to implement, since there is no data shared by the cores, and it leads to an increased throughput with the cost of a higher end-to-end latency.

For many interactive vision-based applications, where the end-to-end latency is a concern, another approach that allows us to keep the latency smaller consists of dividing the input images into equal strips and assigning them to each one of the cores, using a domain decomposition or data parallelism technique. However, several experiments suggest (Humenberger et al. 2009) that doubling the number of processors do not double the speed. For each partition, a set of pixels needs to be accessed by two of the cores, causing an overhead.

Experiments show that for pixel-based computations (such as convolutions) on N cores, the time consumed per frame gets reduced by a factor of approximately 0.8 ∗ N to 0.9 ∗ N (Bordallo López et al. 2014) The results show that using the four cores on a processor, the computations are about 3.6 times faster. The overhead in using more than one core can be caused by multiple factors such as inefficiencies in the operating system, cache utilization or contention in the access of the data shared by several cores. These results are in line with previous observations in mobile multicore systems (Blume et al. 2008).

5.1.4 Heterogeneous Multi-Core Architectures

Mobile CPU architectures are starting to include together with several homogeneous powerful cores, different complementary low power processors that are meant to reduce the power and heat dissipation in modern SoCs (Greenhalgh 2011) (Rajovic et al. 2013). The different approaches for these kinds of architectures can be summarized in three strategies:

In the symmetric clustering approach, the CPU architectures couples a relatively slow energy-efficient processor with a powerful core, clocked at a higher frequency. This processor couple is able to adjust better to dynamic computing needs, increasing the energy efficiency in respect to the approaches that use only clock scaling. In this kind of coupled architecture, a cache memory is shared between both cores, and the tasks are transferred from the slower to the faster processor depending on the load. Only one of the processors is powered and running at the same time.

Asymmetric clustering organizes the processors in non-symmetrical groups, where one fast core can be tied together with several low power cores or vice versa. Although the approach offers increased flexibility, only either fast or slow cores can be running at the same time, keeping the others unpowered.

Heterogeneous multiprocessing architectures allow the concurrent use of all cores, assigning high throughput tasks to faster cores and tasks with less priority or computational needs to the slower low power ones. The advantage of this approach is that all physical cores can be used concurrently.

5.2 Application Domain Specific Processors

To provide for optimized solutions for specific tasks, mobile SoC has been increasingly integrating several processors directed to the execution of a set of algorithms on an application domain such as signal, graphics or image processing. Application Domain- Specific Processors (ADSPs) rely upon notions of concurrency and parallelism to satisfy performance and cost constraints resulting from increasingly complex applications and architectures. ADSPs are essentially programmable devices that aim to combine the efficiency of the hardware with the flexibility of the software. Several of these ADSPs, such as DSPs, ISPs, or GPUs have been included in mobile SoCs.

A Digital Signal Processor (DSP) is a microprocessor-based system with a set of instructions and hardware optimized for data intensive applications. Although not exclusively used in mobile devices, DSPs are often used in mobile and embedded systems, where they integrate all the necessary elements and software. DSPs are able to exploit parallelism both in instruction execution and data processing by adopting a Harvard architecture and Very Long Instruction Words (VLIW) that allow the execution of instructions on each clock cycle. Although many DSPs have floating-point arithmetic units, fixed-point units fit better in battery-powered devices. Formerly, floating-point units were slower and more expensive, but nowadays this gap is getting smaller and smaller.

Mobile Graphics Processing Units (GPUs) are specialized co-processors for graphic processing, employed to reduce the workload of the main microprocessor. They implement highly optimized graphic operations or primitives. GPUs have several independent processing units (cores) working on floating point data. Due to their higher level of parallelism, when computing graphics tasks, they have a higher operation throughput than modern microprocessors, while running at lower clock rates.

Image Signal Processors (ISPs) are subsystems designed to apply real-time image enhancement algorithms like de-mosaicking and noise reduction to war images taken by a high resolution camera sensor. Mobile ISPs aim to achieve cost, power and performance objectives by implementing most of the algorithmic and compression tasks in dedicated hardwired processing chains using minimal software.

To cope with the future needs of mobile devices, current devices are integrating other domain-specific processors such as audio processors, sensor processors or radio and network processors. Therefore, the number of ADSPs included in mobile SoCs is only expected to rise, increasing the heterogeneity of mobile processing.

6. DISCUSSION

The main contribution of this chapter is the analysis of alternative implementation principles for vision-based interactivity. The identified challenges in terms of latency, throughput and energy efficiency and their intertwining characteristics result in the proposal of the exploitation of a set of heterogeneous processors using asymmetric multiprocessing, maximizing the use of all the computing resources available on a mobile device.

Figure 9. The evolution of mobile SoC. The increased heterogeneity calls for new toolchains.
Adapted from Goodacre (2009).

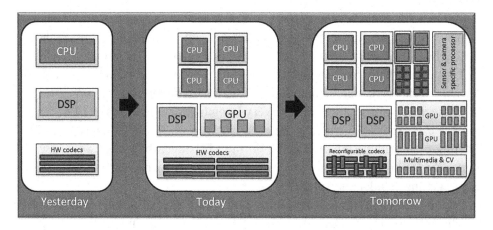

The guidelines for high performance computing in mobile devices substantially differ from the strategies utilized in non-battery devices, such as desktop computers. The scarcity of the mobile resources calls for the wise use of the available computing devices. Parameters such as the precision or dynamic range of the computed data do not only depend on the application itself, but also on the number and type of available processors. Designing for high throughputs is intrinsically related to the assignation of the most suitable core to the task in hand.

In this context, the extensive knowledge of the system timing in terms of performance and latency is paramount for the creation of high performance applications. A careful design and distribution of tasks could hide the possible latencies and increase the total algorithmic throughput.

However, even the highest throughput solution might not be the most suitable. The energy-efficiency of mobile SoCs has become the limiting factor in performance. Even if battery capacity problems could be mitigated, the thermal envelope that keeps heat dissipation under control will still require low power consumption. In this context, the inclusion of even more heterogeneous lower frequency components in SoCs is the natural path. Figure 9 depicts the evolution of mobile SoCs towards heterogeneity.

The increased heterogeneity calls for a simplification and standardization of the ways of using all the included computing resources, while still providing for low level access to them. The different tools to address this task that are at the designer's disposal range from macro-micro architecture design, to dynamic resource management and automatic application partitioning, with the granularity of the tasks depending on the specific architecture.

REFERENCES

Abolfazli, S., Sanaei, Z., Gani, A., Xia, F., & Yang, L. T. (2013). Rich mobile applications: Genesis, taxonomy, and open issues. *Journal of Network and Computer Applications*.

Akenine-Möller, T., & Johnsson, B. (2012). Performance per what?. *Journal of Computer Graphics Techniques*, *1*(1), 37–41.

Amdahl, G. M. (1967) Validity of the single processor approach to achieving large scale computing capabilities. *Proceedings of theJoint Computer Conference*. ACM.

Balfour, J., Dally, W. J., Black-Schaffer, D., Parikh, V., & Park, J. (2008). An energy-efficient processor architecture for embedded systems. *Computer Architecture Letters*, *7*(1), 29–32. doi:10.1109/L-CA.2008.1

Blume, H., Livonius, J., Rotenberg, L., Noll, T. G., Bothe, H., & Brakensiek, J. (2008). OpenMP based parallelization on an mpcore multiprocessor platform–a performance and power analysis. *Journal of Systems Architecture*, *54*(11), 1019–1029. doi:10.1016/j.sysarc.2008.04.001

Bordallo López, M., Boutellier, J., & Silvén, O. (2007). Implementing mosaic stitching on mobile phones.*Proc. Finnish Signal Processing Symposium*.

Bordallo López, M., Hannuksela, J., Silvén, J. O., & Vehviläinen, M. (2011b). Multimodal sensing-based camera applications. *Proceedings of SPIE*. The International Society for Optical Engineering. doi:10.1117/12.871934

Bordallo López, M., Hannuksela, J., & Silvén, O. (2011a). Mobile feature-cloud panorama construction for image recognition application. *Proceedings of Mobiphoto, International Workshop on Camera Phone Sensing*.

Bordallo López, M., Hannuksela, J., Silvén, O., & Fan, L. (2012a). Head-tracking virtual 3-d display for mobile devices. *Proc. Computer Vision and Pattern Recognition Workshops (CVPRW), 2012 IEEE Computer Society Conference on*. IEEE.

Bordallo López, M., Hannuksela, J., Silvén, O., & Vehviläinen, M. (2009). Graphics hardware accelerated panorama builder for mobile phones.*Proceeding of SPIE Electronic Imaging 2009*. doi:10.1117/12.816511

Bordallo López, M., Hannuksela, J., Silven, O., & Vehvilainen, M. (2012b). Interactive multiframe reconstruction for mobile devices. *Multimedia Tools and Applications*, 1–21.

Bordallo López, M., Nieto, A., Boutellier, J., Hannuksela, J., & Silvén, O. (2014). Evaluation of LBP computing in multiple architectures. *Journal of Real-Time Image Processing*, 1–34.

Bordallo López, M., Nykänen, H., Hannuksela, J., Silvén, O., & Vehviläinen, M. (2011c) Accelerating image recognition on mobile devices using gpgpu.*Proceeding of SPIE Electronic Imaging 2011*. doi:10.1117/12.872860

Borkar, S. (1999). Design challenges of technology scaling. *Micro, IEEE, 19*(4), 23–29. doi:10.1109/40.782564

Carroll, A., & Heiser, G. (2010). An analysis of power consumption in a smartphone. *Proceedings of the 2010 USENIX conference on USENIX annual technical conference*.

Dabrowski, J., & Munson, E. (2001) Is 100 milliseconds too fast?*Proc. Conference on Human Factors in Computing Systems*.

Dennard, R. H., Gaensslen, F. H., Rideout, V. L., Bassous, E., & LeBlanc, A. R. (1974). Design of ion-implanted mosfet's with very small physical dimensions. Solid-State Circuits. *IEEE Journal of, 9*(5), 256–268.

Doerffel, D., & Sharkh, S. A. (2006). A critical review of using the peukert equation for determining the remaining capacity of lead-acid and lithium-ion batteries. *Journal of Power Sources, 155*(2), 395–400. doi:10.1016/j.jpowsour.2005.04.030

Esmaeilzadeh, H., Blem, E., St Amant, R., Sankaralingam, K., & Burger, D. (2011) Dark silicon and the end of multicore scaling. *Proc. Computer Architecture (ISCA), 2011 38th Annual International Symposium on*. IEEE. doi:10.1145/2000064.2000108

Esmaeilzadeh, H., Blem, E., St Amant, R., Sankaralingam, K., & Burger, D. (2012). Power limitations and dark silicon challenge the future of multicore. *ACM Transactions on Computer Systems, 30*(3), 11. doi:10.1145/2324876.2324879

Fabritius, S., Grigore, V., Maung, T., Loukusa, V., & Mikkonen, T. (2003). *Towards energy aware system design*. Academic Press.

Ferreira, D., Dey, A. K., & Kostakos, V. (2011). Understanding human-smartphone concerns: a study of battery life. In Pervasive Computing (pp. 19–33). Springer. doi:10.1007/978-3-642-21726-5_2

Ferri, C., Viescas, A., Moreshet, T., Bahar, R., & Herlihy, M. (2008) Energy efficient synchronization techniques for embedded architectures.*Proceedings of the 18th ACM Great Lakes Symposium on VLSI*. ACM. doi:10.1145/1366110.1366213

Goodacre, J. (2009). The evolution of mobile processing architectures.*Proc. ARM Holdings*.

Greenhalgh, P. (2011). *Big.little processing with arm cortex-a15 & cortex-a7*. ARM White Paper.

Grochowski, E., Ronen, R., Shen, J., & Wang, P. (2004). Best of both latency and throughput. *Proc. Computer Design: VLSI in Computers and Processors*. IEEE. doi:10.1109/ICCD.2004.1347928

Gustafson, J. L. (1988). Reevaluating amdahl's law. *Communications of the ACM, 31*(5), 532–533. doi:10.1145/42411.42415

Hannuksela, J. (2008). *Camera based motion estimation and recognition for human computer interaction*. (Ph.D. thesis). Acta Univ Oul C 313.

Heikkinen, M. V., & Nurminen, J. K. (2010). Consumer attitudes towards energy consumption of mobile phones and services. *Proc. Vehicular Technology Conference Fall* (VTC 2010-Fall). IEEE. doi:10.1109/VETECF.2010.5594115

Horowitz, M., Alon, E., Patil, D., Naffziger, S., Kumar, R., & Bernstein, K. (2005). Scaling, power, and the future of cmos. *Proc. Electron Devices Meeting*. IEEE. doi:10.1109/IEDM.2005.1609253

Humenberger, M., Zinner, C., & Kubinger, W. (2009). Performance evaluation of a census based stereo matching algorithm on embedded and multi-core hardware. *Proceedings of 6th International Symposium on Image and Signal Processing and Analysis*. doi:10.1109/ISPA.2009.5297702

Kim, N. S., Austin, T., Baauw, D., Mudge, T., Flautner, K., Hu, J. S., & Narayanan, V. et al. (2003). Leakage current: Moore's law meets static power. *Computer, 36*(12), 68–75. doi:10.1109/MC.2003.1250885

Kristof, P., Yu, H., Li, Z., & Tian, X. (2012). Performance study of SIMD programming models on intel multicore processors. *Proc. Parallel and Distributed Processing Symposium Workshops PhD Forum* (IPDPSW). doi:10.1109/IPDPSW.2012.299

Kumar, R., Tullsen, D. M., Jouppi, N. P., & Ranganathan, P. (2005). Heterogeneous chip multiprocessors. *Computer, 38*(11), 32–38. doi:10.1109/MC.2005.379

Leskelä, J., Nikula, J., & Salmela, M. (2009). Opencl embedded profile prototype in mobile device. *Proc. Signal Processing Systems*. IEEE.

Miettinen, A. P., & Nurminen, J. K. (2010). Energy efficiency of mobile clients in cloud computing. *Proceedings of the 2nd USENIX conference on Hot topics in cloud computing*. USENIX Association.

Neuvo, Y. (2004). Cellular phones as embedded systems. *Proc. Solid-State Circuits Conference*. IEEE. doi:10.1109/ISSCC.2004.1332581

Pathak, A., Hu, Y. C., Zhang, M., Bahl, P., & Wang, Y. M. (2011). Fine-grained power modeling for smartphones using system call tracing.*Proceedings of the sixth conference on computer systems*. ACM. doi:10.1145/1966445.1966460

Peukert, W. (1897). Über die abhängigkeit der kapazität von der entladestromstärke bei bleiakkumulatoren. *Elektrotechnische Zeitschrift, 20*, 20–21.

Pickard, W. F., & Abbott, D. (2012). Addressing the intermittency challenge: Massive energy storage in a sustainable future. *Proceedings of the IEEE, 100*(2), 317–321. doi:10.1109/JPROC.2011.2174892

Rajovic, N., Rico, A., Vipond, J., Gelado, I., Puzovic, N., & Ramirez, A. (2013) Experiences with mobile processors for energy efficient HPC.*Proceedings of the Conference on Design, Automation and Test in Europe*. doi:10.7873/DATE.2013.103

Rakhmatov, D., & Vrudhula, S. (2003). Energy management for battery-powered embedded systems. *ACM Transactions on Embedded Computing Systems, 2*(3), 277–324. doi:10.1145/860176.860179

Ronkainen, S. (2010). *Camera based motion estimation and recognition for human computer interaction*. (Ph.D. thesis). Acta Univ Oul C 355.

Satyanarayanan, M. (2005). Avoiding dead batteries. *IEEE Pervasive Computing / IEEE Computer Society [and] IEEE Communications Society, 4*(1), 2–3.

Shye, A., Scholbrock, B., & Memik, G. (2009). Into the wild: Studying real user activity patterns to guide power optimizations formobile architectures.*Proceedings of the 42nd Annual IEEE/ACM International Symposium on Microarchitecture*. ACM. doi:10.1145/1669112.1669135

Silvén, O., & Rintaluoma, T. (2007). Energy efficiency of video decoder implementations. In *Mobile Phone Programming and its Applications to Wireless Networking*. Springer. doi:10.1007/978-1-4020-5969-8_23

Sutter, H. (2005). The free lunch is over: A fundamental turn toward concurrency in software. *Dr. Dobb's Journal, 30*(3), 202–210.

Texas-Instruments. (2011). *Omap3530 power estimation spreadsheet*. Technical Report. Author.

Tolia, N., Andersen, D. G., & Satyanarayanan, M. (2006). Quantifying interactive user experience on thin clients. *Computer, 39*(3), 46–52. doi:10.1109/MC.2006.101

Wolf, W. (2004). The future of multiprocessor systems-on-chips. *Proc. Design Automation Conference*. IEEE. doi:10.1145/996566.996753

Zhang, L., Tiwana, B., Qian, Z., Wang, Z., Dick, R. P., Mao, Z. M., & Yang, L. (2010). Accurate online power estimation and automatic battery behavior based power model generation for smartphones. *Proceedings of the eighth IEEE/ACM/IFIP international conference on Hardware/software codesign and system synthesis*. ACM. doi:10.1145/1878961.1878982

Zhou, F., Duh, H. B. L., & Billinghurst, M. (2008). Trends in augmented reality tracking, interaction and display: A review of ten years of ismar. *Proceedings of the 7th IEEE/ACM International Symposium on Mixed and Augmented Reality*. IEEE Computer Society.

Chapter 3
Fish Tracking with Computer Vision Techniques:
An Application to Vertical Slot Fishways

Alvaro Rodriguez
University of Umeå, Sweden

Juan R. Rabuñal
University of A Coruña, Spain

Angel Jose Rico-Diaz
University of A Coruña, Spain

Marcos Gestal
University of A Coruña, Spain

ABSTRACT

Vertical slot fishways are hydraulic structures which allow the upstream migration of fish through obstructions in rivers. Their design depends on the interplay between hydraulic and biological variables to match the requirements of the fish species for which they are intended. However, current mechanisms to study fish behavior in fishway models are impractical or unduly affect the animal behavior. In this chapter, we propose a new procedure for measuring fish behavior in fishways using Computer Vision (CV) techniques to analyze images obtained from the assays by means of a camera system designed for fishway integration. It is expected that this technique will provide detailed information about the fish behavior and will help to improve fish passage devices. A series of assays have been performed in order to validate this new approach in a full-scale fishway model and with living fishes. We have obtained very promising results that allow reconstructing correctly the movements of the fish within the fishway without disturbing fish.

DOI: 10.4018/978-1-5225-0889-2.ch003

1. INTRODUCTION

One of the most important and significant changes in the river ecosystems are related with the construction of water resources management works, such as dams, weirs, water diversions. These works provide many advantages to exploit the water resources, but they also present drawbacks, the main related with the fish natural movements because these structures constitute a physical barrier, what negatively impacts their populations. In fact, this interruption of free passage has been identified as the main reason for the extinction or the depletion of numerous species in many rivers (Jackson, Marmulla, Larinier, Miranda, & Bernacsek, 2001).

Among several solutions used to solve this problem, some of the most versatile are known as vertical slot fishways that are basically a channel divided into several pools separated by slots. Their main advantage lie in its ability to handle large variations in water levels, since the velocity and turbulence fields in the pools are independent of the discharge. Moreover, it allows fish to swim at their preferred depth and to rest in low-velocity areas, in contrast to other types of fishways.

An effective vertical slot fishway must allow fish to enter, pass through, and exit safely with minimum cost to the fish in terms of time and energy. Thus, the achievement of the best biological requirements required for the fishes should drive design and construction criteria for this type of structures. However, only some authors have characterized the flow in vertical slot fishways (Puertas, Pena, & Teijeiro, 2004; Tarrade, Texier, David, & Larinier, 2008; Wu, Rajaratma, & Katopodis, 1999) and others have studied fish swimming performance (Blake, 2004; Dewar & Graham, 1994). Besides, very few works have studied the interaction between the biological and physical processes that are involved in swimming upstream a vertical slot fishway (Puertas et al., 2012). Consequently, the knowledge of fish behavior and its relation with this kind of structures is very limited and the previously noted biological requirements usually rely on the designer's experience, rather than on rational approaches.

In order to address this deficit, it should be required to complete the fishway design methodology with results from experimental assays with living fish. In these tests, fish are introduced into full-scale fishway models (see Figure 1). Their movements and behavior are analyzed. In the tests described in this chapter, the passage success is evaluated and the fish effort is measured by means of blood tests. That value measures the proportion of individuals that passes through the fishway. Nevertheless, these techniques should be used in combination with another that permits detailed characterization of the animal behavior during the assay, determining parameters such as: resting areas, resting times, fish velocities and accelerations, times spent for full ascent and in each pool, etc. Subsequently, these parameters can be linked to the hydraulic data and the results of the blood tests in order to measure the fish biological requirements.

Figure 1. Indoor full-scale (1:1 scale) vertical slot fishway model used in this study
Photo taken at Center for Studies and Experimentation of Public Works, Madrid, Spain.

However, the monitoring of the fish on the fishway during the assay with the current methods gives rise to many difficulties:

- **Direct Observation:** This technique is impractical because of the difficulty of observation due to the water turbulence and the limited validity of the information collected.
- **Placement of Sensors on the Specimens:** This technique is based on the placement of antennas in key positions in order to record the pass of the fish, which will be equipped with a transmitter (Castro-Santos, Haro, & Walk, 1996). Although this technique may be a good alternative when the tests are carried out with a large number of individuals, it provides no information on the full fish trajectory. Besides, the sensors placed externally tend to fall off, and the surgically-implanted sensors affect significantly the animal behavior.

Therefore, it is necessary to develop a new technique to measure the behavior of the fish within the fishway, in a less intrusive way and capable of obtaining more accurate information than direct observation and placement of sensors techniques. To this end, an approach based on optical or acoustic monitoring is the best alternative. Some early examples of these applications are the use of acoustic transmitters and a video camera for observing the behavior of various species (Armstrong, Bagley, & Priede, 1992), or the utilization of acoustic scanners for monitoring fish stocks (Steig & Iverson, 1998).

More recently, different *CV* techniques for the study of the fish behavior have been used; these works use techniques such as stereo vision (Petrell, Shi, Ward, Naiberg, & Savage, 1997), background models (Morais, Campos, Padua, & Carceroni, 2005), shape priors (Clausen et al., 2007), local thresholding (Chuang, Hwang, Williams, & Towler, 2011), moving average algorithms (Spampinato, Chen-Burger, Nadarajan, & Fisher, 2008), particle image velocimetry techniques (Deng, Richmond, Guest, & Mueller, 2004), pattern classifiers applied to the changes measured in the background (Lines et al., 2001) or Artificial Neural Networks (*ANN*). Finally, some techniques based on infrared imaging (Baumgartner et al., 2010) or *LIDAR* (Light Detection and Ranging or Laser Imaging Detection and Ranging) technologies (Mitra, Wang, & Banerjee, 2006) have also been applied in the field.

However, it should be noted that most of the published techniques have been carried out in calm water conditions and with controlled light sources. Therefore they are not suitable for their use inside a fishway as those presented in the present work. Additionally, some of these techniques use marks or light sources, which may influence fish behavior, while others employ special and expensive sensors, which may be only used in certain points of the structure.

Consequently, since none of the current techniques would be appropriate in the context of this research, a new technique is proposed to study fish behavior in vertical slot fishways. It gathers information at every instant about the position, velocity and acceleration of the fish. To this end, images obtained through a network of video cameras are analyzed using *CV* techniques and artificial neural networks. As a part of the technique proposed, a new algorithm to extract the mass center of the fishes in the images segmented by the neural network is presented, as well as a procedure to integrate the different cameras used in the assays. These characteristics will allow to perform in the feature studies about different parameters or similar structures.

2. PROPOSED TECHNIQUE

The proposed technique uses the recorded images of the assay in order to calculate the position of the fish on the fishway at every instant along of the 7 pools that build the full vertical fishway structure.

To this end, a camera system equipped with fisheye lenses that provide a 180° viewing angle has been installed. The cameras were placed in an overhead perspective and partially submerged so that the entire fishway is covered and turbulence and surface reflections are avoided to improve the image acquisition process (Rodriguez et al., 2011).

Figure 2 shows the location of the cameras with water protection structure, illustrating the operation of the camera and the visual angle of the camera slightly reduced by the protection structure.

Figure 2. Recording conditions

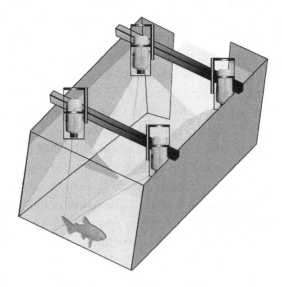

Therefore, a total of 28 cameras have been used, 4 per pool. The cameras have been integrated into the monitoring and data acquisition system so that each camera has been connected to a hard disk (it improves the write operation times) and the recording of all disks has been synchronized. Furthermore, in order to facilitate the control of the process, each hard disk has been connected to a central computer and a monitor through a video quad and video multiplexer in order to facilitate the control of the process. This structure defined for the data acquisition process is schematized in the Figure 3.

The images taken by the data acquisition system, will allow us to calculate the position, velocity and acceleration of the fish.

Once we have defined the structure for the image acquisition, several steps should be done in order to get valuable results for those images. These steps are summarized here and explained more in-depth in the following subsections:

1. Camera calibration.
2. Segmentation:
    a. Background modelling,
    b. Edge analysis,
    c. Region analysis.
3. Representation and Interpretation.
4. Tracking.
5. Filtering.
6. Data Processing.

Figure 3. Overview of the data acquisition system

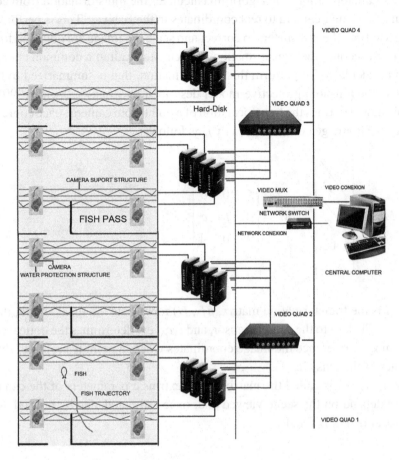

One of the main advantages of this approach is the scalability of the system. According to this, the images of each camera are analyzed in parallel with a distributed architecture system. Furthermore, the most computationally expensive steps of the algorithm such as the edge and region analysis in the segmentation step, or the representation and interpretation step do not use temporal information from previous outputs of the system, so different frames may be analysed concurrently and can take advantage of multicore processing to reduce the computation times.

2.1 Camera Calibration

Cameras acquire images with a certain distortion, so it should be eliminated. Furthermore, several cameras are used to track the fish movement, so a projective model is designed to integrate measurements from the different cameras into a common coordinate space in order to improve the visualization.

First of all, the calibration algorithm calculates the transformation from coordinates in a particular camera to real coordinates in the fishway. This is performed in two stages: first, the parameters to correct and scale the image are obtained for each camera and second, the transformation of each camera into a common coordinate system is calculated.To perform this transformation, that is summarized in Figure 4, we use the pin-hole projective model described by Zhang (Zhang, 1999). The pin-hole model defines the transformation of a point from camera space coordinates (Xc, Yc, Zc) to image coordinates (x_i, y_i), as follows:

$$\begin{bmatrix} x_i \\ y_i \\ 1 \end{bmatrix} = M_{3x3} \times \begin{bmatrix} X_c/Z_c \\ Y_c/Z_c \\ 1 \end{bmatrix} \qquad M = \begin{bmatrix} f_x & 0 & c_x \\ 0 & f_y & c_y \\ 0 & 0 & 1 \end{bmatrix} \qquad (1)$$

where M is the transformation matrix, $f(fx, fy)$ represents the focal length, the distance from the lens to the camera sensor, and $c(cx, cy)$ determines the optical center, establishing as reference the image coordinates where a point is projected through the center of the lens Oc.

The matrix M is called the matrix of the extrinsic parameters of the camera, it does not depend on the scene viewed and, once estimated, can be re-used as long as the focal length is fixed.

Figure 4. Projection of a fish in a pin-hole camera model. The point (xi,yi) represent a pixel of a fish in a digital image, and (xc,yc) are the corresponding projected coordinates in the space. The image is projected through the center of the lens or optical center Oc.

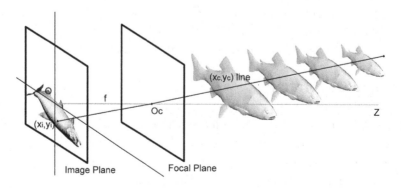

In practice, due to small imperfections in the lens and other factors, some distortions are integrated into the image. These distortions can be modeled using the following parametric equations (Weng, Cohen, & Herniou, 1992):

$$
\begin{aligned}
dr_x(x) &= xk_1r^2 + xk_2r^4 + xk_3r^6 \\
dr_y(y) &= yk_1r^2 + yk_2r^4 + yk_3r^6 \\
dt_x(x,y) &= k_3\left(r^2 + 2x^2\right) + 2k_4xy \\
dt_y(x,y) &= 2k_3xy + k_4\left(r^2 + 2y^2\right)
\end{aligned}
\tag{2}
$$

where x and y are spatial coordinates, r is the distance to the lens optical center, dr is the radial distortion, dt is the tangential distortion and k_i are the distortion parameters to be determined.

The distortion coefficients do not depend on the scene viewed, thus they also belong to the intrinsic camera parameters. And they remain the same regardless of the captured image resolution.

Additionally, the refraction of light in the water must be considered. Thus, cameras should be calibrated underwater or refraction should be modeled with an additional transformation. In this case, an affine model is employed to perform this task.

In the second process, the measurements obtained by each camera are projected to a common coordinate system, the entire pool being covered. Thus, applying an equation of general projective geometry, the transformation M_2 between the global coordinate space c' and the coordinate space c, obtained from a concrete camera, can be expressed as follows:

$$
\begin{bmatrix} x_{c'} \\ y_{c'} \\ 1 \end{bmatrix} = M_2 \times \begin{bmatrix} x_c \\ y_c \\ 1 \end{bmatrix} \qquad M_2 = \begin{bmatrix} a & b & c \\ d & e & f \\ g & h & 1 \end{bmatrix}
\tag{3}
$$

To solve the equation above, a number of visual marks have been placed in the areas where the vision field of the cameras overlaps (Figure 5).

2.2 Segmentation

Image segmentation is the process of dividing an image into multiple parts, in this case, with the aim of separating the fish from the background. Firstly, every segmentation algorithm must addresses the criteria used to get a good partition and the

Figure 5. Camera overlapping vision fields. The image shows a pool of the fishway formed with the projected images from the four cameras which are covering the pool. Each polygon represents the field of each different camera.

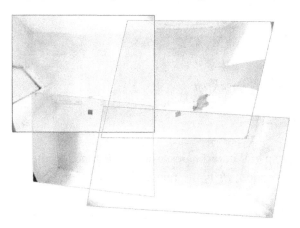

method for achieving an efficient one (Yilmaz, Javed, & Shah, 2006). In statistics, this problem is known as cluster analysis and is a widely studied area with hundreds of different algorithms (Szeliski, 2011).

Therefore, it will be necessary to find the subset of features which allows a robust separation of the fish from the background and then to choose a technique to classify the image according to the selected features.

In the state of the art, most common criteria to detect fish in images are based on color features and a *priori* knowledge of the background. However, these techniques do not perform well in underwater images, even for calm water and high quality images, due to the low levels of contrast (Lines et al., 2001). This problem increase in the fishway study so the water is continually moving. Besides, acquired images in this study will be characterized by extreme luminosity changes and huge noise levels, being texture and color information useless.

Taking this into account, different techniques are considered in this work. They are detailed in the results section and provide a comparative framework for evaluating the performance of the system. They are based on the discontinuities in the intensity of the image (edge-based classification) or on the intensity similarity of pixels (region-based classification). Due to the need to operate the system by non-experts, only non-supervised techniques have been considered and, given the huge amount of images to be analysed, computational complexity was decided to be a critical factor.

Figure 6. Segmentation tests with different SOM neural networks

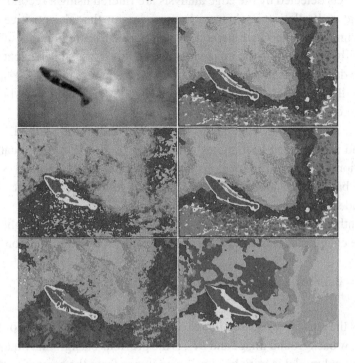

One of these techniques, previously developed in (Rodriguez et al., 2011), consists of a *SOM* (Self-Organizing Map) neural network (Kohonen, 1982). The *SOM* model is aimed at establishing a correlation between the numerical patterns supplied as an input and a two-dimensional output space, named topological map. This characteristic can be applied to image segmentation, and *SOM* networks have been widely used in the image analysis field (Ahmed & Farag, 1997; Dong & Xie, 2005; Ngan & Hu, 1999; Verikas, Malmqvist, & Bergman, 1997; Waldemark, 1997). Although promising results were obtained in this early work, the *SOM* approach is slow compared with more straightforward techniques and it heavily depends on the training patterns selected. Examples of classification with different SOM networks can be seen in Figure 6.

In this work, a combination of two simple techniques is selected, together with an image preprocessing procedure and a dynamic background modeling, to overcome the limitations of the *SOM* approach. The first selected technique is a modern implementation of the *Canny* edge detector, which resulted less noisy than other edge-finding methods such as the *Sobel* or the *Prewitt* operators. In our case, the edges will correspond to the frontiers between fish and background.

The objects detected by the edge analysis are filtered using a second segmentation technique. It allows to achieve a lower value for the false positive rate. This second technique is the *Otsu* method, which performs a region classification by automatically thresholding the image histogram. It is a fast and efficient technique to separate dark objects in a white background (Sezgin & Sankur, 2004). The final outcome will include only the objects detected by the edge algorithm which overlap 95% with those found with the region technique.

So as to include knowledge about the background in the method, a dynamic background is calculated forming a synthetic image. Before the application of the segmentation technique, the image is normalized and the foreground is extracted using this background model. This procedure is known in Computer Vision as background subtraction.

The synthetic background is constructed dynamically to handle light and long-term scene changes. It is calculated according to the following equation:

$$BI_i(x,y) = 0.5 \times BI_{i-1}(x,y) + 0.5 \times I_i(x,y) \tag{4}$$

where, I_i is the current processed image, corresponding to the frame i of the video, BI_i is the new background image and BI_{i-1} is the previous background image. For $i=1$ the background model is initialized using an image from the camera with no fish.

In order to enhance the image quality, the images are preprocessed using a standard contrast-limited adaptive histogram equalization technique. Besides, the borders where the waterproof cases of the cameras produced a black region (without information) were masked.

2.3 Representation and Interpretation

As a result of the segmentation process, the image is divided in different regions representing the background and a possible location of the fish. At this point, it is possible to use a higher level processing, adding knowledge extracted from the characteristics of real fish, to interpret the segmented image. To this end, the objects detected in the previous step are translated into convenient descriptors, which can be used to perform different operations: its area, its centroid (calculated as the average position of the body pixels) and the minimum ellipse containing the body.

Subsequently, an algorithm classifies each detected body into fish or non-fish categories. The operation of this algorithm is divided in three stages as shown in Figure 7. In the first stage, the detected bodies are discarded or classified as either fish or small bodies. To this end, a shape criteria based on value ranges of the above descriptors is defined for each fish species. In the second stage, close fish bodies

Figure 7. Diagram of the algorithm used to interpret the segmented image

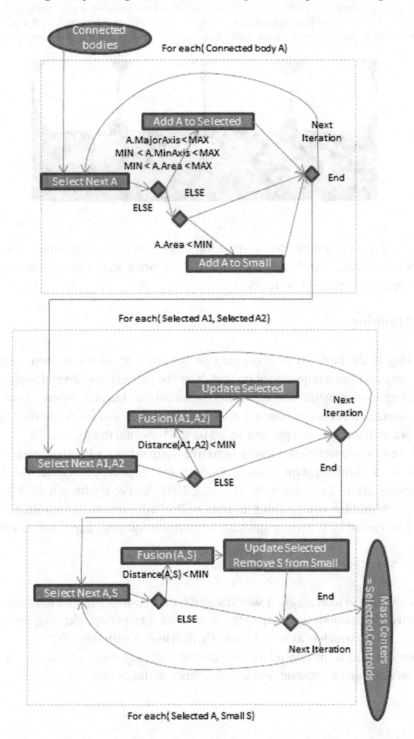

Figure 8. Obtained results after segmentation and interpretation steps

Original images are shown at the top of the figure and their corresponding segmentation is shown at the bottom. Each detected body is marked in white and each fish center is marked with a small dark square inside the body. Note that some bodies have been interpreted as parts of the same fish.

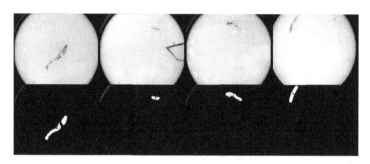

are joined if the resulting body verifies the shape criteria. Finally, small bodies are either joined with detected fish or discarded. Figure 8 shows the obtained results when applying image interpretation.

2.4 Tracking

Tracking is the problem of generating an inference about the motion of one or more objects from a sequence of images. It can be solved using several approaches, including motion estimation and feature matching techniques. Some of the most important approaches consider a statistical point of view and formulate the problem as a prediction correction process based on the Bayesian theory.

A well-known technique in this group is the Kalman filter, which has been selected in this work (Arulampalam, Maskell, Gordon, & Clapp, 2002; Stenger, Mendonca, & Cipolla, 2001; Yu, Watson, & Arrillaga, 2005; Yun & Bachmann, 2006). It addresses the problem of estimating the state $x \in R^n$ of a discrete-time controlled process that is governed by the linear stochastic difference equation, expressed as follows:

$$x(t+1) = Ax(t)+w(t) \tag{5}$$

where A is a nxn matrix called state transition matrix, which relates the state of the system at the previous time step to the state at the current step, and w represents the process noise, which is assumed normally distributed with mean 0.

For the state transition matrix, we consider the equations of two dimensional motion assuming a constant acceleration between time steps:

$$x_{t+1} = x_t + v_{x,t} + \frac{1}{2} a_x t^2$$

$$y_{t+1} = y_t + v_{y,t} + \frac{1}{2} a_y t^2 \qquad\qquad (6)$$

$$v_{x,t+1} = v_{x,t} + a_x t$$

$$v_{y,t+1} = v_{y,t} + a_y t$$

where (x, y) is the fish position, $(v_x v_y)$ is the velocity and $(a_x a_y)$ is the acceleration, which is assumed constant in the time interval t (equal to the frequency of the image acquisition, i.e., *0.04* s).

We consider also an observation model described by the following equation:

$$z(t) = Hx(t) + v(t) \qquad\qquad (7)$$

where $z \in R^m$ represents the measurement, H is a *mxn* matrix called observation matrix and v is a measurement error assumed independent of w and normally distributed with mean 0.

After the calibration process, it is assumed that real world positions can be inferred from observed positions in the image. In addition, the acceleration term is considered to have a zero mean, so the model equations can be expressed as follows:

$$\begin{bmatrix} x_{t+1} \\ y_{t+1} \\ v_{x,t+1} \\ v_{y,t+1} \end{bmatrix} = \begin{bmatrix} 1 & 0 & t & 0 \\ 0 & 1 & 0 & t \\ 0 & 0 & 1 & 0 \\ 0 & 0 & 0 & 1 \end{bmatrix} \begin{bmatrix} x_t \\ y_t \\ v_{x,t} \\ v_{y,t} \end{bmatrix} + w(t)$$

$$\qquad\qquad (8)$$

$$\begin{bmatrix} z_x \\ z_y \end{bmatrix} = \begin{bmatrix} 1 & 0 & 0 & 0 \\ 0 & 1 & 0 & 0 \end{bmatrix} \begin{bmatrix} x_t \\ y_t \\ v_{x,t} \\ v_{y,t} \end{bmatrix} + v(t)$$

The Kalman filter works in a two-step recursive process. First, it estimates the new state, along with their uncertainties. Once the outcome of the next measurement (corrupted with noise) is observed, these estimates are updated using a weighted average. The higher weight is given to the estimates with higher uncertainty. The algorithm can, therefore, run in real time using only the current input measurements and the previously calculated state. In the present work, the implementation of the Kalman filter was performed according to (Welch & Bishop, 2006), obtaining an empirical estimate of the measurement error and the process noise covariances.

The Kalman filter is designed to track multiple objects, which are referred to as fish or tracks. The essential problem which is solved at this point is the assignment of detections to fish. In order to associate detections to tracks, a cost is assigned to every possible pair fish-detection. The cost is understood as the probability of that detection to correspond to the current fish position. It is calculated using the distance from the detected position to the predicted position and to the last confirmed position of the fish. To this end, the minimum of the Euclidean distances is selected as cost metric.

Therefore, every detection is assigned to the track with the lower cost, provided that it is lower than a selected value, and each track can only be assigned to one detection. When a new detection is assigned to a fish, the predicted position for that instant is confirmed and corrected. Detections which remain unassigned to any existing fish are assumed to belong to new tracks. Additionally, if a fish remains unassigned for too long, its track is closed, so no new assignments can be made to that fish. Fish without enough detections are assumed to be noise and deleted. The operation of the assignment algorithm is described in the schematic of Figure 9 and the results obtained in a situation with two fish are shown in Figure 10.

In conclusion, this technique does not only obtain trajectories from detections, but also allows filtering some of the false positives of the system and estimating the fish position when it is not detected in the images.

2.5 Filtering

The result of the process so far is the vector of positions of every detected fish along time, representing its full trajectory on the fishway. However, it is expected that these results will still show certain undesirable phenomena, caused by the small variability of the calculated position of the centroid, the parts of fish which are hidden by bubbles and the errors in perspective and alignment of planes, when the fish moves from a field of view of a camera to another.

In order to solve these problems, and to remove some of the noise still present in the results, a complex filtering process is required. First, the relative position of the cameras is taken into account to solve differences between simultaneous observations. Thus, when the fish is detected simultaneously by two or more cameras, its position is the average of all the observed positions. In order to determine if two observations from different cameras belong to the same target, the trajectories resulting from the Kalman filter are compared. If they start and end in adjacent cameras in similar times, they are then merged. When more than one fish crosses simultaneously from one camera field of view to another, the distance from the last predicted position in the old camera to the first position in the new camera is used as a cost function.

Figure 9. Diagram of the algorithm used to assign detections to fishes

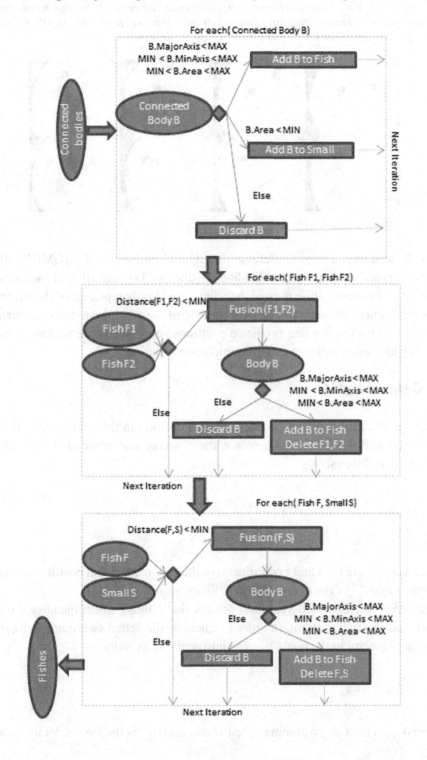

Figure 10. Obtained results with Kalman filtering in a sequence of images
Image order is from left to right and from the top to the bottom. Fish detections are shown as dark areas
superimposed to the images. Black circles and labels indicate tracked fishes. Note that the position of
the two fishes is calculated even if they are not detected in the image.

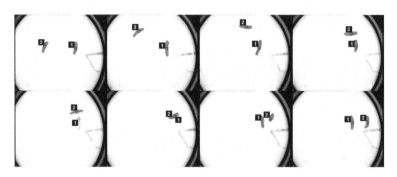

In the next step, a moving average filtering process is applied (SIGMUR, 2003) and outliers are detected by thresholding the distance between filtered and original positions. Therefore, while normal detections are simply replaced by their filtered ones, the outliers are substituted by the average of the previous and next confirmed detections. This implies that predicted positions near outliers are no longer valid, and they are hence replaced using interpolation techniques.

2.6 Data Analysis

As the result of the previous process, the fish position in the fishway over time is obtained. From the fish position vector, the observed instantaneous velocities are calculated as follows:

$$\overline{v}_{obs} = \left(\frac{X_i - X_{i-1}}{t_i - t_{i-1}}, \frac{Y_i - Y_{i-1}}{t_i - t_{i-1}} \right) \tag{9}$$

where X_i and Y_i are the x and y coordinates of the fish in the global coordinate system in time t_i, and $\overline{v}_{obs}$ is the observed fish velocity vector.

However, the observed velocities are not really those which quantify the real effort made by fish to swim. In order to calculate the actual swimming velocities, the water velocity in the pools is taken into account, as follows:

$$\overline{v}_{swim} = \overline{v}_{obs} - \overline{v}_{flow} \tag{10}$$

where $\overline{v}_{swim}$ is the fish swimming speed vector and $\overline{v}_{flow}$ is the flow velocity vector.

Figure 11. Example of fish ascent trajectory

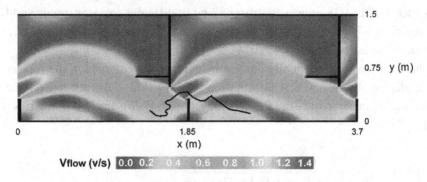

The water velocity in the fishway can be evaluated by means of experimental studies (J. Puertas et al., 2004; Tarrade et al., 2008; Wu et al., 1999) or numerical models (Cea, Pena, Puertas, Vázquez-Cendón, & Peña, 2007; Chorda et al., 2010; Heimerl, Hagmeyer, & Echteler, 2008). In this case, the velocity field in the pools is computed with a numerical model based on the 2D depth averaged shallow water equations. The experimental validation of this model in 16 different fishway designs, as well as a detailed description of the model equations, can be found in (Bermúdez, Puertas, Cea, Pena, & Balairón, 2010). Figure 11 shows the computed velocity field in two consecutive pools of the fishway model.

In addition, further information regarding fish behavior can be obtained, such as ascending and resting times, accelerations, total distance covered or preferential areas for rest. Although further research is needed, the analysis of these parameters can contribute to the definition of key factors in fish passage through these devices.

3. EXPERIMENTAL RESULTS

In the following subsections the results of the proposed techniques will be analyzed according three different aspects: the quality of the results taking into account statistical measures as precision, recall or true or false positive rate; the tracking characteristic performance to generate valid trajectories from fish and the biological measures used to test the fish behaviors and stress.

3.1 Performance of the System

In order to measure and compare the achievement of the system, several experiments were performed in a full-scale vertical slot fishway model located in the CEDEX laboratory. From these experiments, a dataset was created to apply the proposed technique and other well-known methods. The dataset is composed of 135 videos with a total of 11,028 images, corresponding to different cameras, pools and fishway regions, as well as different daylight conditions and fish species (Rodriguez, Bermúdez, Rabuñal, & Puertas, 2014).

These videos were manually labeled by experts who marked in the images the fish center positions, and this information served as ground-truth to evaluate the techniques. In order to measure the accuracy, the *Precision* and *Recall* metrics were used:

$$\text{Precision} = \frac{\text{True Positive}}{\text{True Positive} + \text{False Positive}}$$

$$\text{Recall} = \frac{\text{True Positive}}{\text{True Positive} + \text{False Negative}} \qquad (11)$$

$$\text{False Positive Rate} = 1 - \text{Precision}$$

$$\text{False Negative Rate} = 1 - \text{Recall}$$

With the aim to compare the proposed technique with other algorithms, some widely used non-supervised segmentation approaches have been implemented and tested by means of the previous metrics.

Specifically, the following techniques have been used:

- **Region:** A region segmentation algorithm based on the *Otsu* method.
- **Edge:** A modern implementation of the *Canny* edge detector.
- **Edge-Region:** A combination of the two previous techniques. It is the one proposed in this research.
- **SOM-Pix:** A *SOM* neural network based on the *RGB* intensity values of the image from the neighborhood of each pixel.
- **SOM-Avg:** A *SOM* neural network which input is the local average of the RGB values in a window centered in the neighborhood of the pixel.
- **SOM-Feat:** A *SOM* neural network that uses two different image features: the local average of the *RGB* values in a window centered in the neighborhood of the pixel and the standard deviation of the *RGB* values in the column and file of the pixel.

Three different versions of each technique were implemented: one without background information and another two in which a background is used to normalize the image. In the latter case, either a static frame without fish or the proposed dynamic background technique was used to model the background. In every case, images were enhanced with a standard contrast-limited adaptive histogram equalization technique.

When using the *SOM* techniques, a three-layer topology with 3 processing elements (neurons) in each layer was selected and a 3 by 3 window was used for each input. To mitigate the dependence of the results on the selected training patterns, all networks were trained using 3 different datasets. Additionally, the *SOM* network proposed in (Rodriguez et al., 2011) was considered in the comparative.

The results obtained after the representation and interpretation step for the different techniques are shown in Table 1. It can be observed that the results are strongly dependent on the background model. It should be take into account that only the proposed technique performed well without background modeling and, in general, dynamic background achieved better results than the static one.

Table 1. Results obtained for the selected techniques without tracking

	Average Results	Precision	Recall	False Pos. Rate	False Neg. Rate	Time (s/ Frame)
No Backgnd.	SOM Pixel	0.43	0.29	0.57	0.71	1.38
	SOM Avg.	0.55	0.35	0.45	0.65	3.60
	SOM Feat.	0.63	0.26	0.37	0.74	11.63
	Edge	0.86	0.73	0.14	0.27	0.34
	Region	0.40	0.39	0.60	0.61	0.40
	Edge – Region	0.93	0.71	0.07	0.29	0.31
Static Backgnd.	SOM Pixel	0.91	0.49	0.09	0.51	1.55
	SOM Avg.	0.96	0.72	0.04	0.28	3.41
	SOM Feat.	0.96	0.62	0.04	0.38	11.22
	SOM (Rodriguez et al., 2011)	0.85	0.69	0.15	0.31	3.37
	Edge	0.65	0.75	0.35	0.25	0.35
	Region	0.94	0.81	0.06	0.19	0.19
	Edge – Region	0.94	0.82	0.06	0.18	0.32
Dyn. Backgnd.	SOM Pixel	0.96	0.78	0.04	0.22	1.15
	SOM Avg.	0.96	0.61	0.04	0.39	11.62
	SOM Feat.	0.96	0.72	0.04	0.28	3.61
	Edge	0.67	0.78	0.33	0.22	0.32
	Region	0.95	0.78	0.05	0.22	0.17
	Edge - Region (proposed)	0.95	0.82	0.05	0.18	0.31

Table 2. Results obtained with tracking operating as a filter. Selected techniques are used with background modeling after tracking and filtering steps and using only confirmed detections.

	Average Results	Precision	Recall	False Pos. Rate	False Neg. Rate	Time (sec./ Frame)
Static Backgnd.	SOM Pixel	0.97	0.81	0.03	0.19	1.14
	SOM Avg.	0.98	0.74	0.02	0.26	3.71
	SOM Feat.	0.97	0.64	0.03	0.36	11.97
	SOM (Rodriguez et al., 2011)	0.88	0.75	0.12	0.25	3.27
	Edge	0.70	0.83	0.30	0.17	0.33
	Region	0.97	0.84	0.03	0.16	0.18
	Edge - Region	0.97	0.84	0.03	0.16	0.31
Dyn. Backgnd.	SOM Pixel	0.97	0.80	0.03	0.20	1.15
	SOM Avg.	0.98	0.74	0.02	0.26	3.67
	SOM Feat.	0.97	0.63	0.03	0.37	11.87
	Edge	0.75	0.85	0.25	0.15	0.33
	Region	0.97	0.81	0.03	0.19	0.17
	Edge - Region (proposed)	0.98	0.85	0.02	0.15	0.31

It can also be noted that the worst results in terms of accuracy are obtained with the *Edge* technique. On the other hand, *SOM* models based on features achieve good accuracy. However the presents a high disvantage, because this kind of techniques requires a higher computational time. Finally, although the *Region* technique obtained quite good results, the proposed technique yielded the same level of precision with the best recall, and without increasing significantly the execution time.

Once the representation and interpretation step is completed, fish detections are processed with the tracking algorithm. As explained above, this algorithm can operate as a filter, using the confirmed positions of the tracked fish. The results obtained using this configuration are shown in Table 2. Techniques without background have been discarded, as they generally achieved low accuracy.

However, the tracking technique can also estimate hidden positions of the fish. This is done by the Kalman algorithm, which predicts fish locations based on the motion model (6). Following this procedure, the results include both confirmed and estimated positions (Table 3).

Table 3. Performance with filtering and interpolation tracking. Selected techniques are used with background modeling after tracking and filtering steps. Both confirmed and predicted detections are used.

	Average Results	Precision	Recall	False Pos. Rate	False Neg. Rate	Time (sec./ Frame)
8tatic Backgnd.	SOM Pixel	0.93	0.91	0.07	0.09	1.14
	SOM Avg.	0.95	0.86	0.05	0.14	3.71
	SOM Feat.	0.93	0.80	0.07	0.20	11.97
	SOM (Rodriguez et al., 2011)	0.73	0.88	0.27	0.12	3.27
	Edge	0.44	0.93	0.56	0.07	0.33
	Region	0.94	0.94	0.06	0.06	0.18
	Edge - Region	0.94	0.94	0.06	0.06	0.31
Dyn. Backgnd.	SOM Pixel	0.94	0.91	0.06	0.09	1.15
	SOM Avg.	0.95	0.86	0.05	0.14	3.67
	SOM Feat.	0.94	0.80	0.06	0.20	11.87
	Edge	0.48	0.93	0.52	0.07	0.33
	Region	0.94	0.93	0.06	0.07	0.17
	Edge - Region (proposed)	0.95	0.94	0.05	0.06	0.31

The precision of the system is increased significantly if the algorithm operates only as a filter. However, the use of predicted positions improves the recall, without losing precision when compared to the results before the tracking step (Table 1).

It must be taken into account that some of the new false positives that appear when using predictions are not errors. In fact, they may reflect the position of the fish when it is not observable in the images and the fish center position has not been manually marked.

In conclusion, the proposed technique obtains the best results within the selected techniques. It achieves one of the lowest false positive rates and the lowest false negative one, with one of the best execution times. That confirms that proposed technique obtains very reliable results finding the true positions of the fish, with a high probability and detecting the fish in most of the situations.

Hence, the technique is considered to obtain reliable results: it detects the fish in most situations and finds their true positions with a high probability.

Additionally, the capability of the system to observe fish along time was studied. Here, the ability of the system to avoid noise detections to be tracked as a fish is usually related with the ability to tracking fish without losing it. These two error have been analysed together in long sequences with a single fish and in short sequences with two fishes. The obtained results show a very low error rate, with one tracking error every 5000 frames or more. These results confirm that the proposed system is suitable for obtaining fish trajectories from recorded images.

It must be taken into account that, when two or more fishes interact during some time, causing occlusions and overlapping in the images. This results in the assignment of some of the fishes to the wrong trajectory, and this type of error is not visually observable by human operators, since they usually correspond to changes in the relative position of fish when they are occluded by turbulence or bubbles. Under these conditions, fish are not visually distinguishable from each other. However, interaction among fish was barely observed in high-velocity areas and it does not affect the global analysis of fish behavior in resting zones.

3.2 Biological Results

The proposed system was applied to 15 assays conducted for two years in the full-scale vertical slot fishway model located at the CEDEX laboratory (Figure 1). During the corresponding migration period, four different species (a total of 259 fishes) were tested: Iberian barbel (*Luciobarbus bocagei*), Mediterranean barbel (*Luciobarbus guiraonis*), Iberian straight-mouth nase (*Pseudochondrostoma polylepis*) and brown trout (*Salmo trutta*), as shown in Figure 12. The recordings of each assay last approximately 12 hours, and the recording frequency is 25Hz.

Overall, passage success during the experiments was low, regardless of species, and varied considerably with fish size (Table 4). In general, larger individuals presented a higher rate of success in ascending the entire fishway, relative to small specimens of the same species.

On the other hand, the path chosen by fish moving from one pool to another and the specific resting zones actually exploited by the fish were identified. In the experiments, the individuals avoided high-velocity areas and used regions where velocity and turbulence levels are lower, to move within the pool and for resting before

Figure 12. Fish species used in the assays. From left to right: Iberian barbel, Mediterranean barbel, Iberian straight-mouth nase and brown trout.

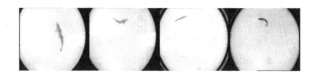

Table 4. Overall passage success during the experiments

Specie	Size (cm)	Number of Fishes	Passage Success (%)
Iberian barbel	0 - 15	12	33.3%
	15 - 20	12	75.0%
	20 - 25	5	80.0%
	>25	34	41.2%
Mediterranean barbel	0 - 15	6	0.0%
	15 - 20	8	0.0%
	20 - 25	11	54.6%
	>25	12	25.0%
Iberian straight-mouth nase	0 - 15	61	9.8%
	20 - 25	34	41.2%
Brown Trout	0 - 15	5	0.0%
	15 - 20	43	14.0%
	20 - 25	14	42.9%
	25-30	2	100.0%
Total		259	28.6%

ascending through the higher velocity area of the slot. Thus, a preliminary analysis of the fish trajectories revealed that, when ascending the fishway, fish spent the vast majority of time in low velocity areas that seems to be used as rest areas.

Besides, low-velocity areas were not frequented uniformly by fish, which stayed most frequently in the zone located just downstream from the slot and behind the small side baffle (zone A in Figure 13). The exploitation of low-velocity areas for the four species can be seen in Table 5. The frequency of use of resting zones is expressed as the proportion between the time spent in a specific one and the total resting time during the ascent.

In addition, the trajectories during the pool ascents were analyzed. In general, two modes of successful ascents were observed, depending on the location of the individual within the pool before traversing the slot and the area used to approach it (Figure 14). The results suggest that all the selected fish species tend to follow similar trajectories, and exploit the same flow regions during the ascent.

Finally, the observed speed, swimming speed and acceleration have been calculated as described in section 2.6. Figure 15 shows a sample of obtained velocities and accelerations (in modulus), which are represented as a function of the traveled distance, and their respective polynomial fitting curves.

Figure 13. Location of the resting zones considered in this work

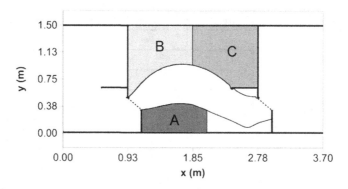

Table 5. Exploitation of resting areas for the four species; resting zones are labeled as in Figure 13

Specie	Frequency of Use (%)			Avg. Resting Time (s)
	A	B	C	
Iberian barbel	68.5	28.5	2.9	161
Mediterranean barbel	88.4	10.5	1.1	325
Iberian straight-mouth nase	99.8	0.0	0.2	269
Brown trout	82.7	16.7	0.6	1271
Total	84.1	15.1	0.8	585

Figure 14. Examples of the two typical successful ascents used by fishes

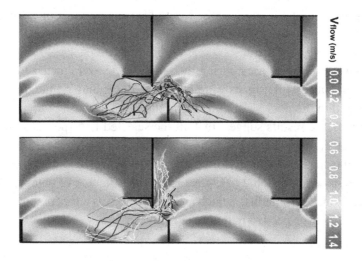

Figure 15. Fish velocities and accelerations. Velocities and accelerations calculated for a set of pool ascents observed in the experimental tests. Ds is the traveled length from the slot section.

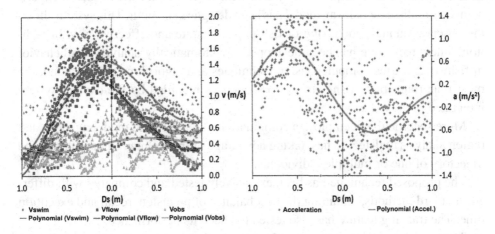

A clear trend is observed in fish swimming velocities, with a peak occurring immediately prior to crossing the slot and significant decrease in velocity once the fish passes to the next pool. This pattern is strongly influenced by the water velocities that fish is confronted to in the different regions of the fishway.

On the other hand, fish acceleration data are more scattered, being maximum accelerations observed when fish approach the slot. This is due to the fact that fish usually come from a resting area and need to reach a certain speed to traverse the slot. After crossing this high velocity area, they usually decelerate.

Average maximum swimming speeds and accelerations can be seen in Table 6. Observed fish velocities are low relative to the flow velocity in the slot region, as shown in Figure 15. Hence, maximum swimming velocities are only slightly higher than the water velocity in the slot, regardless the fish species.

Table 6. Average maximum speeds and accelerations for the four species

Specie	Swimming Speed (m/s)		Acceleration (m/s2)	
	Avg. Maximum	Std. Deviation	Avg. Maximum	Std. Deviation
Iberian Barbel	1.51	0.27	1.13	0.60
Mediterranean Barbel	1.51	0.25	0.95	0.60
Iberian straight-mouth nase	1.52	0.26	1.08	0.54
Brown Trout	1.60	0.25	1.31	0.74

4. CONCLUSION

In this chapter, a data acquisition system with video monitoring to record experiments on a full-scale fishway model has been designed and built. This system allows the observation and monitoring of fish in an accurate and effective way. In addition, a new technique has been developed to automatically analyze fish behavior in fishways. It uses computer vision techniques and algorithms to detect and, the most important track, fishes in video sequences recorded by the camera system integrated in the fishway.

More specifically, it employs a combination of background modeling, edge and region analysis to detect fishes, taking advantage of the Kalman filter to obtain the trajectory of one or multiple individuals.

The proposed technique has been extensively tested and compared with different standard methods, obtaining the best balance of precision, recall and execution time. The tracking feature has also tested to check its performance.

The system has been applied to 15 assays performed along two years and using more than 250 living fishes. It has provided valuable information regarding fish behavior, including fishway efficiency, swimming trajectories, swimming velocities and accelerations, resting times and preferential resting areas.

Although in these preliminary results the parallel performance was not discussed. The described structure makes very simple to use a distributed computing approach based on multicore processing. According to this structure, we analyzed concurrently the sequence obtained in each camera. In a lower level, we used Matlab parallel computing support to successfully exploit the independence in the segmentation representation and interpretation tasks to improve the response times. Using that improvement, it would even be possible in future stages of the project to run this application in a real time environment.

REFERENCES

Ahmed, M. N., & Farag, A. A. (1997). Two-stage neural network for volume segmentation of medical images. *Pattern Recognition Letters*, *18*(11-13), 1143–1151. doi:10.1016/S0167-8655(97)00091-3

Armstrong, J. D., Bagley, P. M., & Priede, I. G. (1992). Photographic and acoustic tracking observations of the behavior of the grenadier Coryphaenoides (Nematonorus) armatus, the eel Synaphobranchus bathybius, and other abyssal demersal fish in the North Atlantic Ocean. *Marine Biology*, *112*(4), 1432–1793. doi:10.1007/BF00346170

Arulampalam, M. S., Maskell, S., Gordon, N., & Clapp, T. (2002). A tutorial on particle filters for online nonlinear/non-Gaussian Bayesian tracking. *IEEE Transactions on Signal Processing, 50*(2), 174–188. doi:10.1109/78.978374

Baumgartner, L., Bettanin, M., McPherson, J., Jones, M., Zampatti, B., & Beyer, K. (2010). *Assessment of an infrared fish counter (Vaki Riverwatcher) to quantify fish migrations in the Murray-Darling Basin*. Retrieved from Australia: www.dpi. nsw.gov.au

Bermúdez, M., Puertas, J., Cea, L., Pena, L., & Balairón, L. (2010). Influence of pool geometry on the biological efficiency of vertical slot fishways. *Ecological Engineering, 36*(10), 1355–1364. doi:10.1016/j.ecoleng.2010.06.013

Blake, R. W. (2004). Fish functional design and swimming performance. *Journal of Fish Biology, 65*(5), 1193–1222. doi:10.1111/j.0022-1112.2004.00568.x

Castro-Santos, T., Haro, A., & Walk, S. (1996). A passive integrated transponder (PIT) tag system for monitoring fishways. *Fisheries Research, 28*(3), 253–261. doi:10.1016/0165-7836(96)00514-0

Cea, L., Pena, L., Puertas, J., Vázquez-Cendón, M. E., & Peña, E. (2007). Application of several depth-averaged turbulence models to simulate flow in vertical slot fishways. *Journal of Hydraulic Engineering, 133*(2), 160–172. doi:10.1061/(ASCE)0733-9429(2007)133:2(160)

Chorda, J., Maubourguet, M. M., Roux, H., Larinier, M., Tarrade, L., & David, L. (2010). Two-dimensional free surface flow numerical model for vertical slot fishways. *Journal of Hydraulic Research, 48*(2), 141–151. doi:10.1080/00221681003703956

Chuang, M.-C., Hwang, J.-N., Williams, K., & Towler, R. (2011). *Automatic fish segmentation via double local thresholding for trawl-based underwater camera systems* Paper presented at the IEEE International Conference on Image Processing (ICIP). doi:10.1109/ICIP.2011.6116334

Clausen, S., Greiner, K., Andersen, O., Lie, K.-A., Schulerud, H., & Kavli, T. (2007). *Automatic segmentation of overlapping fish using shape priors*. Paper presented at the Scandinavian conference on Image analysis, Aalborg, Denmark. doi:10.1007/978-3-540-73040-8_2

Deng, Z., Richmond, C. M., Guest, G. R., & Mueller, R. P. (2004). *Study of Fish Response Using Particle Image Velocimetry and High-Speed, High-Resolution Imaging*. Academic Press.

Dewar, H., & Graham, J. (1994). Studies of tropical tuna swimming performance in a large water tunnel – Energetics. *The Journal of Experimental Biology, 192*(1), 13–31.

Dong, G., & Xie, M. (2005). Color clustering and learning for image segmentation based on neural networks. *IEEE Transactions on Neural Networks, 16*(4), 925–936. doi:10.1109/TNN.2005.849822 PMID:16121733

Heimerl, S., Hagmeyer, M., & Echteler, C. (2008). Numerical flow simulation of pool-type fishways: New ways with well-known tools. *Hydrobiologia, 609*(1), 189–196. doi:10.1007/s10750-008-9413-1

Jackson, D. C., Marmulla, G., Larinier, M., Miranda, L. E., & Bernacsek, G. M. (2001). *Dams, fish and fisheries. Opportunities, challenges and conflict resolution.* Academic Press.

Kohonen, T. (1982). Self-organized formation of topologically correct feature maps. *Biological Cybernetics, 43*(1), 59–69.

Lines, J. A., Tillett, R. D., Ross, L. G., Chan, D., Hockaday, S., & McFarlane, N. J. B. (2001). An automatic image-based system for estimating the mass of free-swimming fish. *Computers and Electronics in Agriculture, 31*(2), 151–168. doi:10.1016/S0168-1699(00)00181-2

Mitra, V., Wang, C.-J., & Banerjee, S. (2006). Lidar Detection of Underwater Objects Using a Neuro-SVM-Based Architecture. *IEEE Transactions on Neural Networks, 17*(3), 717–731. doi:10.1109/TNN.2006.873279 PMID:16722175

Morais, E. F., Campos, M. F. M., Padua, F. L. C., & Carceroni, R. L. (2005). *Particle filter-based predictive tracking for robust fish count.* Paper presented at the Brazilian Symposium on Computer Graphics and Image Processing (SIBGRAPI). doi:10.1109/SIBGRAPI.2005.36

Ngan, S.-C., & Hu, X. (1999). Analysis of functional magnetic resonance imaging data using self-organizing mapping with spatial connectivity. *Magnetic Resonance in Medicine, 41*(5), 939–946. doi:10.1002/(SICI)1522-2594(199905)41:5<939::AID-MRM13>3.0.CO;2-Q PMID:10332877

Petrell, R. J., Shi, X., Ward, R. K., Naiberg, A., & Savage, C. R. (1997). Determining fish size and swimming speed in cages and tanks using simple video techniques. *Aquacultural Engineering, 16*(1-2), 63–84. doi:10.1016/S0144-8609(96)01014-X

Puertas, J., Cea, L., Bermudez, M., Pena, L., Rodriguez, A., Rabuñal, J., & Aramburu, E. et al. (2012). Computer application for the analysis and design of vertical slot fishways in accordance with the requirements of the target species. *Ecological Engineering*, *48*, 51–60. doi:10.1016/j.ecoleng.2011.05.009

Puertas, J., Pena, L., & Teijeiro, T. (2004). An Experimental Approach to the Hydraulics of Vertical Slot Fishways. *Journal of Hydraulic Engineering*, *130*(1), 10–23. doi:10.1061/(ASCE)0733-9429(2004)130:1(10)

Rodriguez, A., Bermúdez, M., Rabuñal, J., & Puertas, J. (2014). Fish tracking in vertical slot fishways using computer vision techniques. *Journal of Hydroinformatics*. doi:0.2166/hydro.2014.034

Rodriguez, A., Bermudez, M., Rabuñal, J., Puertas, J., Dorado, J., & Balairon, L. (2011). Optical Fish Trajectory Measurement in Fishways through Computer Vision and Artificial Neural Networks. *Journal of Computing in Civil Engineering*, *25*(4), 291–301. doi:10.1061/(ASCE)CP.1943-5487.0000092

Sezgin, M., & Sankur, B. (2004). Survey over image thresholding techniques and quantitative performance evaluation. *Journal of Electronic Imaging*, *13*(1), 146–165. doi:10.1117/1.1631315

SIGMUR. (2003). *Filtering techniques. Geography degree. Tele detection.* Retrieved from http://www.um.es/geograf/sigmur/teledet/tema06.pdf

Spampinato, C., Chen-Burger, Y.-H., Nadarajan, G., & Fisher, R. (2008). *Detecting, Tracking and Counting Fish in Low Quality Unconstrained Underwater Videos.* Paper presented at the Int. Conf. on Computer Vision Theory and Applications (VISAPP).

Steig, T. W., & Iverson, T. K. (1998). Acoustic monitoring of salmonid density, target strength, and trajectories at two dams on the Columbia River, using a split-beam scaning system. *Fisheries Research*, *35*(1-2), 43–53. doi:10.1016/S0165-7836(98)00058-7

Stenger, B., Mendonca, P. R. S., & Cipolla, R. (2001). *Model-Based Hand Tracking Using an Unscented Kalman Filter.* Paper presented at the British Machine Vision Conference. doi:10.5244/C.15.8

Szeliski, R. (2011). *Computer Vision: Algorithms and Applications.* Springer. doi:10.1007/978-1-84882-935-0

Tarrade, L., Texier, A., David, L., & Larinier, M. (2008). Topologies and measurements of turbulent flow in vertical slot fishways. *Hydrobiologia*, *609*(1), 177–188. doi:10.1007/s10750-008-9416-y

Verikas, A., Malmqvist, K., & Bergman, L. (1997). Color image segmentation by modular neural networks. *Pattern Recognition Letters, 18*(2), 173–185. doi:10.1016/S0167-8655(97)00004-4

Waldemark, J. (1997). An automated procedure for cluster analysis of multivariate satellite data. *International Journal of Neural Systems, 8*(1), 3–15. doi:10.1142/S0129065797000033 PMID:9228572

Welch, G., & Bishop, G. (2006). *An Introduction to the Kalman Filter*. Academic Press.

Weng, J., Cohen, P., & Herniou, M. (1992). Camera calibration with distortion models and accuracy evaluation. *IEEE Transactions on Pattern Analysis and Machine Intelligence, 14*(10), 965–980.

Wu, S., Rajaratma, N., & Katopodis, C. (1999). Structure of flow in vertical slot fishways. *Journal of Hydraulic Engineering, 125*(4), 351–360. doi:10.1061/(ASCE)0733-9429(1999)125:4(351)

Yilmaz, A., Javed, O., & Shah, M. (2006). Object Tracking: A Survey. *ACM Computing Surveys, 38*(4), 13, es. doi:10.1145/1177352.1177355

Yu, K. K. C., Watson, N. R., & Arrillaga, J. (2005). An adaptive Kalman filter for dynamic harmonic state estimation and harmonic injection tracking. *IEEE Transactions on Power Delivery, 20*(2), 1577–1584. doi:10.1109/TPWRD.2004.838643

Yun, X., & Bachmann, E. R. (2006). Design, Implementation, and Experimental Results of a Quaternion-Based Kalman Filter for Human Body Motion Tracking. *IEEE Transactions on Robotics, 22*(6), 1216–1227. doi:10.1109/TRO.2006.886270

Zhang, Z. (1999). *Flexible Camera Calibration By Viewing a Plane From Unknown Orientations*. Paper presented at the International Conference on Computer Vision (ICCV), Kerkyra, Greece. doi:10.1109/ICCV.1999.791289

Chapter 4
Computer Vision Based Classification on Commercial Videos

B. Rebecca Jeya Vadhanam
SRM University, India

V. Sugumaran
VIT University Chennai, India

Mohan S.
Al Yamamah University, Saudi Arabia

Vani V.
Al Yamamah University, Saudi Arabia

V. V. Ramalingam
SRM University, India

ABSTRACT

Computer vision is a study which is concerned with automatic mining, analysis, perception, and extraction of the essential information from a single frame or image and a sequence of frames. It focuses on the development of automatic visual perception systems to reconstruct and interpret a three-dimensional scene from two-dimensional images through the properties of the structures in the scene. This is a challenging task for the contemporary computer vision system. Hence, this chapter explores the essential information, processing, analysis, and understanding necessary for computer vision. This enables users to retrieve product-based advertisement content and efficient browsing of desired shows. The final goal of this chapter is to design electronic embedded systems focused on technology integration with a domestic utility concept.

DOI: 10.4018/978-1-5225-0889-2.ch004

1. INTRODUCTION

Technological developments and applications have provided the satellite TV channels with an advanced quality, huge production, and transmission capabilities. In the massive collection of digital video processing, video indexing and retrieval, browsing, video categorization and video classification are the mainstream techniques are the key areas of interest for researchers and scholars. The primary objective of the computer vision is to formulate the computers for efficient perception, processing, and understanding visual information of the frames in videos. The ultimate goal is for computers to imitate the perceptual ability of human eyes and brains. Also, it exceeds the human capability and be an assistant for the human in many ways. Computer vision is applied in the field of robotics, medicine, security, transportation, image and video database and human-computer interface.Interpreting the multimedia information is a broad area of research. Nowadays people have access to a tremendous amount of videos on YouTube through the internet and Television. The recent technologies in multimedia used to deliver the audio and video be it streaming, progressive download, webcasting, IP conferencing, podcasting, video blogging. It is aboutusing the right mix of multiple distribution technologies to reach the right audience with the right type of content. Videos can be delivered in an accurate live stream. There are some potential problems with delivering video and audio. To overcome the problem, video streaming or video classification is the best initiative in the multimedia industry. In the review of video classification, a significant number of techniques have been attempted in performing video indexing and retrieval systems, summarization, browsing, spatial - temporal continuity, video annotation, concept-based video retrieval and content-based video retrieval, etc. The research on video classification has intended of classifying the entire videos into broad genre classification, limited domain classification, and semantic content classification. At the top level of hierarchy, video database can be organized into a different genre such as cartoon, sports, commercials, news, and music. At the second tier, domain videos can be categorized into different subcategories. At the floor level, a video sequence itself can be segmented and classified as its semantic contents. Video classification helps new technology to support more effective video access over a large scale database and also for supporting more powerful video search engines. An advanced technology development is needed for the available video databases.Many different attempts have been tried by the researchers with great success. Brezeal et al. (2008) presented a detailed literature study about automatic video classification approaches and also described the low level features such as text features (closed caption, speech recognition and OCR), audio features and visual features (color based features, MPEG, short based feature, motion and object based feature) and statistical methods for video classification. Sadlier et al.

(2002) explained the relationship between audio silences and black frames. This audio break and black frames were used as an indicator of commercial boundaries to detect the advertisement frames from the MPEG stream. Lienhart et al. (1997) specified the country regulations about commercial broadcast and used a set of features to discriminate advertisement from the general television programs (TV) programs. Mostly, the video classification study attempts to classify videos into one of the many broad categories; however, some research work has been chosen to focus their efforts on identifying particular video among another video genre. Kobla et al. (1997) described the replay, text and motion features to determine the sports video from all other video genres from the compressed domain of the MPEG. The authors quoted and explained well about the two major problems in content-based video retrieval systems (i) Semantic-sensitive video classification problem and (ii) Integrated video access problem. A hierarchical video database indexing and summary presentation technique was carried out to access videos from the large data set. However, an attempt was made to generate semantic video scenes with two measurements, such as visual similarity and semantic similarity. Semantics-sensitive video classifier was employed for classification and relevance analysis was used to reduce the gap between low level visual features and high level semantic features. The study achieved the considerable success and presented the future issues in video classification and indexing system. Support Vector Machine (SVM) classifier was employed to classify the advertisement shot and the general program shot with a series of content based features. These content based features were expanded from the audio and video based features. The post processing and scene grouping methods were used to identify the advertisement shots. Gaucha et al. (2006) described about the repeated video sequence detection and feature based classification to detect the advertisement frames. Qi et al. (2000) utilized SVM classifier to classify the different types of news stories from the stream of news videos. Audio and visual features were used to detect the news video from the video shots. The closed captions and text in the scenes were detected by OCR features utilized by the SVM classifier to classify news stories. Silence ratio, noise ratio and background noise ratio were considered as the audio features. Editing feature, motion feature and color feature were considered as the visual features to classify the different video genre and the study explained rough set rule based classification system in a suitable manner. The pooled audio and visual features were used for classification of video genre like, sports, cartoon, news, commercial and music. The audio features were extracted from 14 Mel-Frequency Cepstrum Coefficient (MFCC). The visual features were drawn from the mean and standard deviation of the MPEG motion vectors. Principal component analysis was applied for dimensionality reduction and the classification was carried out by HMM to classify the different video genre. Different number of mixture components were implemented and tested to achieve the best results. The reasonable results were obtained with more components. The importance of principal component analysis for dimensionality reduction was illustrated and utilized to reduce the size of the data. An attempt has been made to bring out the temporal relationship of video through Hidden Markov Model (HMM) with the block intensity comparison code used as the input feature set. The results obtained from the experiments prove that the BICC features have performed well when compared to other features like, edge, motion and histogram features. In the study, a novel text frame classification method was demonstrated by Probable Text Block Selection (PTBS), Probable Text Pixel Selection (PTPS), Mutual Nearest Neighbour based Symmetry (MNNS). The combined methods of PTBS and MNNS were experimented for text frame classification. The wavelet and median moment with k-means clustering technique was used to identify the text blocks in videos. Moreover, the study illustrated the effectiveness of existing text detection techniques considered to misclassify non-text frames at both block and frame levels. Advertisement content is a paid proclamationconveyed through newspaper, broadcast channels, glossy magazine, etc by means of words, pictures, music and action. Even though, the creating, producing, editing and broadcasting a TV advertisement are astounding, television is one of the best cost effective media (Vilanilam et al, 2004). In recent days, advertisements have become essential for many clients in the satellite and cable television. Advertisements are stuffed in 10 to 15 minutes of a 30-minutes television program. With increasing amount of product and service hasbeen caused a revolution in digital video recordings and play back systems. Plenty of research work has focused on automatic detection of commercials which helps to develop a "commercial skip" type of applications (Mizutani et al, 2005).

1.1. Video Analytics

The video analytics science has scaled with advances in machine vision, multi-lingual speech recognition and rules-based decision engines. Intense interest exists in prescriptive analytics driven by real-time streams of rich video content. Video analytics is the automatic algorithmic extraction and logical analysis of information found in video data using digital image processing techniques. A video is a set of signals sensed by the human eye and processed by the visual cortex in the brain creating a vivid experience of a scene that is instantly associated with concepts and objects previously perceived and recorded in one's memory. To a computer, images are either a raster image or a vector image. Simply put, raster images are a sequence of pixels with discreet numerical values for color; vector images are a set of color-annotated polygons. To perform analytics on images or videos, the geometric encoding must be transformed into constructs depicting physical features, objects and movement represented by the image or video. These constructs can then be logically analyzed

by a computer. In particular, Video signal is basically any sequence of time varying images. A still image is a spatial distribution of intensities that remain constant
with time, whereas a time varying image has a spatial intensity distribution that
varies with time.

In early 1890's, Thomas A Edison invented the motion pictures and in 1895,
the motion picture camera was invented by Louis Lumiera. Video signal is treated
as a series of images called frames. An illusion of continuous video is obtained by
changing the frames in a faster manner which is generally termed as frame rate.
Frame rate is defined as the number of still pictures per unit time of video which is
usually 6-8 frames for old mechanical cameras and 25 or more frames per second
for new professional cameras. Digital video provides the picture information is digitized both spatially and temporally and theresultant pixel intensities are quantized.

1.1.1. A Hierarchical Video Representation

Video data can be structured into a hierarchy consisting of scenes, shots and frames
as shown in Figure 1.The brief description is given in the following subsections.

Figure 1. A hierarchical video representation

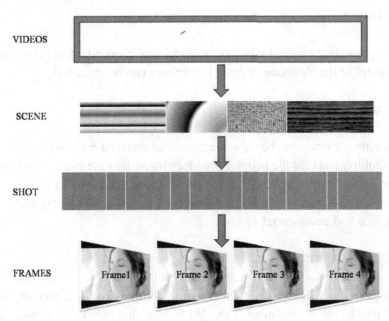

A HIERARCHICAL VIDEO REPRESENTATION

1.1.2. Scene

Video scene is defined as a collection of semantically related and temporally adjacent shots depicting and conveying a high-level concept. However, though shots are marked byphysical boundaries, scenes are marked by semantic boundaries. There are a variety of complex scene changes used in video production, but the basic premise is a change in visual content. Scene change in a video sequence can either be abrupt or gradual. Abrupt scene changes result from fast cuts, distance cuts, and inter cutting and detecting them is called cut detection.

1.1.3. Shot

The shot is defined as a series of interconnected successive frames taken continuously in a single camera. Hence, a shot represents uninterrupted action in time and space. Video shot is a consecutive sequence of frames recorded from a single camera. The shot is the building block of video streams. Between two adjacent shots, there is a shot boundary. Shot boundaries or shot transitions can be classified as abrupt or gradual. An abrupt shot change occurs in a sudden transition from one shot to another shot. Gradual shot transitions includes special effects like dissolves and fades in, fadeout, wipes and blends (see Figure 1).

1.1.4. Frames

A frame represents the salient visual content of a shot. Depending on the complexity of the content of the shot, one or more key frames can be extracted.

1.2. Broadcast Videos

In broadcasting, a video can be view as a broadcast material created to attain certain specific requirements for the people. Broadcasting videos are categorized as news, sports, music and entertainment, movies, game shows, serial, reality shows, general entertainment and human interest, documentary, religion, discovery, analysis and interpretation and commercial videos.

1.3. Video Streaming

Streaming video is where the content is sent in compressed form over the Internet and displayed by the viewer in real time. With streaming video or streaming media, a web user does not have to wait to download a file to play it. Instead, the media is sent in a continuous stream of data and is played as it arrives. The user needs a player, which is a special program that uncompressed and sends video data to the display and audio data to speakers. A player can be either an integral part of a browser or downloaded from the software maker's web site.Streaming video is usually sent from pre-recorded video files. But, it can be distributed as part of a live broadcast feed. In a live broadcast, the video signal is converted into a compressed digital signal and transmitted from a special web server that is able to multicast, sending the same file to multiple users at the same time.

1.4. Overview of Advertisement Videos

Advertisement videos are usually more prominent and mind attractive than the other general television programs. The action rate of the advertisement videos is always very high. The volume of the audio signal is turned up during the allocation time of advertisement. in television. Visual style of the advertisement video shows the dominating colours and particularly the drastic light variations are the main distinguish factor for advertisement videos. Technical characteristics of advertisement videos are defined and separated by the blank frames, silence break, Scene Change, Shot abrupt change, Cuts per minute.

1.4.1. Need for Classification of Advertisement Videos

The need for efficient storing, indexing, retrieval, browsing, and recognition and videos classification has been emphasized by researchers having mass of video collections such as, live stream television videos, youtube videos, video archives, video libraries, video-on-demand services for many years. There are many significant problems are highlighted, where research is required, including the representation of video data, feature extraction, video indexing, video query based retrieval and classification. These depicted problems can be achieved through enhancing the existing methods and developing new technologies for efficient video classification.Classification of video content is a significant streamline process in the growing volume of image and video data in the digital field. The digital video data has become an appropriate source of information for all users those who are in a great demand to search the contents through the database for their requirement. In particular, the image and video indexing, retrieval and classification intelligence infrastructure facilitate the end users interactively search and retrieve their desired content. Video classification and retrieval has evolved and become the greatest multimedia research area in the last two decades. It is getting extensive focus for an user to retrieve the required information, automatic classification and categorization of the video content is essential. Advertising is a systematic way of communicating information about an item or product for consumption or service which a business concern or individual needs to prop up to reach the people. TV advertising is omnipresent, and economically it is an essential for the current business world.

This research work focused, to detect the advertisement videos from the live stream television videos with the efficient visual feature. Hence, great effort has been taken to identify advertisement blocks itself. The motivations andpotential applications of advertisementand non advertisement videos classification and identification are summarized as follows.

- All advertisers pay more money, and hence, it is essential to verify that their commercials are broadcasted as per contract. What is necessary is, a broadcast advertisement monitoring system.
- However, the latest trend in design of electronic embedded systems focuses on technology integration with a domestic utility concept. The emergence of automated classification of advertisement from the general program videos as an essential task is expected to support the television (TV) viewers to have a seamless unhampered visual experience of commercial advertisement videos. The demand for automated classification of advertisement system is gaining momentum, thus enabling the viewers to skip the commercials and move automatically to another channel.
- It is applied to identify, trace out new commercials, summarizing the commercials and removing the repeated commercials within the limited period.
- To conceptualize ideas, products and services to enhance the business data effectively. Thus, it helps to classify the advertisement videos with respect to the advertisement products or services. Besides, it helps to carry out the advertisement filtering towards personalized consumer services through MMS message on the specified advertisements of interest to registered customers or targeted customers sent to their mobile phone or electronic mail.
- It enables the user to retrieval of product based advertisement content, efficient browsing for their desired shows, you tube search strategy of the videos with advertisement content or without advertisement content.

2. FRAMEWORK

The present research work, is to show about how, when a TV tuner card connected to a computer system is used to conduct the experiments. To record the live stream videos a set up file is installed. Then, the videos are recorded in MPEG4 format of size 1024×1024. After that, the videos are recorded from various Tamil channels directly from the TV live stream videos. Nevertheless, all kinds of advertisement are recorded under the category of ADD class. The news videos, sports videos, cartoon videos, movie videos, music videos, cookery shows, dance shows and adventure shows are recorded for NADD class. Thereafter, the advertisement and non advertisement videos are processed and segmented into 10 seconds videos each. Thus, the image frames are extracted at the rate of 25 frames per second from each 10 seconds video. The complete framework of the present study is shown in Figure 2.

Figure 2. Frame work for the present study

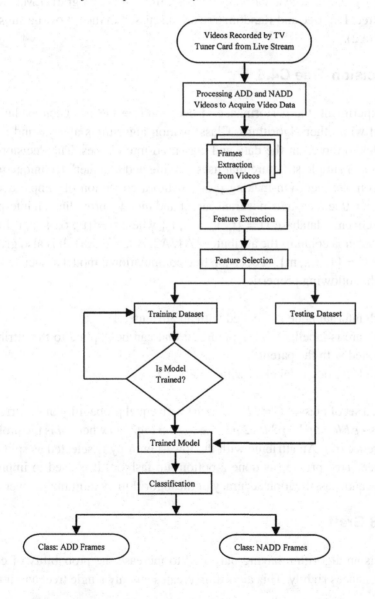

3. CLASSIFIERS

The objective of this present study aimed to investigate the performance of different classification algorithm for ADD and NADD video classification. Classification algorithms could be compared by predictive accuracy, robustness, scalability and interpretability criteria. The performance of different techniques must be evaluated to attain the ultimate model for video classification. The best model can be built with the aid of machine learning algorithm to obtain the end results. The performance applicability and their evaluation of decision tree C4.5, J48 graft, LMT, Random tree, BF tree, Rep tree and Random tree are discussed in the following subsections (see Figure 2).

3.1. Decision Tree C4.5

In this experiment, the performance of decision tree J48 has been evaluated and compared with other algorithms. Classification algorithms always find a rule or set of rules to represent the data and classified into classes. The decision tree is a popular and simple structure that uses "divide and conquer" technique to break down a complex decision-making process into a collection of simple decisions. The decision tree mechanism is transparent and thereby providing an interpretable solution. Given a database $D = \{t_1, t_2, \ldots, t_n\}$ where $t_i = \{t_{i1}, t_{i2}, \ldots, t_{ih}\}$ and the database schema contains the attributes $\{A1, A2, A3, \ldots, Ah\}$. It is also given a set of classes $C = \{1, \ldots, m\}$. A decision tree computational model associated with D that has the following properties;

- Each internal node is labelled with an attribute, *Ai*.
- Each arc is labelled with a predicate that can be applied to the attribute associated with the parent.
- Each leaf node is labelled with a class, *Cj*.

Given a set of classes $C = \{1, \ldots, m\}$ with equal probability of occurrence the entropy is $- p1 \, log2 \, p1 - p2 \, log2 \, p2 \ldots \ldots - pm \, log2 \, pm$ where *pi* is the probability of occurrence of *i*. An attribute with the lowest entropy is selected as split criteria for the tree. Tree pruning is done a bottom-up fashion. It is used to improve the prediction and classification accuracy of the algorithm by minimizing over-fitting .

3.2. J48 Graft

J48graft is an algorithm having purposed to increase the probability of classifying the instances rightly. This algorithm creates an only single tree, and it reduces prediction error. J48 grafting algorithm for generating grafted decision tree from a J48 tree algorithm. The purpose of this grafting algorithm is to increase the probability of correctly classifying instances that fall outside the areas covered by the training data. The grafting technique is an inductive process which adds nodes to infer decision trees with the purpose of reducing prediction errors. The J48 grafting algorithm provides the best general prediction accuracy over a representative selection of the learning process .

3.3. Logistic Model Tree (LMT)

A logistic model tree (LMT) consists of a standard decision tree structure with logistic regression functions at the leaves. The LMT contains a tree structure that is made up of a set of inner or non-terminal nodes and a set of leaves or terminal nodes. The Logistic Model Tree algorithm makes a tree with binary and multiclass target variables, numeric and missing values. LMT is a combination of induction trees and logistic regression. LMT uses cost-complexity pruning. This algorithm is significantly slower than the other algorithms .

3.4. Best First Tree (BF)

In Best-first (BF) decision tree algorithm, the tree expands by selecting the node which maximizes the impurity reduction among all the existing nodes to split. In this algorithm, the impurity could be measured by the Gini index and information gain. BF trees are constructed in a divide-conquer method similar to the standard depth-first decision trees. The primary step for building the best-first tree is given below.

- Select an attribute to place at the root node and make some branches for this attribute based on some criteria.
- Split training instances into subsets, one for each branch extending from the root node.
- The constructing process continues until all nodes are pure, or a specific number of expansions are reached.

3.5. Reduced Error Pruning Tree (REP)

Reduced Error Pruning Tree (REP) Tree is the simplest and most understandable technique in decision tree pruning. It is a fast decision tree learner, which builds a decision or a regression tree using information gain as the splitting criterion and prunes it using reduced error pruning. Using REP algorithm, the tree traversal has performed from bottom to top and then checks for each internal node and replace it with most frequently class with the most concern about the tree accuracy, which must not reduce. This procedure will continue until any further pruning decreases the efficiency.

3.6. Random Tree (RT)

Random tree (RT) is an efficient algorithm for constructing a tree with K random features at each node. Random tree is a tree which drawn at random from a set of possible trees. Random trees can be generated efficiently, and the combination of large sets of random trees leads to accurate models. Random tree models have been extensively developed in the field of machine learning to build a suitable and reliable model for video classification.

4. PROPOSED TECHNIQUES

In the context of the advertisement(ADD) frames detection from the stream, live videos is a great challenge in content-based video retrieval and video classification. The internet user may attempt their search in many ways, such as the movie or serial content without commercials or with commercials, non-stop music channelsand 24x7 news channels without commercial breaks. To facilitate the users' desires, the present study attempts two novel techniques to develop a system to detect the advertisement frames from the general programs. The system should provide; for easy access to multimedia content, competent browsing, the retrieval of desirable videos and implication of appropriate video content. The initial work of the present study started with video segmentation. Video segmentation is the process of dividing the videos into smaller units. Then the segmented videos were considered for the further process.

In the present study, Block Intensity Comparison Code technique and key frame rate technique have been proposed to detect the ADD frames. BICC is a low-level visual feature which is based on spatial analysis of the video frames, and Key Frame Rate technique is a high-level feature is based on temporal analysis of the frames. These techniques are essential for video genre classification, scene understanding, event recognition, content-based image retrieval, content-based video indexing, and retrieval system. The major work focused was on the robustness of the algorithm and competence by utilizing the low-level visual features and the high-level semantic features.

4.1. Block Intensity Comparison Code Technique

In video classification, proper representation of the visual attributes is essential. Visual data exhibits numerous types of features that could be used to recognize or represent the information it reveals. These features exhibit both static and dynamic properties. Classification or recognizing an appropriate video relies on the proficient use of these features that provide discriminative information useful for high-level classification. The technique to compute the block intensity comparison code (BICC) is used to characterizes the intensity variations between blocks in a video frame. The method to generate the BICC is motivated by the fact that the intensity distribution of video frame in a genre is unique. The intensity between blocks of a frame characterizes an object. The human visual system perceives the objects based on these intensity changes. Based on this, the intensity changes between blocks of a frame is represented by block intensity comparison code. To extract the BICC features, each image is divided into k × k blocks, each of size M/k× N/k, whereM ×N is the size of the image (refer Figure 3.).

BICC feature is extracted from each frame of advertisement videos and non-advertisement videos. Each frame is divided into various block sizes like, *2×2, 3×3, 4×4, 5×5, 6×6, 7×7, 8×8, 9×9* and *10×10* of the frame size *320×240*. Obtained feature set as 4, 9, 16, 25, 66, 49, 64, 81 and 100 features for the block sizes 2x2, 3x3, 4x4, 5x5, 6x6, 7x7, 8x8, 9x9 and 10x10 respectively. The average intensity values are calculated for each block of a frame and compared with all the other blocks in the frame (refer Figure 4 and Figure 5) .

The blocking model of the frames capitulates proof over the occurrence of changes between the present frame and the future reference frame. The comparison is done through the block intensity comparison code which is a very useful code to

Figure 3. Sample frames divided into various block size

Block 2×2   Block 3×3   Block 4×4

Block 5×5   Block 8×8   Block 10×10

Figure 4. Frames extracted from cartoon video: divided into 2x2 block size

Figure 5. Block intensity average value comparison of block size of 2x2 frame

44	44	44	44	44	44	44	44	44	44	44	44	44	44	44	44	44	44
44	44	44	44	44	44	44	44	44	44	44	44	44	44	44	44	44	44
44	44	44	44	44	44	44	44	44	44	44	44	44	44	44	44	44	44
44	44	44	44	44	44	44	44	44	44	44	44	44	44	44	44	44	44
44	44	44	44	44	44	44	44	44	44	44	44	44	44	44	44	44	44
44	44	44	44	44	44	44	44	44	44	44	44	44	44	44	44	44	44
44	44	44	44	44	44	44	44	44	44	44	44	44	44	44	44	44	44
43	43	44	45	45	45	44	44	42	41	41	41	42	44	47	48	42	42
52	52	52	52	52	51	50	50	55	53	50	47	45	46	47	48	49	50
105	105	104	104	103	101	99	98	89	84	77	70	66	64	65	66	68	69
132	132	131	130	128	125	123	122	113	107	97	87	81	79	79	81	84	85
128	128	127	125	122	119	117	115	110	104	94	84	78	77	78	80	86	88
131	130	129	127	125	122	119	118	109	104	95	87	82	81	83	85	88	89
129	129	128	126	124	121	119	117	115	110	103	96	92	91	93	95	93	94
131	131	130	128	126	124	121	120	113	109	102	96	92	92	93	94	95	96
132	131	130	128	126	124	123	122	113	110	105	100	97	96	96	97	102	102
132	131	130	128	126	124	123	122	116	113	107	103	99	98	98	99	102	102
132	131	130	128	126	124	123	122	118	115	110	105	102	101	101	102	102	102
132	131	130	128	126	124	123	122	120	117	112	107	103	102	103	103	103	103
132	131	130	128	126	124	123	122	120	116	111	106	103	102	102	103	103	103
132	131	130	128	126	124	123	122	120	116	111	106	103	102	102	103	104	104
132	131	130	128	126	124	123	122	121	117	112	107	104	103	103	104	104	104
132	131	130	128	126	124	123	122	122	118	113	108	105	104	104	105	104	104
130	129	128	127	125	124	122	122	120	117	113	108	105	103	103	103	104	104
130	130	128	127	125	124	123	122	120	117	113	108	105	103	103	103	104	104
131	130	129	127	126	124	123	122	120	117	113	108	105	103	103	103	104	104

design the feature vector from the derived average block intensity values. The blocking pattern leads an efficient approach to improve the performance evaluation of the video classification. Therefore, the database has been created for advertisement and non advertisement frames from the extracted BICC features.

4.1.1. Algorithm Implementation of BICC Technique

Block intensity comparison code (BICC) algorithm contains four phases, namely dividing the frames into various block sizes, selecting the promising block size, calculating the average intensity value for each block and comparing the average intensity value of neighbouring blocks and constructing the feature vector.

Step 1: Each image or frame is divided into $K \times K$ blocks, where $K = 2, 3, 4, 5,$
  $6, 7, 8, 9, 10$.Each of size $M/K \times N/K$, where M, N is the size of the image.
Step 2: Select 8×8 block of image of size 320×240 used for the experimental study
  and test.The average intensity value is calculated for each block of a frame and
  compared with every other block in the frame.
Average Intensity Value,
qhere $q=16$ here;
Step 3: Feature vector has been designed as follows:

$$Y [((i-1)*M) + 1: ((i*M),(j-1)*N)+1):(j*N)],$$

where, $M \times N$ size of the image. i, j is the average intensities of ith and j^{th} block respectively.

BICC features are the best evidence for both static and dynamic properties. Classification or identifying proper video by using BICC features that provide meaningfully and discriminative data is advantageous for high order precision.

4.2. Key Frame Rate Technique

Key frame extraction is an essential technique in video searching, classification and knowledge, and understanding of video content. In this present work, a novel approach has been attempted through the key frame extraction technique to reduce the gap between high-level semantic understanding of visual features and low-level visual features and it helps to conquer any hindrance between semantic interpretations and furthermore, low-level features. More research effort has been done regarding key frame extraction. Existing key-frame extraction techniques usually follow two ways to choose the key frames such as random key frame selection and uniform key frame selection at predefined intervals. A few approaches attempted to collect the group of frames with similar characteristics and select the frames closer to the centre of the cluster frame as the key frame. For example, Zhang et al. (1997) Utilized color feature to check, whether the current frame belongs to the cluster of available frames. Li et al. (2003) reported about a triangle model of perceived motion energy (PME) for modelling motion patterns for the key frame extraction. Gresle and Huang (1997) computed the histograms for intra frame and the reference frame. Subsequently, an activity indicator was also computed. The local minima were selected as the key frame based on their activity curve. Ferman and Tekalp illustrate the off-line fuzzy clustering method to attain the optimum level of the hierarchical digest and after that, they generated coarser digest to find the matching for a basic level of browsing of the user desires. Wolf (1996) calculated the optical flow of each frame from the sequence of frames and then utilized a motion metric to estimate the differences in the optical flow. Key frames are then extracted at the point of the metric is found as the local minima. Hanjalic et al. (1996) computed histogram difference of successive frames from the shot of the complete sequence. From each shot of the sequence, a key frame gets allotted based on their percentage of total histogram differences. The above-discussed evidence of low-level visual feature based approaches is widely used in video content analysis. Although, they are not efficient enough for human observation because of their inconsistency. An automatic recognition system of video content is essential for the contemporary computers. To reduce the semantic gap of video content to achieve the best automatic detection system for video advertisement frames from the stream live video is the core study of this research work. To attain the core concept of the study, an attempt has been taken to measure the frame rates of the advertisement videos. In an advertisement, the key frames will change more rapidly compared to Non-advertisement videos. Hence, the difference in two key frames at a particular interval is expected to be different in advertisement frame than the Non-advertisement frame. The frame rate can be computed through the motion acceleration of the frames. It depends on the speed of frame change.The following steps are used to compute the key frame rate feature, such as

- Input videos,
- Shot segmentation,
- Key frame extraction,
- Difference of extracted key frames,
- Divide the frame into 16 macro blocks,
- Compute the frame rate.

Initially, the input videos are segmented as shots. Then, the key frames from each shot in a sequential fashion in the ratio of 1:4, 1:8 and 1:12. from each shot.

Figure 6. Key frames extracted from advertisement videos

Among,1:12 is selected as the promising one for the further study. Sequential fashion is the best way to bring out the motion information. The resultant frame obtained from the difference of current frame and every 12th position of the frame in a shot is divided into 4x4 macroblocks. Macro blocks provide the reduction of the temporal redundancy. Finally, the frame rate is computed from the average intensity values of each column of the frame. The extracted key frames are shown in Figure 6.

4.2.1. Algorithm Implementation of Key Frame Rate Technique

The frame rate can be measured by extracting the key frames from the each shot of an advertisement videos and non advertisement video as well. The following procedure has been followed to extract the key frame rate feature and utilized to detect the advertisement frames based on the frame rate.

Step 1: Key frame set X = {KF$_j$; j= 1,12,24,...K+12}
Step 2: Shot from set S = {F$_i$; i = 1,2,3,...N}
Step 3: Extract the key frames from each shot. K={k1,k2,k3...}
Step 4: Difference of key frames = KFj - Fi.
It can be written as difference (KFj, Fi)
dij = d(KFj, Fi) ;
where dij is the difference metrics of the frame(F) of shot S.
Step 5: Divided the frames into 4x4 = 16 blocks
Step 6: Compute the average magnitude of intensity of each macro block.
Sum of Average magnitude
where n = number of macro blocks
Step 7: Construct feature vector (f) = {f1,f2,...f16}.

5. EXPERIMENTAL ANALYSIS

To evaluate the efficiency of the BICC and key frame rate algorithm, the training and testing process has been carried out. The experimental results of the family tree classifiers such as C4.5 decision tree, decision tree graft, Logistic Model Tree (LMT), Random tree, Best first tree (BF) and REP tree classifier for BICC feature are discussed in the following subsections. Using the same procedure for training and testing process are taken over the key frame rate features set to evaluate the performance of the family tree classifiers. The performance of the classifiers with BICC and key frame rate feature set are assessed in terms of classification accuracy and discussed in the conclusion section.

5.1. Experimental Analysis for BICC Feature

Feature selection is an important process in machine learning. The feature selection process can be used for either to improve estimators (classifiers) accuracy scores or to boost their performance on very high-dimensional datasets. With sufficient data and time, it is good to use all the input features, including those irrelevant features, to approximate the primary function between the input and the output. There are two problems with the irrelevant features; (i) It will induce greater computational cost, (ii) The irrelevant input features may mislead the training process. Hence, those input features with little effect on the output may be ignored to keep the size of the approximation model small. Hence, the feature selection process plays a vital role in predicting the classification accuracy. All the features need not necessarily reveal the required information. Some features may yield more information than others. The process of selecting such excellent features which reveal more details for classification is called feature selection. This process is also known as 'dimensionality reduction as each feature adds a dimension in feature space and selecting a few features reduces the dimension.

In the present study, C4.5 decision tree algorithm was utilized for dimensionality reduction and best-performing feature selection to improve the accuracy of video classification. The decision tree was first generated by a training data set for the block intensity comparison code features. The feature which stays on the top of the tree is called root, and that feature is the most important feature for classification based on entropy reduction. Then next nodes down the root were considered. As the number of features increases the classification accuracy increases up to a certain level, then it starts falling. Here, all the features that appear in the decision tree have been chosen. With the pruned J48 algorithm, there were 19 well performing features (h1, h5, h8, h10, h15, h20, h27, h31, h39, h42, h47, h50, h52, h54, h55, h56, h57, h58 and h61) selected out of 64 features derived from BICC features of 8x8 block size of the frame. The remaining features were consciously ignored in the future study.

5.1.1. Significance of Decision Tree (C4.5) Algorithm

A decision tree is a good automatic rule discovery technique. It produces a set of branching decisions that ends in a classification. In the present study, the effect of various block sizes of frames was analyzed with BICC feature. BICC is applied for each and every individual frame of the two video genre used for classification of ADD video and NADD video. The decision tree has been used to evaluate the results for various block sizes of frames on their classification accuracy. From the graph (Refer Figure 7.) one can find that the block size of *8×8* gives maximum classification accuracy. Decision tree algorithm has been attempted to classify the ADD frames and NADD frames with BICC features. In the first stage of the experiment, individual frames of the advertisement video and non advertisement video genre are used for the analysis. There were 20000 frames used for training and 5000 frames used for the testing process. The feature set has obtained as 4, 9, 16, 25, 66, 49, 64, 81 and 100 features for the block sizes *2× 2, 3×3, 4×4, 5×5, 6×6, 7×7, 8×8, 9×9 and 10×10* respectively. BICC is applied for all the training and testing frames to derive the feature vector for the above mentioned block sizes. Among all, the block size *8×8* has achieved 94.3% of classification accuracy when the minimum number of the object is fixed as 2. In this case, the obtained classification accuracy is not being taken into consideration since the result seems over fitting and unsuitable for the larger dataset. Further, the feature selection process has been carried out through the decision tree algorithm to select the best features out of 64 features which are derived from the *8×8* block size of ADD and NADD frames. From the 64 features, 19 features performed well and thus formed the feature subset which is the input for the different classifiers. Hence, the decision tree C4.5 algorithm was employed to find out the best promising block size, best contributing features selection and classification of ADD and NADD frames.

Allotting an object to a certain class based on its similarity to previous examples of the objects. As with most data mining solutions, a classification usually comes with a degree of certainty. It might be the probability of the object belonging to the class or it might be some other measures of how closely the object resembles other examples from the class. Classification is the final stage of machine learning approach. After feature selection process, the selected features are classified using a feature classifier. Classification is a two-phase process: training and testing. Training is the process of learning to label from the samples. Training can be in supervised mode or unsupervised mode. Unsupervised training is used in situations where the target class information is not available. In the study the target class information is available. Hence, the supervised mode is used for training. Testing is the process of checking how well the classifier has learned to label the unseen samples.

Figure 7. Effect of block size vs classification accuracy

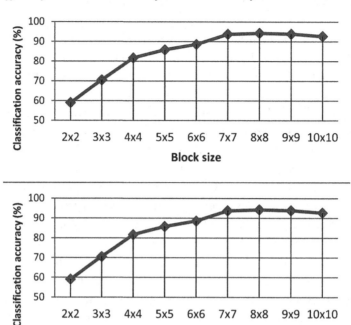

5.2. Experimental Analysis for Key Frame Rate Feature

Information theory says different frames consist much information than the same kind of frames. As a result of key frame extraction mainly produced the dissimilarity of the two frames. Here, the input videos are segmented as many different shots. From each shot, the key frames are extracted in the ratio 1:12. The representative key frames start from the first frame of the shot and every twelfth frame of each shot. The resultant frame is obtained from the difference of two frames. Then it is divided into 4x4 blocks to obtain 16 macro blocks. The average intensity value is calculated for each block of the resultant frame and yields 16 features like f1, f2, f3, f4, f5, f6, f7, f8, f9, f10, f11, f12, f13, f14, f15 and f16. The C4.5 algorithm has been employed to select the best performing features. All 16 features were contributed well and selected the whole as the well-performing features utilized for the present study.

The decision tree is a traditional and straightforward structure that uses "divide and conquer" technique to break down a complicated decision-making the process into a collection of simple decisions. To select the well-performing feature set and classification, Decision tree J48 algorithm has been employed simultaneously. The selected features were classified using the C4.5 decision tree algorithm. The classification accuracy was found using the 10-fold cross-validation. A significant advantage of the 10-fold cross validation method is that all observations are used for both training and validation, and each view is used for validation exactly once. This leads to a more accurate way to measure the accuracy, based on training set data.

5.2.1. Effect of Number of Features on Classification Accuracy

The 16 extracted feature set has an effect on classification accuracy. The feature selection process can be validated using the effect of a number of features on the classification accuracy study. It is investigated here. The features are taken in the order of importance from one feature to the maximum number of features, and the classification accuracy for a particular algorithm was noted down. The first feature (f1) in the decision tree was selected for classification. The first feature alone was classified using a decision tree algorithm and the classification accuracy was noted down. Then the first feature was clubbed with the second feature in the in the decision tree. The clubbed two features were classified using a decision tree algorithm and the classification accuracy was noted again. Referring to Table 1, the accuracy is increasing. This procedure was repeated for all selected attributes. Remaining

Table 1. Effect of number of features on classification accuracy

No. of Features	Classification Accuracy (%)
	C4.5 Decision Tree Algorithm
f1	57.81
f2	57.81
f3	57.67
f4	57.97
f5	59
f6	58.83
f7	58.78
f8	59.19
f9	58.86
f10	58.83
f11	59.33
f12	59.72
f13	59.49
f14	59.13
f15	59.49
f16	60

key frame rate features were also clubbed with the other feature sets, and the corresponding classification accuracy was also noted down.

Hence, the maximum classification accuracy of 60% was achieved with all 16 features.

6. RESULTS AND DISCUSSIONS

This section includes the results of the tree family classifiers with BICC features. The similar procedures are followed to measure the performance of the tree family classifiers with key frame rate feature. Finally, a comparative analysis of BICC and key frame rate feature with other visual features has been presented in subsection 6.8 . The study concluded that the Random tree model performs better than others. The random tree with BICC feature provided better classification accuracy for advertisement frames.

6.1. Result Analysis of BICC Feature

To investigate the performance of the selected classification algorithm from decision tree family, the same experimental procedures have been followed as suggested by WEKA tool. Decision tree classifier algorithms are potentially powerful predictors and characterize the structure of the dataset. In the present study, a large data set which contains 20,000 instances of the ADD and NADD class. The classification has been done using 10-fold cross-validation with the default percentage split is 66% for all the classifiers is summarized in the following subsections.

6.2. Experimental Results on Decision Tree C4.5

The decision tree C4.5 algorithm is employed to build the model for class ADD and NADD. Here, the applied algorithm evaluates the BICC feature and prepares a decision table which demonstrates and distinguishes a total number of instances into two different classes of ADD and NADD classes. With BICC feature, the classification accuracy was generated using decision tree C4.5 algorithm. The minimum number of objects (variable parameter) required to form class (M) was varied from 1 to 10000 (total no.of.instances per class) and the corresponding classification accuracy were noted down for further study. The value of 'M' which gives the maximum classification accuracy was fixed and confidence factor was varied from 0 to 1 in steps of '0.1'. The best classification accuracy of 83.69% of the block size *8x8* of frames was achieved with M value of 100 and confidence factor of '0.25'.

6.3. Experimental Results on J48 Graft

In this experimental study, Class for building a model by J48 graft algorithm shows the same level of accuracy which obtained in decision tree J48 classifier algorithm. There was no significant difference in their experimental results. But, J48 classifier takes less time to build the model than J48 graft classifier. J48 graft algorithm takes 1.92 seconds to build the model, and J48 classifier only takes 1.50 seconds to build the model. Here also, the minimum number of objects (variable parameter) required to form class (M) was varied from 1 to 10000 (total no.of.instances per class) and the corresponding classification accuracy were noted down for further study. The value of 'M' which gives the maximum classification accuracy was fixed and confidence factor was varied from 0 to 1 in steps of '0.1'. The best classification accuracy of 83.69% of the block size 8x8 of frames was achieved with M value of 100 and confidence factor of '0.25'.

6.4. Experimental Results on LMT

Class for building an LMT decision tree classifier contains a standard decision tree structure with logistic regression function at the leaves. LMT is significantly outperforming when compared with other models. A minimum number of instances (variable parameter) was varied from the default value 15 to 10000 in steps of 5 and the corresponding classification accuracy was noted down for further experimental study. The best classification accuracy of 91.34% of the block size 8x8 of frames was achieved in 10-fold cross validation with the default percentage split 66%. Looking at this ranking for classification accuracy, one could find LMT and Random tree very close to the top and achieved the best classification accuracy. The computational efficiency of the LMT is very slow compared to the other algorithms. This is due to the slow estimation process for the parameters of the logistic model performed by the LogitBoost algorithm. If the computational efficiency is increased, LMT would be the best model for video classification.

6.5. Experimental Results on BF Tree

In this experimental study, the same training dataset was used to evaluate the performance of BF tree. The Best-first decision tree performs the best split in the tree based on boosting algorithms. The minimum number of instances (variable parameter) was varied from the default value 2 to 10000 in steps of 1 and the corresponding classification accuracy was noted down. The best classification accuracy of 83.51% for the block size 8x8 of frames was achieved with M value of 100 in 10-fold cross validation with the default percentage split 66%.

6.6. Experimental Results on REP Tree

Observing in the result of accuracy and compilation efficiency, one can also easily find that the REP tree model has taken only minimum compilation time of 0.52 seconds to build the model. A minimum total weight of instances (Variable parameter) was varied from 2 to 10000 in the step of 1. The REP tree model has achieved the classification accuracy of 80.64% of the block size 8x8 of frames with M value of 100 in 10-fold cross validation with the default percentage split 66%.

6.7. Experimental Results on Random Tree

An extensive investigation has been attempted with random tree classifier. The random tree model produced a high predictive performance, which is competitively compared with other algorithms. The performance of the random tree model is evaluated with the tuning of parameters like k-value, maximum depth, and the number of folds. K-value sets the number of randomly chosen attributes, and maximum depth defines the maximum depth of the tree, and the number of folds determines the amount of data used for back fitting. The variations of the classification accuracy on default K-value = 15 is shown in the Figure 8. The random tree classifier has achieved the overall maximum classification accuracy is found to be 99.48%.

The K-values varied from 1 to 19(total no. of. best performing features) and the corresponding classification accuracies were noted down. The value of K =15, which gives the maximum classification accuracy was fixed with the consideration of the apparent structure of the decision tree and the value of maximum depth was varied from 0 to 19 in steps of 1.

Figure 8. Classification performance of random tree model

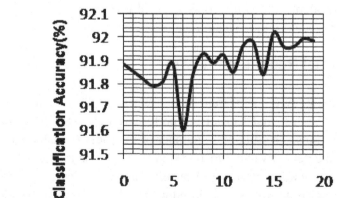

The variation of classification accuracy with respect to maximum depth of the tree and folds is shown in Figure 9 and Figure 10. The number of folds varied in the decreased order from 11 to 0 with a fixed value of k =15 and depth = 19. Thus, the random tree classifier is able to achieve the maximum classification accuracy of 99.48% with the minimum default folds.

Confusion matrix is a specific table layout to demonstrate the actual and predicted classifications of the classifier is shown in Table 2. From the observations, 485 data points of ADD class were misclassified as NADD class. And 1098 data points of NADD class were misclassified as ADD class. The training data for two classes of advertisement video data and the non advertisement video data shows the user accuracy of 95.15% and 89.02% respectively.

Figure 9. Performance of random tree depth vs classification accuracy

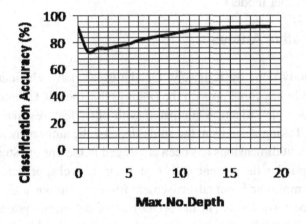

Figure 10. Performance of random tree folds vs classification accuracy

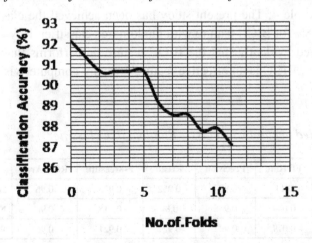

Table 2. Confusion matrix: Random tree classifier

Class	ADD	NADD
ADD	9515	485
NADD	1098	8902

With reference of Table 3, one can consider the calculation of true positive values, true negative values, and false positive and false negative values. All measures of sensitivity, specificity and accuracy can be calculated based on these values. Finding the TP rates and FP rates is very essential part to conclude the best model. The TP rate should be close to '1' and FP should be close to '0' for better classification accuracy. From the given Table 3, one can realize the closeness of TP rate to '1' and FP rate to '0'. Thus, both values confirm that the built model is the best one, among the other models.

6.8. Comparative Analysis

In an earlier study done by Kalaiselvi Geetha et. al., have elucidated the BICC feature. The study has come up with the findings that the BICC feature is best and suitable for video classification compared with other features like edge, motion and histogram. Taking a cue from the study done by the authors mentioned above, a study of different dimensions has been envisaged in the present study. The BICC technique is applied in the present study to develop a novel approach to classify the advertisement frames and non advertisement frames from the stream live videos. BICC feature performs better in the ADD frames detection system. The results found in the earlier study is compared with the result obtained in the present study is shown in Figure 11.

Referring Table 4, The present study has been achieved the classification accuracy of 99.48% for BICC feature with random tree classifier. However, the present study proved evidently that the BICC feature outperforms than other visual features. Hence, BICC is an effective feature formany computer vision based applications.

Table 3. Detailed accuracy by class – Random tree classifier

TP Rate	FP Rate	Precision	Recall	F-Measure	ROC Area	Class
0.952	0.11	0.897	0.952	0.923	0.96	ADD
0.89	0.049	0.948	0.89	0.918	0.96	NADD
0.921	0.079	0.922	0.921	0.921	0.96	Weighted Avg

Figure 11. Performance of various visual features with BICC

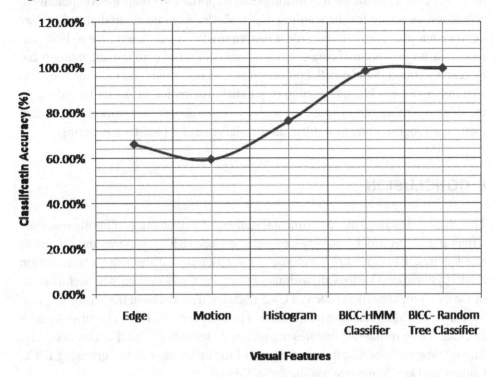

Table 4. Performance comparison of other visual features

Edge	Motion	Histogram	BICC-HMM Classifier	BICC- Random Tree Classifier
66.07%	59.46%	76.29%	98.4%	99.48%

7. MULTICORE IMPLEMENTATION OF C4.5 ALGORITHM

Many researchers have proposed the parallism in implementing various decision tree algorithms, implementing on multicore is challenging as it is limited to the software support. In recent research, there are various models have been implemented for classification, such as support vector machine, neural networks and markov models, decision tree and genetic algorithms. In particular, decision trees are the best appropriate for data mining approach. The performance ability of the decision tree is relatively higher when compared with other classifiers. In the current generation, there is a massive growth of image and videos in television and internet. It is essential to manage the huge volume of data stored in computer memory. Hence, a great need for an efficient classification algorithms and important to comprise computational efficiency, accuracy for the solution and scalable. Automatic parallelization may be more feasible solution to decrease the required computational time to build the model for huge volume of datasets. The concept of multi core implementation can be achieved through the parallel processing of decision tree construction. The decision tree nodes can be built parallel or parallel distribution of the training data. At the time of writing this chapter, the authors of this chapter are working on Matlab multicore programming to implement the algorithm for parallel computing.

8. CONCLUSION

This chapter describes the experimental study for the evaluation of family tree classifiers applied on Block Intensity Comparison Code (BICC) features and key frame rate features. BICC feature benchmarks the efficiency of the video classification model by exploiting various algorithms for labelling the video data. The performance of the different classifiers' such as C4.5 decision tree, decision tree graft, Logistic Model Tree (LMT), Random tree, Best first tree (BF) and REP tree classifier for both BICC and Key frame rate features are presented regarding classification accuracy. The summary of classification accuracies of the mentioned classifiers using BICC features and key frame rate are shown in Table 5.

From the experimental evaluation of the above discussed classifiers, the Random tree classifier gives the maximum classification accuracy with BICC features. In particular, Random tree with K-value and the number of folds achieved maximum classification accuracy as 99.48%. The obtained result of the study is application

Table 5. Summary of classification accuracy of BICC and key frame rate features

S. No.	Name of the Classifiers	Classification Accuracy (%)	
		BICC Feature	Key Frame Rate Feature
1.	Decision Tree C4,5	83.69	60.94
2.	J48 Graft	83.69	62.08
3.	Reduced error pruning (REP)	80.64	59.11
4.	Best First (BF)	83.51	62.28
5.	Logistic Model Tree (LMT)	91.35	71.01
6.	**Random Tree**	**99.48**	**71.95**

oriented for the given data set. The probability plot or a goodness-of-fit test can be used to verify the built model. A tree based machine learning unique Random tree model for classification of ADD and NADD videos was demonstrated which proved the efficiency of BICC feature. The effectiveness of the BICC feature was analysed, the efficiency was proven and validated.

REFERENCES

Aha, D. W., Kibler, D., & Albert, M. K. (1991). Instance-based Learning Algorithms. *Machine Learning*, 6(1), 37–66. doi:10.1007/BF00153759

Bauer, E., & Kohavi, R. (2004). An empirical comparison of voting classification algorithms: Bagging, Boosting, And Variants. *Machine Learning*, 36(1-2), 105–139.

Brezeal, D., & Diane, J., & Cook. (2008). Automatic Video Classification: A Survey of the Literature. *IEEE Transactions on Systems, Man and Cybernetics. Part C, Applications and Reviews*, 38, 3.

Dai1, W., & Ji, W. (2014). A Map Reduce Implementation of C4.5 Decision Tree Algorithm. *International Journal of Database Theory and Application*, 7(1), 49-60.

David, A., & Sadlier. (2002). Automatic TV advertisement detection from MPEG bit stream. *Journal of the pattern Recognition Society*.

Gresle, T., & Huang, S. (1997). Gisting of video documents: a key frames selection algorithm using relative activity measure. *The 2nd International Conference On Visual Information System*.

Hanjalic, A., Lagendijk, R. L., & Biemond, J. (1996). A new key-frame allocation method for representing stored video-streams. *Proc. 1st Int.Workshop Image Databases Multi Media Search*.

Hua, X. (2005). Robust Learning-based TV Commercial Detection. *Proc. of ICMF*.

Jianping, F., & Elmagarmid, K. (2004). Class View: Hierarchical Video Shot Classification, Indexing and Accessing. *IEEE Transactions on Multimedia*, 6, 1.

John, M. (2006). Finding and identifying unknown commercials using repeated video sequence detection. *Computer Vision and Image Understanding*, 103(1), 80–88. doi:10.1016/j.cviu.2006.03.002

Kalaiselvi Geetha, M., Palanivel, S., & Ramalingam, V. (2009). Department of Computer science and Engineering and Technology, Annamalai University, TamilNadu. A Novels block intensity comparison code for video classification and retrieval. *Expert Systems with Applications*, 6415–6420. doi:10.1016/j.eswa.2008.07.047

Kobla, V., Doermann, D., Lin, K-I., & Faloutsos, C. (1997). Compressed domain video indexing techniques using DCT and motion vector information in MPEG video. *Proc. Storage Retrieval Image video Databases(SPIE)*.

Le, X., Chow, M., Timmis, J., & Leroy, S. (2007). Power Distribution Outage Cause Identification With Imbalanced Data Using Artificial Immune Recognition System (AIRS) Algorithm. *IEEE Transactions on Power Systems*, *22*(1), 198–204. doi:10.1109/TPWRS.2006.889040

Li, W., & Xing, C. (2010). Parallel Decision Tree Algorithm Based on Combination. *International Forum on Information Technology and Applications*.

Lienhart, R. (1997). On the detection and recognition of television commercials. *Proc of IEEE Conf on Multimedia Computing and Systems*. doi:10.1109/MMCS.1997.609763

Nilsson, J. (1999). *Introduction to Machine Learning*. Academic Press.

Nuno, A., & Gama, J., & Silva, F. (2002). Parallel implementation of decision tree learning algorithm. *Chapters in Progress in Artificial Intelligence*, *2258*, 6–13.

Qi, W., Gu, L., Jiang, H., Chen, H., & Zhang, H. J. (2000). Integrating visual, audio and text analysis for news video. *Proc. 7th IEEE Int. Conf. Image Process. (ICIP), 520-523*. doi:10.1109/ICIP.2000.899482

Quinlan, J. R. (1986). Introduction of decision trees. *Machine Learning*, *1*(1), 81–106. doi:10.1007/BF00116251

Sadlier, D. A. (2000). Automatic TV advertisement detection fro MPEG bitstream. *Journal of the Pattern Recognition Society*, *35*(12), 2–15.

Shivakumara, P., Dutta, A., Phan, T., Tan, C., & Uma, P. (2011). A novel mutual nearest neighbor based symmetry for text frame classification in video. *Pattern Recognition*, *44*(8), 1671–1683. doi:10.1016/j.patcog.2011.02.008

Sugumaran, V., Muralidharan, V., & Ramachandran, K. I. (2007). Feature selection using Decision Tree and classification through Proximal Support Vector Machine for fault diagnostics of roller bearing. *Mechanical Systems and Signal Processing*, *21*(2), 930-942.

Timmis, J., Neal, M., & Hunt, J. (2000). An artificial immune system for data analysis. *Bio Systems, 55*(1-3), 143–150. doi:10.1016/S0303-2647(99)00092-1 PMID:10745118

Watkins, A., & Timmis, J. (2002). Artificial immune recognition system(AIRS): revisions and refinements.*1st International Conference on Artificial Immune Systems (ICARIS2002).*

Watkins, A., Timmis, J., & Boggess, L. (2004). Artificial immune recognition system (AIRS): An immune-inspired supervised learning algorithm. *Genetic Programming and Evolvable Machines, 5*(3), 291–317. doi:10.1023/B:GENP.0000030197.83685.94

Wolf, W. (1996). Key frame selection by motion analysis.*Proc. IEEE Int. Conf. Acoust., Speech Signal Proc.*

Xu, L. Q., & Li, Y. (2003). Video classification using spatial-temporal features and PCA.*Proc. Int. Conf. Multimedia Expo(ICME)*, 485-488.

Zhang, H. J., Wu, J., Zhong, D., & Smoliar, S. W. (1997). An integrated systemfor content-based video retrieval and browsing. *Pattern Recognition, 30*(4), 643–658. doi:10.1016/S0031-3203(96)00109-4

Chapter 5
Creating Sound Glyph Database for Video Subtitling

Chitralekha Ganapati Bhat
TCS Innovation Labs, India

Sunil Kumar Kopparapu
TCS Innovation Labs, India

ABSTRACT

Accessibility of speech information in videos is a huge challenge for the hearing impaired, making a visual representation such as text subtitling essential. Unavailability of a good Automatic Speech Recognition (ASR) engine, makes automatic generation of text subtitles for resource deficient languages such as Indian languages, extremely difficult. Techniques to build such an ASR using audio and corresponding transcription in the form of broadcast news or audio books have been proposed; however, these techniques require transcriptions corresponding to the audio in editable text format, which are unavailable for resource deficient languages. In this chapter, a novel technique of building a sound-glyph database for a resource deficient language has been described. The sound-glyph database can be used effectively to subtitle videos in the same language script. Considering large volumes of data that need to be processed, we propose a parallel processing method in a multiresolution setup, harnessing the multi-core capacity of present day computers.

DOI: 10.4018/978-1-5225-0889-2.ch005

INTRODUCTION

Science may have found a cure for most evils; but it has found no remedy for the worst of them all - the apathy of human beings. – Helen Keller

Accessibility is one of the key design aspects for any product, to ensure that people with disabilities are able to use the product, indicates a societal growth wherein, Helen Keller's worst fears have a chance of being addressed. With increasing attention being dedicated to making any digital content accessible, text subtitling or closed captioning for videos, TV programmes, is gaining significance. Several countries have mandated that all broadcasted videos be made accessible. The most common mode of making videos accessible to hearing impaired, is to provide visual cues corresponding to audio through subtitles in text format. The process of manually creating text subtitles for a video is long drawn and tedious. Alternatively, an Automatic Speech Recognition (ASR) engine can be employed to convert the audio into text and then use the text to subtitle the video, either in real-time or in the offline mode. This mechanism is efficient for resource rich languages like English. However, for resource deficient languages, especially Indian languages, this is not possible because of the absence of a good ASR in that language. This is primarily due to the non availability of a good speech corpus.

A speech corpus is a collection of speech audio files and their corresponding transcription. The sanctity of the speech corpus is measured by the quality of audio in terms of noise, accuracy of time alignment of audio and its corresponding text. Current state-of-the-art ASR technologies use audio and transcription in editable text format. There exists a wealth of open access audio and corresponding transcription in the form of news data, audio books etc. for various Indian languages. However, the transcripts of the news audio for several Indian languages are only available in non-editable form, meaning the transcripts corresponding to the audio cannot be converted into text to build a speech corpus. We propose a technique by which, using the audio and the corresponding transcripts in the image form (non-editable) to build a sound and word-glyph database. We derive a correlation between audio clips and images of the script corresponding to these audio clips by exploiting speech and image processing techniques. The central idea is to be able to build a database which represents the audio in terms of images of the script. Considering large volumes of image data that needs to be processed, we use multiresolution techniques on a multi-core processor to provide speed up in the process. The main contribution of this chapter is to build a sound-glyph database for a resource-deficient language to aid making video/audio accessible. We use multiresolution technique to reduce the size of the image and exploit inherent parallelism in the nature of the method of building the sound-glyph database.

The rest of the chapter is organized as follows, a background of the existing techniques for building a speech corpus for resource deficient language and their limitations are provided, followed by the methodology used in building the sound-glyph database using multiresolution and multi-core techniques.

Background

Through this work, we intend to address the building of a novel type of speech corpus comprising sound and its corresponding word-glyph, with special focus on Indian languages. This speech corpus is intended to be used to create video subtitles automatically. An ASR is essentially a pattern recognition engine using two types of reference models known as (a) Acoustic models and (b) Language models. These reference models or training data, are generated using a speech corpus specific to a language.

The accuracy of a state-of-the-art ASR engine is dependent on the quality and quantity of the speech corpus. A high quality speech corpus contains clean, non-noisy audio data and corresponding accurate time aligned text transcription, in addition, it has to be phonetically balanced and consist of speech spoken by diverse speakers in order to bring in an element of as much generalization as possible, for the ASR to perform optimally. For resource deficient languages, such as Indian languages, such data is not readily available. Building such a corpus from scratch is tedious and expensive.

In the absence of a good speech corpus, researchers have been looking at addressing the problem of enabling a good ASR by careful construction of language models and adaption of acoustic models. Authors outline a process of adapting language models using machine translated data from English to Icelandic to reduce the word error rate of an ASR significantly (Jensson, Iwano & Furui, 2008). A method of designing a text corpus by estimating the phone error distribution of an existing fully transcribed speech corpus and growing this corpus by collecting data for sentences with phone occurrence distribution equivalent to the phone error distribution to enhance the performance of a Japanese ASR has been described (Murakami, Shinoda, & Furui, 2011). A likelihood-based, cross-lingual adaptation scheme to adapt a Chinese language model using a corpus of contemporary English news articles, thereby addressing the resource scarceness (Kim & Khudanpur, 2003) has been proposed to achieve good ASR recognition accuracy.

Techniques to build acoustic models differently for small speech corpus is another method by which ASR performance for resource deficient languages is enhanced. A maximum a posteriori adaptation approach was proposed in (Lu, Ghoshal, & Renals. 2012), wherein the authors focus on the adaptation of phonetic subspace parameters and thus used the globally shared parameters from languages other than target language (resource deficient) to improve ASR performance. In (Chen, Mak, Leung, & Sivadas, 2014), triphone acoustic models are estimated in parallel with trigrapheme acoustic models, as a joint task in a multitask learning (MTL) framework using deep neural network (DNN), on small amount of training data for a resource deficient language and the approach was evaluated on three resource deficient South African languages. Subspace Gaussian mixture model (SGMM) approach is also being used for cross-lingual ASR design, where subspace parameters are estimated on multiple source languages and then transferred to the target language (Miao, Metze, & Waibel, 2013). In Miao, Metze, and Rawat, (2013), authors discuss the advantage of using deep maxout networks (DMN) for resource deficient conditions with application to a large vocabulary continuous speech recognition (LVCSR) task.

Apart from building intelligent language models and acoustic models for low-resource languages, efforts are being made towards building speech corpus for resource deficient languages frugally.The Norwegian speech corpus RUNDKAST (Amdal, Strand, Almberg, & Svendsen, 2008) with approximately 77 hours of data contains both read and spontaneous speech, dialogues and multipart discussions. However, only one hour of read and spontaneous speech has been manually annotated. The article (Jongtaveesataporn, Wutiwiwatchai, Iwano, and Furui, 2008) discusses the first Thai broadcast news speech corpus, containing about 17 hours of speech data. The preliminary results of ASR using models built on this data yielded a word error rate of 20% for clean and planned speech.

More recently, authors used the audio and the corresponding transcripts available on the internet to build a corpus using frugal methods (Kopparapu & Ahmed, 2013). The problem of building the corpus by automatically annotating the long audio using the transcript is non trivial (Kopparapu & Ahmed, 2013; Prahallad & Black, 2011). As a part of the development of a frugal method for building speech corpus for Indian languages, the option of using the All India Radio (AIR) news data (All India Radio News Archives, 2015) that is available in the form of audio and corresponding text transcript has been explored. However, the transcripts of the news audio for several Indian languages are only available in the form of non-editable PDFs, meaning the transcripts corresponding to the audio cannot be converted into text to build a speech corpus.

OCR engines such as Tesseract are available to convert documents in a variety of image format into editable text format. Tesseract is available in 60 languages including Hindi (Tesseract, 2015), however the accuracy is very low, as the conjunct character combinations of Hindi language are not easily separable due to partial overlapping. Attempts are being made to improve the OCR technology for Hindi by researchers (Yadav, S´anchez-Cuadrado, & Morato, 2013; Bansal & Sinha, 2001; Yadav, Sharma, & Gupta, 2007; Mishra, Patvardhan, Lakshmi, & Singh 2012), however the results are not yet on par with the results for the English language. CDAC-Pune has built *'Chitrankan',* an OCR for Hindi and Marathi (CDAC-Pune, 2015). *'Parichit'* (Parichit, 2015) is another project that aims at OCR development for several Indian language, *'Parichit'* also provides training data for several of these languages. CDAC has also released *'Nayana'* (CDAC, 2015), which is an OCR for Malayalam language.

However, the work on OCR for Indian languages is still in nascent stages.

Our objective is to build an automatic video subtitling engine for Indian languages. Major roadblocks towards this are -

- Non availability of a speech corpus to build an ASR engine to perform with high accuracy.
- Non availability of transcriptions in editable text format for building speech corpora using freely available web resources.
- Non availability of an OCR engine to convert the transcriptions from a non-editable format into editable text to build a speech corpus.

In this book chapter, we address these concerns by proposing a novel type of speech corpus, 'sound-glyph' database comprising speech utterances and their corresponding word-glyph images. Thus we build a speech corpus using image processing and audio processing techniques, thereby eliminating the need for OCR while still harnessing the freely available web resources.

BUILDING A SOUND-GLYPH DATABASE

The entire process of building the sound-glyph database (Bhat & Kopparapu, 2014) can be broken into three major steps and needs to be carried out in that order, namely

1. Processing of the image transcripts using image processing techniques to first segment the transcript image into similar words.
2. Identifying segments in the audio corresponding to the words identified in step 1.
3. Building the sound-glyph database.

We outline the process of building such a database and then describe an approach that makes use of mutliresolution image analysis and multi-core implementation of the image processing operations.

Figure 1. Correspondence between Image of the transcript and audio
Bhat and Kopparapu (2014)

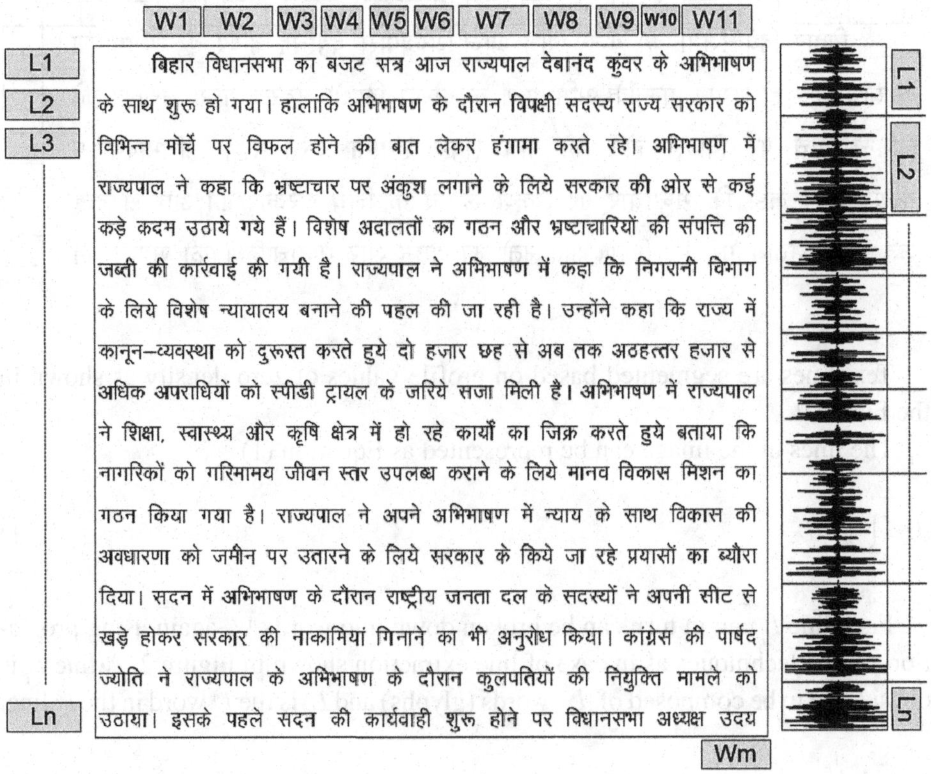

Let the audio be represented as $A(t)$; $0 < t < T$ where T is the duration of the audio; typically T is of the order of five to six minutes (All India Radio News Archives, 2015). The transcript $\left\{\sum I_{x,y}\right\}, \left\{\sum_{x,y}^{m,n} = 1,1\right\}$ is an image of size $m \times n$ pixels as shown in Figure 1 and is assumed to represent the information contained in the audio $A(t)$.

The image transcript consists of lines (marked as L_1, L_2, ..., L_N in Figure 1). These lines are extracted from the image using a technique based on projection profiles that are commonly used to segment printed documents (Likforman-Sulem, Zahour, and Taconet, 2007). The transcript image is binarized by applying a global threshold. Vertical projection profile is computed for each column of the transcript image $\left\{\sum I_{x,y}\right\}, \left\{\sum_{x,y}^{m,n} = 1,1\right\}$ as

$$profile(y) = \sum_1^m I(x,y)$$

Figure 2. Vertical and horizontal projection profiles for transcript image
Bhat and Kopparapu (2014).

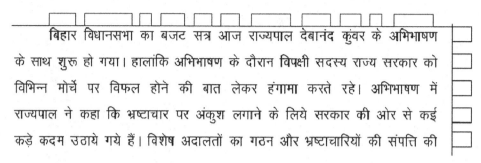

Text lines are segmented based on profile values of zero density as shown in the Figure 2.

The lines in the image can be represented as Equation (1).

$$I = \bigcup_{i=1}^{N} L_i \tag{1}$$

Each line L_i can in turn can be broken down into words W, again using projection profile techniques as in case of line extraction shown in Figure 2. A line L_i is considered to be composed of $|L_i|$ words (glyphs) and L_{ij} is the jth word in the ith line.

$$L_i = \bigcup_{j=1}^{|L_i|} L_{ij} \tag{2}$$

The transcript image can be viewed as,

$$I_{x,y} = \bigcup_{i=1}^{N} \bigcup_{j=1}^{|L_i|} L_{ij}$$

such that each word-glyph L_{ij} is an image with height H_{ij}, breadth B_{ij} in pixels and can be represented as

$$L_{ij} = f(H_{in}, B_{ij})$$

Note that H_{ij} of all the word-glyph is more or less the same, while B_{ij} in pixels varies depending on the length of the word. We now derive a correspondence between the audio utterance $A(t)$ and word-glyph under the following assumptions.

1. $A(t) \equiv I_{x,y}$ as shown in Figure 1. If the transcription contains a total of $\sum_{i=1}^{N} |L_i|$ words, then corresponding audio must also contain the same number segments corresponding to these image-glyph.
2. The audio is spoken at a uniform speaking rate.
3. The breadth B_{ij} of a word in the transcript image is proportional to the time taken to utter that word in $A(t)$.
4. There are repetitive occurrences of words in image transcript and hence the audio.

The news audio, available at (All India Radio News Archives, 2015), generally comprises of music at the beginning, followed by self-introduction of the news reader, the news, conclusion by the news reader and ending with music. The transcripts correspond only to the portion where the actual news is being read. The audio corresponding to the actual news is extracted automatically as mentioned in (Soni, Ahmed, and Kopparapu, 2014).

Under these assumptions it is clear that,

$$T \equiv \sum_{i=1}^{N} \sum_{j=1}^{|L_i|} B_{ij}$$

namely the total duration of the audio T is equivalent to the sum of the breadth of all the word-glyphs in the transcript image. Or, the length of the audio segment corresponding to these word-glyphs can be represented as

$$t_{ij} = \frac{B_{ij} \times T}{\sum_{i=1}^{N} \sum_{j=1}^{|L_i|}} B_{ij} \tag{3}$$

Note that using (3), it is clear that one can identify the exact location of the word-glyph in the audio stream. Also note that these segments of speech are not perfect because of the constant speaking rate assumption made. We now try to identify more accurate location of the audio segment corresponding to the word-glyph.

The word-glyphs are clustered into groups using word spotting techniques as described in (Rath and Manmatha, 2003). A set of four profile features, as described below are extracted from the binarized word-glyphs.

1. **Vertical Projection Profile:** Number of ink pixels in each column.
2. **Upper Word Profile:** The distance from the upper boundary to the closest ink pixel in each column.

3. **Lower Word Profile:** The distance from the upper boundary to the closest ink pixel in each column.

4. **Transition Profile:** The number of transitions from ink to background per column.

We have for each word-glyph I, a feature set F_I of dimension $4 \times B_I$, where B_I is the breadth of the word-glyph in terms of number of columns.

Dynamic time warping (DTW) algorithm (Müller, 2007) is used to measure the similarity between word-glyphs represented by the feature set F_I and thus clusters of similar word-glyphs is built. This results in the total number of word-glyphs $\sum_{i=1}^{N} |L_i|$, being clustered into some T clusters such that similar word-glyphs in the image transcript, belong to the same cluster. The goodness of our algorithm in creating clusters is measured in terms of precision and recall as defined below.

$$Precision = \frac{Number\ of\ relevant\ images\ retrieved}{Total\ number\ of\ images\ retrieved}$$

$$Recall = \frac{Number\ of\ relevant\ images\ retrieved}{Total\ number\ of\ relevant\ images}$$

It is expected that similar patterns will be displayed in the audio as well, wherein if the image is repeated within the transcript, the corresponding utterance will also be repeated within the audio. We harness this pattern correlation between audio and transcript-image for building the sound-glyph database.

Essentially, we now have multiple audio segments corresponding to a particular word-glyph (cluster) from the transcript. These audio segments are identified based on the uniform speaking rate assumption and hence the starting and ending points of the audio corresponding to a word-glyph will not be accurate, however it will be in the vicinity of the identified audio segment. We make use of the repetitive pattern within the audio to narrow down the exact location using sliding DTW techniques (Mantena, Bollepalli, and Prahallad. 2011), wherein we consider twice the length of audio segments of audio pertaining to a particular word-glyph. This locates the vicinity of the required audio. The shortest path of the DTW algorithm marks the closest match between the two audio segments, giving a better estimate of the starting and ending points of the required audio segments.

We use these audio segments to train a sound model corresponding to the word-glyph. Let $U_W = [u_1, u_2, ..., u_n]$ be the set of audio utterances that represent the word-glyph W. Using U_W, we train a Hidden Markov Model (HMM) for U_W which is representative of the word-glyph W. The sound-glyph database is the word W and U_W pair.

Limitations of Single Core Implementation

The sound-glyph database is built using freely available AIR Hindi news data for several regions as well as using news data over a period of several years. The process of building the sound-glyph database as outlined above involves several image processing techniques operating on several GBs of data, making the process computationally expensive, as well as time consuming when implemented on a single core. Since the web resource being used is one that is incremental in nature with time, the sound-glyph database can also be updated in an incremental fashion, making this process a repetitive one. Of the three major steps used to build the sound-glyph database, the first step of breaking the transcription-image into individual images and then clustering to identify similar images as a word-glyph is the most time and resource consuming. Hence, an approach to process the images at a lower resolution using multi-core becomes imperative.

Advances in hardware and computer industry have made it possible to take advantage of the multi-core processors for computationally intensive processes. Multi-core implementations are generally used in image processing for processing of high resolution images such as image segmentation as described in (Happ, Ferreira, Bentes, Costa, & Feitosa, 2010), where a speed up of 2.6 was obtained using a multithreading parallel implementation of a region growing algorithm. In (Kim, Kim, and Lee, 2014), authors present an efficient parallel implementation of a 2D convolution algorithm, giving a speed up of 6.2 times using the SIMD (Single Instruction Multiple Data) extension (SSE) technology and TBB (Threading Building Block) run time library in Intel multi-core processors. In their work (Saxena, Sharma, and Sharma. 2013), authors present a multi-core processing approach to several image processing algorithms such as segmentation, noise reduction, features calculation, histogram equalization and comparative study with some sequential image processing algorithm. A speed up of 200% on a dual core and 400% on a quad core processor was reported for the parallel implementation of cubic convolution interpolation algorithm in (Liu, and Gao, 2010).

Parallel implementation of image processing algorithms to harness the multi-core processors has been done using OpenMP (Open Multi Processing) which is an industry standard, parallel programming.

API for shared memory multi-processors, including multicore processors (Slabaugh, Boyes, and Yang, 2010). A lock free multithreading approach developed using Visual C++ with Microsoft Foundation Class (MFC) support was implemented for contrast enhancement using fuzzy technique and edge detection (Kamalakannan & Rajamanickam, 2013). Authors have used the inherent multthreading available in Java language to implement several image processing algorithms and have compared the performance on a single-core and multi-core CPUs in (Kika & Greca, 2013).

Existing literature and methodologies indicate that a speed up, that is desirable in building the sound-glyph database can be achieved by using the multi-core processing.

MULTIRESOLUTION: MULTICORE APPROACH TO BUILDING SOUND-GLYPH DATABASE

We discuss a method that takes advantage of two ways in which speed up can be achieved

- Multiresolution processing of the transcription-image.
- Multi-core approach to image processing operation – breaking down image transcriptions into lines and words.

Multiresolution Processing of Transcription Image

The first step towards building the sound-glyph database comprises breaking the transcription-image first into lines and then into individual words, as described in the previous section. Experiments were conducted using the multiresolution analysis using the *Daubechies' wavelets* (Daubechies, 1992) on MATLAB.

Using the Daubechies wavelet on the original image, results in a reduction in the transaction image size by half. The height and width of an individual word-glyph is now $H_1 / 2$ and $B_1 / 2$ respectively. This in turn reduces the size of the feature set F_1 by two. Also, since the features are computed over the column, a reduction in height automatically translates into additional speed up.

Figure 3 shows a decomposed image of transcription image.

The reduction in resolution compromises the precision and recall of the clustering process, however a speed up is achieved by the reduction in resolution. Although, the reduced resolution is acceptable for clustering, the image to be used for subtitling needs to be clear enough for the user to be able to read. Hence the word-glyph representing a cluster needs to be reconstructed to the original resolution when stored in the sound-glyph database.

Figure 3. Multiresolution analysis of transcription image

आकाशवाणी ईटानगर

Time : 7:45 PM Duration - 5 mnts 01-02-2013

राष्ट्रपति प्रणब मुखर्जी ने कहा कि सम्मिलित विकास और गरीबी दूर करने के लिए कृषि क्षेत्र और खाद्य उत्पादन में वृद्धि सबसे महत्वपूर्ण है। नई दिल्ली में एक कृषि सम्मेलन को संबोधित करते हुए श्री मुखर्जी ने कहा कि इससे गांवों में रोजगार के अवसर पैदा होंगे, शहरों की और पलायन रुकेगा और खाद्य सुरक्षा उपलब्ध होगी। उन्होंने कहा कि खाद्य उत्पादन बढ़ने से भण्डारण और परिवहन सुविधाओं में निवेश बढ़ेगा और कृषि प्रसंस्करण उद्योग को भी बढ़ावा मिलेगा। राष्ट्रपति ने कहा कि खाद्य उत्पादन को बढ़ाकर दोगुना करना एक बड़ी चुनौती है और इसके लिए देश को दूसरी हरित क्रांति की जरूरत है। श्री मुखर्जी ने खेती में नई तकनीकों के इस्तेमाल पर जोर दिया।

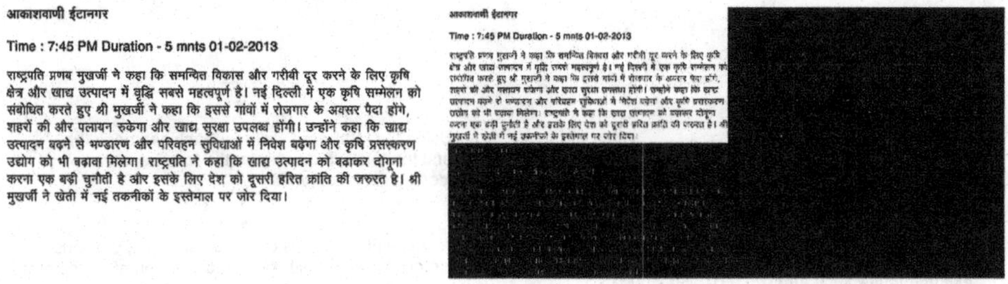

(a)

(b)

Multi-Core Processing of Transcription Image

Building the sound-glyph database involves processing of large amounts of transcription images. A multi-core approach applied to the image processing algorithms is expected to provide speed up, especially since the process is not one time and is expected to be an iterative one, whenever incremental data is available.

Parallel Computing Toolbox (PCT) on MATLAB, provides several high-level programming constructs to convert applications to take advantage of computers equipped with multicore processors. The number of workers in the PCT was set to 2 since we use a dual core processor. However, the algorithm can be easily modified to work on processors with higher number of cores. A divide and conquer approach was used to achieve parallel computing. The first step to the process of building the sound-glyph database involves breaking the transcription image into individual word-glyphs. Each transcription image was divided into two parts and processed by two separate MATLAB workers, since this process can be conducted independently for the two halves. However, an index of the lines needs to be maintained in order to keep the speech audio and the image transcription synchronized.

Algorithm used for the process of building the sound-glyph database using multiresolution – parallel processing is shown in Figure 4.

Figure 5 shows the implementation of the Multiresolution; multi-core approach.

EVALUATION OF THE MULTIRESOLUTION AND MULTI-CORE APPROACH

In order to evaluate the proposed method of building the sound-glyph database, we used 23 Hindi news audio files from (All India Radio News Archives, 2015), each of duration between 5 and 6 minutes, spoken by two male and two female speakers. There were a total of 781 lines and 19773 word-glyphs. The precision and recall for clustering of word-glyphs was evaluated over a sample set.

Figure 4. Multiresolution; multi-core approach to construct a sound-glyph database

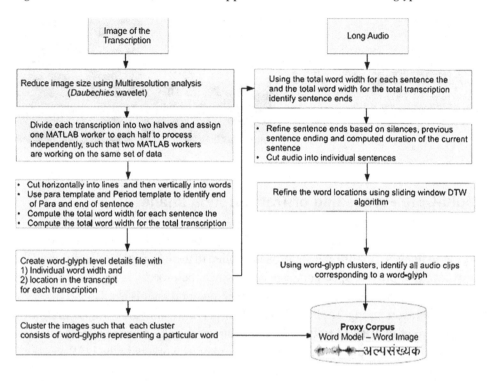

Figure 5. Implementation of the Multiresolution; multi-core approach

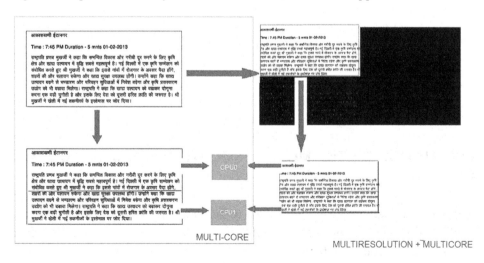

Figure 6. Recognition Accuracy of Sound-Glyph database
Bhat and Kopparapu (2014).

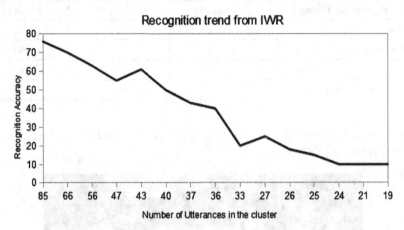

20 clusters with word-glyphs of B > 160 were selected for experimentation. The audio segments corresponding to these clustered word-glyphs were extracted. Each cluster had a maximum of 86 and minimum of 20 utterances corresponding to each image, which is our training set to build U_w. Training was performed for each of the 20 clusters of word-glyphs by dividing the utterances into training and testing sets, so as to be able to perform using five-fold cross validation method. HMMs were created for each word-glyph cluster; word-glyph and the corresponding HMM formed the sound-glyph database. Testing was carried out using the testing sets created, for each cluster. The recognition results are shown in the Figure 6.

It can be seen clearly from the graph that higher the number of training instances corresponding to each word-glyph, the better is the sound model corresponding to the word-glyph.

In this work, we focus on the speed up that is achieved using multiresolution and multi-core approaches described in the previous sections.

Three sets of experiments were performed on the data discussed, to understand the speed up that can be achieved. In the multiresolution approach, word-glyphs of width around 75 to 80 pixels (half of 160, which was the original width considered for single resolution) were considered for further processing. A comparative analysis of the methods used, in terms of speed up, precision and recall are listed in Table 1. This is representative of only the first step of sound-glyph database creation as mentioned in the section 'Building a sound-glyph database'. The rest of the process, steps 2 and 3 are run sequentially. It can be seen from Table 1 that a trade off in precision and recall has been done to achieve speed-up in the multi-resolution approach as well as the mixed approach.

Table 1. Speed up and precision-recall using multiresolution, multi-core approach

Experimental Setup	Speedup	Precision (%)	Recall (%)
Single resoultion	1	93	95
Multiresolution	2	87	90
Multi-core	1.6	95	97
Multiresolution + Multi-core	2.3	85	88

Figure 7. Sample video clip with subtitles built using sound-glyph database
Bhat and Kopparapu (2014).

Figure 7 shows an example of how the word-glyphs that form a part of the sound-glyph database are used to build the text subtitle for a Hindi news video.

CONCLUSION

Video subtitling is a significant step towards providing access to the spoken content and other audio cues in the video. Video subtitling can be done automatically with the help of a state-of-the-art ASR. However, no such ASR is available for resource-deficient languages such as Indian languages. Research work with focus on harnessing publicly available data for low resource languages is currently being pursued by several research groups. However, they assume the availability of editable text transcripts. Immediate non availability of tools for converting the scripts in Indian languages, becomes an impediment. Hence, we chose to harness the correspondence between the transcripts in image (JPEG) form and audio. Using the proposed technique, based on image and speech processing, a sound-glyph database has been built. A mapping between word-glyph of the transcript and sound models was created by harnessing the correlation between word image breadth and time taken for the utterance of the sound. The repetitive pattern of the word-glyphs and hence the audio utterance help in building HMMs. We envision that this database can be used for subtitling in the following way, the audio is compared with all the HMMs of the sounds corresponding to the word-glyphs, the word-glyph corresponding to the best matched HMM is returned as the (image) title corresponding to the audio. This technique has the advantage of being unsupervised as well as being less dependent on the linguistic framework of the language for which the database is being built. When such a database is built using large amounts of data, the better is suited for video subtitling application, since it would cover a larger vocabulary in a particular language. However, processing of large amounts of data is computationally expensive as well as time consuming. This is also an iterative process and needs to be done whenever new data is available in order to upgrade the database. Hence multiresolution and multi-core approaches were used to provide speed up to the process, however a trade off needed to be done between speed up and precision and recall.

REFERENCES

Ahmed, I., & Kopparapu, S. K. (2013). Technique for automatic sentence level alignment of long speech and transcripts. In *Proceedings of INTERSPEECH*. Retrieved June 29, 2015 from http://www.newsonair.com/

Amdal, I., Strand, O. M., Almberg, J., & Svendsen, T. (2008). RUNDKAST: An Annotated Norwegian Broadcast News Speech Corpus. *In Proceedings of Sixth International Conference on Language Resources and Evaluation.*

Bansal, V., & Sinha, R. M. K. (2001). A Complete OCR for Printed Hindi Text in Devnagari Script. In *Proceedings ofSixth International Conference on Document Analysis and Recognition*. IEEE.

Bhat, C., & Kopparapu, S. K. (2014). Constructing a Sound-Glyph Database for Subtitling Videos. In *Proceedings of Oriental COCOSDA*.

CDAC. (n.d.). *Nayana*. Retrieved June 29, 2015 from https://sites.google.com/site/cibu/ocr

CDAC-Pune. (n.d.). *Chitrankan*. Retrieved June 29, 2015 from http://cdac.in/index.aspx?id=mlc_gist_chitra

Chen, D., Mak, B., Leung, C., & Sivadas, S. (2014). Joint acoustic modeling of triphones and trigraphemes by multi-task learning deep neural networks for low-resource speech recognition. In Proceedings of ICASSP. doi:10.1109/ICASSP.2014.6854673

Daubechies, I. (1992). Ten Lectures on Wavelets. CBMS-NSF Regional Conference Series in Applied Mathematics.

Happ, P. N., Ferreira, R. S., Bentes, C., Costa, G. A. O. P., & Feitosa, R. Q. (2010). Multiresolution Segmentation: a Parallel Approach for High Resolution Image Segmentation in Multicore Architectures. In *3rd International Conference on Geographic Object-Based Image Analysis, 2010, Ghent, The International Archives of the Photogrammetry, Remote Sensing and Spatial Information Sciences*. Enshede: ITC.

Jensson, A. T., Iwano, K., & Furui, S. (2008). Language model adaptation using machine-translated text for resource-deficient languages. *EURASIP Journal on Audio, Speech, and Music Processing*, *2008*, 1–7. doi:10.1155/2008/573832

Jongtaveesataporn, M., Wutiwiwatchai, C., Iwano, K., & Furui, S. (2008). Thai Broadcast News Corpus Construction and Evaluation. In *Proceedings of Sixth International Conference on Language Resources and Evaluation*.

Kamalakannan, A., & Rajamanickam, G. (2013). High Performance Color Image Processing in Multicore CPU using MFC Multithreading. *International Journal of Advanced Computer Science and Applications*, *4*(12), 2013. doi:10.14569/IJACSA.2013.041207

Kika, A., & Greca, S. (2013). Multithreading Image Processing in Single-core and Multi-core CPU using Java. *International Journal of Advanced Computer Science and Applications*, *4*(9), 2013. doi:10.14569/IJACSA.2013.040926

Kim, C. G., Kim, J., & Lee, D. (2014). Optimizing image processing on multi-core CPUs with Intel parallel programming technologies. Journal of Multimedia Tools and Applications, 68(2), 237-251. doi:10.1007/s11042-011-0906-y

Kim, W., & Khudanpur, S. (2003). Cross-lingual lexical triggers in statistical language modeling. In *Proceedings of the 2003 Conference on Empirical Methods in Natural Language Processing*. Association for Computational Linguistics. doi:10.3115/1119355.1119358

Kopparapu, S. K., & Ahmed, I. (2013). *Frugal method and system for creating speech corpus*. US Patent App. 13/533,174.

Likforman-Sulem, L., Zahour, A., & Taconet, B. (2007). Text line segmentation of historical documents: a survey. International Journal of Document Analysis and Recognition 9(2-4), 123–138.

Liu, Y., & Gao, F. (2010). Parallel Implementations of Image Processing Algorithms on Multi-Core. In *Proceedings of Fourth International Conference on Genetic and Evolutionary Computing (ICGEC)*.

Lu, L., Ghoshal, A., & Renals, S. (2012). Maximum a posteriori adaptation of subspace gaussian mixture models for cross-lingual speech recognition. In Proceedings of ICASSP. doi:10.1109/ICASSP.2012.6289012

Mantena, G.V., Bollepalli, B., & Prahallad, K. (2011). SWS task: Articulatory phonetic units and sliding DTW. *Mediaeval 2011*.

Miao, Y., Metze, F., & Rawat, S. (2013). Deep Maxout Networks for Low-resource speech recognition. In *Proceedings of IEEE Workshop on Automatic Speech Recognition and Understanding (ASRU)*. doi:10.1109/ASRU.2013.6707763

Miao, Y., Metze, F., & Waibel, A. (2013). Subspace mixture model for low-resource speech recognition in cross-lingual settings. In Proceedings of ICASSP. IEEE. doi:10.1109/ICASSP.2013.6639088

Mishra, N., Patvardhan, C., Vasantha Lakshmi, C., & Singh, S. (2012). Shirorekha Chopping Integrated Tesseract OCR Engine for Enhanced Hindi Language Recognition. International Journal of Computer Applications, 39(6). doi:10.5120/4824-7076

Müller, M. (2007). *Information Retrieval for Music and Motion*. Secaucus, NJ: Springer-Verlag New York, Inc. doi:10.1007/978-3-540-74048-3_4

Murakami, H., Shinoda, K., & Furui, S. (2011). Designing text corpus using phone-error distribution for acoustic modeling. In *Proceedings of Automatic Speech Recognition and Understanding (ASRU), 2011 IEEE Workshop on*. doi:10.1109/ASRU.2011.6163929

Parichit. (n.d.). Retrieved June 29, 2015 from https://code.google.com/p/parichit/

Prahallad, K., & Black, A. W. (2011). Segmentation of monologues in audio books for building synthetic voices. IEEE Transactions on Audio, Speech, and Language Processing, 19(5), 1444–1449. doi:10.1109/TASL.2010.2081980

Rath, T. M., & Manmatha, R. (2003). Features for word spotting in historical manuscripts. In *Proceedings of Seventh International Conference on Document Analysis and Recognition*. doi:10.1109/ICDAR.2003.1227662

Saxena, S., Sharma, N., & Sharma, S. (2013). Image Processing Tasks using Parallel Computing in Multi core Architecture and its Applications in Medical Imaging. International Journal of Advanced Research in Computer and Communication Engineering, 2(4).

Slabaugh, G. G., Boyes, R., & Yang, X. (2010). Multicore Image Processing with OpenMP. IEEE Signal Processing Magazine, 27(2), 134-138.

Soni, S., Ahmed, I., & Kopparapu, S. K. (2014). Automatic segmentation of broadcast news audio using self similarity matrix. In *Proceedings of International Conference for Convergence of Technology (I2CT)*. doi:10.1109/I2CT.2014.7092245

Tesseract. (n.d.). Retrieved June 29, 2015 from https://code.google.com/p/tesseract-ocr/

Yadav, D., S'anchez-Cuadrado, S., & Morato, J. (2013, March). Optical character recognition for Hindi language using a neural-network approach. *Journal of Information Processing Systems*, 9(1), 117–140. doi:10.3745/JIPS.2013.9.1.117

Yadav, D., Sharma, A. K., & Gupta, J. P. (2007). Optical character recognition for printed Hindi text in Devanagari using soft-computing technique. In Proceedings of IASTED International Multi-Conference: Artificial Intelligence and Applications.

Chapter 6

Parallel Computing in Face Image Retrieval:
Practical Approach to the Real-World Image Search

Eugene Borovikov
National Library of Medicine, USA

Girish Lingappa
National Library of Medicine, USA

Szilárd Vajda
National Library of Medicine, USA

Michael C Bonifant
National Library of Medicine, USA

ABSTRACT

Modern digital photo collections contain vast multitudes of high-resolution color images, many containing faces, which are desirable to retrieve visually. This poses a problem for effective image browsing and calls for efficient Content Based Image Retrieval (CBIR) capabilities ensuring near-instantaneous visual query turn-around. This in turn necessitates parallelization of many existing image processing and information retrieval algorithms that can no longer satisfy the modern user demands, when executed sequentially. Hence a practical approach to Face Image Retrieval (FIR) is presented. It utilizes multi-core processing architectures to implement its major modules (e.g. face detection and matching) efficiently without sacrificing the image retrieval accuracy. The integration of FIR into a web-based family reunification system demonstrates the practicality of the proposed method. Several accuracy and speed evaluations on real-word data are presented and possible CBIR extensions are discussed.

DOI: 10.4018/978-1-5225-0889-2.ch006

INTRODUCTION

In 2002 the global capacity of the digital data storage has apparently exceeded that of the analog data storage, which can officially be marked as the beginning of the digital age (Hilbert & López, 2011). Since then the volume of visual data being generated, stored and shared over the Internet has been steadily growing due to the dramatically decreasing prices on the high capacity digital storage and due to the virtually omnipresent high-resolution inexpensive digital cameras. The web image collection today can easily account for millions of high-resolution true-color digital photographs, which calls for very efficient image processing (IP) algorithms involving

- Variable compression rates,
- Important visual feature extraction,
- Smart visual indexing and feature clustering

that would provide for a reasonably instantaneous content based image retrieval (CBIR) user experience in many practical web-based multimedia (MM) applications. The traditional sequential image processing algorithms (accessing one pixel at a time) clearly cannot satisfy the modern performance requirements, and some smart IP acceleration becomes a necessity. Fortunately, many of the IP and MM algorithms can be parallelized using various hardware/software solutions, including multi-core central processing units (CPU) and massively parallel graphics processor units (GPU) currently available in the consumer-level computers (Cullinan, Wyant, & Frattesi, 2012; Prinslow, 2011; Robson, 2008) and even in some mobile devices (Lee, Kyung, Park, Kwak, & Koo, 2015). The set of potential MM applications that can benefit from the accelerated image processing includes family/organization photo-album visual browsers, multi-dimensional medical image organizers, automatic visual surveillance in public areas, visual search for missing people and pets, etc.

In particular, let's consider building a practical face image retrieval (FIR) system for a family reunification application (Thoma, Antani, Gill, Pearson, & Neve, 2012) in disaster scenarios, where information about missing and found people is collected in several modes including semi-structured text (e.g. name, gender, age, location, etc.) and unconstrained images (e.g. digital photos with human faces shot in arbitrary settings), as shown in Figure 1. Such open web collections may contain hundreds of thousands of records, yet multiple simultaneous visual queries need to be instantaneous (i.e. answered within about a second). Such a system should obviously implement an IP module that satisfies all of the mentioned modern CBIR requirements, plus the high-level functions such as accurate and efficient face localization and matching, retrieving the most visually similar candidate faces for the given query face (Borovikov, Vajda, Lingappa, Antani, & Thoma, 2013).

Figure 1. Typical unconstrained digital photos in post-disaster family reunification image data-sets

Given the dynamic nature of the web image datasets, where the number of images can change anytime and we cannot assume to encounter more than one photo per person, we had to take the single image per person (SIPP) approach, which cannot train any person-specific statistical models for face recognition. It rather needs to rely on efficient, yet discriminative image descriptors that capture the essential image features (Jacobs, Finkelstein, & Salesin, 1995; Lowe, 2004; Raoui, Bouyakhf, Devy, & Regragui, 2011; Salembier & Sikora, 2002) in a compact and fast-to-match image signature, providing an instantaneous query turn-around experience. Such an approach needs to formalize the necessary methodology and implement all the mentioned capabilities to work on the unconstrained digital images (as in Figure 1), using various parallel computing techniques utilized on multi-core CPUs and GPUs, and confirm its performance with the experimental results on several public datasets.

The presented face matching methodology efficiently implements the mentioned SIPP approach for FIR in a cross-platform library (FaceMatch), taking advantage of the available multi-core hardware, and serving its image matching functionality via the web services, which are shown to be successfully utilized by a web-based family re-unification system that helps locate people missing/found in natural disasters by significantly reducing the image search space from tens of thousands of photos to about twenty likely ones, effectively deploying visual search along with the text based queries. Aside from the face image retrieval, FaceMatch functionality has shown to be effective in other applications:

- Image repository reduction by near-duplicate image detection.
- Medical image retrieval by content based image matching.
- Face localization in very large document image collections.
- Semi-automatic annotation of image datasets by face and landmark localization.

The mentioned visual search and annotation tools are performing most of the image processing tasks in near real-time due to the high-performance IP algorithms that were implemented using various kinds of parallelism from multi-threading on multi-core CPUs to massively parallel image processing on GPUs. The detailed discussion of all these applications is beyond the scope of this chapter, but we shall describe our FIR approach and its integration to a web-based family re-unification system, emphasizing our multi-core image processing R&D findings and solutions.

The subsequent sections present the background information on multi-core image processing and CBIR, state the problem of face image retrieval and its major challenges, and describe a practical approach to the web-based FIR and a real-life application as a viable realization of the proposed method. The discussed functionality is implemented in a cross-platform *high-performance computing* (HPC) library (utilizing multi-core CPUs and GPUs) and deployed (a) in the desktop settings and (b) via the web services. Scaling to the web-based image collections is discussed in the context of a cloud environment, enabling instantaneous (sub-second) face image queries regardless of the dataset size or the computing platform it resides on.

Background

Modern image processing (e.g. ImageMagick.org, OpenGL.org) and computer vision libraries (e.g. VxL, OpenCV.org) can considerably speed-up their image processing functions by taking advantage of the available hardware, e.g. multi-core CPU (C. Kim, Kim, & Lee, 2014; Sundaram, 2012) and/or GPU (Park, Singhal, Lee, Cho, & Kim, 2011; Pulli, Baksheev, Kornyakov, & Eruhimov, 2012), especially when the library source code is available and can be compiled for particular system configurations.

Custom image processing acceleration (outside of any library) in an intuitive way is also becoming possible with the advent of the parallel processing standards (e.g. OpenACC.org) and tools, providing seamless access to high-performance hardware and significantly easing the transition from the existing sequential code to its parallel variations, allowing the programmer to focus on the algorithms, rather than on the specifics of the available HPC hardware.

Recent decades of R&D in the area of CBIR have produced meaningful web-based image-based query techniques (Dharani & Aroquiaraj, 2013), and modern web search engines (google.com, yandex.ru) now offer search by image, as presented in Figure 2: this query-by-image technique clearly tries to guess the information need expressed by the user, using various image and object features speculating on its possible semantics, but the query results perhaps make the inquirer wonder, as what is considered visually similar or relevant from the search engine's viewpoint.

The same recent decades have also seen a considerable progress in the area of face detection (FD) and face recognition (FR) technologies, in some cases approach-

Figure 2. Image query (larger left-most photo) results (smaller photos to the right of the query)
By images.google.com.

ing human-level accuracy in face detection and verification tasks, especially in the controlled environments (Jafri & Arabnia, 2009; Naruniec, 2010). There emerged some efficient web based FR solutions (facebook.com, plus.google.com) for matching faces within limited image sets of user circles, and although the implementation details of those services are proprietary, we can safely speculate that performing instantaneous image queries on the web scale has to implement parallel image processing in a cloud environment, which can occur on several levels employing multi-core CPU/GPU in distributed systems (Naik & Kusur, 2015), see Figure 3.

In spite of all the recent advances, unconstrained face recognition remains a very challenging problem with an ever-present trade-off between the accuracy and the speed, which typically needs to be balanced depending on the application (Li &

Figure 3. Several levels of parallel image processing with multi-core CPU and GPU stations clusters on a computing cloud

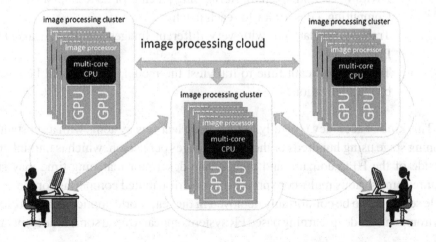

Jain, 2011). Aside from FIR, the FR application set may also include general ID verification (e.g. during passport control), face-based surveillance (e.g. in an airport), witness face reconstruction (e.g. in criminal justice), augmenting face appearance (e.g. in plastic surgery preview), etc. Some of the mentioned applications emphasize accuracy (e.g. ID verification) above speed, while others may favor speed (e.g. face-based surveillance), but most of them benefit from high performance image processing, even if the amount of the available data is not that large.

Some recent publications describe FR systems that exhibit remarkable accuracy using web-scale datasets, approaching human-level recognition rates or sometimes even beating it on certain datasets. Let us discuss these two recent systems in more detail:

- **DeepFace:** (Taigman, Yang, Ranzato, & Wolf, 2014) is closing the gap to human-level performance in face verification, where faces are assumed to be localized and use fairly high resolution (120 pixels across or better). The method is claimed to verify faces as accurately as humans do, improving the state of the art by a couple of percentage points and featuring:
    - Solid 2D (6 points) & 3D (>60 points) alignment procedure with hard commitment;
    - Multi-layer deep network approach with pre-processing;
    - Data-driven feature extraction, piece-wise affine frontalization;
    - Representation stage trained on 4M pictures with an average of 1K images per person using Social Face Classification (SFC) dataset;
    - Smart knowledge transfer step for particular datasets, Labeled Faces in the Wild database (LFW), YouTube Faces (YTF) datasets.
- **GaussianFace:** (Lu & Tang, 2014) claims to solve the face verification problem (with pre-training)
    - Normalizing each face into a 150×120 pixel image,
    - Dividing each image into overlapping patches of 25 x 25 pixels
    - Computing a descriptor for each patch
    - Training on datasets with very different images (Multi-PIE and Life Photos)
    - Taking significant time to train/test the model, which could be solved by parallelization.

This kind of accuracy typically implies deep learning systems with a substantial training stage using hundreds or thousands images per person, which is unthinkable outside of the HPC domain, and their image descriptor matching time may still require some serious multi-core processing and distributed computing for the large scale searches. To be comfortably deployed in the real-world applications in a cloud environment, the deep learning based FR systems appear to need some time to mature.

In the subsequent sections, we state the problem of the real-world face image retrieval, note its major challenges, discuss possible approaches, suggest a solution and present some of our R&D findings, expressed in the experimental results per each section.

Problem: SIPP Face Image Retrieval in Dynamic Data-Sets

Traditionally, the face recognition (FR) problem would be solved in one of the two common formulations (Zhou et al., 2014): verification (answering, if the two given photos depict the same person or not, i.e. verifying the ID by picture) or identification (searching a static set of individuals for the one closest in appearance to the query image).

Traditional FR systems require some form of statistical face model training (e.g. principal component analysis (PCA), linear discriminant analysis (LDA), etc.) or image feature based classifiers (e.g. support vector machines (SVM), artificial neural networks (ANN), hidden Markov models (HMM), etc.) typically using multiple photos per individual (Li & Jain, 2011), which is not the case in the SIPP scenarios and may be quite impractical for hundreds of thousands of individual classes.

Typical face verification systems take another route and work with a set of visual attributes extracted from images then imposing (or learning) a measure of visual similarity (Li & Jain, 2011), attempting to model (in some ways) human perception of faces, which are more applicable to the large-scale FIR, but may need routine re-training given the *dynamic* nature of the web-based datasets, hence may lack the immediate ingest/query/remove response required for addressing the problem we solve here.

While modern automatic face identification and verification systems can work quite well on good quality face images (somewhat unconstrained, but well-lit and sharp, 80×80 pixels and above), their matching performance degrades as the image quality drops (Scheirer, Kumar, Iyer, Belhumeur, & Boult, 2013) due to the significant degeneration of the visual attributes they rely on because of blurring, scaling, re-compression, etc. Unless they utilize HPC techniques, their speed of matching often renders them impractical for the real-world applications due to the amount of data they need to process.

In the web-based SIPP photo collection (implying no person-specific model training) scenario, one has to re-formulate the face matching problem in a FIR framework: given a query face photo, match it against the dynamic gallery of faces, and return the most similar (preferably of the same individual) faces, thus efficiently reducing the user's browsing space from millions to just tens of likely candidates. This dynamic (open gallery) approach gives up person-specific training and uses face match accuracy evaluation methods that are more typical of CBIR (e.g. top-N hit-rate or recall-at-threshold) rather than those traditionally used in FR (e.g. ROC: receiver operating characteristic).

A practical FIR methodology necessitates porting the available face detection and matching algorithms into the parallel computing domain, utilizing the available multi-core hardware and distributed systems. We show that this approach is feasible by implementing our SIPP face image retrieval methodology in a real-world face retrieval system (FaceMatch), putting no restrictions on input images, detecting and matching faces in arbitrary poses or lighting conditions. When scaling to web-based photo collections, FaceMatch requires no person-specific model training while dealing with open sets of images, yet it remains instantaneous and robust to the image data variability.

Let us now discuss some of the major challenges along our route to the real-world face image retrieval system, which needs to be sped-up considerably with respect to its sequential implementation, yet it needs to remain accurate and robust to any input imagery.

Unconstrained Face Detection and Matching Challenges

Unconstrained face images typically imply real-world photographs made by casual photographers using amateur photo equipment, e.g. point-and-shoot cameras. Such images typically portray faces in arbitrary head poses and with various facial expressions, typically shot in sub-optimal illumination with some degree of blurring and other image noise interfering with face detection and matching. According to the face recognition survey (Jafri & Arabnia, 2009), the facial appearance variations may be intrinsic (due to the physical nature of the face, independent of the observer) or extrinsic (due to observer-dependent factors, such as optics, lighting, viewpoint, etc.) A robust FIR system needs to deal with both categories.

In addition to the mentioned challenges, some photo collections may contain old paper photographs re-captured using some consumer-level scanners or mobile device cameras, which introduces additional noise and distortions to usually imperfect originals, hence adversely affecting any face recognition process in both accuracy and speed. Figure 4 presents some unconstrained images that pose a challenge to the modern face detection utilities (Viola & Jones, 2004) that may run at near real-time speeds on gray-scale images, but require some significant pre- and post-processing to boost their accuracy on unconstrained color images, which in-turn calls for parallel execution to run in real time.

In spite of all the FR progress reported in the literature (Naruniec, 2010; Zhou et al., 2014), there are still very few publicly available SIPP face image retrieval systems that work efficiently and accurately with dynamic collections of millions of unconstrained face images (as in Figure 1 and Figure 4), as there may still be

Figure 4. Challenging unconstrained images for modern face detection tools: Circles denote candidates, where false negatives may be caused by unconstrained head pose or facial hair, while false positives may indicate face-like patterns

many challenges to successfully implement such a system in practice, especially targeting open-to-public applications, such as post-disaster recovery (Thoma et al., 2012):

- (Extrinsic) sub-optimal quality of both query and data-set images (e.g. blur, noise, and compression) affect face detection and matching by interfering with the feature extraction;
- (Extrinsic) partial face occlusion, non-frontal head poses or partial face damage cause some of the key features to be absent from the detection or matching process;
- (Intrinsic) inconsistency in face appearance (e.g. expression, aging, facial hair, glasses, jewelry, etc.) confuse face detectors and matchers with extra features that are not present in the original.

Many of those challenges are being addressed by the modern FR systems thanks to the emergence of the annotated datasets with unconstrained images and the various face image matching competitions (Beveridge et al., 2013; G. B. Huang, Ramesh, Berg, & Learned-Miller, 2007). The modern face image matching techniques working with unconstrained images utilize image features that are robust to illumination, scale and affine transformations, hence relying on a set of global and local image descriptors cultivating the mentioned properties (Bicego, Lagorio, Grosso, & Tistarelli, 2006; Dreuw, Steingrube, Hanselmann, & Ney, 2009; Rublee, Rabaud, Konolige, & Bradski, 2011). To employ the newly developed face matching techniques in the real-world systems, one inevitably needs to use parallel image processing that allows instantaneous response application behavior without compromising the image descriptor matching accuracy.

Challenges in Instantaneous Face Image Retrieval

Sizes of the modern photo collections easily reach millions of photos with multiple near-duplicates (visually very similar, but not exact copies, e.g. due to resampling or recompression). The larger the datasets become, the more one needs to advance the image processing algorithms implementations to the HPC domain, utilizing the available multi-core hardware architectures and distributed systems.

Any real-world face image retrieval system typically involves a large number of basic image processing tasks (e.g. smoothing, resampling, color space conversion, histogram equalization), non-trivial image processing steps (e.g. face/landmark localization, saliency map computing, key-spot detection, visual descriptor computing and comparison), and maintenance processing (e.g. near-duplicate image detection, descriptor clustering, bucketing and indexing), many of which can and should take advantage of parallel computing techniques.

Given a query face image, the goal is to match its visual descriptor against the repository of the existing face descriptors, and output a list of likely face candidates ordered by similarity. Practical FIR methods usually cannot assume that many faces of the same subject are present in the database, thus no person-specific model can be utilized for recognition, but rather some HPC image matching algorithms should be utilized to maintain instantaneous response behavior within the acceptable retrieval accuracy requirements.

Solution: Practical Face Image Retrieval System

Given the availability of multi-core computing systems often equipped with GPUs and connected via fast networks, it is possible to address many of the mentioned CBIR challenges and build a practical system handling web-based image collections, providing meaningful visual query results at real-time turn-around periods.

Here we focus on a SIPP face matching methodology and present a real-world face image retrieval system (FaceMatch) that implements it, putting no restrictions on its input images, detecting and matching faces in arbitrary poses or lighting conditions, requiring no person-specific models while dealing with open sets of digital photos. Handling web-based photo collections, FaceMatch utilizes parallel computing power from the available multi-core CPUs and GPUs, and serves its functionality efficiently via the web services, hence taking advantage of the distributed system architecture. The major components of the FaceMatch system are:

- **Color-Based Skin Tone Mapper:** (FaceRegionDetector) component for color based image segmentation trained to return skin presence probability for each pixel in the image, implemented as Artificial Neural Net (ANN).

- **Color-Aware Face Detector:** (FaceFinder) component for localization of faces/profiles and their major landmarks, e.g. eyes, ears, nose, and mouth.
- **Color-Aware Face Matcher:** (ImageMatcherFaceRegions) component for extraction of face descriptors, indexing them and answering face-specific visual queries.
- **Color-Aware Image Matcher:** (ImageMatcherWhole) component for extraction of image descriptors, indexing them and answering whole-image visual queries and detecting near-duplicates.

All of the mentioned components are implemented and assembled in a cross-platform FaceMatch library (FM.lib) and are described in details in the subsequent sub-sections. Figure 5 presents a high-level overview FM.lib, its major modules and their dependencies: most of the image processing is opportunistically pushed to the available GPU boards via OpenCV and its CUDA SDK bindings, while multi-core CPU gets utilized for macro operations via dynamic and intuitive OpenMP multi-threading. Our experience with OpenCV (utilizing multi-core Intel.com CPU via OpenMP.org and NVIDIA.com GPU via CUDA SDK) suggests that such custom compilation is quite advisable, as our performance results indicate similar (to CPU) accuracy with a considerable increase in the computing speed: image resampling (×15), color-space conversion (×20), visual descriptor computing and comparison (×18) with respect to the serial CPU processing.

In the following sub-sections, we present the major components of our FaceMatch system in order of the information flow and discuss our experimental results. We further describe how we deployed FaceMatch in a web-based family re-unification system to help fuse text-based searches with the visual search modality by drasti-

Figure 5. FaceMatch library major modules and their dependencies

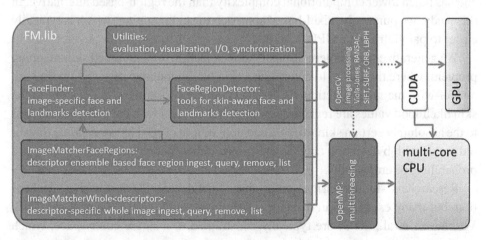

cally reducing the search space to just a few relevant records for the user (e.g. a hospital worker or a relative) to review, minimizing the manual browsing time. Each section describes a FaceMatch module, its underlying methodology, provides relevant citations and comparisons to the existing systems via experimental results, including the accuracy assessments, as well as the corresponding speed-up figures from the employed HPC techniques.

Color Based Skin Tone Mapping

Robust color blob segmentation is an important image processing task that can be used in the early stages of object segmentation. Automatic skin detection is an important special case of the two-class image segmentation (Bouwmans, 2014), as it can help in many human-centric machine vision tasks, including face detection and tracking. It has been shown empirically that the human skin color under non-extreme lighting lies in a specific color range (Vezhnevets, Sazonov, & Andreeva, 2003), but that does not mean that automatic skin detection is a trivial problem, as many existing skin detection systems often face extra challenges, e.g. confusing surfaces with skin-like tones, abnormal lighting conditions, facial make-up, specular reflections due to moisture, incorrect camera settings, etc.

Image processing researchers typically distinguish between color classification methods for skin detection: pixel-based (Chaves-González, Vega-Rodríguez, Gómez-Pulido, & Sánchez-Pérez, 2010; Kakumanu, Makrogiannis, & Bourbakis, 2007; Khan, Hanbury, Stöttinger, & Bais, 2012), operating on individual pixels, and region-based (Kruppa, Bauer, & Schiele, 2002), considering both color information and location information. Region-based methods are typically slower, but may be more accurate as they account for more context than their pixel-based competitors. However, pixel-based color classification is more robust to the affine transforms and has much lower computational complexity than the region-based alternative. In this study, we pursue the pixel-based approach to skin mapping, which is typically easier to parallelize on a GPU.

We generalize the problem of binary skin detection to real-valued skin mapping problem, where the task is to determine a skin likelihood map over any image with a pixel-wise mapping function $s: C \to [0,1]$, where C is some color space and the skin likelihood values are real numbers in the range $[0,1]$ with the extremes mapped to the absolutely certain skin, $s(c)=1$, and non-skin, $s(c)=0$. The appropriate threshold for skin blob detection can be determined either theoretically (e.g. when s is a probability) or empirically.

Researchers studied various color spaces (Malacara, 2002) for skin localization, but many existing skin detectors (Kakumanu et al., 2007; Khan et al., 2012; Vezhnevets et al., 2003) are typically constrained to a single color space, which may limit the classification accuracy. To overcome this, we combine values from several color spaces in a composite feature vector by concatenating the individual color band values. Machine learning (ML) solutions (Khan et al., 2012) may be quite accurate at skin color detection. With the data-driven approach, we researched a variety of skin mapping methods (parametric and non-parametric), and decided to develop an ML solution based on artificial neural network (ANN), as the most accurate in our experiments.

Artificial Neural Network Based Skin Mapper

An artificial neural network (ANN) can learn a skin likelihood map using a labeled dataset (Jones & Rehg, 2002) with skin and non-skin pixels. A fully connected multi-layer perceptron based (T. Kim & Adali, 2002) ANN with a single hidden layer is proposed to model the binary decision surface in Extended Color Space (ECS: a composite multi-dimensional color space, e.g. [RGB, HSV, Lab]), as shown in Figure 6. The input layer corresponds to the number of color components describing the analyzed pixel, while the output layer contains two neurons (units) to distinguish between skin and non-skin.

The number of units in the hidden layer was set experimentally to 15. The neural training adapts its weights during each epoch (a step in the training process of an artificial neural network) invoking back-propagation learning strategy, which assures a certain optimum. In our experiments, the learning rate $\alpha = 0.02$ and the momentum $\beta = 0.08$ were considered during ANN training.

Figure 6. An artificial neural network (ANN) architecture for skin classification in Extended Color Space (ECS)

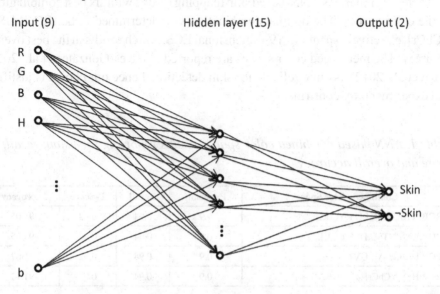

Skin Mapper Experiments

The ANN-based skin classifier was evaluated on images acquired by the family re-unification system (Thoma et al., 2012) during various disaster events (Haiti, Turkey, New Zealand, Japan, etc.) The images include a large range of skin tones, environments, cameras, resolutions, and illumination conditions. The quality of the images varies significantly in illumination, resolution and sharpness. Overall, 7680 images were used with 7M skin and 5M non-skin pixels. A three-fold cross validation scenario was considered. The pixels used in training/testing do not overlap, as they come from different images. Several metrics from information retrieval were considered:

Precision = TP / (TP+FP), Recall = TP / (TN+FN),
Accuracy = (TP+TN) / (TP+TN+FP+FN), and
F-score = 2×Precision×Recal / (Precision + Recall),

where the respective counts are TP = true positive, i.e. skin pixels classified as skin; TN = true negative, i.e. non-skin pixels classified as non-skin; FP = false positive, i.e. non-skin classified as skin; and FN = false negative, i.e. skin classified as non-skin.

We have experimented with ANN-based skin mapper in several commonly used color spaces, e.g. RGB, Lab, NTSC, HSV, Luv, and YCbCr (Kakumanu et al., 2007) and picked the ones that were most discriminative in our tests. We have injected the sampled RGB color point into ECS, which provided a more robust skin tone clustering, highly effective feature analysis, and subsequent skin tone classification.

Table 1 summarizes ANN-based skin mapping results with six best combinations of the color spaces. The optimal combination was determined to be [RGB, HSV, YCbCr], effectively spanning a 9-dimensional ECS, which results in the best overall accuracy. The mentioned color spaces are reported (Chaves-González et al., 2010; Khan et al., 2012) as quite reliable for skin detection, hence our choice is justified and experimentally confirmed.

Table 1. ANN based combined color spaces results reporting precision, recall, F-score and overall accuracy

Combined Color Space	Precision	Recall	F-Score	Accuracy
[RGB,NTSC,HSV,LUV,YCbCr]	0.9	0.94	0.92	91.05
[RGB,LAB,NTSC,HSV,LUV]	0.9	0.94	0.92	91.05
[RGB,LAB,HSV,LUV]	0.9	0.94	0.92	91.07
[RGB,HSV,YCbCr]	0.9	0.94	0.92	**91.12**

The major advantage of this data-driven approach is its generalization power to modeling of the unknown skin tone distribution, resulting in the higher skin mapping accuracy, compared to the histogram or parametric based approaches. The main limitation is its low (sequential) computing speed and much longer training time, compared to the competing methods. We decided to overcome this shortcoming by implementing our ANN on a GPU (Bharangar, Doeger, & Mittal, 2013), efficiently parallelizing the matrix-vector multiplications in single or double floating point number precision, depending on the available hardware.

Propagation of an input vector from one ANN layer to the next can see significant speed-ups on large networks. On smaller networks, however, if input feature vectors are copied on to the GPU individually, the cost of data move operations between the CPU and GPU can vastly outweigh any gains from parallelizing the matrix multiplication. To alleviate this crippling slowness, pixel data can be moved onto the GPU in groups (matrices with each row being a feature vector), and propagated through ANN in parallel, essentially performing a matrix × matrix multiplication in parallel at each layer of the network, so that the final output matrix gives an output row vector for each of the input row vectors.

The ANN for FM skin mapper has an input layer of size 9, which feeds to a layer of 15 hidden nodes to an output layer of size 2. When fully parallelized we can feed our data through ANN in larger batches to produce further speed-ups reaching about ×10 using 1K input vectors, as shown in Figure 7.

Figure 7. GPU vs. CPU based ANN speed-up levels for progressively larger input batches

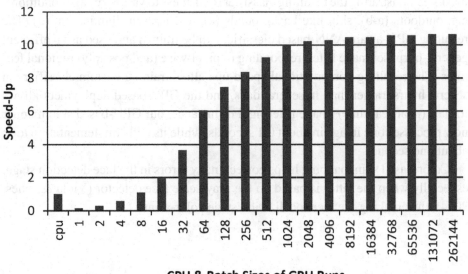

CPU & Batch Sizes of GPU Runs

Figure 8. Skin mapping using ANN: green pixels denote skin above threshold

Note that running less than 8 signals through the network at a time performs slower than the CPU because of the expensive CPU/GPU memory transfer. Starting at 16 input vectors, the GPU starts performing better (at 2 times of the CPU speed) and rises in performance from there with increasing batch sizes up to 1024, before speed-up increases slow down at 2K inputs, where the speed limiting factor is the size of our ANN. Speed-up can be greater for larger networks, for instance running the same input against a $9 \times 1024 \times 1024 \times 2$ network, the GPU can better parallelize the network and get a speed-up of about 100 times the CPU's performance.

Our experiments clearly show the GPU's ability to handle large ANNs (e.g. convolution networks for deep learning), but for our skin mapping purposes, one hidden layer double the size of the input suffices to reach the desired accuracy. The CPU in use was an Intel Xeon W3520, 2.67GHz and the GPU in use was an NVIDIA GeForce GTX 750Ti, 640 cores, 1020 MHz GPU.

Figure 8 illustrates the ANN-based skin mapping labeling skin pixels as green masks demonstrating the resulting classifier robustness to various image conditions, e.g. outdoors (a-b), skin-like backgrounds (c), and uneven illumination (d). The resulting GPU-aware ANN-based classifier can be trained and used as an efficient general-purpose image filter, responding to pixel-wise (and possibly) regional features. The resulting computational speed-ups allow training custom classifiers in several hours, rather than in several days, and the GPU-based deployment allows for fast (near real time) image filtering. For instance, our GPU-based skin mapper now processes one image in about 0.1 seconds, while its CPU implementation took about one second.

Color-based skin mapping helps correct many errors in the face detection stage, especially when the latter is based on the gray-scale face detector (Viola & Jones, 2004), thus making the face localization stage color-aware.

Color-Aware Face Detection

Reliable face localization is the first critical step in any face matching application. Color-blind face detection has been well researched and some efficient detectors have been developed (Zhang & Zhang, 2010). Some of those detectors can run in near-real time even sequentially (Viola & Jones, 2004). However, they typically come with pre-trained models that may work well for the near-frontal views of faces, but fail on many unconstrained images where faces could be arbitrarily positioned, occluded, blurred or sub-optimally lit, as in Figure 4: skin color mapping can correct those detection errors.

To improve on this base-line face detection accuracy, we propose to use color as one the most important cues for face (and its landmarks) presence or absence (Deng & Pei, 2008; Hsu, Abdel-Mottaleb, & Jain, 2002). To have the resulting color-aware detector run at similar near real-time speeds as the base, we propose to utilize GPU boards for gray-scale face detection, skin color mapper and basic image processing, while running these major components on separate CPU cores using OpenMP multi-threading techniques, thus keeping our code very readable and portable.

Efficient facial features (landmarks) detection quickly gains importance for the ever increasing dominance of the high-resolution face images. A survey on facial features detection (Naruniec, 2010) presents a good overview of the face and landmark localization algorithms divided in the following groups:

- **Appearance Based Methods:** Allow arbitrary image pattern detection, some run in real-time, but depend on a representative training set, and could require long training time, e.g. weeks if not accelerated.
- **Knowledge-Based Algorithms:** Are simple and fast, but their accuracy is often worse than the others.
- **Geometric Models:** Are often bound to one face/profile and usually allow localization of only one face in the image with the advantage that in most of the solutions no unrealistic shapes can appear.
- **3D Vision Based Models:** Deliver more information than 2D and therefore allow more efficient classification, but usually assume, that the tip of the nose is the closest point to the device, and their data acquisition is often expensive and slow, if precise; or coarse and error prone, if fast.

An interesting method for the hierarchical classification approach to face detection (Hoffmann, Naruniec, Yazdani, & Ebrahimi, 2008) was made via Discrete Gabor Jets (DGJ) being used for extracting brightness-related features (for preliminary classification) with a skin detection algorithm employed, showing that the use of color efficiently reduces the number of false positives while maintaining a high true positive rate. In comparison with the Viola-Jones Face Detector (VJFD), this method shows higher correct detection rates. Our face detection strategy (although not using DGJ) goes further and attempts to recover some false negatives by locally enhancing the likely skin patches for the VJFD to re-iterate.

In the following sub-sections we present our multi-threaded approach to face localization and present some experimental results, comparing it to other modern commercial and open-source face detection systems.

FaceFinder Assembly

Our face localization sub-module (called FaceFinder) is an ensemble of three algorithms working together: gray-scale face detector, real-valued skin mapper, and color-based landmark detector. As shown in Figure 9, taking advantage of the available hardware that allows parallel execution for more flexible asynchronous computation.

All of the major components take advantage of any number of GPU boards (when they are available), and multi-core CPU dynamically assigning threads to the available hardware modules, using a named lock array to synchronize the execution. For example, when two GPU boards are available, we schedule two CPU threads to run the GPU-aware versions of our base detector in parallel: one for detecting the frontal views, and another for the profile views. The landmarks (eyes, nose, mouth, ears) for each detected face region are also detected in parallel using dynamic thread

Figure 9. FaceFinder major components (blue boxes) with data items (gray boxes) and parallel execution flow

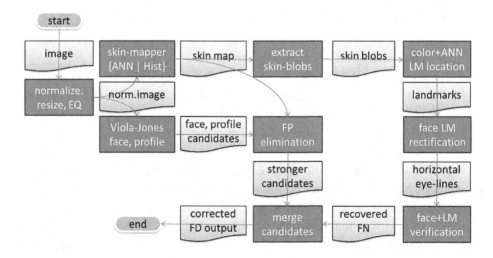

Figure 10. Corrected face detection using real-valued skin map and landmarks

scheduling intuitively using OpenMP parallel loop facilities, opportunistically using GPU, assembling the detection results and reporting all thread-specific exceptions after the final synchronization point, properly locking the accumulators of the results.

Our base gray-scale detector (Viola & Jones, 2004) aside from detecting frontal and profile views in parallel, is also made robust to rotation by executing it (also in parallel) on rotated versions of the input image with the angular step of πk/6, k=0:11. All angle-specific steps are performed in separate threads utilizing GPU, e.g. for image rotation as well as for less trivial object detection. Since GPU-aware face detection is about 12-times faster than CPU-based, the overall process recalls more face/profile candidates and runs at about the same speed as the non-GPU aware single position version, hence resulting in an average ×12 speed-up with good robustness to rotations.

Our real-valued skin mapping module (run in parallel with the base detector) helps diminish the non-skin regions (reducing some false alarms) and enhance the large skin blobs (recovering some missing face candidates). The color enhanced large skin blobs are then run through the color-based landmark (eyes, mouth) detector (Hsu et al., 2002), which helps identify them as face candidates that can be rectified by their eye lines and re-inspected by another instance the base face localizer for new possible faces not found originally by the gray-scale face detector.

We observe the results of our FaceFinder major steps in Figure 10: base detection (a) gets corrected by computing the real-valued skin color map (b), which is used to remove the false detection and recover the missing candidates by landmark localization and eye-line rectification (c) to produce the output (d).

FaceFinder Experiments

To evaluate the face detection accuracy of FaceFinder, we have considered a variety of image collections:

- **HEPL-500 Data Collection:** A set of 500 Haiti 2010 Earthquake images, containing a large variety of (small and large) faces in unconstrained environments. Many of them are over-exposed, blurry or occluded as shown in Figure 1.
- **FDDB:** A benchmark image collection (http://vis-www.cs.umass.edu/fddb/) containing 5,171 faces in 2,845 images with variable quality photos, challenging lighting and expressions (V. Jain & Learned-Miller, 2010).
- **Caltech Face Collection:** (http://www.vision.caltech.edu/html-files/archive.html) Containing some 450 images of 27 different persons.

For evaluation, we have used the traditional for information retrieval metrics: R=Recall, P=Precision and F=F-score, defined as

$$R = M/S, P = M/D, F = 2PR/(P+R),$$

where respective counts are M=Match, S=Source, and D=Destination. M was incremented every time there was enough of overlap between the detected and the source region, known from the pre-annotated ground-truth data. The overlap of two rectangular face regions A and B can be calculated as $L = \dfrac{|A \cap B|}{|A \cup B|}$, and if $L > 0.5$, we considered that a match.

Table 2 summarizes the accuracy figures for the baseline (VJFD) system, our skin-/landmark-aware FaceFinder, a leading OpnSrc (Zhu & Ramanan, 2012) system, a commercial mobile face detector (CmrMbl), and a commercial face SDK (FaceSDK). Overall, our FaceFinder accuracy is on par with or better than the leading commercial and open-source face detectors we tested. The benefits of our face detection sub-system tested on real-world data can be summarized as follows:

- Recovering faces missed by the base-line detection stage,
- Overruling false alarms by eliminating non-skin regions,
- Detecting rotated faces by recovering their landmarks.

Our color-aware face detection method is robust to the affine transformations, lighting and image noise. Provided enough of the CPU/GPU power, our adaptive cross-platform multi-core implementation is more accurate than its base-line Viola-Jones (VJ) face detector, yet it runs on average at about the same speed as the CPU-based VJ implementation on the same hardware, effectively providing the 10-12 times speed-up due to the multi-core utilization.

Table 2. Face detection accuracy on different data-sets

Data	Methods	Recall	Precision	F-Score
HEPL-500	VJFD	0.76	0.87	0.81
	FaceFinder	**0.81**	0.84	**0.82**
	CmrMbl	0.68	0.87	0.76
	FaceSDK	0.73	0.87	0.79
	OpnSrc	0.33	0.92	0.49
FDDB	VJFD	0.6	0.8	0.69
	FaceFinder	0.74	**0.88**	**0.80**
	CmrMbl	0.63	0.76	0.69
	FaceSDK	**0.64**	**0.85**	**0.73**
	OpnSrc	0.61	0.79	0.69
CalTech	VJFD	0.95	0.88	0.91
	FaceFinder	**0.98**	**0.97**	**0.98**
	CmrMbl	0.97	0.98	0.97
	FaceSDK	0.96	0.94	0.95
	OpnSrc	0.97	**0.97**	0.97

The described FaceFinder functionality is utilized in the subsequent color-aware face matching and retrieval stages, whenever reliable face detection is needed, e.g. during ingest or query requests.

Color-Aware Face Matching and Retrieval

The FaceMatch (FM) system understands *face matching* as SIPP face recognition (FR) approach utilized for near real-time searches in large collections of face images shot in unconstrained environments, i.e. arbitrary resolution, scale, illumination, etc. Our *face retrieval* problem is different from a typical FR problem set, being neither 1:1 verification (as our decision is not binary) nor 1:N identification (as our image sets are dynamic and SIPP).

Face recognition (FR) in general conditions remains to be an open problem that's being researched actively (Azeem, Sharif, Raza, & Murtaza, 2014; Jafri & Arabnia, 2009; Sharif, Mohsin, & Javed, 2012). Beham (Beham & Roomi, 2013) gives a good overview of FR techniques and divides them in the following major groups (holistic, feature-based, and soft-computing), providing normalized accuracy (NA) figures, pointing out their advantages and disadvantages.

Unconstrained SIPP face retrieval from a large, dynamically changing (open-set) reference gallery basically requires its face matching to be

- Training-less, or quickly and incrementally trainable
- Robust to noise, pose, occlusion, expression and lighting
- Very fast to be scalable

essentially modeling human perception of unfamiliar faces from a single photo and utilizing very fast visual indexing for efficiency.

Several very promising methods (Gao & Qi, 2005; A. K. Jain, Klare, & Park, 2012; Tan, Chen, Zhou, & Zhang, 2006) have been proposed over the past decade. Ma et al. (Ma, Su, & Jurie, 2014) presented a biologically inspired approach to person re-identification and face verification that relies on the combination of Gabor filter and some covariance features, which can be robust to background and illumination variations, capable of working with a single photo per person. However, FaceMatch uses a much cheaper to compute ensemble of features deployed in a multi-core parallel processing framework.

In the following sub-sections we present and discuss our face image retrieval facility called ImageMatcher that is robust to image noise, transformations, lighting and occlusions.

ImageMatcher: Efficient and Robust Face Image Retrieval

Given a dynamically changing repository of images, we propose a methodology for scalable visual search, effectively solving the face image retrieval problem. Face matching queries can be performed after the face/profile regions in the image collection are localized and their descriptors are indexed. The proposed method accommodates wide variations in face appearance mentioned in the introduction.

We experimented with several image descriptor-based object matching techniques, e.g. SIFT-based (Lowe, 2004) energy minimization method called SoftCBIR (Luo, Dementhon, Yu, & Doermann, 2006), Local Binary Pattern Histograms (LBPH) (Ahonen, Hadid, & Pietikäinen, 2004). Among the training-less single-descriptor face matching methods, we decided to focus on rotation and scale invariant key-spot descriptor based matching (e.g. SIFT, SURF, and ORB), compare them with the holistic descriptors (color HAAR and LBPH), and then consider an ensemble of image descriptors.

Figure 11 presents two key-spot matching examples with SIFT descriptors. The left pair shows matches between two different photos of the same person: the number of correctly matched locations is relatively high. The right pair shows the faces that belong to different people: there are evidently fewer sensible matching

Figure 11. Key-point matching based on face and its landmarks

 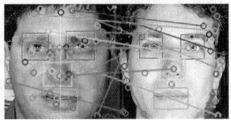

locations, e.g. note the wrongly matched key-spots at the boundaries the faces. After experiments with several datasets, we realized that

- Single descriptor is insufficient for accurate retrieval,
- Some key-spot matches need to be filtered as outliers,
- Face landmarks help filter and weigh the matches, and
- Running matchers based on different descriptors in parallel is efficient.

Having several image descriptors per face (HAAR, SURF, SIFT, ORB, LBPH), we experimented with similarity distance-based and similarity rank-based feature combination strategies.

While dealing with multiple face image datasets (with about 20K images per set), our system is required to retrieve face images within sub-second turn-around time intervals. To accomplish that, we researched and developed the *attribute bucketing* strategy, utilizing multi-core parallel processing. We have noticed that along with the images our records typically carry gender and age groups meta-information, which allowed us to partition the search space into a number of age and gender groups (called buckets), which we *query in parallel* using dynamic multi-threading. This allowed us to speed-up our query turn-around times by a factor of 3×3=9 (the number of age times gender buckets), as in Figure 12: typical bucket levels are shown in different colors.

Face Image Retrieval Experiments

To balance out the uneven levels in the buckets, we introduced sub-bucketing within groups (dynamically limiting the sub-bucket size around 1K records) and have enough of CPU cores to handle the parallel queries, whose results were merged also in *parallel* (Knuth, 1998) dynamically allocating multiple processing cores: as soon as one thread finishes, it is assigned to a more populated bucket or to a pending results merge chunk.

Figure 12. Bucketing by attribute values (age and gender) with the typical levels of records in each bucket

	male	female	unknown
youth	low	low	medium
adult	low	low	medium
unknown	medium	medium	high

This allowed us to boost the speed-ups to ×20 compared to the sequential execution (as was shown in our experiments using multiple runs of 100 parallel image queries), while keeping basically the same accuracy, as shown in Table 3. FaceMatch FIR accuracy figures on CalTech Faces (vision.caltech.edu/html-files/archive.html) and ColorFERET (nist.gov/itl/iad/ig/colorferet.cfm) sets are similar, reaching the statistically guaranteed retrieval in top-20 queries; and the accuracy on IndianFacesDB (vis-www.cs.umass.edu/~vidit/IndianFaceDatabase/) is lower due to the wider out-of-plane rotations of the head. We define the top-n hit rate as

$$HitRate(n) = HitCount(n,Q)/|Q|$$

i.e. the average number of successful top-n hits for the query set Q of size |Q|.

FaceMatch System Integration

The core FaceMatch (FM) imaging code is written in C++. It relies on open source libraries (e.g. STL, OpenCV, OpenMP) and on some proprietary ones (CUDA), taking advantage of the available multi-core and accelerated graphics hardware. This makes it usable for desktop applications or over the internet as web services. The key focus during the web integration into a web-based family re-unification system was to ensure the top performance across all FaceMatch operations:

Table 3. FaceMatch top-N hit rate accuracy figures on several data-sets

Top-N	CalTech	IndianFacesDB	ColorFERET
1	0.98	0.79	0.98
3	0.98	0.85	0.98
5	0.99	0.87	0.99
10	0.99	0.90	0.99
20	1	0.92	1

- **List:** Print out the contents of an index with various levels of detail.
- **Ingest:** Extract face image descriptors and index them to answer subsequent visual queries.
- **Query:** Visual query into the visual index using face image descriptors.
- **Remove:** Delete a range of visual index entries, specified by the caller.

FaceMatch web services link to FM.lib and expose its HPC functionality to the client applications executing its major components asynchronously and can answer multiple queries while ingesting or removing descriptors with a sub-second turn-around time, regardless of the data-set size, provided enough of the CPU cores and the GPU threads.

Figure 13 shows an example of a visual query performed using FaceMatch integrated into a publicly available system for family re-unification (via the exposed web services): the results are shown in the order of increasing visual distance to the query image: the first row shows the faces that are most similar to the query face left-to-right, the second row results are more distant, then the ones in the first, etc.

Figure 13. Sample visual query using FaceMatch web services integrated in a family re-unification web application

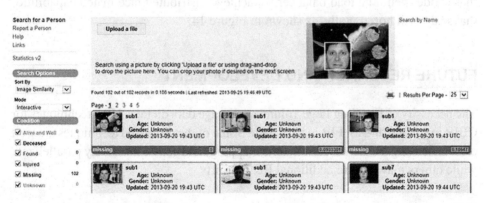

The next logical step would be to discuss FaceMatch adaptation to the cloud environment, and discuss its scalability with respect to the unknown (and potentially unlimited) web-based unconstrained image data-sets.

Face Image Retrieval Cloud

The proposed face image retrieval core library typically runs on as single computing node (with a multi-core CPU and a set of GPUs), and it can be deployed in a public cloud, such as Azure Service Bus (AWS), via a distributed system adaptor that enables the system to scale horizontally, which we call FaceMatch Service Bus (FSB). FSB proposes to leverage local (ActiveMQ, JMS) or public cloud based Queue Services (Azure Service Bus or Amazon Simple Queue Service) to save and distribute asynchronous inbound conversations with any FaceMatch node to other nodes in its cluster.

Each node in the FSB architecture is made aware of the other nodes in its cluster and manages a private message queue for each node present in its configuration file. The queues store the incoming image ingest requests with the face localization values. These requests are then forwarded asynchronously to other nodes in the cluster.

A dedicated thread running in each node's FaceMatch web service pops the ingest messages for each node and forwards it by a web service call to that node. Once the ingest returns successfully, it marks the message as processed before moving on to the next message that needs to be forwarded. This process continues until it has finished processing all the remaining unmarked messages from its queue.

In the event the destination node becomes unavailable, messages for it are sent at a later time when it comes back online. Since ingests with localized faces are very efficient at every node in the system, the entire system rapidly becomes coherent and consistent across all nodes. Thus horizontal scalability is cheaply achieved.

When a query request comes in, it is handled at a single node as it has the complete index and is processed at its node with no forwarding necessary. By placing these nodes behind a load balancer we achieve distributed face match capabilities that scale well horizontally, as shown in Figure 14.

FUTURE RESEARCH AND DEVELOPMENT

The necessity of handling large volumes of image data dictates HPC techniques for CBIR in general and for FIR in particular. Some of the discussed techniques are well established (e.g. ANN-based skin tone mapping) and can be massively parallelized, while others may require additional R&D efforts.

Figure 14. Face image retrieval cloud architecture with multiple FaceMatch (FM) nodes

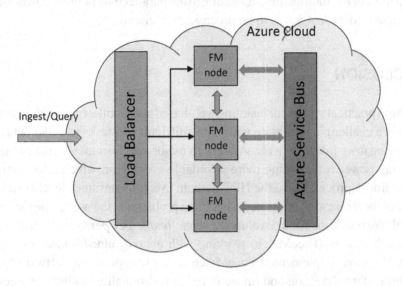

We plan to expand on the parallel processing within FaceMatch, making it even faster and more adaptable to the existing hardware. For example, one could take advantage of the GPU streaming (J. Kim, Kim, Lee, & Lee, 2011) when ingesting and indexing large batches of image descriptors in parallel. Generalization power of the GPU-aware fast ANN makes it possible to train and use image filters for multi-class object segmentation and recognition tasks that take into account more complex features than pixel color.

A more general purpose classification with elements of deep learning becomes a possibility as well, e.g. for automatic gender, age and ethnicity estimation. Modeling visual perception of object appearance also becomes possible, e.g. learning the implicit face/object visual similarity function given a large number of similar and dissimilar examples. We also plan to expand the number of applications for our public FaceMatch services. Those may include visual search for missing children and pets, as well as detecting disaster scenes and segmenting people in them.

We are currently researching the *human-in-the-loop* (HiL) approach for naturally merging FIR with annotation, making both more efficient via semi-supervised and incremental machine learning techniques as well as via more natural human-computer interactions, which may include the development of more convenient game-like visual annotation tools, and use of crowd-sourcing for developing more comprehensive testing and evaluations data sets, including video, because mobile technology tends to generate an increasing amount of moving pictures often with characteristic audio tracks, quite useful for practical face and object image retrieval. All of this requires moving most of the multimedia processing to the parallel multi-core hardware, given the amount of data that needs to be processed efficiently.

CONCLUSION

Targeting a practical system for handling web-based photo collections with real-world images is a challenging problem with many difficult sub-tasks to solve, where the size of often nosy image data is considered a major one. Fortunately, the multi-core processing power is becoming more affordable every year, which allows pushing much of image processing to the HPC domain even on consumer-level computers.

One of the interesting multimedia handling problems is the web-scale face image retrieval. We researched and developed a *single-image-per-person* (SIPP) query-by-photo methodology (FaceMatch) working with unconstrained images of variable quality. We have implemented FaceMatch as a cross-platform software library, exposing its face detection and image retrieval functionality via the web-services, which can be consumed by real-world applications, such as efficient photo collection search for the disasters management, missing children location, and medical images management.

To achieve the user-friendly instantaneous performance on the web-based image data-sets (e.g. 20K records per disaster event or more, as in family reunification system), we parallelized our critical image processing and information retrieval algorithms taking advantage of the available multi-core CPUs and massively parallel GPUs, providing for a practical FIR system. In particular, we have implemented accurate

- GPU-aware ANN-based color mapper for skin detection
- GPU-aware, multi-core CPU driven object detector for face localization
- Multi-core CPU driven face image matching and retrieval

with an average ×10 (or more) speed-up across the system in presence of the appropriate hardware. The system is expected to scale virtually linearly with the number of the available GPU accelerators and CPU cores and can be deployed in the cloud environment, handling web-based image datasets of virtually any size without sacrificing its performance in accuracy or speed.

The proposed FaceMatch methodology compares favorably to some of the available FR solutions (e.g, facebook.com, plus.google.com) in several ways, exhibiting these major advantages:

- Training-less, as dictated by SIPP that works with dynamic image sets with cheap re-indexing.
- Robust to input image quality, resolution, compression.
- Cross-platform, yet very light-weight and efficient.
- Tolerant to the affine and non-linear image transformations.
- Easily deployable on any scale from desktop to the cloud.

Some of the FaceMatch features can also bring various limitations to the system that uses its functionality, for example:

- Managing descriptors (not images) shifts the image management to the client.
- Lack of training may cause suboptimal recognition rates, compared to trainable systems.
- Suggested cloud architecture may require custom integration of the exposed web-services.

In our view, the overall positive impact outweighs the shortcomings of the approach, which may be improved with some additional R&D efforts in the directions of incremental learning for skin mapping, face detection (C. Huang, Ai, Yamashita, Lao, & Kawade, 2007; Sharma, Huang, & Nevatia, 2012) and matching (S. Kim, Mallipeddi, & Lee, n.d.; Ozawa, Toh, Abe, Pang, & Kasabov, 2005), as well as further image processing and computer vision tasks parallelization using multi-core computing.

ACKNOWLEDGMENT

This research is supported by the Intramural Research Program of the National Library of Medicine, National Institutes of Health. We would like to express our special thanks to Michael Gill and Lan Le for helping with image annotation efforts.

REFERENCES

Ahonen, T., Hadid, A., & Pietikäinen, M. (2004). Face recognition with local binary patterns. In *Proceedings of the European Conference on Computer Vision* (pp. 469–481). Springer.

Azeem, A., Sharif, M., Raza, M., & Murtaza, M. (2014). A survey: Face recognition techniques under partial occlusion. *Int. Arab J. Inf. Technol., 11*(1), 1–10.

Beham, M. P., & Roomi, S. M. M. (2013). A Review Of Face Recognition Methods. *International Journal of Pattern Recognition and Artificial Intelligence*, 27(4). doi:10.1142/S0218001413560053

Beveridge, J. R., Phillips, P. J., Bolme, D. S., Draper, B., Givens, G. H., Lui, Y. M., ... Cheng, S. (2013). The challenge of face recognition from digital point-and-shoot cameras. In *Biometrics: Theory, Applications and Systems (BTAS), 2013 IEEE Sixth International Conference on* (pp. 1–8). http://doi.org/ doi:<ALIGNMENT.qj></ALIGNMENT>10.1109/BTAS.2013.6712704

Bharangar, D. S., Doeger, A., & Mittal, Y. K. (2013). Implementation of Fast Artificial Neural Network for Pattern Classification on Heterogeneous System. *International Journal of Scientific and Engineering Research*, 4(1).

Bicego, M., Lagorio, A., Grosso, E., & Tistarelli, M. (2006). On the use of SIFT features for face authentication. In *Conference on Computer Vision and Pattern Recognition Workshop* (pp. 35–35). IEEE. doi:10.1109/CVPRW.2006.149

Borovikov, E., Vajda, S., Lingappa, G., Antani, S., & Thoma, G. (2013). Face Matching for Post-Disaster Family Reunification. In *IEEE International Conference on Healthcare Informatics* (pp. 131–140). http://doi.org/ doi:<ALIGNMENT.qj></ALIGNMENT>10.1109/ICHI.2013.23

Bouwmans, T. (2014). Traditional and recent approaches in background modeling for foreground detection: An overview. *Computer Science Review*, 11, 31–66. doi:10.1016/j.cosrev.2014.04.001

Chaves-González, J. M., Vega-Rodríguez, M. A., Gómez-Pulido, J. A., & Sánchez-Pérez, J. M. (2010). Detecting skin in face recognition systems: A colour spaces study. *Digital Signal Processing*, 20(3), 806–823. doi:10.1016/j.dsp.2009.10.008

Cullinan, C., Wyant, C., & Frattesi, T. (2012). *Computing performance benchmarks among CPU, GPU, and FPGA (No. 030212-123508)*. MathWorks.

Deng, P., & Pei, M. (2008). Multi-View Face Detection Based on AdaBoost and Skin Color. In *Intelligent Networks and Intelligent Systems, 2008. ICINIS '08. First International Conference on* (pp. 457–460). doi:10.1109/ICINIS.2008.60

Dharani, T., & Aroquiaraj, I. L. (2013). A survey on content based image retrieval. In *Pattern Recognition, Informatics and Mobile Engineering (PRIME), 2013 International Conference on* (pp. 485–490). http://doi.org/ doi:10.1109/ICPRIME.2013.6496719

Dreuw, P., Steingrube, P., Hanselmann, H., & Ney, H. (2009). SURF-Face: Face Recognition Under Viewpoint Consistency Constraints. In *British Machine Vision Conference*. doi:10.5244/C.23.7

Gao, Y., & Qi, Y. (2005). Robust Visual Similarity Retrieval in Single Model Face Databases. *Pattern Recognition, 38*(7), 1009–1020. doi:10.1016/j.patcog.2004.12.006

Hilbert, M., & López, P. (2011). The World's Technological Capacity to Store, Communicate, and Compute Information. *Science, 332*(6025), 60–65. doi:10.1126/science.1200970 PMID:21310967

Hoffmann, U., Naruniec, J., Yazdani, A., & Ebrahimi, T. (2008). Face Detection using Discrete Gabor Jets and Color Information. In P. A. A. Assunção & S. M. M. de Faria (Eds.), *SIGMAP* (pp. 76–83). INSTICC Press.

Hsu, R.-L., Abdel-Mottaleb, M., & Jain, A. K. (2002). Face detection in color images. *IEEE Transactions on Pattern Analysis and Machine Intelligence, 24*(5), 696–706. doi:10.1109/34.1000242

Huang, C., Ai, H., Yamashita, T., Lao, S., & Kawade, M. (2007). Incremental Learning of Boosted Face Detector. In *Computer Vision, 2007. ICCV 2007. IEEE 11th International Conference on*. doi:10.1109/ICCV.2007.4408850

Huang, G. B., Ramesh, M., Berg, T., & Learned-Miller, E. (2007). *Labeled faces in the wild: A database for studying face recognition in unconstrained environments*. Amherst, MA: University of Massachusetts.

Jacobs, C. E., Finkelstein, A., & Salesin, D. H. (1995). Fast multiresolution image querying. In *Proceedings of the 22nd annual conference on Computer graphics and interactive techniques* (pp. 277–286). New York, NY: ACM.

Jafri, R., & Arabnia, H. R. (2009). A Survey of Face Recognition Techniques. *JiPS, 5*(2), 41–68.

Jain, A. K., Klare, B., & Park, U. (2012). Face Matching and Retrieval in Forensics Applications. *MultiMedia, IEEE, 19*(1), 20–20. doi:10.1109/MMUL.2012.4

Jain, V., & Learned-Miller, E. (2010). *FDDB: A Benchmark for Face Detection in Unconstrained Settings (No. UM-CS-2010-009)*. Amherst, MA: University of Massachusetts.

Jones, M., & Rehg, J. M. (2002). Statistical Color Models with Application to Skin Detection. International Journal of Computer Vision.

Kakumanu, P., Makrogiannis, S., & Bourbakis, N. (2007). A survey of skin-color modeling and detection methods. *Pattern Recognition*, *40*(3), 1106–1122. doi:10.1016/j.patcog.2006.06.010

Khan, R., Hanbury, A., Stöttinger, J., & Bais, A. (2012). Color based skin classification. *Pattern Recognition Letters*, *33*(2), 157–163. doi:10.1016/j.patrec.2011.09.032

Kim, C., Kim, J., & Lee, D. (2014). Optimizing image processing on multi-core CPUs with Intel parallel programming technologies. *Multimedia Tools and Applications*, *68*(2), 237–251. doi:10.1007/s11042-011-0906-y

Kim, J., Kim, H., Lee, J. H., & Lee, J. (2011). Achieving a Single Compute Device Image in OpenCL for Multiple GPUs. *SIGPLAN Not.*, *46*(8), 277–288. doi:10.1145/2038037.1941591

Kim, S., Mallipeddi, R., & Lee, M. (n.d.). Incremental Face Recognition: Hybrid Approach Using Short-Term Memory and Long-Term Memory. In T. Huang, Z. Zeng, C. Li, & C. Leung (Eds.), *Neural Information Processing* (Vol. 7663, pp. 194–201). Springer Berlin Heidelberg. doi:10.1007/978-3-642-34475-6_24

Kim, T., & Adali, T. (2002). Fully complex multi-layer perceptron network for nonlinear signal processing. *Journal of VLSI Signal Processing Systems for Signal, Image and Video Technology*, *32*(1-2), 29–43.

Knuth, D. E. (1998). The Art of Computer Programming: Sorting and Searching (2nd ed.; vol. 3). Redwood City, CA: Addison Wesley Longman Publishing Co., Inc.

Kruppa, H., Bauer, M. A., & Schiele, B. (2002). Skin Patch Detection in Real-World Images. In *Annual Symposium for Pattern Recognition of the DAGM* (LNCS), (vol. 2449, pp. 109–117). Springer.

Lee, K. Y., Kyung, G., Park, T. R., Kwak, J. C., & Koo, Y. S. (2015). A design of a GP-GPU based stream processor for an image processing. In *Telecommunications and Signal Processing (TSP), 2015 38th International Conference on* (pp. 535–539). http://doi.org/ doi:10.1109/TSP.2015.7296320

Li, S. Z., & Jain, A. K. (2011). *Handbook of Face Recognition* (2nd ed.). Springer Publishing Company, Incorporated. doi:10.1007/978-0-85729-932-1

Lowe, D. G. (2004). Distinctive Image Features from Scale-Invariant Keypoints. *International Journal of Computer Vision*, *60*(2), 91–110. doi:10.1023/B:VISI.0000029664.99615.94

Lu, C., & Tang, X. (2014). *Surpassing Human-Level Face Verification Performance on LFW with GaussianFace*. CoRR, abs/1404.3840

Luo, M., Dementhon, D., Yu, X., & Doermann, D. (2006). *SoftCBIR: Object Searching in videos combining keypoint matching and graduated assignment*. Academic Press.

Ma, B., Su, Y., & Jurie, F. (2014). Covariance descriptor based on bio-inspired features for person re-identification and face verification. *Image and Vision Computing*, *32*(6–7), 379–390. doi:10.1016/j.imavis.2014.04.002

Malacara, D. (2002). *Color vision and colorimetry: theory and application*. SPIE Press.

Naik, V. H., & Kusur, C. S. (2015). Analysis of performance enhancement on graphic processor based heterogeneous architecture: A CUDA and MATLAB experiment. In *Parallel Computing Technologies (PARCOMPTECH), 2015 National Conference on* (pp. 1–5). doi:10.1109/PARCOMPTECH.2015.7084519

Naruniec, J. (2010). A Survey on Facial Features Detection. *International Journal of Electronics and Telecommunications*, *56*(3), 267–272. doi:10.2478/v10177-010-0035-y

Ozawa, S., Toh, S. L., Abe, S., Pang, S., & Kasabov, N. (2005). Incremental learning for online face recognition. In *Neural Networks, 2005. IJCNN '05. Proceedings. 2005 IEEE International Joint Conference on* (Vol. 5, pp. 3174–3179). http://doi.org/ doi:10.1109/IJCNN.2005.1556435

Park, I. K., Singhal, N., Lee, M. H., Cho, S., & Kim, C. W. (2011). Design and Performance Evaluation of Image Processing Algorithms on GPUs. *Parallel and Distributed Systems. IEEE Transactions on*, *22*(1), 91–104. doi:10.1109/TPDS.2010.115

Prinslow, G. (2011). *Overview of Performance Measurement and Analytical Modeling Techniques for Multi-Core Processors*. Retrieved from http://www.cse.wustl.edu/ jain/cse567-11/ftp/multcore/

Pulli, K., Baksheev, A., Kornyakov, K., & Eruhimov, V. (2012). Real-time Computer Vision with OpenCV. *Communications of the ACM*, *55*(6), 61–69. doi:10.1145/2184319.2184337

Raoui, Y., Bouyakhf, E. H., Devy, M., & Regragui, F. (2011). Global and Local Image Descriptors for Content Based Image Retrieval and Object Recognition. *Applied Mathematical Sciences*, *5*(42), 2109–2136.

Robson, D. (2008). From CPU to GPU. *High Performance Computing for Science*, (1), 8.

Rublee, E., Rabaud, V., Konolige, K., & Bradski, G. (2011). ORB: An efficient alternative to SIFT or SURF. In *IEEE International Conference on Computer Vision* (pp. 2564 –2571). doi:10.1109/ICCV.2011.6126544

Salembier, P., & Sikora, T. (2002). *Introduction to MPEG-7: Multimedia Content Description Interface* (B. S. Manjunath, Ed.). New York, NY: John Wiley & Sons, Inc.

Scheirer, W. J., Kumar, N., Iyer, V. N., Belhumeur, P. N., & Boult, T. E. (2013). How reliable are your visual attributes? In Proceedings of SPIE (Vol. 8712, pp. 87120Q–87120Q–12). http://doi.org/ doi:10.1117/12.2018974

Sharif, M., Mohsin, S., & Javed, M. Y. (2012). A Survey: Face Recognition Techniques. *Research Journal of Applied Sciences. Engineering and Technology, 4*(23), 4979–4990.

Sharma, P., Huang, C., & Nevatia, R. (2012). Efficient incremental learning of boosted classifiers for object detection. In *Pattern Recognition (ICPR), 2012 21st International Conference on* (pp. 3248–3251).

Sundaram, N. (2012, May). *Making computer vision computationally efficient.* EECS Department, University of California, Berkeley. Retrieved from http://www.eecs.berkeley.edu/Pubs/TechRpts/2012/EECS-2012-106.html

Taigman, Y., Yang, M., Ranzato, M. A., & Wolf, L. (2014). DeepFace: Closing the Gap to Human-Level Performance in Face Verification. In *Proceedings of the IEEE Computer Society Conference on Computer Vision and Pattern Recognition.* doi:10.1109/CVPR.2014.220

Tan, X., Chen, S., Zhou, Z.-H., & Zhang, F. (2006). Face recognition from a single image per person: A survey. *Pattern Recognition, 39*(9), 1725–1745. doi:10.1016/j.patcog.2006.03.013

Thoma, G., Antani, S., Gill, M., Pearson, G., & Neve, L. (2012). People Locator: A system for family reunification. *IT Professional, 14*(3), 13–21. doi:10.1109/MITP.2012.25

Vezhnevets, V., Sazonov, V., & Andreeva, A. (2003). *A Survey on Pixel-Based Skin Color Detection Techniques.* GRAPHICON.

Viola, P., & Jones, M. (2004). Robust real-time face detection. *International Journal of Computer Vision, 57*(2), 137–154. doi:10.1023/B:VISI.0000013087.49260.fb

Zhang, C., & Zhang, Z. (2010). *A Survey of Recent Advances in Face detection.* Microsoft.

Zhou, H., Mian, A., Wei, L., Creighton, D., Hossny, M., & Nahavandi, S. (2014). Recent Advances on Singlemodal and Multimodal Face Recognition: A Survey. *Human-Machine Systems. IEEE Transactions on*, *44*(6), 701–716. doi:10.1109/THMS.2014.2340578

Zhu, X., & Ramanan, D. (2012). Face Detection, Pose Estimation, and Landmark Localization in the Wild. In *Proceedings of the IEEE Computer Society Conference on Computer Vision and Pattern Recognition*.

KEY TERMS AND DEFINITIONS

Image Descriptor: Description of the visual features of the image contents capturing elementary characteristics such as shape, color, texture, etc.

Object Classification: Supervised partitioning of a set of objects by observable attributes (features) into (disjoint) similarity classes.

Object Clustering: Unsupervised partitioning of a set of objects by observable attributes (features) into (disjoint) similarity classes, sometimes constituting a hierarchical structure.

Object Detection: In a large set of objects, finding out all those belonging to a certain similarity class.

Object Identification: (A particular case of recognition) proving that a given object indeed belongs to a similarity class being declared.

Object Recognition: For a given object, answering to what of (a priori defined) similarity classes it belongs to.

Object Verification: Asserting that the two (or more) sampled instances do represent/belong to the same (declared) identity/class.

Retrieval Hit-Rate: Percentage of the correct top-N records retrieved.

Chapter 7
Fish Monitoring, Sizing, and Detection Using Stereovision, Laser Technology, and Computer Vision

Angel Jose Rico-Diaz
University of A Coruña, Spain

Jeronimo Puertas
University of A Coruña, Spain

Alvaro Rodriguez
University of Umeå, Sweden

Maria Bermudez
University of A Coruña, Spain

ABSTRACT

Stereovision and laser techniques allow for getting knowledge about fish, mostly when they are combined with computer vision. This kind of techniques avoid to use traditional procedures such as direct observation, which are impractical or can affect the fish behavior, in task such as aquarium and fish farm management or fishway, like vertical slot fishway, evaluation. This chapter describes in a first stage, the use stereovision join with computer vision to fish monitoring and measure size of fishes. In the second part, using laser technology and computer vision to fish detection, especially in slot fishways. Vertical slot fishways are structures that are placed in rivers to allow fish to avoid obstacles such as dams, hydroelectric plants. Then, it shows a results section and finally authors' conclusions.

DOI: 10.4018/978-1-5225-0889-2.ch007

1. INTRODUCTION

Inspection of the appearance or behavior of fishes can provide a variety of information regarding the fish species, including their health and development, and its relations with the ecosystem. In particular it can be used to provide early indications of health problems, estimating growth rates and predicting the optimal development stage for an eventual commercial exploitation.

Non invasive fish inspection is an important issue in fields related with fish studies; such as marine biology or oceanography, where it is common to maintain specimens of different fish species in closed and controlled ecosystems, which need to be managed.

Additionally, fish size inspection is a critical question in fish farming applications consisting of raising fish in tanks or enclosures, usually to be used in the food industry. In this applications, the optimum fish size and the parameters concerning fish growth have to be studied and monitored (Leon-Santana & Hernandez, 2008).

In rivers, fish passage structures (e.g., vertical slot fishways) allow fish to move upstream obstacles such as dams or weirs. Along the years, several researches have studied fishways and fish passage, including water flow features (Puertas, Pena, & Teijeiro, 2004; Tarrade, Texier, & David, 2008; Wu, Rajaratnam, & Katopodis, 1999), fish swimming abilities (Blake, 2004; Dewar & Graham, 1994) or fish behavior within them (Rodríguez et al., 2011).

In order to detect the fish, several techniques have been applied. One of them is the sonar, which detects submerged objects presence and situation through acoustic waves. From the sixties this technique has been used in applications to detect fish (Craig & Forbes, 1969) or study fish features (Ehrenberg, 1972). More recently, systems as the DIDSON (Dual-frequency identification sonar), have reduced the previous acoustic systems limitations, obtaining higher quality images, and favoring the development of new studies for fish detection and counting (Balk & Lindem, 2000; Belcher, Matsuyama, & Trimble, 2001; Han, Honda, Asada, & Shibata, 2009; Holmes, Cronkite, Enzenhofer, & Mulligan, 2006).

In other works techniques based on infrared laser have been used for fish detection (Mitra, Wang, & Banerjee, 2006). One of the most well-known fish counter, the *Riverwatcher Fish Counter* (Baumgartner et al., 2010), is based on this technique.

Finally, other authors have obtained promising results using submarine cameras combined with computer vision techniques (White, Svellingen, & Strachan, 2006; Boaz Zion, Alchanatis, Ostrovsky, Barki, & Karplus, 2007) or Artificial Neural Networks (ANN) (Storbeck & Daan, 2001). Computer Vision is a rapid, economic, consistent, objective, and non-destructive inspection technique which may consti-

Figure 1. Proposed stereovision system

tute a more efficient alternative (Cappo, Harvey, Malcolm, & Speare, 2003). It has been already widely used in the agricultural and food industry, and its potential in this field has been analyzed in works such as (Brosnan & Sun, 2002; Costa, Scardi, Vitalini, & Cataudella, 2009).

Computer Vision techniques have also been applied with success in underwater scenarios and in fish related research. Early examples of these applications are the use of acoustic transmitters and a video camera for observing the behavior of various species (Armstrong, Bagley, & Priede, 1992). More recently, different computer vision techniques have been used to study fish swimming trajectories (Rodriguez, Bermudez, Rabuñal, & Puertas, 2015), classify fish species (B. Zion, Shklyar, & Karplus, 1999, 2000), fish sizing (Israeli & Kimmel, 1996; Petrell, Shi, Ward, Naiberg, & Savage, 1997) or monitoring fish behavior (Ruff, Marchant, & Frost, 1995).

This chapter proposes two techniques in order to resolve the fish detection and the fish size measurement without human supervision and both of them could be mixed in the future.

To estimate, without human supervision, distribution of fish sizes in a small water environment, the first proposed technique uses a stereo camera system and different computer vision (Figure 1).

To detect fish, the second proposed technique combines, on the one hand, the use of an infrared laser sensor to make the fish detection and, on the other hand, computer vision techniques to prove that the object detected by the laser is really a fish. In this way, a fish detection system in real time is obtained, reducing the computational time of Artificial Neural Networks, and at a reduced cost, since an expensive assembly is not required (Figure 2).

Figure 2. Proposed laser system

2. FISH MONITORING AND SIZING USING STEREOVISION AND COMPUTER VISION

Principles of stereopsis can be explained considering a point *P* in the real 3D space, being projected simultaneously in two image (Figure 1) points p and p' through two camera projection centers *C* and *C'*. The points *P, p, p', C* and *C'* lie in a plane called epipolar plane. The epipolar plane, intersects each image in a line. This lines correspond to the projection of the rays through *p* and *P*, and *p'* and *P*. They are called the epipolar lines. This projection is described by epipolar geometry (Hartley & Zisserman, 2004) (Figure 3).

In practice this process is done in two steps. First, the estimation of the intrinsic parameters of each camera is performed. The intrinsec parameters, determine the process how a point in the real space is projected on the image plane in a single optical system. This projection process can be precisely described using *Pin-hole* mathematical model (Abad, Abad, Andreu, & Vives, 2002; Martin, Perez, Aguilera, & Lahoz, 2004).

$$
\begin{bmatrix} p_x \\ p_y \\ 1 \end{bmatrix} = \begin{bmatrix} f_x & 0 & c_x \\ 0 & f_y & c_y \\ 0 & 0 & 1 \end{bmatrix}_M * \begin{bmatrix} p_x/p_z \\ p_y/p_z \\ 1 \end{bmatrix} \tag{1}
$$

where p is a point in the image with coordinates p_x, p_y, f represents the focal length of the camera (which can be view as the distance from the lens to the camera sensor) and *c* determines the image coordinates where a point is projected through the

Figure 3. Epipolar geometry

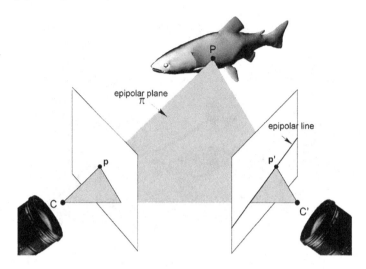

center of the lens C. Therefore, the matrix M models the projection from a point in the image, through a camera system to the real 3D space, obtaining a projection line pP, as shown in (Figure 3) with plane coordinates $(P_x/P_z, P_y/P_z)$.

Additionally, the pin-hole model describes the projection of a point in a perfect optical system. In practice, the real position of the point differs from the ideal one because imperfections in camera lenses introduce some distortions in the image. These distortions follow simple mathematical Formulas (2) depending on a reduced number of parameters D *(Zhang, 1999)*.

$$
\begin{aligned}
dr_x &= xk_1r^2 + xk_2r^4 \\
dr_y &= yk_1r^2 + yk_2r^4 \\
dt_x &= k_3\left(r^2 + 2x^2\right) + 2k_4xy \\
dt_y &= sk_3xy + k_4\left(r^2 + 2y^2\right) \\
D &= [k_1\ k_2\ k_3\ k_4]
\end{aligned}
\tag{2}
$$

where a distortion for a point in the image, in coordinates *(x,y)* is modeled, and being $r = \sqrt{x^2 + y^2}$

The final step to estimate the epipolar geometry of the camera system is the estimation of the translation and rotation of the second camera relative to the first one.

$$\begin{bmatrix} C'_x \\ C'_y \\ C'_z \end{bmatrix} = \begin{bmatrix} r_{11} & r_{12} & r_{13} \\ r_{21} & r_{22} & r_{23} \\ r_{31} & r_{32} & r_{33} \end{bmatrix}_R * \begin{bmatrix} C_x \\ C_y \\ C_z \end{bmatrix} + \begin{bmatrix} t_1 \\ t_2 \\ t_3 \end{bmatrix}_T \qquad (3)$$

Taking this into account, the complete camera model depends on a limited number of parameters which can be solved using a set of known correspondences in both cameras. This is achieved using a calibration pattern of known geometry and easily detectable feature points, and then minimizing the total re-projection error for all the points in the available views from both cameras using the Levenberg-Marquardt optimization algorithm (Figure 4).

Once the camera model has been obtained, to estimate a 3D map from an observed scene, it is necessary to perform a matching process, with the aim of solving the correspondence of the images obtained in the same moment by the two cameras. The result of this process will be the estimation of a disparity map (Figure 5), referred to the difference in image location the pixels seen by the left and right cameras.

Figure 4. (a) Calibration process (b) calibration pattern

Figure 5. (a) Real image (b) disparity map image

Disparity is inversely related with the distance from the cameras. Furthermore, using the previously estimated camera model, it can be used to obtain the 3D position of the objects observed in the scene.

To estimate the disparity map, a parallelized implementation of the Block-Matching algorithm, available in OpenCV ("OPENCV: Open Source Computer Vision") has been used. This technique analyses the statistical similarity of pixel values in each region (block) of the image. The purpose is to solve the correspondence problem for each block, finding in the next image the region representing the most likely displacement.

Numerically, the point (i', j') corresponds to (i,j) after applying the displacement $d(i,j)=(dx,dy)$, which may be described as described in (4).

$$(i',j') = (i+x, j+y) \tag{4}$$

This approach is based on the assumption expressed in (5).

$$I(i,j) + N = I'(i+x, j+y) \tag{5}$$

N being a noise factor following a specific statistical distribution, I the image obtained from camera C and I' the one obtained from camera C'.

In this point, a segmentation based on disparity thresholding of the scene, will provide us with the objects located in the field of view of the cameras and located at a distance of interest.

2.1 Estimating Fish Size

The first stage in the proposed algorithm is the detection of fish. This step will be based on the use of stereopsis, which allows the system to obtain measurements in the real world of objects located at different distances from the cameras.

However, the real time obtained disparity map may not be accurate enough to estimate the fish size properly and may not possess enough information to distinguish fish from other objects. The proposed technique uses a segmentation technique to detect fish in the region of the RGB space corresponding to the fish location in the disparity map, and combining both analysis, fish are then properly detected and sized.

The fish segmentation technique consists in a background subtraction process using a dynamic background modelling technique. According to this, every pixel of the scene must be matched to the background or foreground category. To this end a widely used model based in estimate the RGB color space probability distribution for every pixel in the image has been chosen. The segmentation algorithm works using Bayesian probability to calculate the likelihood of a pixel x_{ij} (t), at time t

in coordinates *(i,j)*, being classified as background *(B)* or foreground *(F)*. This is expressed as follows:

$$p\ (B\ |x) = \frac{p(x\ |B)\,p\ (B)}{p(x\ |B)\,p\big(B\big) + p(x\ |F)\,p\ (F)} \tag{6}$$

$$p(x|B) \sim x_{ij}(t)^T H_{ij}(t) \tag{7}$$

where $H_{ij}(t)$ is an histogram estimation in time *t* for *(i,j)*. This estimation is based in a set of observations $\chi_{ij} = \{x_{ij}(t\text{-}T), ..., x_{ij}(t)\}$ where *T* is a time period used to adapt to changes. According to this, new samples are added to the set and old ones are discarded, while the set size does not exceed a certain value. Therefore, the estimated probability distribution will be adapted to changes in the scene. This is performed by using weighting values depending on a decaying factor that is used to limit the influence of the old data.

Background subtraction through the estimation of pixel distributions has been studied in several works. Most of these works are based in the use of parametric models to estimate the probability distribution of pixel values (Coifman, Beymer, McLauchlan, & Malik, 1998; Horprasert, Harwood, & Davis, 1999). These techniques are based commonly on the use of single Gaussian distribution models or mixture of Gaussian models, according to the complexity of the scene (KaewTraKulPong & Bowden, 2002; Zivkovic, 2004).

In this work, a nonparametric algorithm proposed in (Godbehere, Matsukawa, & Goldberg, 2012) has been used. Therefore, the distribution itself is estimated and updated, assuming a priori probabilities *p(B)=p(F)=0.5*. Thus, a pixel is classified as a background *if p(x—B)>0.8*. The weights of the model are updated according to the following equation:

$$H_{ij}(t+1) = (1-\alpha)H_{ij}(t) + \alpha x_{ij}(t) \tag{8}$$

where $x_{ij}(t)$ is the current sample and α is a constant value, equivalent to *1/T*, as expressed above. α was set by default to *0.025*. Given that, the new weighting value in the histogram for a sample y observed *k* frames in the past and which had a weight *w*, will be $w(1 - \alpha)^k$.

At this point, a thresholding will be performed on the result, obtaining a binary representation of the candidate foreground objects. Finally, a representation and interpretation phase is conducted, using the edges of the detected objects, whose aim is determining if they can be considered as fish.

In this stage objects that do not achieve certain restrictions are eliminated, these restrictions are defined as valid ranges on the object size, its area, and its length-height ratio, defined empirically according to the fish species.

Finally, if the segmented object is accepted as a fish the camera calibration and the disparity map are used to measure the fish size.

3. FISH DETECTION IN SLOT FISHWAYS USING LASER TECHNOLOGY AND COMPUTER VISION

In this work a technique to detect and monitor the fish density that goes through a vertical slot fishway, with low cost and in real time, is proposed. To this end, computational and Computer Vision techniques are used to analyze the data obtained with a laser sensor and a camera.

Therefore, a system with different components has been designed. It uses two kinds of sensors: a conventional camera and a laser sensor, focused on the same fishway section. Therefore, the camera captures images from the objects detected when interfering with the beam emitted by the laser sensor (Figure 1).

This information is downloaded in a storage unit where the computer vision software application is executed. In addition, a control and a display unit are employed to allow the interaction of the user with the application.

The technique can be divided into two stages that are described in detail as follows:

3.1 Object Detection Stage with the Laser Sensor

The sensor is placed in a fishway section of interest to study the crossing fish. Laser measurements are encoded as grey scale images (Figure 6a), where the grey level in a point represents the measured distance by the laser in that point. These values are stored in a buffer, in a way that each time the sensor sends data, they are introduced at the end of the buffer and the rest of the vectors are moved (Figure 7). In this way it is obtained a distance image from the laser influence area that is refreshed in real time.

After the image is obtained, the computer vision process is executed, it includes the following stages: pre-processing, segmentation and recognition and interpretation.

The image pre-processing is focused in improving the image quality for future treatment and to facilitate the image analysis in subsequent stages. In this first stage the image background is eliminated using a smoothed sample scan of the fishway. This sample is subtracted to each data vector that the sensor sends. The canvas where the image is then represented is defined as black for subsequent stages (Figure 6b).

Figure 6. Applied computer vision process: (a) Generated image, (b) image after the pre-processing, (c) image after the segmentation process, and (d) image with the selected candidate objects

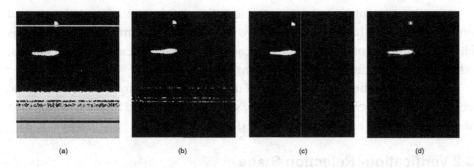

(a)   (b)   (c)   (d)

Figure 7. Functioning of the sensor reading value input in the buffer

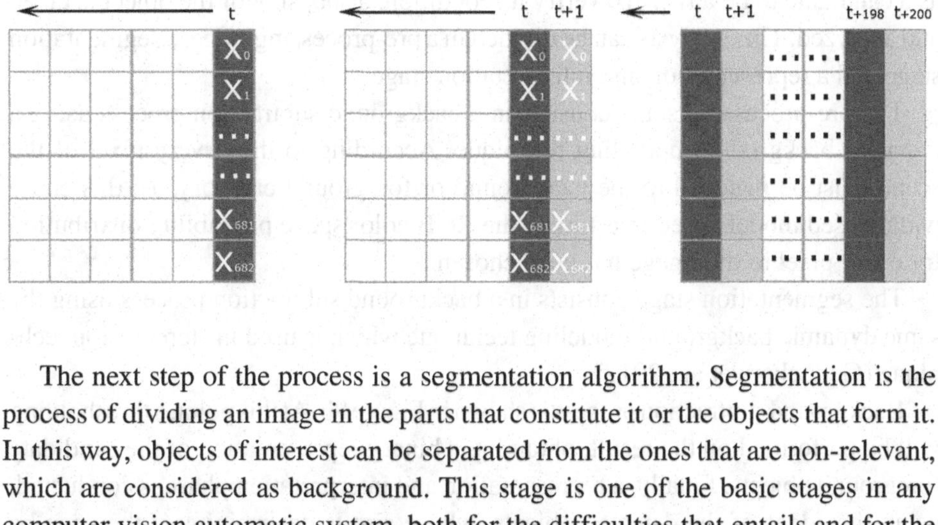

The next step of the process is a segmentation algorithm. Segmentation is the process of dividing an image in the parts that constitute it or the objects that form it. In this way, objects of interest can be separated from the ones that are non-relevant, which are considered as background. This stage is one of the basic stages in any computer vision automatic system, both for the difficulties that entails and for the importance of its results.

Here, the binary thresholding technique, that allows making the segmentation in real time, has been used.

With the aim of improving the results obtained in the previous step, morphological operations are applied (Haralick, Sternberg, & Zhuang, 1987) to the image in the next step. Mathematical morphology is a theoretical framework for non-linear processing of digital images. With this technique, it is possible to quantify and filter specific geometric structures contained in an image (Morales & Azuela, 2011). In this case opening and closing operations have been used (Coifman et al., 1998; Horprasert et al., 1999) to improve the detected object edges. The opening operation allows filtering the smallest objects and the closing operation fills the gaps that appear in the remaining objects of interest. In this way, a combination of one opening operation followed by three closing operations is used to remove noise and optimize the result (Figure 6c).

After the segmentation phase, a representation and description stage is executed on the objects that have been previously segmented. The aim at this technique is choosing a useful computational representation of selected features of the objects, which remain invariant to geometric transformations.

This representation is made through the minimum rectangle that contains the object, allowing a second filtering stage, where each object is selected for the next stage, or dismissed according to its size (Figure 6d).

3.2 Verification- Rejection Stage

In the previous stage an object has been detected in the water and it has been marked as a candidate to be a fish. To verify its condition, a snapshot of the object is taken and analyzed. This analysis can be divided in a pre-processing stage, a segmentation stage and a representation and interpretation stage.

The pre-processing stage consists in a background subtraction process using a dynamic background modelling technique. According to this, every pixel of the scene must be matched to the background or foreground category. To this end a widely used model based in estimate the RGB color space probability distribution for every pixel in the image has been chosen.

The segmentation stage consists in a background subtraction process using the same dynamic background modeling technique which is used in stereovision technique (Godbehere et al., 2012).

Background subtraction process is shown in Figure 8b. At this point, a thresholding will be performed on the result, obtaining a binary representation of the candidate foreground objects. Finally, a representation and interpretation phase is conducted, using the edges of the detected objects, whose aim is determining if they can be considered as fish (Figure 8c). To this end, the detected objects will be compared with a data base of models that represent a fish shape.

Firstly, the segmented objects that do not achieve certain restrictions are eliminated, these restrictions are defined as valid ranges on the object size or its area, defined according to the fish species. In the remaining objects, the seven Hu moments (Ochoa Somuanom, Pérez Lara, Toscano Martínez, & Pereyra Ramos, 2013) are calculated and used to compare the shape of the object with the fish models. Spatial moments (Pajares Martinsanz & De la Cruz García, 2007) are statistical measurements that describe regions (objects) in terms of its interior points. The Hu moments are the normalized moments that are invariant under translation, changes in scale and under rotation.

Figure 8. Applied computer vision process in verification-rejection stage: (a) Original image, (b) Foreground objects after background subtraction, and (c) Fish representation. Color has been modified for visualization.

The similarity between the compared figure and the segmented object is compared using the similarity value defined as follows:

$$f\left(A,B\right) = \max_{i=1:7} \frac{\left|m_i^A - m_i^B\right|}{\left|m_i^A\right|} \qquad (9)$$

where A is the segmented object and B is a model of a fish in the database, being m_i^A the i moment of Hu calculated in the object A.

The segmented object A is accepted as a fish (fish counter is increased) if the similarity value with any of the fish models in the database reach a threshold, set by default to 0.31; otherwise it is discarded.

4. RESULTS

4.1 Stereovision Technique

To measure the performance of the proposed system a set of experiments were conducted with living fishes in different fish tanks.

To this end, five experiments were conducted in a fish tank located in the Centre of Technological Innovation in Construction and Civil Engineering (CITEEC) of A Coruña, using specimens of European perch (*Perca fluviatilis*) and brown trout (*Salmo trutta*) Figure 9; and two experiments were conducted in a pool located in the Finisterrae Aquarium of A Coruña, using specimens of Atlantic wreckfish (*Polyprion americanus*) Figure 10.

Figure 9. Example of obtained results: (a) Image of a detected wreckfish recorded in Centre of Technological Innovation in Construction and Civil Engineering (CI-TEEC) of A Coruña and (b) Segmented and processed Image

Figure 10. Example of obtained results: (a) Image of a detected European perch recorded in the Finisterrae Aquarium of A Coruña and (b) Segmented and processed Image

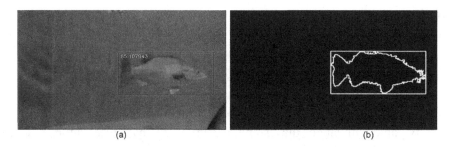

Near 2000 images were used in the experiments, and the obtained results were achieved comparing the measurements obtained by the system with a manual labeling of the different fish specimens conducted by experts.

Obtained results are summarized in Table 1.

False positive, were automatically marked as anomalous detections which estimated length L is outside the limits $[\mu - 2\sigma, \mu + 2\sigma]$. Being μ, σ the average and standard deviation respectively of the estimated sizes in the assay.

Two types of experimental tests have been conducted. In the first experiment, the laser sensor behavior in the water has been measured. The second type of tests is focused in evaluating the performance of the computer vision software.

Analyzing the results it may be observed that, in general, a 10% of error in estimated fish size was achieved. Obtaining a low standard deviation of error and a precision rate near the 90%.

Table 1. The average results obtained with the different techniques

Results	European Perch	Brown Trount	Atlantic Wreckfish
Avg. Measured Size	8.8	6.5	92.6
Std.Dev. Measured Size	0.8	0.8	8.4
Avg. Absolute Error (cm)	0.6	0.9	6.5
Std.Dev. Absolute Error (cm)	0.6	0.7	5.2
Avg. Relative Error	0.07	0.12	0.07
Std.Dev. Relative Error	0.09	0.09	0.06
True Positives	620	600	182
Detected False Positives	44	31	47
Precision	0.9	1.0	0.8
False Positive Ratio	0.1	0.0	0.2

The absolute error in measurements of European perch and brown trout is less than 1cm, which constitute a very promising result. However, a higher absolute error is observed when measuring Atlantic wreckfish, this is motivated to the big size of the used specimens (some bigger than 1m), which caused some detections when a part of the fish was outside the visual frame. Although this situation, will be managed in future versions of this work, obtained results are still accurate enough to study this kind of fishes.

Summarizing, it can be stated that the proposed technique can obtain a reliable measurement of fish size regarding the variability in luminosity changes, environmental conditions and fish species.

A higher absolute error is observed when measuring Atlantic wreckfish than with other species, this is motivated.

In general, it can be seen that a very low false positive rate is achieved, so obtained results are very reliable, and detected fishes represent real fishes with a high probability.

Finally, the obtained error in the measurements is very low, achieving also a low standard deviation of the error. These results indicate that the proposed technique may be used in real conditions.

4.2 Laser Detection Technique

4.2.1 Laser Performance

Two types of hydraulic channels have been used for this test: a 93 liters swimming pool and a circular channel with an engine that moves the water in a certain speed in a closed circuit. The tests have been made firstly with clean water to measure the laser range and afterwards it has been added turbidity (through the incorporation of slime silica) to analyze the relation of water turbidity with laser range.

With these measurements it could be analyzed how the sensor behaves in different circumstances, comparing the measurement values from the sensor with the real position of the fish, allowing to establish a relationship between the variables.

Four turbidity levels have been defined. The first level represent clean water and at each level the turbidity is increased till reaching level four, where there is not enough visibility to see objects with direct observation.

During the experiments it has been confirmed that the laser behavior in the water makes the sensor measurement higher than the real distance of the object. Additionally, the sensor loses accuracy when the distance of the object exceeds a certain limit. This aspect has been taken into account to calibrate the system to obtain a distance estimation according to reality.

It has also been confirmed that the materials that behave better are glass and quartz glass, since they allow measuring farther correct distances than the measurements that methacrylate offers.

4.2.2 Software Analysis

These tests have been conducted on a 1:8.3 scale model of a vertical slot fishway, built in methacrylate and connecting two fish tanks, where around ten fish of different colors and types were introduced to evaluate the implemented software efficiency.

Different tests have been conducted in this scenario. Each one of them lasted from 1 to 3 hours to produce enough fish crossings along the fishway to be significant.

Additionally, different non fish bodies have been introduced in the assay, ranging from wood pieces to methacrylate and steel bodies, in order to determine the rate of false positives of the system.

Finally, to measure the behavior of the system in these assays, the obtained images of the detected objects have been stored and analyzed by experts. Around 200 images of crossing objects were analyzed (Table 2). The images where the complete object cannot be seen or the object is out of the shot have been discarded to obtain a reliable measure of the systems performance.

Table 2. Test results

Fish	Data	%
Precision	0.97	97.18%
Recall	0.73	72.63%
False positive rate	0.03	2.18%
False negative rate	0.27	27.36%

The metrics used to analyses the behavior of the system are *Precision* and *Recall*, shown in the following equations (Equations 10-13):

$$Precision = ((True\ Positives) / (True\ Positives + False\ Positives)) \tag{10}$$

$$Recall = ((Right\ Positives) / (True\ Positives + False\ Negatives)) \tag{11}$$

$$False\ Positive\ Ratio = 1 - Precision \tag{12}$$

$$False\ Negative\ Ratio = 1 - Recall \tag{13}$$

5. CONCLUSION

In this chapter, two non invasive solutions to detect and estimate fish size in underwater environments are proposed, aimed to the optimization of aquarium and fish farm management.

First technique, stereovision, combines stereo imaging with computer vision techniques to detect and to measure fish in images, without need of fish marking or direct fish observation.

The accuracy and performance of the proposed technique has been tested, conducting different assays with living fishes. The results obtained with this system have been very promising, as they allowed us to obtain the fish size in the image with a low error rate.

In future stages of this work, the segmentation and detection algorithms will be optimized, to improve the reliability of the system and a tracking algorithm will be defined to manage measurements according to each specimen. Additionally, further experiments will be conducted and the functionality of the proposed technique will be extended to estimate the distribution of fish weights and sizes.

Second technique, fish detection and counter system using laser technology and computer vision techniques, offers a non-invasive method, working in real time, and without the visual limitation problem of direct observation techniques.

From the analysis of the different materials in which the laser was submerged, it could be concluded that quartz glass or glass should be used to operate, since they allow accurate measures with a higher range with the sensor beam. In addition, the refraction effect in water must be taken into account, since it causes the distances to be overestimated by the device.

A very high accuracy has been obtained; the system is able to detect the 73% of the fishes, with a 0.03% rate of wrong objects marked as fish.

The main advantages of this technique are the following. The assembly size of the entire system is reduced, and the only required devices are: a laser sensor, a camera and a laptop with the software that makes the computer vision process.

In conclusion, the proposed technique can be carried out with low cost, and allows us to sample a fishway section in real time with high precision.

The proposed method has been tested in a laboratory, simulating unfavorable conditions and obtaining promising results. Nevertheless, in next stages of this research, the system should be optimized and tested in a real scenario and in a real river. It may provide a useful fish counter tool to detect and study fish in their natural environment.

In future work, the mixture of these two techniques will do a better and more accurate technique.

ACKNOWLEDGMENT

Angel Jose Rico-Diaz gratefully acknowledges financial support from the Spanish Ministry of Education (FPI grant Ref. BES-2013-063444)

Maria Bermudez gratefully acknowledges financial support from the Spanish Regional Government of Galicia (Postdoctoral grant reference ED481B 2014/156).

REFERENCES

Abad, F. H., Abad, V. H., Andreu, J. F., & Vives, M. O. (2002). *Application of Projective Geometry to Synthetic Cameras*. Paper presented at the XIV International Conference of Graphic Engineering.

Armstrong, J. D., Bagley, P. M., & Priede, I. G. (1992). Photographic and acoustic tracking observations of the behavior of the grenadier Coryphaenoides (Nematonorus) armatus, the eel Synaphobranchus bathybius, and other abyssal demersal fish in the North Atlantic Ocean. *Marine Biology, 112*(4), 1432–1793. doi:10.1007/BF00346170

Balk, H., & Lindem, T. (2000). Improved fish detection in data from split-beam sonar. *Aquatic Living Resources, 13*(05), 297–303. doi:10.1016/S0990-7440(00)01079-2

Baumgartner, L., Bettanin, M., McPherson, J., Jones, M., Zampatti, B., & Beyer, K. (2010). Assessment of an infrared fish counter (Vaki Riverwatcher) to quantify fish migrations in the Murray-Darling Basin. *Industry & Investment NSW. Fisheries Final Report Series, 116*, 47.

Belcher, E., Matsuyama, B., & Trimble, G. (2001). *Object identification with acoustic lenses.* Paper presented at the OCEANS, 2001. MTS/IEEE Conference and Exhibition.

Blake, R. W. (2004). Fish functional design and swimming performance. *Journal of Fish Biology, 65*(5), 1193–1222. doi:10.1111/j.0022-1112.2004.00568.x

Brosnan, T., & Sun, D.-W. (2002). Inspection and grading of agricultural and food products by computer vision systems—a review. *Computers and Electronics in Agriculture, 36*(2-3), 193–213. doi:10.1016/S0168-1699(02)00101-1

Cappo, M., Harvey, E., Malcolm, H., & Speare, P. (2003). *Potential of video techniques to monitor diversity, abundance and size of fish in studies of Marine Protected Areas.* Paper presented at the Aquatic Protected Areas - what works best and how do we know? World Congress on Aquatic Protected Areas, Cairns, Australia.

Coifman, B., Beymer, D., McLauchlan, P., & Malik, J. (1998). A real-time computer vision system for vehicle tracking and traffic surveillance. *Transportation Research Part C, Emerging Technologies, 6*(4), 271–288. doi:10.1016/S0968-090X(98)00019-9

Costa, C., Scardi, M., Vitalini, V., & Cataudella, S. (2009). A dual camera system for counting and sizing Northern Bluefin Tuna (Thunnus thynnus; Linnaeus, 1758) stock, during transfer to aquaculture cages, with a semi automatic Artificial Neural Network tool. *Aquaculture (Amsterdam, Netherlands), 291*(3-4), 161–167. doi:10.1016/j.aquaculture.2009.02.013

Craig, R. E., & Forbes, S. T. (1969). *Design of a sonar for fish counting.* Academic Press.

Dewar, H., & Graham, J. (1994). Studies of tropical tuna swimming performance in a large water tunnel - Energetics. *The Journal of Experimental Biology, 192,* 13–31. PMID:9317243

Ehrenberg, J. E. (1972). *A method for extracting the fish target strength distribution from acoustic echoes.* Paper presented at the Engineering in the Ocean Environment, Ocean 72-IEEE International Conference on. doi:10.1109/OCEANS.1972.1161176

Godbehere, A. B., Matsukawa, A., & Goldberg, K. (2012). *Visual tracking of human visitors under variable-lighting conditions for a responsive audio art installation.* Paper presented at the American Control Conference (ACC). doi:10.1109/ACC.2012.6315174

Han, J., Honda, N., Asada, A., & Shibata, K. (2009). Automated acoustic method for counting and sizing farmed fish during transfer using DIDSON. *Fisheries Science, 75*(6), 1359–1367. doi:10.1007/s12562-009-0162-5

Haralick, R. M., Sternberg, S. R., & Zhuang, X. (1987). Image analysis using mathematical morphology. *IEEE Transactions on Pattern Analysis and Machine Intelligence,* (4), 532-550.

Hartley, R. I., & Zisserman, A. (Eds.). (2004). *Multiple View Geometry in Computer Vision.* Cambridge University Press. doi:10.1017/CBO9780511811685

Holmes, J. A., Cronkite, G. M., Enzenhofer, H. J., & Mulligan, T. J. (2006). Accuracy and precision of fish-count data from a "dual-frequency identification sonar" (DIDSON) imaging system. *ICES Journal of Marine Science: Journal du Conseil, 63*(3), 543–555. doi:10.1016/j.icesjms.2005.08.015

Horprasert, T., Harwood, D., & Davis, L. S. (1999). *A statistical approach for real-time robust background subtraction and shadow detection.* Paper presented at the IEEE ICCV.

Israeli, D., & Kimmel, E. (1996). Monitoring the behavior of hypoxia-stressed Carassius auratus using computer vision. *Aquacultural Engineering, 15*(6), 423–440. doi:10.1016/S0144-8609(96)01009-6

KaewTraKulPong, P., & Bowden, R. (2002). *An improved adaptive background mixture model for real-time tracking with shadow detection.* Paper presented at the Video-Based Surveillance Systems.

Leon-Santana, M., & Hernandez, J. M. (2008). Optimum management and environmental protection in the aquaculture industry. *Ecological Economics, 64*(4), 849–857. doi:10.1016/j.ecolecon.2007.05.006

Martin, N., Perez, B. A., Aguilera, D. G., & Lahoz, J. G. (2004). *Applied Analysis of Camera Calibration Methods for Photometric Uses*. Paper presented at the VII National Conference of Topography and Cartography.

Mitra, V., Wang, C.-J., & Banerjee, S. (2006). Lidar detection of underwater objects using a neuro-SVM-based architecture. *Neural Networks. IEEE Transactions on*, *17*(3), 717–731.

Morales, R. R., & Azuela, J. H. S. (2011). Procesamiento y análisis digital de imágenes (Ra-Ma Ed.). Ra-Ma.

Ochoa Somuanom, J., Pérez Lara, C., Toscano Martínez, J. H., & Pereyra Ramos, C. G. (2013). *Clasificación de objetos rígidos a partir de imágenes digitales empleando los momentos invariantes de Hu*. Paper presented at the X Congreso Internacional sobre Innovación y Desarrollo Tecnológico, Cuernavaca Morelos, México. Retrieved from http://opencv.org

Pajares Martinsanz, G., & De la Cruz García, J. (2007). Visión por computador imágenes digitales y aplicaciones (Ra-Ma Ed. 2ª ed.). Ra-Ma.

Petrell, R. J., Shi, X., Ward, R. K., Naiberg, A., & Savage, C. R. (1997). Determining fish size and swimming speed in cages and tanks using simple video techniques. *Aquacultural Engineering*, *16*(1-2), 63–84. doi:10.1016/S0144-8609(96)01014-X

Puertas, J., Pena, L., & Teijeiro, T. (2004). Experimental Approach to the Hydraulics of Vertical Slot Fishways. *Journal of Hydraulic Engineering*, *130*(1), 10–23. doi:10.1061/(ASCE)0733-9429(2004)130:1(10)

Rodríguez, A., Bermúdez, M., Rabuñal, J., Aff, M. A. S. C. E., Puertas, J., Dorado, J., & Balairón, L. et al. (2011). Optical Fish Trajectory Measurement in Fishways through Computer Vision and Artificial Neural Networks. *Journal of Computing in Civil Engineering*, *25*(4), 291–301. doi:10.1061/(ASCE)CP.1943-5487.0000092

Rodriguez, A., Bermudez, M., Rabuñal, J., & Puertas, J. (2015). Fish tracking in vertical slot fishways using computer vision techniques. *Journal of Hydroinformatics*, *17*(2), 275–292. doi:10.2166/hydro.2014.034

Ruff, B. P., Marchant, J. A., & Frost, A. R. (1995). Fish sizing and monitoring using a stereo image analysis system applied to fish farming. *Aquacultural Engineering*, *14*(2), 155–173. doi:10.1016/0144-8609(94)P4433-C

Storbeck, F., & Daan, B. (2001). Fish species recognition using computer vision and a neural network. *Fisheries Research*, *51*(1), 11–15. doi:10.1016/S0165-7836(00)00254-X

Tarrade, L., Texier, A., David, L., & Larinier, M. (2008). Topologies and measurements of turbulent flow in vertical slot fishways. *Hydrobiologia, 609*(1), 177–188. doi:10.1007/s10750-008-9416-y

White, D., Svellingen, C., & Strachan, N. (2006). Automated measurement of species and length of fish by computer vision. *Fisheries Research, 80*(2), 203–210. doi:10.1016/j.fishres.2006.04.009

Wu, S., Rajaratnam, N., & Katopodis, C. (1999). Structure of flow in vertical slot fishways. *Journal of Hydraulic Engineering, 125*(4), 351–360. doi:10.1061/(ASCE)0733-9429(1999)125:4(351)

Zhang, Z. (1999). *Flexible Camera Calibration By Viewing a Plane From Unknown Orientations*. Paper presented at the International Conference on Computer Vision (ICCV). doi:10.1109/ICCV.1999.791289

Zion, B., Alchanatis, V., Ostrovsky, V., Barki, A., & Karplus, I. (2007). Real-time underwater sorting of edible fish species. *Computers and Electronics in Agriculture, 56*(1), 34–45. doi:10.1016/j.compag.2006.12.007

Zion, B., Shklyar, A., & Karplus, I. (1999). Sorting fish by computer vision. *Computers and Electronics in Agriculture, 23*(3), 175–187. doi:10.1016/S0168-1699(99)00030-7

Zion, B., Shklyar, A., & Karplus, I. (2000). In-vivo fish sorting by computer vision. *Aquacultural Engineering, 22*(3), 165–179. doi:10.1016/S0144-8609(99)00037-0

Zivkovic, Z. (2004). *Improved adaptive Gaussian mixture model for background subtraction*. Paper presented at the International Conference on Patern Recognition (ICPR 2004). doi:10.1109/ICPR.2004.1333992

Chapter 8
Controlling Prosthetic Limb Movements Using EEG Signals

V. V. Ramalingam
SRM University, India

V. Sugumaran
VIT University, India

Mohan S.
Al Yamamah University, Saudi Arabia

Vani V.
Al Yamamah University, Saudi Arabia

B. Rebecca Jeya Vadhanam
SRM University, India

ABSTRACT

This chapter focuses on replacing natural arms with artificial arms with movement controlled by EEG signals. The selected features were classified using C4.5 decision tree algorithm, best first decision tree algorithm, Naïve Bayes algorithm, Bayes net algorithm, K star algorithm and ripple down rule learner algorithm. The results of statistical and histogram features are discussed and conclusions of the study are presented.

1. INTRODUCTION

The loss of human limb is a major issue that intensely limits the everyday capabilities and interaction of the persons. There can be two types of signals that are of direct use for the above purpose: EMG and EEG. EMG signals are available in the muscles and they contain a large amount of information for the purpose of limb movements. However, there are many instances where the subject loses most part of the limb.

DOI: 10.4018/978-1-5225-0889-2.ch008

In such cases, the EMG signals that are available near the affected area (shoulder, upper arm) may not be of great use. Moreover, EMG signals are secondary signals, whereas EEG signals are primary signals. Since the EEG signals originate from brain activities, the characteristics remain almost same irrespective of the extent of amputation. This gives a feeling that EEG signal is better candidate for controlling movements of artificial limbs. It is not fully true because of the fact that the EEG signals are a product of some thought process. This complicates the decoding process of EEG signals. Now, the challenge is to decode effectively the information buried inside the EEG signals. A review of the techniques brings out merits and demerits. The need and scope of the present work also evolve from this. The main objective of the study is used to replace the natural arms with an artificial arm with movements of different right hand limb movements like finger open (fopen), finger close (fclose), wrist clockwise (wcw) and wrist counterclockwise (wccw) from EEG signals. These EEG signals can be used to build a model to control the prosthetic limb movements. Cluster analysis is a multivariate statistical analysis method; it is a statistical classification approach that groups signals into different fault categories on the basis of the similarity of the characteristics or features they possess. It seeks to minimize within-group variance on the one hand and maximize between-group variance on the other. The result of cluster analysis is division into a number of groups with homogeneous contents. Multilayer Perceptron Neural Network (MLPNN) architecture was employed to classify the EEG signals. Three sets set-A, set-D and set-E of EEG signals were used for classification. Lyapunov exponents were extracted from the EEG signals given as the inputs to the MLPNNs. Finally, the features were trained with Levenberg-Marquadt algorithm and achieved good classification accuracy (Elif Derya Ubeyli, 2009). Che Wan Fadzal et al. (2012) reported that the Power Spectral Density (PSD) was the well suited method to distinguish right and left hand writing movements using EEG signals. The controlling process of prosthetic limb movements based on surface EMG signals extracted from remnant muscles are the promising ones in the analysis of EMG signals. There were three feature extraction techniques, namely autoregressive coefficients, mean frequency and EMG histogram used in the study. The combined features of mean frequency and EMG histogram were given as the input to neural networks classifier. Hence, it is noticed from this study that the EMG histogram feature vector performed well for the classification of prosthetic limb movements (Aishwarya et al., 2013). Adeli et al. (2003) reported that the wavelet was an effective time–frequency analysis tool for analyzing EEG signals and most capable technique to extract features from EEG signals. The main idea of time series modeling is to fit the waveform data to a parametric time series model and extract features based on this parametric model. There are two popular mathematical models, namely, Auto-Regressive (AR) model and the Auto-Regressive Moving Average (ARMA) model. AR model is established by the time difference and EEG amplitude. In practice, however, application of the AR model or ARMA model is difficult due to the complexity in modeling, especially the need to determine the order of the model (Andrew, 2006). Least Square Support Vector Machine (LS-SVMs) was proposed by (Elif Derya Ubeyli, 2010). To classify normal and epilepsy patients during epileptic seizures, for feature extraction, spectral analysis of the EEG signal was carried out with three model-based methods namely, Burg autoregressive-AR, moving average – MA, Yule- walker autoregressive moving average-ARMA methods. The author has proved that the Burg AR coefficients were the best features to represent the characteristics of EEG signals. Shiliang et al. (2007) systematically evaluated the performance of the three ensemble methods for EEG signal classification of mental imaginary tasks. K-nearest-neighbor, decision tree and support vector machine were used as the classifiers and the experiments are carried out upon real EEG recordings from the mental imaginary task. Artificial Intelligence (AI) techniques have been increasingly applied to control prosthetic limb movements and have shown improved performance over conventional approaches. Numerous attempts have been made to improve the accuracy and efficiency of prosthetic limb movements by employing AI techniques. Various supervised learning techniques have been applied for controlling prosthetic limb movements. Ubeyli et al. (2007) used a diverse and composite input features of EEG signals obtained by the eigenvectors. The classification was performed on diverse features (modified mixture of expert-MME) and composite feature (mixture of experts-ME) with five data set (set-A, set-B, set-C, set-D, and set-E). The result demonstrated that the MME trained on diverse features have achieved a higher level of classification accuracy than ME. Ocak (2008) new scheme was presented to classify the EEG signals. Features were extracted using fourth-level Wavelet Packet Decomposition (WPD). Genetic Algorithm (GA) was used for feature selection and identified the best performing features to form the optimal feature subset. The approximate entropy values were derived as the feature vector and a Learning Vector Quantization (LVQ) was used as the classifier to attain the best classification accuracy for the normal and epileptic epoch. A review of recent developments in applications of ML techniques for controlling prosthetic limb movements was given by Bhattacharyya et al. (2015), Ericka et al. (2015), Monalisa et al. (2015), Enrique et al., (2015), and Siddique et al. (2003). To make the training and testing of the techniques (classifiers) more effective, feature selection was employed using Decision Tree (DT) (Suykens et al, 2003).

1.1 Scope of the Present Work

Literature review highlighted that only the minimum number of machine learning techniques with few features has been used for EEG signal classification. Many of the researcher used statistical, histogram and ARMA features. In machine learning approach more than 50 classification algorithms are available. The researchers used a very few classifiers for EEG signal classification (Decision tree, Support vector machine, K-nearest-neighbor, Multilayer Perceptron Neural Network and Least Square Support Vector Machine etc.). Even these classifiers are not used with all features combinations. Hence, it is difficult to comment on the best machine learning system (feature – classifier pair) to classify EEG signals for the purpose of controlling prosthetic limb movements. To find the solution to this problem, one needs to extract all possible features and classify them with all classification algorithms with same EEG signals (dataset). Practically, it is very difficult to execute all features with more than 50 classification algorithms. Hence, in this study only frequently used features like statistical features and histogram features were considered. Similarly, 6 classifiers namely, decision tree, best first tree, Naïve Bayes, Bayes net, K star and ripple down rule learner classifier were used. The classification algorithms are chosen based on their performance in the other studies reported in the literature. The main objective of carrying out this study is to identify the best 'feature-classifier' combination among the above listed features and classifiers.

The problem is modeled as a 'machine learning' problem. The steps involved here are as follows:

1. The EEG signals pertaining to various right hand limb movements were acquired.
2. Various features were extracted there from.
3. Prominent amongst the features were selected.
4. The selected features were input to the various classifiers to determine the classification accuracy of the classifiers.

2. DATA ACQUISITION AND SYSTEM ARCHITECTURE

In the present study, an effort is taken for data collection process. EEG signals were recorded from 27 healthy volunteers while performing the four different limb movements. These four limb movements are the predominant physiological measures of the human being. Thus, the four limb moments viz., finger open, finger close, wrist clockwise and wrist counterclockwise are considered for the study. The complete architecture of the present study is shown in Figure 1.

EEG signals were recorded for the four classes using the standardized electrode placement method. The experiments have been conducted using the EEG data acquisition kit (make: RMS). Signals from electrodes C3, C4, CZ, FZ and PZ contain the information related to right hand movements and thus is selected in this study to identify the different limb movements.

Figure 1. System architecture of prosthetic arm

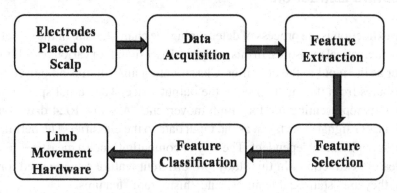

2.1 Channel Selection

The dataset described in section two was taken and the statistical parameters were computed for each channel. Then C4.5 algorithm was used to perform the dimensionality reduction and classification with the default confidence factor value is 0.25 and the minimum number of object is 2. From the conducted experiments, amongst the channels C3, C4, CZ, FZ and PZ, the best classification accuracy was achieved by C4 channel. Hence, only the C4 channel has been considered for the rest of the study. This is evident from Figure 2.

Figure 2. Channels vs. classification accuracy

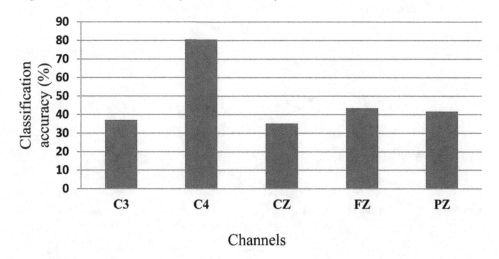

2.2 Feature Extraction

Feature extraction is the process of determining the characteristic of the signal using some mathematical measures. In this study, the EEG signals of various conditions are consider as the input to the classifier. Classification algorithm is employed to map the attributes from the input space to the output space. The output space contains four regions representing the four limb movements. A set of 1024 data points of digitized EEG signals was taken as the input data to the classifier. The definition of features is application dependent. The way of computing, such a measure is referred to as 'feature extraction'. In this study two different feature sets are used for EEG signals, they are "statistical features" and "histogram" features.

2.3 Feature Selection

The main idea of feature selection is to choose a subset of input variables by eliminating features with little or no predictive information. The features can be any measure of data points or the signal; however the relevance of them will depend on how well they help in the process of classification. The process of selecting the best features from a pool of features is called 'feature selection'. The good feature will have feature values with minimum variation within a class and maximum variation between the classes. Many techniques are used for feature selection; among them decision tree was widely used. For all cases of the study, decision tree has been used for feature selection (see Figure 3).

Figure 3. Decision tree

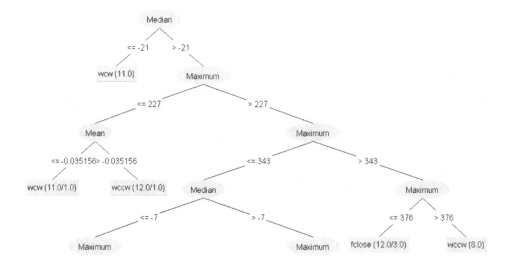

2.4 Time Domain Features

The parameters or measures computed directly from the acquired time domain signals are called 'time domain features'. The following three sets of time domain features are significant ones in prosthetic limb control of machine components:

- Statistical features
- Histogram features

2.4.1 Statistical Features

Statistical analysis of EEG signals yields different parameters which provide the physical characteristics of time domain data. Statistical analysis of EEG signals with different parameter combinations was used to elicit information McFadden and Smith (1984). Such procedures use allied logic often based on physical considerations. A fairly wide set of these statistical parameters was selected as a basis for the study. They are mean, standard error, median, standard deviation, sample variance, kurtosis, skewness, range, minimum, maximum, and sum. In this study, these parameters were extracted from EEG signals and used as features.

2.4.2 Histogram Features

Observing the magnitude of the time domain signal, it is found that the range of EEG amplitude varies from class to class. A better graph to show the range of variation is the histogram plot. The information derived from a histogram plot can be used as features in the prosthetic arm control. A representative sample from each condition (class) is taken and the histogram is plotted. The selection of bin involves two criteria.

The bin range should accommodate the amplitude range of signals obtained from all conditions of limb movements and the same were analyzed. The EEG amplitude range is divided into a set of sub ranges starting from the minimum value to the maximum value of the EEG signal. The sub-ranges are known as bins from the x-axis of the histogram. The number of data points whose EEG amplitude value falls within a particular bin is counted and the count forms the y-axis of the histogram. The histograms for each hand movement condition are plotted using EEG signals as separate plots. The objective here is to find out the bins whose y-axis values are same for a particular class but different from other classes. These values for a particular condition of the hand movements may be small but for another condition they may be large. The bin range selected should accommodate all conditions. i.e., the bin range should start from the minimum of minimum amplitude of different classes and go up to maximum of maximum amplitude of different classes. The procedure for computing the minimum of minimum amplitude is as follows:

1. Find out the minimum amplitude of each signal in a particular class.
2. Repeat step (1) for all classes. Find the minimum of those minimum amplitudes.

The procedure for computing the maximum of maximum amplitude is similar to this.

The width of the bin should be fixed such that the height of bins is different for different condition of the hand movements. It needs not be true for all width of the bins, but at least a few of them should follow this criterion so that it can be used as a feature for distinguishing various conditions (classes). Bin width is a set of limiting values that should be in ascending order so that the program counts the number of data points between the current bin number and the adjoining higher bin, if any. The bin width need not be always constant; however, in this study a constant bin width is used.

Following the above criteria, the bin width and bin range were selected and histogram was plotted. Figure 4 refers to a typical bin of the histogram plot illustrating the variations in bin width and bin height, etc.

Figure 4. Sample histogram of a rectangular distribution

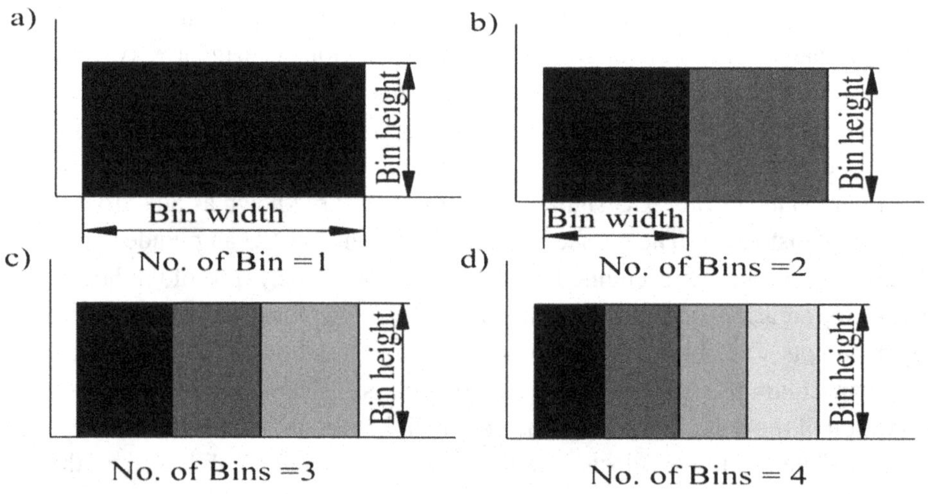

3. FEATURES SUGGESTED BY C4.5 DECISION TREE ALGORITHM

The level of contribution by individual features is given by a statistical measure within the parenthesis in the decision tree (Figure 3). The first number in the parenthesis indicates the number of data points that can be classified using that feature set. The second number indicates the number of samples against this action. If the first number is very small compared to the total number of samples, then the corresponding features can be considered as outliers and hence ignored. Referring to the Figure 3, one can identify three such most dominant features and their significance as follows:

- Mean,
- Maximum,
- Median.

3.1 Feature Classification Using C4.5. Decision Tree

The C4.5 decision tree algorithm determines the features that dominate as prosthetic limb movements system. Knowledge structure in the decision tree is used for the classification of future events Saimurugan et al. (2011) and Ravikumar et al. (2011). A classifier has to satisfy the following two contracting objectives, to obtain better classification accuracy. During the training process, the algorithm should not over fit the data. Over fitting seems to give better classification results for the training data set; however, such algorithm tends to give lower classification accuracies for the test data set (unseen samples). If the parameters are adjusted to avoid over fitting, the algorithm results in lower prediction accuracy. In order to have higher prediction accuracy and to avoid over fitting of data, a numerous set of experiments are carried out to design the classifier and the results are discussed below.

When the minimum number of objects is small the tree tends to grow faster, leading to more branching activity. More branching may lead to higher classification accuracy; however, it may tend to over fit the data. For the given situation, it is preferable to have less number of branches and have good classification accuracy. For that the minimum number of objects required to form a class should be less so that the branching is minimum. This process is called pruning (Jingnian et al., 2009).

The minimum number of objects required for forming a class was varied from 1 to 27. Referring Figure 5, a series of experiments were conducted to investigate the effect of minimum number of objects on classification accuracy by keeping confidence factor at its default value (0.25). The performance of the features has achieved better accuracy when the minimum number of objects is fixed at 2. Even though it produced better accuracy, it leads to over fitting. Hence, the minimum number of objects was fixed at 5. Keeping the minimum number of objects as 5 and by varying the confidence factor from 0.1 to 1 at an interval of 0.1, the experiments have been conducted to study the effect of confidence factors. The experiments reveal that confidence factor has an effect only between 0.1 and 0.6 and it reaches the saturation stage. Any further increase in confidence factor does not reflect on the classification accuracy. Hence, '0.6' is fixed as the confidence factor. The variation of classification accuracy with respect to confidence factor is shown in (Figure 6).

The above encouraging results have been achieved through the 10-fold cross validation. The overall classification accuracy of the decision tree classification algorithm using statistical features is 79.62%.

3.2 Best First Tree (BF Tree)

The selected top three features, namely, mean, median and maximum was trained and tested by using a best first tree algorithm with pre pruning and post pruning processes. From the decision tree, three features that are contributed for classification were only selected for training and testing. Summary of pre pruning and post pruning operation is given in Table 1. Referring the Table 1, best first tree with post pruning process gives a better classification accuracy (79.62%) than that of the pre pruning processes. The best first decision tree gives a maximum classification accuracy of 79.62% for a selected number of features.

Figure 5. Minimum no. of objects vs. classification accuracy: decision tree algorithm

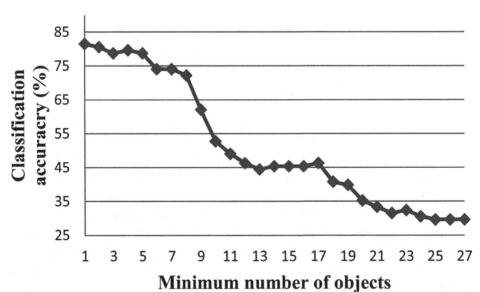

Figure 6. Confidence factor vs. classification accuracy: decision tree

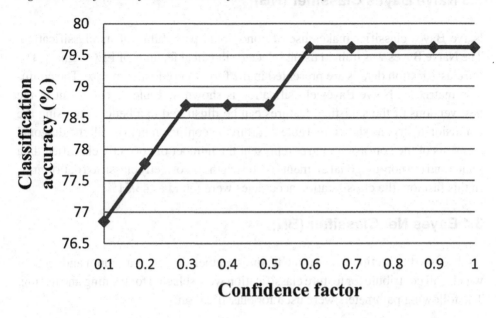

Table 1. Effect of number of features on classification accuracy

No. of Features	Classification Accuracy (%)	
	Best First Tree (Pre Pruning)	Best First Tree (Post Pruning)
1	50.00	75.92
2	62.96	76.85
3	58.33	75.00
4	58.33	75.00
5	58.33	75.00
6	70.37	77.77
7	70.37	**79.62**
8	77.77	79.62
9	74.07	79.62
10	**78.70**	79.62
11	78.70	79.62
12	78.70	79.62

3.3 Naïve Bayes Classifier (NB)

Naïve Bayes classifier makes use of conditional probability of its classification. The Naïve Bayes was trained using selected statistical features of EEG signals. The misclassification details are presented in the form of confusion matrix. The confusion matrix for Naïve Bayes classification is shown in Table 2. The result of the best versions of the statistical features can be illustrated in a better way using the confusion matrix as shown in Table 2. From the confusion matrix, all the diagonal elements of the confusion matrix represent the number of correctly classified data points and the non-diagonal elements represent the incorrectly classified data points. In this fashion, the classification accuracies were found as 43.51%.

3.4 Bayes Net Classifier (BN)

As discussed in section 3, top three features, namely, mean, maximum and median which will contribute for feature classification were selected for training and testing. The following parameters were used for classification.

- **Estimator:** Simple estimator is used for estimating the conditional probability tables of a Bayes network once the structure has been learned. A parameter α (0.1 to 0.9) was used for estimating the probability tables and can be interpreted as the initial count on each value. The classification accuracy was maximum when $\alpha = 0.4$.
- **Search Algorithm:** This Bayes Network learning algorithm uses hill climber search for finding a well scoring Bayes network structure.
- **Maximum Number of Parents:** The maximum number of parents of a node in the Bayes net was set at 1.

The Bayes net algorithm with the above parameters was trained using a selected number of statistical features of EEG signals. Classification accuracy of the Bayes net algorithm was calculated as 57.40%.

Table 2. Confusion matrix: Naïve Bayes algorithm

Class	fclose	fopen	wccw	wcw
fclose	16	7	0	4
fopen	11	8	8	0
wccw	7	8	11	1
wcw	4	3	8	12

3.5 K Star (K*) Algorithm

The selected three features were used to train the K* algorithm and the following parameters were selected for classification.

1. Global blend parameter values were taken between 0 and 100.
2. Missing mode was used to treat the missing attribute values. There are four modes to treat missing values:
    a.   Ignore the instances with missing values.
    b.   Treat missing values as maximally different.
    c.   Normalize over the attributes.
    d.   Average column entropy curve.

The global blend value was changed from 0 to 100 and the corresponding classification accuracy was noted down. The maximum classification accuracy was obtained when the global blend value was 50. All the four missing modes have the same effect on the classification accuracy. Hence, the classification accuracy of the K Star algorithm was found to be 82.40%.

3.6 Ripple Down Rule Lerner (RIDOR) Algorithm

The effect of number of features on classification accuracy was found using decision tree. The selected three features were classified by using RIDOR. The following parameters were used for the classification.

-   **Folds (F):** Determines the amount of data used for pruning. One fold is used for pruning, the rest for growing the rules.
-   **Majority Class:** Whether the majority class is used as default
-   **minNo (N):** The mi nimum total weight of the instances in a rule.
-   **Seed:** The seed used for randomizing the data.
-   **Shuffle (S):** Determines how often the data is shuffled before a rule is chosen. If > 1, a rule is learned multiple times and the most accurate rule is chosen (1).

Totally 12 rules were generated for classification.
Ripple Down Rules:

1. Class = fclose (108.0/81.0): Default Rule
2. Except (Maximum <= 260.5) and (Median > -7) => class = wccw (22.0/0.0) [11.0/0.0]

3. Except (Mean <= 0.065918) and (Mean > -2.106934) => class = wcw (8.0/0.0) [4.0/0.0]
4. Except (Maximum > 225.5) and (Mean > 2.34668) => class = fopen (4.0/0.0) [3.0/0.0]
5. Except (Mean <= 0.37793) and (Median <= -10.5) => class = wcw (16.0/0.0) [6.0/1.0]
6. Except (Mean <= -0.338868) => class = fopen (7.0/1.0) [4.0/1.0]
7. Except (Maximum <= 313.5) and (Mean <= -2.134278) => class = fopen (6.0/0.0) [1.0/0.0]
8. Except (Median > -9) => class = wccw (4.0/1.0) [1.0/0.0]
9. Except (Maximum > 386) => class = wccw (5.0/0.0) [3.0/0.0]
10. Except (Median <= -12) => class = wcw (8.0/0.0) [3.0/0.0]
11. Except (Median <= -6) and (Median > -7.5) => class = fopen (8.0/1.0) [3.0/1.0]
12. Except (Mean <= -0.828613) and (Mean > -1.646484) => class = wcw (2.0/0.0) [1.0/0.0]

Here, the ten-fold cross validation technique was used to find the classification accuracy.Hence, classification accuracy for RIDOR was found to be 80.55%.

4. SUMMARY

The statistical features were taken and feature selection was performed using C4.5 algorithm. Three statistical features were selected for classification. The summary of classification accuracies of different classifiers using statistical features have been presented in Table 3.

Table 3. Summary of classification accuracy using statistical features

Classifier	Classification Accuracy (%)
	Statistical Features
C4.5 Decision tree	79.62
Best Fist Tree	79.62
Naïve Bayes	43.51
Bayes Net	57.40
K Star	82.40
Ripple down rule learner	80.55

It can be noticed that the classification accuracy is maximum in K star classifier (**82.40%**) among the six classifiers.

5. APPLICATION OF DECISION TREE (C4.5 ALGORITHM)

The value between the maximum and minimum of the EEG signal was divided into number of frequency ranges called as bins. Totally 50 bins were extracted from the EEG signal. All the 49 bin ranges (2-50) were classified one by one using a decision tree algorithm. Fig. 5.1 shows the classification accuracy for various bin ranges. Referring Figure 7, the classifier gives maximum classification accuracy for the 38th bin (frequency) ranges.

Thirty-eight frequency ranges were used as input to C4.5 decision tree algorithm. The contributing bin values are namely, "C4h34", "C4h11", "C4h25", "C4h31", "C4h28", "C4h22", "C4h20", "C4h18" and "C4h33". The features were selected based on entropy reduction and information gain. The information gain is a measure of the discriminating capability of a feature of the given data set.

5.1 Feature Classification Using C4.5 Decision Tree Algorithm

C4.5 Decision tree algorithm performs both feature selection and the feature classification simultaneously. Classification results were presented as confusion matrix. Among the extracted 49 Bins, 9 most important feature set were identified using decision tree. The selected features were classified using the C4.5 decision tree al-

Figure 7. Number of bins vs. classification accuracy

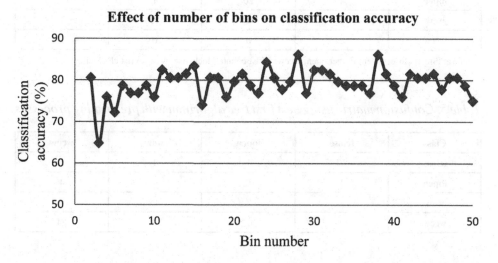

gorithm. The classification accuracy was found using the 10-fold cross validation. A big advantage of the 10-fold cross validation method is that all observations are used for both training and validation, and each observation is used for validation exactly once. This leads to a more accurate way to measure the accuracy, based on training set data. The classification and misclassification details are presented as a confusion matrix as shown in Table 4.

From the confusion matrix in Table 4. The first row first element shows that there are 26 instances classified correctly as 'fclose' class and 1 instance is misclassified as 'fopen, wccw, and wcw. Similarly, the second row, second element shows that there are 20 instances classified correctly as 'fopen' and 7 instances misclassified as rest of the class. Hence, all the diagonal elements of the confusion matrix table show the correctly classified instances of the class. Thus, the classification accuracy was calculated. However, C4.5 decision tree gives better classification accuracy (85.18%) for a selected number of histogram features.

5.2 Best First Tree (BF Tree)

The selected nine features were classified using best first tree with different kernels. Classification and misclassification details for best first decision tree algorithm with pre pruning and post-pruning processes were presented in Tables 5 and 6 respec-

Table 4. Confusion Matrix: C4.5 Decision tree algorithm

Class	fclose	fopen	wcw	wccw
fclose	26	1	0	0
fopen	4	20	1	2
wcw	5	2	19	1
wccw	2	0	0	25

fclose: Finger close; fopen: Finger open; wccw: Wrist counterclockwise; wcw: Wrist clockwise

Table 5. Confusion matrix using best first tree algorithm with pre pruning processes

Class	fclose	fopen	wcw	wccw
fclose	20	1	1	5
fopen	1	22	0	4
wcw	1	2	15	9
wccw	2	1	0	24

Table 6. Confusion matrix: Best first tree algorithm with post pruning processes

Class	fclose	fopen	wcw	wccw
fclose	21	1	2	3
fopen	3	22	0	2
wcw	3	2	21	1
wccw	1	1	2	23

tively. The following parameters were used for classification. Hence, the selected features were classified and the classification accuracy was achieved as 80.55%.

- **Minimum Number of Objects:** 2.
- **Number of Folds:** 5.
- **Pruning Strategy:** Post pruning.
- **The Training Set Size:** 1.
- **Splitting Criterion:** Gini index.

5.3 Naïve Bayes (NB) Classifier

Naïve Bayes classifier makes use of conditional probability of its classification. Among the 49 extracted bins, top nine bins are selected as features. The selected features were classified using the Naïve Bayes algorithm. Table 7 shows the classification and misclassifications details.

As there was some misclassification, the classification accuracy of the Naïve Bayes algorithm was calculated as 49.07%.

5.4 Bayes Net (BN) Classifier

The Bayesian network uses simple estimator for estimating the conditional probability tables of a Bayes network once the structure has been learned. It estimates

Table 7. Confusion matrix: Naïve Bayes (NB) algorithm

Class	fclose	fopen	wcw	wccw
fclose	10	3	3	11
fopen	10	14	0	3
wcw	0	1	11	15
wccw	3	0	6	18

probabilities directly from data. The selected features were classified using the Bayes net (BN) classifier. The following parameters were considered for the classification process.

1. **Estimator Algorithm:** Four estimator algorithms were used for finding the conditional probability tables of the Bayes network.

    a.   Bayes net estimator ($\alpha = 0.5$).
    b.   BMA estimator ($\alpha = 0.5$).
    c.   Multi nominal BMA estimator ($\alpha = 0.5$).
    d.   Simple estimator ($\alpha = 0.5$).

The estimator algorithm has no effect on the classification accuracy. Hence a Bayes net estimator was chosen.

Search algorithm: Search algorithm was used for searching network structures. Here, the hill climber search algorithm was used to identify the best Bayesian network model.The total classification accuracy was found to be 72.22%.

5.5 K Star (K*) Algorithm

The K Star algorithm uses entopic auto blend. The parameter for global blend has been chosen as 20. One advantage of K Star algorithm is it normalizes the missing attribute values. The selected features were classified using K Star algorithm. The classifier uses 10-fold cross validation for classification. The classification accuracy was obtained as 82.40% using K Star algorithm. The classification and misclassification details were presented in the form of a confusion matrix as shown in Table 8.

Table 8. Confusion matrix: K Star algorithm

Class	fclose	fopen	wcw	wccw
fclose	22	3	2	0
fopen	3	21	2	1
wcw	3	1	23	0
wccw	0	2	2	23

5.6 Ripple Down Rule Learner (RIDOR) Algorithm

The effect of a number of features on classification accuracy was found using the decision tree. Among the 49 bins, nine features were selected for classification. The following parameters were used for the classification.

- **Folds (F):** Determines the amount of data used for pruning. One fold is used for pruning, the rest for growing the rules. (3)
- **Majority Class:** Whether the majority class is used as default
- **minNo (N):** The minimum total weight of the instances in a rule (2).
- **Seed:** The seed used for randomizing the data (1).
- **Shuffle (S):** Determines how often the data are shuffled before a rule is chosen. If > 1, a rule is learned multiple times and the most accurate rule is chosen (1).

The selected nine features were classified using ripple down rule learner (RODOR) algorithm. Totally 13 rules were generated for classification.

Ripple Down Rules:

1. Class = wccw (108.0/81.0)
2. Except (c4h25 > 7.5) and (c4h31 > 13.5) => class = fclose (22.0/0.0) [13.0/0.0]
3. Except (c4h25 <= 13) => class = fopen (15.0/0.0) [7.0/0.0]
4. Except (c4h18 > 146) => class = wcw (8.0/0.0) [3.0/0.0]
5. Except (c4h28 > 6.5) and (c4h33 <= 1.5) => class = fopen (18.0/0.0) [8.0/0.0]
6. Except (c4h20 <= 231.5) => class = fclose (5.0/0.0) [3.0/1.0]
7. Except (c4h20 > 314.5) => class = fclose (8.0/1.0) [2.0/0.0]
8. Except (c4h18 <= 91.5) => class = wcw (3.0/0.0) [1.0/0.0]
9. Except (c4h18 > 130) => class = fclose (2.0/0.0) [1.0/0.0]
10. Except (c4h22 > 31) and (c4h22 <= 35) => class = wcw (8.0/0.0) [4.0/0.0]
11. Except (c4h20 <= 345) => class = fclose (12.0/0.0) [6.0/0.0]
12. Except (c4h11 > 5) => class = fopen (5.0/0.0) [2.0/0.0]
13. Except (c4h18 <= 31) and (c4h18 > 23.5) => class = wcw (2.0/0.0) [1.0/0.0]

Here the ten-fold cross validation technique was used to find the classification accuracy. Hence, the classification accuracy for RIDOR was found to be 82.40%.

The histogram features were taken and feature selection was performed using C4.5 decision tree algorithm. Nine features were selected for classification. Their performance in classification has been presented. The summary of classification accuracies of different classifiers using histogram features have been presented in Table 9.

Table 9. Summary of classification accuracy using histogram features

Classifier	Classification Accuracy (%)
	Histogram Features
C4.5 Decision tree	85.18
Best Fist Tree	80.55
Naïve Bayes	49.07
Bayes Net	72.22
K Star	82.40
Ripple down rule learner	82.40

Among the 6 classifiers considered, the C4.5 Decision tree model gives the maximum classification accuracy with histogram features.

6. MULTICORE IMPLEMENTATION OF C4.5 ALGORITHM

Many researchers have proposed the parallism in implementing various decision tree algorithms by Li Wenlong and Xing Changzheng (2010), Wei Dai and Wei Ji (2014), and Nuno et al. (2002). Implementing on multicore is challenging as it is limited to the software support. In recent research, there are various models have been implemented for classification, such as Naïve bayes, bayes net, neural networks, decision tree and K-Star. In particular, C4.5 decision tree is the best appropriate for data mining approach. The performance ability of the decision tree is relatively higher when compared with other classifiers. Parallelization may be a more feasible solution to decrease the required computational time to build the model for prosthetic limb with movements using EEG signals. The concept of multi core implementation can be achieved through the parallel processing of decision tree construction. The decision tree nodes can be built parallel or parallel distribution of the training data. At the time of writing this chapter, the authors of this chapter are working on Matlab multicore programming to implement the algorithm for parallel computing.

7. CONCLUSION

Machine learning has three important phases, namely, feature extraction, feature selection and feature classification. At each phase, techniques were considered with the aim to identify the best possible 'feature-classifier' pair of the EEG signals. The classification results are concisely presented in Table 10.

Table 10. Summary of classification accuracy

Classifier	Classification Accuracy (%)	
	Statistical Features	Histogram Features
C4.5 Decision tree	79.62	85.18
Best Fist Tree	79.62	80.55
Naïve Bayes	43.51	49.07
Bayes Net	56.48	72.22
K Star	82.40	82.40
Ripple down rule learner (RIDOR)	80.55	82.40

Among the thirteen classifiers considered in the present study, C4.5 Decision tree with Histogram features produced maximum classification accuracy as 85.18%. More specifically, C4.5 Decision tree model performs better with histogram features compared to statistical features. Hence, from the results presented above, one can confidently conclude that 'histogram-C4.5 Decision tree' combination can be considered as a best 'feature-classifier' pair of the EEG signals can be used for controlling the prosthetic limb movements at least amongst the pairs considered for this work.

REFERENCES

Adeli, H., Zhou, Z., & Dadmehr, N. (2003). Analysis of EEG records in an epileptic patient using wavelet transform. *Journal of Neuroscience Methods, 123*(1), 69–87. doi:10.1016/S0165-0270(02)00340-0 PMID:12581851

Aishwarya, R., Prabhu, M., Sumithra, G., & Anusiya, M. (2013). Feature Extraction for EMG based Prosthesis contro. *ICTACT Journal on Soft Computing, 3*(2).

Bhattacharyya, S., Debabrota, B., Konar, A., & Tibarewala, D. N. (2015). Interval type-2 fuzzy logic based multiclass ANFIS algorithm for real-time EEG based movement control of a robot arm. *Robotics and Autonomous Systems, 68*, 104–115. doi:10.1016/j.robot.2015.01.007

Bhattacharyya, S., Konar, A., & Tibarewala, D. N. (2014). A differential evolution based energy trajectory planner for artificial limb control using motor imagery EEG signal. *Biomedical Signal Processing and Control, 11*, 107–113. doi:10.1016/j.bspc.2014.03.001

Che Wan Fadzal, C. W. N. F., Mansor, W., & Khuan, L. Y. (2012). Analysis of EEG Signal from Right and Left Hand Writing Movements. *IEEE Control and System Graduate Research Colloquium (ICSGRC).*

Dai, W., & Ji, W. (2014). A MapReduce Implementation of C4.5 Decision Tree Algorithm. *International Journal of Database Theory and Application, 7*(1), 49–60. doi:10.14257/ijdta.2014.7.1.05

Dornhege, G., Millan, J. R., Hinterberger, T., Mc Farland, D. J., & Muller, K. R. (2007). *Toward Brain-Computer Interfacing* (1st ed.). MIT Press.

Enrique, H., Iáñez, E., Úbeda, A., Carlos, P., & José, M. (2015). Combining a Brain–Machine Interface and an Electrooculography Interface to perform pick and place tasks with a robotic arm. *Robotics and Autonomous Systems, 72,* 181–188. doi:10.1016/j.robot.2015.05.010

Ericka, J.R., & Huosheng, H. (n.d.). Bio-signal based control in assistive robots: a survey. *Digital Communications and Networks, 1*(2), 85-101.

Herrmann, C. S., Arnold, T., Visbeck, A., Hundemer, H. P., & Hopf, H. C. (2001). Adaptive frequency decomposition of EEG with subsequent expert system analysis. *Computers in Biology and Medicine, 31*(6), 407–427. doi:10.1016/S0010-4825(01)00017-8 PMID:11604148

Koley, B., & Dey, D. (2012). An ensemble system for automatic sleep stage classification using single channel EEG signal. *Computers in Biology and Medicine, 42*(12), 1186–1195. doi:10.1016/j.compbiomed.2012.09.012 PMID:23102750

Li & Xing. (2010). Parallel Decision Tree Algorithm Based on Combination. *International Forum on Information Technology and Applications.*

Monalisa, P., Bhattacharyya, S., Konar, A., & Tibarewala, D. N. (2015). An interval type-2 fuzzy approach for real-time EEG-based control of wrist and finger movement. *Biomedical Signal Processing and Control, 21,* 90–98. doi:10.1016/j.bspc.2015.05.004

Muralidharan, V., & Sugumaran, V. (2012). A comparative study of Naïve Bayes classifier and Bayes net classifier for fault diagnosis of mono-block centrifugal pump using wavelet analysis. *Journal of Applied Soft Computing, 12*(8), 2023–2029. doi:10.1016/j.asoc.2012.03.021

Nuno, A., Joao, G., & Fernando, S. (2002). Parallel implementation of decision tree learning algorithm. *Chapters in Progress in Artificial Intelligence, 2258,* 6–13.

Ocak, H. (2008). Optimal Classification of epileptic seizures in EEG using wavelet analysis and genetic algorithm. *Signal Processing, 88*(7), 1858–1867. doi:10.1016/j.sigpro.2008.01.026

Shiliang, S., Changshui, Z., & Dan, Z. (2007). An experimental evaluation of ensemble methods for EEG signal classification. *Pattern Recognition Letters, 28*(15), 2157–2163. doi:10.1016/j.patrec.2007.06.018

Sugumaran, V., Muralidharan, V., & Ramachandran, K. I. (2007). Feature selection using Decision Tree and classification through Proximal Support Vector Machine for fault diagnostics of roller bearing. *Mechanical Systems and Signal Processing, 21*(2), 930–942. doi:10.1016/j.ymssp.2006.05.004

Ubeyli, E. D. (2008). Analysis of EEG signals by combining eigenvector methods and multiclass support vector machines. *Computers in Biology and Medicine, 38*(1), 14–22. doi:10.1016/j.compbiomed.2007.06.002 PMID:17651716

Ubeyli, E. D. (2009). Statistics over features: EEG signals analysis. *Computers in Biology and Medicine, 39*(8), 733–741. doi:10.1016/j.compbiomed.2009.06.001 PMID:19555931

Übeyli, E. D. (2010). Least squares support vector machine employing model-based methods coefficients for analysis of EEG signals. *Expert Systems with Applications, 37*(1), 233–239. doi:10.1016/j.eswa.2009.05.012

Chapter 9
A Technical Assessment on License Plate Detection System

Jeena Rita K. S.
SCMS School of Engineering and Technology, India

Bini Omman
SCMS School of Engineering and Technology, India

ABSTRACT

Identifying the region of interest from an image is an important task in the field of computer vision. This process is referred as Object Detection. Locating the object can be done by extracting the features from the image and the features depend on the application. Image retrieval and surveillance are two important applications of Object Detection. Surveillance is an active research topic in computer vision that tries to detect, recognize and track objects over images. An interesting application of it is License Plate Recognition module in Intelligent Transportation System. The speedy developments in economic and social life bring on for a large increase in the number of vehicles in the city. This makes the traffic management difficult. It has great impact on human life as it aims to increase the transportation safety through innovative technologies. An important function that need for majority of ITS application is to identify the vehicle using LPR. This chapter presents assessment on different methods in detecting the license plate and discusses a case study on it.

DOI: 10.4018/978-1-5225-0889-2.ch009

INTRODUCTION

Object detection is the process of discovering the instances of real-world objects in images or videos. Object detection algorithms use mined features and learning algorithms to recognize instances of an object (Gossian & Gill, 2014). Human can easily recognize the objects in a scene but not for the computer. It is difficult to implement the algorithms that identify the object. Many difficulties are there for detecting the object from an image. View point variation, illumination, occlusion, scale change, deformation or articulation, background clutter are some of the challenges that face in object detection task. In general approach, object detection methods first learn from positive and negative samples that which all images have the particular object. Positive samples are the samples that contain the object of interest and negative samples are that do not possess object of interest. After learning from these samples it determines the object of interest from the new image. Object detection has application in the areas like image retrieval, surveillance, vehicle navigation and the like. Surveillance is an active research topic in computer vision that tries to detect, recognize and track objects over images. An interesting application of it is License Plate Recognition (LPR) module in Intelligent Transportation System (ITS). Here the object of interest is License Plate (LP).

The quick economic development and social progress pay way for a large increase in the number of vehicles in the city. This makes the traffic management difficult (Dong & Feng, 2014). ITS plays an important role in the field of traffic security. It has great impact on human life as it aims to increase the transportation safety through innovative technologies. Arterial management, Emergency management, Traveller information, Electronic payment, Road weather management, Driver assistance system, Collision notification system are some of the key applications of ITS. An important function that need for majority of ITS application is to identify the vehicle. For this LPR system is requiring. As the efficiency of LPR increases the ITS applications outputs good result. So it becomes a vital slice in Intelligent Transportation System.

Detecting the number plate region and recognizing the characters of the number plate is an interesting. It is technique that identifies the vehicles by their license plates. The system uses a camera to capture the front or rear of the vehicle which contain the LP. Then the LPR system processes that image and extracts the information. This information is then used for different applications. The main applications of LPDS come in: parking areas, to detect the vehicles that are in over speed, control in restricted areas, electronic toll collection etc. Licence plate is like a unique identifier (Comelli et al., 1995). No two vehicles have the same license plate. So there is no need for additional hardware fitted to the vehicle to hold its identity. The difficulties in detecting the license plate detection systems faces are poor lighting due to shadows, weather conditions, the image quality, plate model and color, processing time etc.

With the popularity of Intelligent Transportation System, automatic identification of vehicle becomes an important area. Generally, two ways are there to identify a vehicle. One is through electronic devices and other through image processing techniques. In the case of electronic devices, RFID tag is attached to the vehicle and using this identification is performed. An external antenna sends out microwave signal and this signal extract the unique information from the tag. With this information the vehicle identification process is performing. In the other case, camera catches the image of a vehicle and the LPR module extract the number plate information which is unique for each vehicle.

BACKGROUND

As the need for automatic recognition of license plate arises, in 1995 P. Comelli *et al.* in (Comelli et al., 1995) introduced a system that automatically recognizes the characters of motor vehicle license plate. It mainly consists of three main modules. First module segments the region where the license plate is located within the image. As the second step feature projection estimates certain parameters and normalizes the license plate characters. Lastly, using character recognizer some feature points was extracted and template matching produces better solutions. Here the image acquisition is done by a CCD TV camera fitted at a toll gate. A quasi-static image is then obtained and it is then converted into a digital signal to process. Acquired image is of the size 256 x 512 in grayscale level. The estimated image portion containing license plate from first phase is not accurate. It only retrieves the plate area, not the single characters. This finding is based on some characteristics of the image like rectangular regions, black characters on white background etc. the algorithm finds the area which have maximum local contrast that probably contain the rectangular region. The gradient analysis on that finds the rectangle and which is then isolated from the image. This phase results the coordinates of the center of the window containing the license plate. The next phase is called as pre-processing stage. It performs filtering and histogram stretching to produce enhanced image, character size estimation and evaluation of the license plate and the bilinear resampling of the image to obtain the standard dimensions. This pre-processing stage also removes the noises. It detects the centres and normalizes the license plate image and finds all the information from that image region. The output from this phase is an image representing the isolated and normalized whole license plate. Final phase is the recognizing phase. Here a simple template matching technique on gray level images has been used. This method obtained a recognition rate of 91%.

In (Nabaee & Zadeh, 2007) M. Nabaee *et al.* proposed a method for license plate detection based on improved gradient and match filtering. Authors put on a sequence of match filters on the image after eliminating the regions that have a low probability. The filters correspond to various possible sizes of license plate. It generates candidate regions and from these regions finalize license plate region. This method is based on match filtering that means to find a particular pattern, a filter with an impulse response equal to the time reversed of that pattern can be used. In the first step, a simple pre-processing is applied to discard the regions that don't have the features of a license plate. For that improved gradient operator is applied to remove the edges of those regions. The result of this is high values of intensity and gradient are the main features. Subsequently, the size of the plate area is not known, input image is filtered with a spatial domain filter with different window sizes. After filtering down-sampled output images were obtained. The detection of candidate regions is based on the correlation of the region around pixel with filter window for a specific scale. After extracting the candidate regions, properties like elongation and fitness of the regions are used for discarding the inappropriate regions. From the remaining candidate regions density of vertical edges and the portion of length to width are used to find the regions that contain license plate and regions excluding any license plate.

License plate detection based MSER (Maximally Stable Extremal Region) is proposed by W. Wang *et al.* in (Yu & Kim, 2000). Here the proposed method first pre-process the input image and then find the candidate regions based on the pixel sum, scale, length-with ratio. As the next step, the method finds the upper and lower borders of the license plate. Initially the input image undergoes gray scaling and stretching with appropriate parameters. The extremal regions are computed from this output. From this the connected component analysis is performed and obtains the license plate region. Using gray level jump and projection the left and right borders of the license plate is determined. Most of the license plate detection system faces difficulties in handling the illumination changes, complex background or alignment variations. Since the camera observation angle will connect the LP characters with various adornments such as frames, screws, the identification of the characters in LP will be a difficult task. So a colour gradient based method locate the license plate area was proposed in (Huang, 2014) to detect LP. Here a colour gradient map was developed using the colour gradient method. Then by applying the Niblack's method on the map the candidate LP regions will retrieve. After that a template matching will perform to remove the background noises. The color gradient map can keep the license plate character regions completely and also it removes the color variations. This produces a clear character edge details. Niblack's method process low complexity images. It depends on local mean and standard deviation, which is delicate to local abnormal intensity change.

In (Deb et., 2008), authors presented a license plate detection method based on sliding concentric windows and HIS color model. It is based on the fact that the license plate extraction is based on the natural properties by determining the vertical and horizontal edges from the image. The method comprises of three modules. In first step they find the candidate regions using the segmentation technique called as sliding concentric windows. Then the candidate regions are verified based on the hue and intensity in HIS color model. And finally verify the license plate region using position histogram. This system is based on the Korean license plate. There are various styles of license plate in Korea. Each one has different foreground and/ or background color like white, green, yellow, black, blue. Edges show unevenness in the intensity of the image. Using this information a Sliding Concentric Window is used to detect the rectangular regions. The HSI color model is used here because some color show different in different lighting conditions in RGB model and in HIS model there is no difference

In (Deb et., 2008) a region-based license plate detection method is proposed. It firstly generates candidate regions using mean shift segmentation. Then decides if a region of interest really contains a license plate based on the feature analysis of candidate regions. Features of each region are to be extracted in order to correctly differentiate the license plate regions from others. Matas and Zimmermann proposed an algorithm in (Matas & Zimmermann, 2005) which detects license plates under various conditions. Algorithm uses a new class of locally threshold separable detectors based on external regions. The detector selects a category-relevant subset of external regions. External regions as basic units of LPs, which make the algorithm quite robust to viewpoint and illumination. However, this algorithm could hardly highlight characters overlapping from the true LPs.

Most of the works in License plate detection are under constrained conditions, such as static illumination, limited vehicle speed, selected routes, and motionless backgrounds. In (Chang et al., 2004) S. -L. Chang et al. proposed an algorithm which utilizes fuzzy disciplines and color edge to extract license plates from a given input image. LPR strategy comprises of two key modules: a license plate locating module and a license number identification module. The previous characterized by fuzzy disciplines tries to extract license plates from an input image, while the second, conceptualized in terms of neural subjects intends to recognize the number present in a license plate. It can only be used with certain colours. In (S. Kim et al., 2008) S. Kim et al. proposed a system which separate car license plate from images with complex background and comparatively poor quality. It mainly focuses on images that were taken under weak lighting conditions. It consists of two steps. First it searches for the candidate areas from the input image using gradient information and the second is finding the plate area among the candidates and adjusting the boundary of the area by introducing a plate template. In some cases, general LP templates are very difficult to be constructed and algorithm can work on a fixed scale. Hence, the application of this algorithm is restricted. In (Yu & Kim, 2000), M. Yu and Y. D. Kim proposed an algorithm that uses the vertical edge match to determine the license plate from a grayscale image. It uses Prewitt mask to obtain the edge map from grayscale image. A size-and-shape filter based on seed-filling algorithm removes some noisy areas that do not satisfy some restricted conditions. The algorithm is able to identify license plates in standard shape, as well as plates that are out of shape due to the viewpoint.

OBJECT DETECTION

Object detection is a computer technology associated to computer vision and image processing that deals with discovering occurrences of semantic objects of a definite class such as humans, buildings, or cars in digital images and videos. It is one of the fundamental challenges in computer vision. It is because objects in such categories can vary greatly in appearance. Variations arise due to the changes in illumination and viewpoint, non-rigid deformations, and intra-class variability in shape and other visual properties. The object recognition problem can be defined as a labelling problem based on models of known objects. Formally, given an image containing one or more objects of interest (and background) and a set of labels corresponding to a set of models known to the system, the system should assign correct labels to regions, or a set of regions, in the image.

The various object detection techniques are template matching, colour based, active and passive, shape based and local and global features. Template matching is a technique for recognizing small fragments of an image which match a template image. In this technique template images for distinctive objects are stored (Khurana & Awasthi, 2013). At the point an input image is given to the system, it is matched with the kept template images to find the object in the input image. Color offers strong data for object recognition. A basic and effective object detection structure is to characterize and match images on the basis of color histograms. Object detection in passive manner does not include local image samples mined during scanning. Two main object-detection methods that pay passive scanning are Window-sliding approach, it uses passive scanning to check if the object is existing or not at all positions of a uniformly spaced grid, and the other is Part-based approach, it uses passive scanning to decide the interest facts in an image. In active scanning native samples are used to guide the scanning procedure. At the present scanning location of a native image sample is mined and mapped to a shifting vector indicating the next scanning position. The method takes succeeding samples to the expected object location, while skipping regions improbable to comprise the object. The shape features are more conspicuous as compared to local features like SIFT because most object categories are better defined by their shape then texture. Thus shape features are often used as an extra or complement to local features.

Challenges in Object Detection

The various challenges in the process of object detection are the following:

- **Illumination:** The illumination may change with the course of day. The elements that influence with the illumination are climate condition, shadows and so forth.
- **Rotation:** The object can be in pivoted structure. The framework must be skilled to handle such trouble.
- **Partial Occlusion:** The condition during which the image isn't fully visible is referred as occlusion. The system of object tracking should handle such conditions.

Applications of Object Detection

- **Biometric Recognition:** Biometric technology uses human physical or activity traits to acknowledge somebody for security and authentication. Biometrics is that the identification of a personal supported distinguished biological features like fingerprints, hand geometry, tissue layer and iris patterns, DNA, etc. For biometric analysis, Object recognition methods like template matching may be used.
- **Surveillance:** Objects will be recognized and tracked for varied video police investigation systems. Object recognition is needed in order that the suspected person or vehicle as an example is tracked.
- **Industrial Inspection:** Parts of machinery will be recognized object recognition and might be monitored for run-down or injury.
- **Content-Based Image Retrieval (CBIR):** When the retrieval is predicated on the image content it's referred as CBIR. A supervised learning system, referred to as OntoPic, which provides an automatic keyword annotation for pictures and content-based image retrieval.
- **Robotic:** The analysis of autonomous robots is one in all the foremost necessary problems in recent years. The automaton mechanism football game competition is extremely widespread. The mechanism football game players have confidence their vision systems terribly heavily after they are within the unpredictable and dynamic environments. The vision system will facilitate the mechanism to gather numerous atmosphere information because the terminal

knowledge to complete the functions of mechanism localization, mechanism plans of action, barrier avoiding, etc. It will decrease the computing efforts, to acknowledge the vital objects within the contest field by object features which may be obtained simply by object recognition techniques.

- **Medical Analysis:** Neoplasm detection in imaging pictures, Carcinoma detection will be some samples of medical imaging for object detection.
- **Optical Character/Digit Recognition:** Characters in scanned documents will be recognized by recognition techniques.
- **Human Computer Interaction:** Human gestures will be hold on within the system, which might be used for recognition within the period atmosphere by computer to try and do interaction with humans. The system will be any application on interactive games, etc.
- **Intelligent Transportation Systems:** Intelligent vehicle systems square measure required for traffic sign detection and recognition, particularly for vehicle detection and tracking.

Intelligent Transportation System and License Plate Detection

ITS uses License Plate Recognition to spot the vehicles. License Plate Recognition is an image process technology wont to identify the vehicles by their license plates. It's gaining worth in security and traffic installations (Bradley & Roth, 2007). Technology assumes that each one vehicle have already got the License Plate. Thus no further transmitter or any device is requiring to be put in on the vehicle. System uses a camera to require the photographs of the front or rear of the vehicle. Then image process computer code analyses the image and extract the plate info. This info is employed for various the applications.

The main difficulties in vehicle plate Detection Systems are:

- Poor file resolution, actually because the plate is just too secluded however typically ensuing from the utilization of a low-quality camera.
- Blurry pictures, notably motion blur.
- Poor lighting and low distinction attributable to overexposure, reflection or shadows.
- An object obscuring (part of) the plate, very often a tow bar, or dirt on the plate.
- A completely different font, common for self-importance plates (some countries don't enable such plates, eliminating the problem).
- Lack of coordination between countries or states. 2 cars from {different totally completely different completely different} countries or states will have constant variety however different style of the plate.

The different applications are:

- **Payment of Parking Fees:** Once an automobile is moving into a parking region its number plate is browse and hold on. once the automobile can later exit, the automobile plate are going to be read once more and therefore the driver are going to be charged for the time of the parking.
- **Highway Toll Fees:** Number plate is employed to calculate the travel fee in an exceedingly motorway. Victimization the number plate data concerning the vehicle is retrieved from the info and generates the pass price tag.
- **Traffic Control:** Vehicles will be directed to completely different lanes in line with their entry permits. And additionally accustomed turn out a fine on speed or red light-weight systems.
- **Gate Access Control:** Gate mechanically opens for approved members in an exceedingly secured space, exchange a watcher. Events will be saved and will be accustomed search the history of events.
- **Crime Prevention:** A black list can be updated in a real time and provide immediate alarm to the police force.

CASE STUDY

License Plate Detection system will accept image of any size and format. It manly consists of four steps:

1. **Pre-Processing:** Here, the input image is treating to remove the noise and make ready for the further processes. First it converts the image to a size that is fixed for the system. Here it is taken as 352 x 288. Grayscale conversion and thresholding are the two pre-processing methods that used here.
2. **Vertical Edges Detection:** First we need to remove the unwanted lines or noises to find the vertical edges clearly. This can be considered as an enhancement process. Then find the vertical edges.
3. **License Plate Extraction:** License plate extraction means finding the plate region from the selected candidates. Candidate regions can be the probable regions that may contain license plate.
4. **Character Recognition:** Character recognition is done on the final selected candidate region. This candidate region is selected as the license plate region.

1. Pre-Processing

Color images do not provide a good accuracy in natural scenarios. If the input image is color then it will be difficult to process. The Color image takes three times of processing time compared to the grayscale image processing time. And also the noise will be more in the color image. So more wok is needed to code for the color image. Grayscale image is more suitable for the image processing application if the application extracting features other than color for its processing. It is because color combinations are not stable when the lighting conditions change. For example, blue colour seen as black in night scenes. So system processes the vehicle image on grayscale format. Because of these reasons after converting to a uniform size, the image will be converted to grayscale format.

The next sub-process is to apply thresholding to the grayscale image. Thresholding creates a binary representation of the input image. It classifies the image as either dark or light. That means either black or white. In thresholding process, each pixel is compared with a global threshold value. If the pixel value is greater than the threshold, it is assigned as white (or black), otherwise as black (or white). But it is not results good if there are large variations in illumination. For a better result, Adaptive Thresholding method proposed by Bradley and Roth in (Bradley & Roth, 2007) is used for thresholding (Ghaili et al., 2013). In Adaptive Thresholding (AT) each pixel has different threshold value. The threshold for each pixel is computing using the integral image.

Integral image is the sum of all the pixel values above, to the left and the original pixel value. That is integral image at location (i, j) is the sum of the pixels above and to the left of (i, j), inclusive:

$$Int\, Im\, g\left(i, j\right) = \sum_{i' \leq i, j' \leq j}^{n} Im\, g(i', j') \tag{1}$$

where *IntImg(i, j)* is the integral image and *Img(i, j)* is the original image.

$$CumSum(i, j) = CuSum(i, j - 1) + Im\, g(i, j)$$
$$IntImg\left(i, j\right) = IntImg\left(i - 1, j\right) + CumSum\left(i, j\right) \tag{2}$$

where *CumSum(i, j)* is the cumulative row sum, *s(i,-1) = 0*, and *IntImg(-1, y) = 0*. Using (2), the integral image can be computed in one pass over the original image (Comelli et al., 1995). Figure 1 shows an example for integral image. In that (a) shows the pixels values of input image and (b) shows its integral image.

Figure 1. Example for integral image

5	2	5	2
3	6	3	6
5	2	5	2
3	6	3	6

(a)

5	7	12	14
8	16	24	32
13	23	36	46
16	32	48	64

(b)

After computing the integral image, calculate the threshold for each pixel with it. For that we consider a local window with the following boundaries (Khurana & Awasthi, 2013):

$$\left(i+\frac{S}{2},\ j+\frac{S}{2}\right),\ \left(i+\frac{S}{2},\ j-\frac{S}{2}\right),\ \left(i-\frac{S}{2},\ j+\frac{S}{2}\right),\ \left(i-\frac{S}{2},\ j-\frac{S}{2}\right)$$

where S represents the local window size of the integral image and its value is equal to 1/8th of the image width. The intensity summation of each of this local window is computed using the following equation:

$$
\begin{aligned}
sum_{window} = &\ Int\ Im\ g\left(i+\frac{s}{2},j+\frac{s}{2}\right) + Int\ Im\ g\left(i+\frac{s}{2},j-\frac{s}{2}\right) \\
&-Int\ Im\ g\left(i-\frac{s}{2},j+\frac{s}{2}\right) + Int\ Im\ g\left(i-\frac{s}{2},j-\frac{s}{2}\right)
\end{aligned}
\tag{3}
$$

The threshold for pixel at (i, j) is:

$$t(i,j) = (1-T)*sum_{window} \tag{4}$$

where $t(i, j)$ represents the threshold at location $(i. j)$ and T is a constant with value 0. 15. This value for T gives the best thresholding result for the whole images and this testing is shown in Section IV. The adaptive thresholding is then performing using the following criteria:

$$o(i,j) = \begin{cases} 0, & g(i,j)*S^2 < t(i,j) \\ 255, & \text{otherwise} \end{cases} \tag{5}$$

Figure 2. Input and output of adaptive thresholding

where $o(i, j)$ is the adaptive threshold output value of pixel $g(i, j)$, and S^2 represents the computed area of the local window for the selected region. Figure 2 shows the input image and result of the Adaptive Thresholding.

2. Vertical Edges Detection

After pre-processing stage, next step is to enhance the image by eliminating the noises like unwanted lines. As an enhancement process unwanted line elimination algorithm is applying to the image obtained from the adaptive thresholding process. After that, find the vertical edges.

1. **Unwanted Line Elimination Algorithm (ULEA):** From Figure 2 it is clear that image obtained after adaptive thresholding contains many unwanted lines. These lines should be removed otherwise it may interfere in finding the LP (License Plate). Here we consider only the lines with single pixel width otherwise small details of the LP may eliminate. There are four cases to eliminate the lines with one pixel width (Ghaili et al., 2013). Figure 3 shows those four cases. For that a 3 x 3 mask is used. To eliminate these lines, place the mask on each pixel and convert the centre pixel to white if its two neighbours are white as in the Figure 3. It only processes the black pixels i. e.; the mask's central pixel should be black. The output of ULEA is shown in Figure 4.

2. **Vertical Edge Detection Algorithm (VEDA):** This algorithm is used to differentiate the plate detail region (Ghaili et al., 2013). Therefore, the plate details will be easily detected. After thresholding and ULEA processes, the image will only have black and white regions, and the VEDA is processing these regions. It concentrates on black-white region and white-black region as shown in Box 1.

Figure 3. Four cases for eliminating unwanted lines

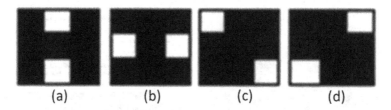

(a)   (b)   (c)   (d)

Figure 4. ULEA output

Table 1. Execution time for each step (in seconds)

AT	ULEA	VEDA	HDD	CRE	PRS & PD
3. 019993	0. 65922	2. 51591	0. 44327	0. 00027	0. 04867

Box 1.

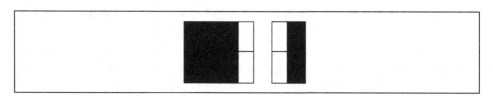

Figure 5. Vertical edge detection mask

x, y-1	x, y	x, y+1	x, y+2
x+1, y-1	x+1, y	x+1, y+1	x+1, y+2

Left   **center**   **right**

A 2x4 mask is proposed for this as in Figure 5. It considers two pixels at a time and it is located at points (0, 1) and (1, 1). The mask is divided into three regions. The first submask is the 2x2 left mask, the second submask is the 2x1 centre mask and the third submask is the 2x1 right mask as marked in Figure 5. The mask starts moving from top to bottom and from left to right.

If the four pixels at locations (0, 1), (0, 2), (1, 1), and (1, 2) are black, then the other mask values are tested if whether they are black or not. If the whole values are black, then the two locations at (0, 1) and (1, 1) will be converted to white. Otherwise, if column 1 and any other column have different values, the pixel value of column 1 will then be taken (Ghaili et al., 2013). Figure 6 shows the output of VEDA.

3. License Plate Extraction

Next we need to find the candidate regions. First step for it is to highlight the desired details in the image. Using that information find the candidate regions and select

Figure 6. VEDA output

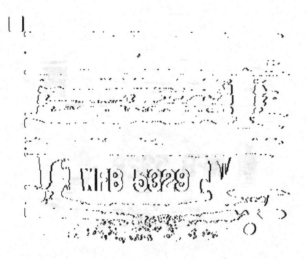

one candidate region as the LP region based on some criteria. The following are the steps for that:

1. **Highlighting Desired Details (HDD):** The output of VEDA is in the form that helps to find the LP easily i. e, it is of the form one 2-pixel width vertical line is followed by 1- pixel width vertical line. When there are two neighbour black pixels and followed by one black pixel, then a horizontal black line will be drawn to highlight that desired details (Ghaili et al., 2013). For drawing the horizontal line two conditions should be satisfied. First, these two vertical edges should be surrounded by a black background, as in the ULEA output image in Figure 4. Second, the value of horizontal distance, the length between the two vertical edges, should be between 1 and 33. After all pixels are scanned, the regions in which the correct LP exists are highlighted, as shown in Figure 7.

2. **Candidate Region Extraction (CRE):** To select the candidate regions first divide the image rows into multiple groups. It is do so to speed up the processing. Rows can be divided using the following equation (Ghaili et al., 2013):

$$number - of - groups = \frac{height}{C}$$

Figure 7. HDD output

Figure 8. CRE output

Here number of groups is the total number of groups, height represents the total number of rows in the image, C represents the candidate region extraction constant and its value is taken as 10. Then count the number of horizontal lines drawn per each row in HDD. Then we set a threshold to select the satisfied group because some groups are not parts of the LP. Each group will be checked by counting the total number of horizontal lines per each group. The threshold is set to 15 lines. If any groups that has atleast 15 lines then it considered as the candidate region. The threshold value is taken as greater than $\frac{1}{20} * 288$ *i.e.,* $\geq 14.4 \approx 15$. If there is any two or more adjacent groups are condition satisfied group then join them and consider as one candidate region. Then draw boundaries of each candidate region. Figure 8 shows this result.

3.   **Plate Region Selection (PRS):** To select one candidate region as LP first check the blackness ratio for each column (Ghaili et al., 2013). If the blackness ratio for the column is greater than 50% of the column height, then it is considered as the part of LP region. Draw a vertical line in that column and make a vote for that column. For each candidate region do the same and the candidate region that has the highest vote will be selected as the correct License Plate. Figure 9 shows the result.

Here, the second candidate region has the maximum vote. So it is the plate region. Figure 10 shows the final result.

Figure 9. PRS output

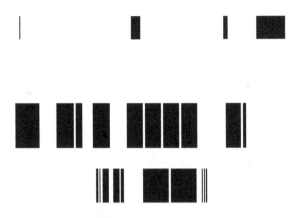

Figure 10. Final result

4. **Character Recognition:** Once the License Plate is correctly located that image part is given as the input to Optical Character Recognition (OCR) module. OCR correctly recognizes the characters in that image patch. Following figure shows the input to this phase.

Figure 11. Input image patch to OCR module

SOLUTIONS AND RECOMMENDATIONS

The License Plate Detection System is running on a system with 8GB RAM and Ubuntu 14. 04 platform with the support of Intel core 3. Python OpenCV library is used for the implementation. The system evaluates the performance of each step and also with the Canny and Sobel edge detection methods.

1. Dataset

The License Plate Detection and Recognition method was applied on more than 100 images that were obtained from (Ghaili et al., 2013)and other sources. Some of them are shown here:

2. Comparison and Evaluation

From 200 samples, the proposed method got 175 correct outputs and it shows 6 seconds as average execution time. Adaptive Thresholding needs the highest time for execution. Figure 13 shows some of the results.

Table 1 shows the execution time for each step.

Figure 12. Input samples

Figure 13. Set of successfully detected license plates

Figure 14. Result of canny and sobel edge detection

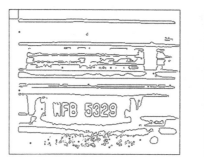 

3. Canny and Sobel Edge Detection Results

When applying the Canny Edge Detection method after the ULEA step, the edges detected are in same pixel width. This will be very difficult to find the LP region correctly. Figure 14 shows the Canny Edge Detection output. If we highlight the details in that image, regions other than LP region may contain more black pixels and that regions may be selected as the LP region. This is the same case for Sobel operator.

Figure 15. Adaptive thresholding output with different values for T

T = 0.05

T = 0.25

T = 0.15

4. Inference

The value for T in Adaptive Thresholding

Its value is taken as 0. 15 in the whole experiment. For different values, the result is not accurate. This is shown in Figure 15 (Figure 15 a: T = 0. 05, b: T = 0. 25).

From these images we can conclude that for the best thresholding performance T = 0. 15 is optimal value.

Threshold for Number of Lines in a Group

Threshold value is used to make sure that the small sized LP is included for a plate searching process. The CRE output and final output for small (1/10th of image height) and large (1/25th of image height) threshold value is shown in Figure 15 and 16. These results show that 1/20th of image height is optimal threshold value for the system.

Figure 16. CRE and final output when threshold = 1/10th of image height

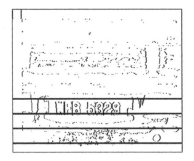

Figure 17. CRE and final output when threshold = 1/20th of image height

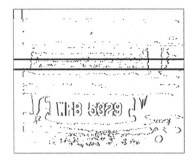

FUTURE RESEARCH DIRECTIONS

The following are some suggestions for future works:

- Reduce the time require for adaptive thresholding by substituting another method which have less processing time.
- LPDS method can also be applied to videos to track a vehicle.
- Apply this method to more complex vehicle images.
- Use with images of more than one license plate.

CONCLUSION

In the field of computer vision and image processing, object detection is an important and difficult task. Process finds the region of interest from the given input image using different methods. It is done by mining different unique features from the image. Features that can clearly define the object of interest are taken as the features for detecting the object and it depends on the applications that perform.

The License Plate Detection System processed the low resolution images. Adaptive thresholding and Unwanted Line Elimination Algorithm eliminates the noise and unwanted long background details from the image. Thus the image is perfect for the edge detection processing. The new algorithm VEDA detects the vertical edge. From the VEDA output the desired details of the plate region were highlighted and candidate regions where selected. VEDA makes the system faster by its output format. System shows less detection rate with samples that contain more background details when compare to other samples. With the 200 input samples system produces 175 correct outputs with 5 seconds as average processing time. Adaptive thresholding shows the higher processing time. This LPDS can be applied to a video to track the vehicle. This work can be done as an extension. Another future work is to track more than one license plate in an image.

REFERENCES

Al-Ghaili, A. M., Mashohor, S., Ramli, A. R., & Ismail, A. (2013). Vertical-edge-based car-license-plate detection method. *Vehicular Technology. IEEE Transactions on, 62*(1), 26–38.

Anagnostopoulos, C. N. E., Anagnostopoulos, I. E., Loumos, V., & Kayafas, E. (2006). A License Plate-Recognition Algorithm for Intelligent Transportation System Applications. *Intelligent Transportation Systems. IEEE Transactions On, 7*(3), 377–392.

Bradley, D., & Roth, G. (2007). Adaptive thresholding using the integral image. *Journal of Graphics, GPU, and Game Tools, 12*(2), 13-21.

Chang, S. L., Chen, L. S., Chung, Y. C., & Chen, S. W. (2004). Automatic license plate recognition. *Intelligent Transportation Systems. IEEE Transactions on, 5*(1), 42–53.

Comelli, P., Ferragina, P., Granieri, M. N., & Stabile, F. (1995). Optical recognition of motor vehicle license plates. *Vehicular Technology. IEEE Transactions on, 44*(4), 790–799.

Deb, K., Chae, H. U., & Jo, K. H. (2008, April). Parallelogram and histogram based vehicle license plate detection. In *Smart Manufacturing Application, 2008. ICSMA 2008.International Conferenceon* (pp. 349-353). IEEE. doi:10.1109/ICSMA.2008.4505550

Dong, Z., & Feng, X. (2014). Research on license plate recognition algorithm based on support vector machine. *Journal of Multimedia, 9*(2), 253–260. doi:10.4304/jmm.9.2.253-260

Gao, Q., Wang, X., & Xie, G. (2007, August). License plate recognition based on prior knowledge. In *Automation and Logistics, 2007 IEEE International Conference on* (pp. 2964-2968). IEEE. doi:10.1109/ICAL.2007.4339089

Gossain, S., & Gill, J. (2014). *A Novel Approach to Enhance Object Detection using Integrated Detection Algorithms*. Academic Press.

Gupta, R. K. (2014). *Object detection and tracking in video image* (Doctoral dissertation). EThesis, NIT Rourkela.

Huang, X. (2014). Automatic license plate detection based on colour gradient map. *Computer Modelling & New Technologies, 18*(7), 393–397.

Jia, W., Zhang, H., & He, X. (2007). Region-based license plate detection. *Journal of Network and Computer Applications, 30*(4), 1324–1333. doi:10.1016/j.jnca.2006.09.010

Khurana, K., & Awasthi, R. (2013). Techniques for Object Recognition in Images and Multi-Object Detection. *International Journal of Advanced Research in Computer Engineering & Technology, 2*(4), 1383.

Kim, J., Han, Y., & Hahn, H. (2008, December). License Plate Detection Using Topology of Characters and Outer Contour. *In Future Generation Communication and Networking Symposia, 2008. FGCNS'08. Second International Conference on* (Vol. 3, pp. 171-174). IEEE. doi:10.1109/FGCNS.2008.53

Kim, S., Kim, D., Ryu, Y., & Kim, G. (2002). A robust license-plate extraction method under complex image conditions. In *Pattern Recognition, 2002. Proceedings. 16th International Conference on* (Vol. 3, pp. 216-219). IEEE.

Luo, L., Sun, H., Zhou, W., & Luo, L. (2009, December). An efficient method of license plate location. In *Information Science and Engineering (ICISE), 2009 1st International Conference on* (pp. 770-773). IEEE.

Malik, M. S., & Klette, R. (2014). *Automatic Detection and Segmentation of License Plates*. The University of Auckland.

Matas, J., & Zimmermann, K. (2005, September). Unconstrained licence plate and text localization and recognition. In Intelligent Transportation Systems, 2005. Proceedings. 2005 IEEE (pp. 225-230). IEEE. doi:10.1109/ITSC.2005.1520111

Nabaee, M., & Hossein-Zadeh, G. A. (2007, November). License Plate Detection in Complex Scenes based on Improved Gradient and Match Filtering. In *Signal Processing and Communications, 2007. ICSPC 2007. IEEE International Conference on* (pp. 564-567). IEEE. doi:10.1109/ICSPC.2007.4728381

Porikli, F., & Tuzel, O. (2006, October). Fast construction of covariance matrices for arbitrary size image windows. In *Image Processing, 2006 IEEE International Conference on* (pp. 1581-1584). IEEE.

Wang, W., Jiang, Q., Zhou, X., & Wan, W. (2011, April). Car license plate detection based on MSER. In *Consumer Electronics, Communications and Networks (CECNet),* 2011 International Conference on (pp. 3973-3976). IEEE.

Yu, M., & Kim, Y. D. (2000). An approach to Korean license plate recognition based on vertical edge matching. In *Systems, Man, and Cybernetics, 2000IEEE International Conference on* (*Vol. 4,* pp. 2975-2980). IEEE.

KEY TERMS AND DEFINITIONS

Adaptive Thresholding: Adaptive thresholding use different threshold for each pixel to convert it into black or white values.

Automatic Number Plate Recognition: It is an innovative technology that uses distinctive strategies to consequently read license plate characters.

Computer Vision: It is an area that contains procedures for obtaining, handling, examining, and understanding images and, high dimensional facts from the real world in order to produce mathematical or representational data.

Image Processing: Processes that receipts images as input and produces images as output. It performs some manipulations to improve image quality.

Intelligent Transportation System: It applies propelled advances of hardware, interchanges, PCs, control and detecting and recognizing in a wide range of transportation framework with a specific end goal to enhance security, effectiveness and administration, and activity circumstance through transmitting constant data.

License Plate Detection: It is a law enforcement framework that optically filters vehicle tags, i. e., license plate. Utilizing settled position cameras on parkways, the framework distinguishes the plate and matches it against a database of stolen and uninsured vehicles, and vehicles enrolled to drivers with suspended licenses.

Object Detection: Object detection is computer technology that related to computer vision and image processing which deals with finding instances of object from a particular class in an image.

Object Recognition: Object recognition is concerned with decisive the identity of associate object being ascertained within the image from a collection of known labels.

Optical Character Recognition: OCR (optical character acknowledgment) is the recognition of printed or composed content characters by a PC.

Compilation of References

Abad, F. H., Abad, V. H., Andreu, J. F., & Vives, M. O. (2002). *Application of Projective Geometry to Synthetic Cameras*. Paper presented at the XIV International Conference of Graphic Engineering.

Abolfazli, S., Sanaei, Z., Gani, A., Xia, F., & Yang, L. T. (2013). Rich mobile applications: Genesis, taxonomy, and open issues. *Journal of Network and Computer Applications*.

Abreu, E., Lightstone, M., Mitra, S. K., & Arakawa, K. (1996). A New Efficient Approach For The Removal Of Impulse Noise From Highly Corrupted Images. *IEEE Transactions on Image Processing*, 5(6), 1012–1025. doi:10.1109/83.503916 PMID:18285188

Adeli, H., Zhou, Z., & Dadmehr, N. (2003). Analysis of EEG records in an epileptic patient using wavelet transform. *Journal of Neuroscience Methods*, 123(1), 69–87. doi:10.1016/S0165-0270(02)00340-0 PMID:12581851

Aha, D. W., Kibler, D., & Albert, M. K. (1991). Instance-based Learning Algorithms. *Machine Learning*, 6(1), 37–66. doi:10.1007/BF00153759

Ahmed, I., & Kopparapu, S. K. (2013). Technique for automatic sentence level alignment of long speech and transcripts. In *Proceedings of INTERSPEECH*. Retrieved June 29, 2015 from http://www.newsonair.com/

Ahmed, F., & Das, S. (2013). Removal of High Density Salt-and-Pepper Noise in Images with an Iterative Adaptive Fuzzy Filter using alpha-trimmed Mean. *IEEE Transactions on Fuzzy Systems*, 22(5), 1352–1358. doi:10.1109/TFUZZ.2013.2286634

Ahmed, M. N., & Farag, A. A. (1997). Two-stage neural network for volume segmentation of medical images. *Pattern Recognition Letters*, 18(11-13), 1143–1151. doi:10.1016/S0167-8655(97)00091-3

Ahonen, T., Hadid, A., & Pietikäinen, M. (2004). Face recognition with local binary patterns. In *Proceedings of the European Conference on Computer Vision* (pp. 469–481). Springer.

Aishwarya, R., Prabhu, M., Sumithra, G., & Anusiya, M. (2013). Feature Extraction for EMG based Prosthesis contro. *ICTACT Journal on Soft Computing*, 3(2).

Akenine-Möller, T., & Johnsson, B. (2012). Performance per what?. *Journal of Computer Graphics Techniques*, *1*(1), 37–41.

Al-Ghaili, A. M., Mashohor, S., Ramli, A. R., & Ismail, A. (2013). Vertical-edge-based car-license-plate detection method. *Vehicular Technology. IEEE Transactions on*, *62*(1), 26–38.

Amdahl, G. M. (1967) Validity of the single processor approach to achieving large scale computing capabilities. *Proceedings of theJoint Computer Conference.* ACM.

Amdal, I., Strand, O. M., Almberg, J., & Svendsen, T. (2008). RUNDKAST: An Annotated Norwegian Broadcast News Speech Corpus. *In Proceedings of Sixth International Conference on Language Resources and Evaluation.*

Anagnostopoulos, C. N. E., Anagnostopoulos, I. E., Loumos, V., & Kayafas, E. (2006). A License Plate-Recognition Algorithm for Intelligent Transportation System Applications. *Intelligent Transportation Systems. IEEE Transactions On*, *7*(3), 377–392.

Andreadisand, I., & Louverdis, G. (2004). Real Time Adaptive Image Impulse Noise Suppression. *IEEE Transactions on Instrumentation and Measurement*, *53*(3), 798–8064. doi:10.1109/TIM.2004.827306

Arakawa, K. (1996). Median Filter Based on Fuzzy Rules and Its Application to Image Restoration. *Fuzzy Sets and Systems*, *77*(1), 3–13. doi:10.1016/0165-0114(95)00122-0

Arce, G. R., Gallagher, N. C., & Nodes, T. (1986). *Median filters: Theory and applications.* Advances in Computer Vision and Image Processing.

Armstrong, J. D., Bagley, P. M., & Priede, I. G. (1992). Photographic and acoustic tracking observations of the behavior of the grenadier Coryphaenoides (Nematonorus) armatus, the eel Synaphobranchus bathybius, and other abyssal demersal fish in the North Atlantic Ocean. *Marine Biology*, *112*(4), 1432–1793. doi:10.1007/BF00346170

Arulampalam, M. S., Maskell, S., Gordon, N., & Clapp, T. (2002). A tutorial on particle filters for online nonlinear/non-Gaussian Bayesian tracking. *IEEE Transactions on Signal Processing*, *50*(2), 174–188. doi:10.1109/78.978374

Astola, J. T., & Campbell, T. G. (1989). On Computation of the Running Median. *IEEE Transactions on Acoustics, Speech, and Signal Processing*, *37*(4), 572–574. doi:10.1109/29.17539

Astola, J. T., & Kuosmanen, P. (1997). *Fundamentals of Nonlinear Digital Filtering.* New York: CRC.

Azeem, A., Sharif, M., Raza, M., & Murtaza, M. (2014). A survey: Face recognition techniques under partial occlusion. *Int. Arab J. Inf. Technol.*, *11*(1), 1–10.

Baha, N., & Touzene, H. (2013). FPGA Implementation for Stereo Matching Algorithm.*IEEE Science and Information Conference (SAI).*

Compilation of References

Balfour, J., Dally, W. J., Black-Schaffer, D., Parikh, V., & Park, J. (2008). An energy-efficient processor architecture for embedded systems. *Computer Architecture Letters*, 7(1), 29–32. doi:10.1109/L-CA.2008.1

Balk, H., & Lindem, T. (2000). Improved fish detection in data from split-beam sonar. *Aquatic Living Resources*, 13(05), 297–303. doi:10.1016/S0990-7440(00)01079-2

Bansal, V., & Sinha, R. M. K. (2001). A Complete OCR for Printed Hindi Text in Devnagari Script. In *Proceedings of Sixth International Conference on Document Analysis and Recognition*. IEEE.

Bauer, E., & Kohavi, R. (2004). An empirical comparison of voting classification algorithms: Bagging, Boosting, And Variants. *Machine Learning*, 36(1-2), 105–139.

Baumgartner, L., Bettanin, M., McPherson, J., Jones, M., Zampatti, B., & Beyer, K. (2010). *Assessment of an infrared fish counter (Vaki Riverwatcher) to quantify fish migrations in the Murray-Darling Basin*. Retrieved from Australia: www.dpi.nsw.gov.au

Baumgartner, L., Bettanin, M., McPherson, J., Jones, M., Zampatti, B., & Beyer, K. (2010). Assessment of an infrared fish counter (Vaki Riverwatcher) to quantify fish migrations in the Murray-Darling Basin. *Industry & Investment NSW. Fisheries Final Report Series*, 116, 47.

Beham, M. P., & Roomi, S. M. M. (2013). A Review Of Face Recognition Methods. *International Journal of Pattern Recognition and Artificial Intelligence*, 27(4). doi:10.1142/S0218001413560053

Belcher, E., Matsuyama, B., & Trimble, G. (2001). *Object identification with acoustic lenses*. Paper presented at the OCEANS, 2001. MTS/IEEE Conference and Exhibition.

Bermúdez, M., Puertas, J., Cea, L., Pena, L., & Balairón, L. (2010). Influence of pool geometry on the biological efficiency of vertical slot fishways. *Ecological Engineering*, 36(10), 1355–1364. doi:10.1016/j.ecoleng.2010.06.013

Beveridge, J. R., Phillips, P. J., Bolme, D. S., Draper, B., Givens, G. H., Lui, Y. M., … Cheng, S. (2013). The challenge of face recognition from digital point-and-shoot cameras. In *Biometrics: Theory, Applications and Systems (BTAS), 2013 IEEE Sixth International Conference on* (pp. 1–8). http://doi.org/ doi:<ALIGNMENT.qj></ALIGNMENT>10.1109/BTAS.2013.6712704

Bharangar, D. S., Doeger, A., & Mittal, Y. K. (2013). Implementation of Fast Artificial Neural Network for Pattern Classification on Heterogeneous System. *International Journal of Scientific and Engineering Research*, 4(1).

Bhat, C., & Kopparapu, S. K. (2014). Constructing a Sound-Glyph Database for Subtitling Videos. In *Proceedings of Oriental COCOSDA*.

Bhattacharyya, S., Debabrota, B., Konar, A., & Tibarewala, D. N. (2015). Interval type-2 fuzzy logic based multiclass ANFIS algorithm for real-time EEG based movement control of a robot arm. *Robotics and Autonomous Systems*, 68, 104–115. doi:10.1016/j.robot.2015.01.007

Bhattacharyya, S., Konar, A., & Tibarewala, D. N. (2014). A differential evolution based energy trajectory planner for artificial limb control using motor imagery EEG signal. *Biomedical Signal Processing and Control, 11*, 107–113. doi:10.1016/j.bspc.2014.03.001

Bicego, M., Lagorio, A., Grosso, E., & Tistarelli, M. (2006). On the use of SIFT features for face authentication. In *Conference on Computer Vision and Pattern Recognition Workshop* (pp. 35–35). IEEE. doi:10.1109/CVPRW.2006.149

Blake, R. W. (2004). Fish functional design and swimming performance. *Journal of Fish Biology, 65*(5), 1193–1222. doi:10.1111/j.0022-1112.2004.00568.x

Blume, H., Livonius, J., Rotenberg, L., Noll, T. G., Bothe, H., & Brakensiek, J. (2008). OpenMP based parallelization on an mpcore multiprocessor platform–a performance and power analysis. *Journal of Systems Architecture, 54*(11), 1019–1029. doi:10.1016/j.sysarc.2008.04.001

Bordallo López, M., Hannuksela, J., & Silvén, O. (2011a). Mobile feature-cloud panorama construction for image recognition application. *Proceedings of Mobiphoto, International Workshop on Camera Phone Sensing.*

Bordallo López, M., Hannuksela, J., Silvén, J. O., & Vehviläinen, M. (2011b). Multimodal sensing-based camera applications. *Proceedings of SPIE*. The International Society for Optical Engineering. doi:10.1117/12.871934

Bordallo López, M., Hannuksela, J., Silvén, O., & Fan, L. (2012a). Head-tracking virtual 3-d display for mobile devices. *Proc. Computer Vision and Pattern Recognition Workshops (CVPRW), 2012 IEEE Computer Society Conference on*. IEEE.

Bordallo López, M., Boutellier, J., & Silvén, O. (2007). Implementing mosaic stitching on mobile phones.*Proc. Finnish Signal Processing Symposium.*

Bordallo López, M., Hannuksela, J., Silvén, O., & Vehviläinen, M. (2009). Graphics hardware accelerated panorama builder for mobile phones.*Proceeding of SPIE Electronic Imaging 2009*. doi:10.1117/12.816511

Bordallo López, M., Hannuksela, J., Silven, O., & Vehvilainen, M. (2012b). Interactive multiframe reconstruction for mobile devices. *Multimedia Tools and Applications*, 1–21.

Bordallo López, M., Nieto, A., Boutellier, J., Hannuksela, J., & Silvén, O. (2014). Evaluation of LBP computing in multiple architectures. *Journal of Real-Time Image Processing*, 1–34.

Bordallo López, M., Nykänen, H., Hannuksela, J., Silvén, O., & Vehviläinen, M. (2011c) Accelerating image recognition on mobile devices using gpgpu.*Proceeding of SPIE Electronic Imaging 2011*. doi:10.1117/12.872860

Borkar, S. (1999). Design challenges of technology scaling. *Micro, IEEE, 19*(4), 23–29. doi:10.1109/40.782564

Compilation of References

Borovikov, E., Vajda, S., Lingappa, G., Antani, S., & Thoma, G. (2013). Face Matching for Post-Disaster Family Reunification. In *IEEE International Conference on Healthcare Informatics* (pp. 131–140). http://doi.org/ doi:<ALIGNMENT.qj></ALIGNMENT>10.1109/ICHI.2013.23

Bouwmans, T. (2014). Traditional and recent approaches in background modeling for foreground detection: An overview. *Computer Science Review, 11*, 31–66. doi:10.1016/j.cosrev.2014.04.001

Bradley, D., & Roth, G. (2007). Adaptive thresholding using the integral image. *Journal of Graphics, GPU, and Game Tools, 12*(2), 13-21.

Brezeal, D., & Diane, J., & Cook. (2008). Automatic Video Classification: A Survey of the Literature. *IEEE Transactions on Systems, Man and Cybernetics. Part C, Applications and Reviews, 38*, 3.

Brosnan, T., & Sun, D.-W. (2002). Inspection and grading of agricultural and food products by computer vision systems—a review. *Computers and Electronics in Agriculture, 36*(2-3), 193–213. doi:10.1016/S0168-1699(02)00101-1

Cappo, M., Harvey, E., Malcolm, H., & Speare, P. (2003). *Potential of video techniques to monitor diversity, abundance and size of fish in studies of Marine Protected Areas.* Paper presented at the Aquatic Protected Areas - what works best and how do we know? World Congress on Aquatic Protected Areas, Cairns, Australia.

Carroll, A., & Heiser, G. (2010). An analysis of power consumption in a smartphone. *Proceedings of the 2010 USENIX conference on USENIX annual technical conference.*

Castro-Santos, T., Haro, A., & Walk, S. (1996). A passive integrated transponder (PIT) tag system for monitoring fishways. *Fisheries Research, 28*(3), 253–261. doi:10.1016/0165-7836(96)00514-0

CDAC. (n.d.). *Nayana.* Retrieved June 29, 2015 from https://sites.google.com/site/cibu/ocr

CDAC-Pune. (n.d.). *Chitrankan.* Retrieved June 29, 2015 from http://cdac.in/index.aspx?id=mlc_gist_chitra

Cea, L., Pena, L., Puertas, J., Vázquez-Cendón, M. E., & Peña, E. (2007). Application of several depth-averaged turbulence models to simulate flow in vertical slot fishways. *Journal of Hydraulic Engineering, 133*(2), 160–172. doi:10.1061/(ASCE)0733-9429(2007)133:2(160)

Chang, J. (1995). Modified 2D median filter for impulse noise suppression in a real-time system. *IEEE Transactions on Consumer Electronics, 41*(1), 73–80. doi:10.1109/30.370312

Chang, S. L., Chen, L. S., Chung, Y. C., & Chen, S. W. (2004). Automatic license plate recognition. *Intelligent Transportation Systems. IEEE Transactions on, 5*(1), 42–53.

Chan, R. H., Ho, C. W., & Nikolova, M. (2005). Salt-and-Pepper Noise Removal by Median-Type Noise Detectors and Detail-Preserving Regularization. *IEEE Transactions on Image Processing, 14*(10), 1479–1485. doi:10.1109/TIP.2005.852196 PMID:16238054

Chaves-González, J. M., Vega-Rodríguez, M. A., Gómez-Pulido, J. A., & Sánchez-Pérez, J. M. (2010). Detecting skin in face recognition systems: A colour spaces study. *Digital Signal Processing*, *20*(3), 806–823. doi:10.1016/j.dsp.2009.10.008

Che Wan Fadzal, C. W. N. F., Mansor, W., & Khuan, L. Y. (2012). Analysis of EEG Signal from Right and Left Hand Writing Movements. *IEEE Control and System Graduate Research Colloquium (ICSGRC)*.

Chen, D., Mak, B., Leung, C., & Sivadas, S. (2014). Joint acoustic modeling of triphones and trigraphemes by multi-task learning deep neural networks for low-resource speech recognition. In Proceedings of ICASSP. doi:10.1109/ICASSP.2014.6854673

Chen, T., Ma, K. K., & Chen, L. H. (1999). Tri-State Median Filter for Image Denoising. *IEEE Transactions on Image Processing*, *8*(12), 1834–1838. doi:10.1109/83.806630 PMID:18267461

Chorda, J., Maubourguet, M. M., Roux, H., Larinier, M., Tarrade, L., & David, L. (2010). Two-dimensional free surface flow numerical model for vertical slot fishways. *Journal of Hydraulic Research*, *48*(2), 141–151. doi:10.1080/00221681003703956

Chuang, M.-C., Hwang, J.-N., Williams, K., & Towler, R. (2011). *Automatic fish segmentation via double local thresholding for trawl-based underwater camera systems* Paper presented at the IEEE International Conference on Image Processing (ICIP). doi:10.1109/ICIP.2011.6116334

Clausen, S., Greiner, K., Andersen, O., Lie, K.-A., Schulerud, H., & Kavli, T. (2007). *Automatic segmentation of overlapping fish using shape priors*. Paper presented at the Scandinavian conference on Image analysis, Aalborg, Denmark. doi:10.1007/978-3-540-73040-8_2

Coifman, B., Beymer, D., McLauchlan, P., & Malik, J. (1998). A real-time computer vision system for vehicle tracking and traffic surveillance. *Transportation Research Part C, Emerging Technologies*, *6*(4), 271–288. doi:10.1016/S0968-090X(98)00019-9

Comelli, P., Ferragina, P., Granieri, M. N., & Stabile, F. (1995). Optical recognition of motor vehicle license plates. *Vehicular Technology. IEEE Transactions on*, *44*(4), 790–799.

Costa, C., Scardi, M., Vitalini, V., & Cataudella, S. (2009). A dual camera system for counting and sizing Northern Bluefin Tuna (Thunnus thynnus; Linnaeus, 1758) stock, during transfer to aquaculture cages, with a semi automatic Artificial Neural Network tool. *Aquaculture (Amsterdam, Netherlands)*, *291*(3-4), 161–167. doi:10.1016/j.aquaculture.2009.02.013

Craig, R. E., & Forbes, S. T. (1969). *Design of a sonar for fish counting*. Academic Press.

Cullinan, C., Wyant, C., & Frattesi, T. (2012). *Computing performance benchmarks among CPU, GPU, and FPGA (No. 030212-123508)*. MathWorks.

Dabrowski, J., & Munson, E. (2001) Is 100 milliseconds too fast? *Proc. Conference on Human Factors in Computing Systems*.

Dail, W., & Ji, W. (2014). A Map Reduce Implementation of C4.5 Decision Tree Algorithm. *International Journal of Database Theory and Application, 7*(1), 49-60.

Compilation of References

Dai, W., & Ji, W. (2014). A MapReduce Implementation of C4.5 Decision Tree Algorithm. *International Journal of Database Theory and Application, 7*(1), 49–60. doi:10.14257/ijdta.2014.7.1.05

Daubechies, I. (1992). Ten Lectures on Wavelets. CBMS-NSF Regional Conference Series in Applied Mathematics.

David, A., & Sadlier. (2002). Automatic TV advertisement detection from MPEG bit stream. *Journal of the pattern Recognition Society.*

Deb, K., Chae, H. U., & Jo, K. H. (2008, April). Parallelogram and histogram based vehicle license plate detection. In *Smart Manufacturing Application, 2008. ICSMA 2008.International Conferenceon* (pp. 349-353). IEEE. doi:10.1109/ICSMA.2008.4505550

Deng, P., & Pei, M. (2008). Multi-View Face Detection Based on AdaBoost and Skin Color. In *Intelligent Networks and Intelligent Systems, 2008. ICINIS '08. First International Conference on* (pp. 457–460). doi:10.1109/ICINIS.2008.60

Deng, Z., Richmond, C. M., Guest, G. R., & Mueller, R. P. (2004). *Study of Fish Response Using Particle Image Velocimetry and High-Speed, High-Resolution Imaging.* Academic Press.

Dennard, R. H., Gaensslen, F. H., Rideout, V. L., Bassous, E., & LeBlanc, A. R. (1974). Design of ion-implanted mosfet's with very small physical dimensions. Solid-State Circuits. *IEEE Journal of, 9*(5), 256–268.

Dewar, H., & Graham, J. (1994). Studies of tropical tuna swimming performance in a large water tunnel – Energetics. *The Journal of Experimental Biology, 192*(1), 13–31.

Dewar, H., & Graham, J. (1994). Studies of tropical tuna swimming performance in a large water tunnel - Energetics. *The Journal of Experimental Biology, 192*, 13–31. PMID:9317243

Dharani, T., & Aroquiaraj, I. L. (2013). A survey on content based image retrieval. In *Pattern Recognition, Informatics and Mobile Engineering (PRIME), 2013 International Conference on* (pp. 485–490). http://doi.org/ doi:10.1109/ICPRIME.2013.6496719

Doerffel, D., & Sharkh, S. A. (2006). A critical review of using the peukert equation for determining the remaining capacity of lead-acid and lithium-ion batteries. *Journal of Power Sources, 155*(2), 395–400. doi:10.1016/j.jpowsour.2005.04.030

Dong, G., & Xie, M. (2005). Color clustering and learning for image segmentation based on neural networks. *IEEE Transactions on Neural Networks, 16*(4), 925–936. doi:10.1109/TNN.2005.849822 PMID:16121733

Dong, Z., & Feng, X. (2014). Research on license plate recognition algorithm based on support vector machine. *Journal of Multimedia, 9*(2), 253–260. doi:10.4304/jmm.9.2.253-260

Dornhege, G., Millan, J. R., Hinterberger, T., Mc Farland, D. J., & Muller, K. R. (2007). *Toward Brain-Computer Interfacing* (1st ed.). MIT Press.

Dougherty, E. R., & Laplante, P. (1995). *Introduction to Real-Time Imaging.* Bellingham, WA: SPIE.

Dreuw, P., Steingrube, P., Hanselmann, H., & Ney, H. (2009). SURF-Face: Face Recognition Under Viewpoint Consistency Constraints. In *British Machine Vision Conference*. doi:10.5244/C.23.7

Ehrenberg, J. E. (1972). *A method for extracting the fish target strength distribution from acoustic echoes*. Paper presented at the Engineering in the Ocean Environment, Ocean 72-IEEE International Conference on. doi:10.1109/OCEANS.1972.1161176

Eng, H. L., & Ma, K. K. (2001). Noise Adaptive Soft-Switching Median Filter. *IEEE Transactions on Image Processing*, *10*(2), 242–251. doi:10.1109/83.902289 PMID:18249615

Enrique, H., Iáñez, E., Úbeda, A., Carlos, P., & José, M. (2015). Combining a Brain–Machine Interface and an Electrooculography Interface to perform pick and place tasks with a robotic arm. *Robotics and Autonomous Systems*, *72*, 181–188. doi:10.1016/j.robot.2015.05.010

Ericka, J.R., & Huosheng, H. (n.d.). Bio-signal based control in assistive robots: a survey. *Digital Communications and Networks*, *1*(2), 85-101.

Esmaeilzadeh, H., Blem, E., St Amant, R., Sankaralingam, K., & Burger, D. (2011) Dark silicon and the end of multicore scaling. *Proc. Computer Architecture (ISCA), 2011 38th Annual International Symposium on*. IEEE. doi:10.1145/2000064.2000108

Esmaeilzadeh, H., Blem, E., St Amant, R., Sankaralingam, K., & Burger, D. (2012). Power limitations and dark silicon challenge the future of multicore. *ACM Transactions on Computer Systems*, *30*(3), 11. doi:10.1145/2324876.2324879

Fabritius, S., Grigore, V., Maung, T., Loukusa, V., & Mikkonen, T. (2003). *Towards energy aware system design*. Academic Press.

Ferreira, D., Dey, A. K., & Kostakos, V. (2011). Understanding human-smartphone concerns: a study of battery life. In Pervasive Computing (pp. 19–33). Springer. doi:10.1007/978-3-642-21726-5_2

Ferri, C., Viescas, A., Moreshet, T., Bahar, R., & Herlihy, M. (2008) Energy efficient synchronization techniques for embedded architectures. *Proceedings of the 18th ACM Great Lakes Symposium on VLSI*. ACM. doi:10.1145/1366110.1366213

Gao, Q., Wang, X., & Xie, G. (2007, August). License plate recognition based on prior knowledge. In *Automation and Logistics, 2007 IEEE International Conference on* (pp. 2964-2968). IEEE. doi:10.1109/ICAL.2007.4339089

Gao, Y., & Qi, Y. (2005). Robust Visual Similarity Retrieval in Single Model Face Databases. *Pattern Recognition*, *38*(7), 1009–1020. doi:10.1016/j.patcog.2004.12.006

Godbehere, A. B., Matsukawa, A., & Goldberg, K. (2012). *Visual tracking of human visitors under variable-lighting conditions for a responsive audio art installation*. Paper presented at the American Control Conference (ACC). doi:10.1109/ACC.2012.6315174

Gonzalez, R. C., & Woods, R. E. (2009). *Digital Image Processing* (3rd ed.). Prentice Hall.

Compilation of References

Gonzalez, R. C., Woods, R. E., & Eddins, S. L. (2004). *Digital Image Processing Using MATLAB*. Prentice-Hall.

Goodacre, J. (2009). The evolution of mobile processing architectures.*Proc. ARM Holdings*.

Gossain, S., & Gill, J. (2014). *A Novel Approach to Enhance Object Detection using Integrated Detection Algorithms*. Academic Press.

Greenhalgh, P. (2011). *Big.little processing with arm cortex-a15 & cortex-a7*. ARM White Paper.

Gresle, T., & Huang, S. (1997). Gisting of video documents: a key frames selection algorithm using relative activity measure. *The 2nd International Conference On Visual Information System*.

Grochowski, E., Ronen, R., Shen, J., & Wang, P. (2004). Best of both latency and throughput. *Proc. Computer Design: VLSI in Computers and Processors*. IEEE. doi:10.1109/ICCD.2004.1347928

Gupta, R. K. (2014). *Object detection and tracking in video image* (Doctoral dissertation). EThesis, NIT Rourkela.

Gustafson, J. L. (1988). Reevaluating amdahl's law. *Communications of the ACM*, *31*(5), 532–533. doi:10.1145/42411.42415

Han, J., Honda, N., Asada, A., & Shibata, K. (2009). Automated acoustic method for counting and sizing farmed fish during transfer using DIDSON. *Fisheries Science*, *75*(6), 1359–1367. doi:10.1007/s12562-009-0162-5

Hanjalic, A., Lagendijk, R. L., & Biemond, J. (1996). A new key-frame allocation method for representing stored video-streams. *Proc. 1st Int.Workshop Image Databases Multi Media Search*.

Hannuksela, J. (2008). *Camera based motion estimation and recognition for human computer interaction*. (Ph.D. thesis). Acta Univ Oul C 313.

Happ, P. N., Ferreira, R. S., Bentes, C., Costa, G. A. O. P., & Feitosa, R. Q. (2010). Multiresolution Segmentation: a Parallel Approach for High Resolution Image Segmentation in Multicore Architectures. In *3rd International Conference on Geographic Object-Based Image Analysis, 2010, Ghent, The International Archives of the Photogrammetry, Remote Sensing and Spatial Information Sciences*. Enshede: ITC.

Haralick, R. M., Sternberg, S. R., & Zhuang, X. (1987). Image analysis using mathematical morphology. *IEEE Transactions on Pattern Analysis and Machine Intelligence*, (4), 532-550.

Hartley, R. I., & Zisserman, A. (Eds.). (2004). *Multiple View Geometry in Computer Vision*. Cambridge University Press. doi:10.1017/CBO9780511811685

Heikkinen, M. V., & Nurminen, J. K. (2010). Consumer attitudes towards energy consumption of mobile phones and services. *Proc. Vehicular Technology Conference Fall* (VTC 2010-Fall). IEEE. doi:10.1109/VETECF.2010.5594115

Heimerl, S., Hagmeyer, M., & Echteler, C. (2008). Numerical flow simulation of pool-type fishways: New ways with well-known tools. *Hydrobiologia*, *609*(1), 189–196. doi:10.1007/s10750-008-9413-1

Herrmann, C. S., Arnold, T., Visbeck, A., Hundemer, H. P., & Hopf, H. C. (2001). Adaptive frequency decomposition of EEG with subsequent expert system analysis. *Computers in Biology and Medicine*, *31*(6), 407–427. doi:10.1016/S0010-4825(01)00017-8 PMID:11604148

Hilbert, M., & López, P. (2011). The World's Technological Capacity to Store, Communicate, and Compute Information. *Science*, *332*(6025), 60–65. doi:10.1126/science.1200970 PMID:21310967

Hodgson, R. M., Bailey, D. G., Nhaylor, M. J., Ng, L. M., & Mc-Cneil, S. J. (1985). Properties, implementations and applications of rank filters. *Image and Vision Computing*, *3*(1), 3–14. doi:10.1016/0262-8856(85)90037-X

Hoffmann, U., Naruniec, J., Yazdani, A., & Ebrahimi, T. (2008). Face Detection using Discrete Gabor Jets and Color Information. In P. A. A. Assunção & S. M. M. de Faria (Eds.), *SIGMAP* (pp. 76–83). INSTICC Press.

Holmes, J. A., Cronkite, G. M., Enzenhofer, H. J., & Mulligan, T. J. (2006). Accuracy and precision of fish-count data from a "dual-frequency identification sonar" (DIDSON) imaging system. *ICES Journal of Marine Science: Journal du Conseil*, *63*(3), 543–555. doi:10.1016/j.icesjms.2005.08.015

Horowitz, M., Alon, E., Patil, D., Naffziger, S., Kumar, R., & Bernstein, K. (2005). Scaling, power, and the future of cmos. *Proc. Electron Devices Meeting*. IEEE. doi:10.1109/IEDM.2005.1609253

Horprasert, T., Harwood, D., & Davis, L. S. (1999). *A statistical approach for real-time robust background subtraction and shadow detection*. Paper presented at the IEEE ICCV.

Hsu, R.-L., Abdel-Mottaleb, M., & Jain, A. K. (2002). Face detection in color images. *IEEE Transactions on Pattern Analysis and Machine Intelligence*, *24*(5), 696–706. doi:10.1109/34.1000242

Huang, C., Ai, H., Yamashita, T., Lao, S., & Kawade, M. (2007). Incremental Learning of Boosted Face Detector. In *Computer Vision, 2007. ICCV 2007. IEEE 11th International Conference on*. doi:10.1109/ICCV.2007.4408850

Huang, G. B., Ramesh, M., Berg, T., & Learned-Miller, E. (2007). *Labeled faces in the wild: A database for studying face recognition in unconstrained environments*. Amherst, MA: University of Massachusetts.

Huang, T. S., Yang, G. J., & Tang, G. Y. (1979). Fast Two-Dimensional Median Filtering Algorithm. *IEEE Transactions on Acoustics, Speech, and Signal Processing*, *1*(1), 13–18. doi:10.1109/TASSP.1979.1163188

Huang, T. S., Yaw, G. J., & Tang, C. Y. (1980). A Fast Two Dimensional Median-Filtering Algorithm. *IEEE Transactions on Acoustics, Speech, and Signal Processing*, *28*, 415–421. doi:10.1109/TASSP.1980.1163426

Compilation of References

Huang, X. (2014). Automatic license plate detection based on colour gradient map. *Computer Modelling & New Technologies, 18*(7), 393–397.

Hua, X. (2005). Robust Learning-based TV Commercial Detection.*Proc. of ICMF.*

Humenberger, M., Zinner, C., & Kubinger, W. (2009). Performance evaluation of a census based stereo matching algorithm on embedded and multi-core hardware. *Proceedings of 6th International Symposium on Image and Signal Processing and Analysis.* doi:10.1109/ISPA.2009.5297702

Hu, Y., & Ji, H. (2009). Research on Image Median Filtering Algorithm and Its FPGA Implementation.*IEEE Conference, Global Congress On Intelligent System.* doi:10.1109/GCIS.2009.130

Ibrahim, H., Kong, N. S. P., & Ng, T. F. (2008). Simple Adaptive Median Filter for the Removal of Impulse Noise from Highly Corrupted Images. *IEEE Transactions on Consumer Electronics, 54*(4), 1920–1927. doi:10.1109/TCE.2008.4711254

Israeli, D., & Kimmel, E. (1996). Monitoring the behavior of hypoxia-stressed Carassius auratus using computer vision. *Aquacultural Engineering, 15*(6), 423–440. doi:10.1016/S0144-8609(96)01009-6

Jackson, D. C., Marmulla, G., Larinier, M., Miranda, L. E., & Bernacsek, G. M. (2001). *Dams, fish and fisheries. Opportunities, challenges and conflict resolution.* Academic Press.

Jacobs, C. E., Finkelstein, A., & Salesin, D. H. (1995). Fast multiresolution image querying. In *Proceedings of the 22nd annual conference on Computer graphics and interactive techniques* (pp. 277–286). New York, NY: ACM.

Jafri, R., & Arabnia, H. R. (2009). A Survey of Face Recognition Techniques. *JiPS, 5*(2), 41–68.

Jain, A. K., Klare, B., & Park, U. (2012). Face Matching and Retrieval in Forensics Applications. *MultiMedia, IEEE, 19*(1), 20–20. doi:10.1109/MMUL.2012.4

Jain, V., & Learned-Miller, E. (2010). *FDDB: A Benchmark for Face Detection in Unconstrained Settings (No. UM-CS-2010-009).* Amherst, MA: University of Massachusetts.

Jensson, A. T., Iwano, K., & Furui, S. (2008). Language model adaptation using machine-translated text for resource-deficient languages. *EURASIP Journal on Audio, Speech, and Music Processing, 2008*, 1–7. doi:10.1155/2008/573832

Jianping, F., & Elmagarmid, K. (2004). Class View: Hierarchical Video Shot Classification, Indexing and Accessing. *IEEE Transactions on Multimedia, 6*, 1.

Jia, W., Zhang, H., & He, X. (2007). Region-based license plate detection. *Journal of Network and Computer Applications, 30*(4), 1324–1333. doi:10.1016/j.jnca.2006.09.010

John, M. (2006). Finding and identifying unknown commercials using repeated video sequence detection. *Computer Vision and Image Understanding, 103*(1), 80–88. doi:10.1016/j.cviu.2006.03.002

Jones, M., & Rehg, J. M. (2002). Statistical Color Models with Application to Skin Detection. International Journal of Computer Vision.

Jongtaveesataporn, M., Wutiwiwatchai, C., Iwano, K., & Furui, S. (2008). Thai Broadcast News Corpus Construction and Evaluation. In *Proceedings of Sixth International Conference on Language Resources and Evaluation.*

KaewTraKulPong, P., & Bowden, R. (2002). *An improved adaptive background mixture model for real-time tracking with shadow detection.* Paper presented at the Video-Based Surveillance Systems.

Kakumanu, P., Makrogiannis, S., & Bourbakis, N. (2007). A survey of skin-color modeling and detection methods. *Pattern Recognition, 40*(3), 1106–1122. doi:10.1016/j.patcog.2006.06.010

Kalaiselvi Geetha, M., Palanivel, S., & Ramalingam, V. (2009). Department of Computer science and Engineering and Technology, Annamalai University, TamilNadu. A Novels block intensity comparison code for video classification and retrieval. *Expert Systems with Applications,* 6415–6420. doi:10.1016/j.eswa.2008.07.047

Kamalakannan, A., & Rajamanickam, G. (2013). High Performance Color Image Processing in Multicore CPU using MFC Multithreading. *International Journal of Advanced Computer Science and Applications, 4*(12), 2013. doi:10.14569/IJACSA.2013.041207

Kasparis, T. N., Tzannes, S., & Chen, Q. (1992). Detail-Preserving Adaptive Conditional Filters. *Journal of Electronic Imaging, 1*(4), 358–364. doi:10.1117/12.61062

Khan, R., Hanbury, A., Stöttinger, J., & Bais, A. (2012). Color based skin classification. *Pattern Recognition Letters, 33*(2), 157–163. doi:10.1016/j.patrec.2011.09.032

Khurana, K., & Awasthi, R. (2013). Techniques for Object Recognition in Images and Multi-Object Detection. *International Journal of Advanced Research in Computer Engineering & Technology, 2*(4), 1383.

Kika, A., & Greca, S. (2013). Multithreading Image Processing in Single-core and Multi-core CPU using Java. *International Journal of Advanced Computer Science and Applications, 4*(9), 2013. doi:10.14569/IJACSA.2013.040926

Kim, C. G., Kim, J., & Lee, D. (2014). Optimizing image processing on multi-core CPUs with Intel parallel programming technologies. Journal of Multimedia Tools and Applications, 68(2), 237-251. doi:10.1007/s11042-011-0906-y

Kim, S., Kim, D., Ryu, Y., & Kim, G. (2002). A robust license-plate extraction method under complex image conditions. In *Pattern Recognition, 2002. Proceedings. 16th International Conference on* (Vol. 3, pp. 216-219). IEEE.

Kim, W., & Khudanpur, S. (2003). Cross-lingual lexical triggers in statistical language modeling. In *Proceedings of the 2003 Conference on Empirical Methods in Natural Language Processing.* Association for Computational Linguistics. doi:10.3115/1119355.1119358

Compilation of References

Kim, J., Han, Y., & Hahn, H. (2008, December). License Plate Detection Using Topology of Characters and Outer Contour.*In Future Generation Communication and Networking Symposia, 2008. FGCNS'08. Second International Conference on* (Vol. 3, pp. 171-174). IEEE. doi:10.1109/FGCNS.2008.53

Kim, J., Kim, H., Lee, J. H., & Lee, J. (2011). Achieving a Single Compute Device Image in OpenCL for Multiple GPUs. *SIGPLAN Not., 46*(8), 277–288. doi:10.1145/2038037.1941591

Kim, N. S., Austin, T., Baauw, D., Mudge, T., Flautner, K., Hu, J. S., & Narayanan, V. et al. (2003). Leakage current: Moore's law meets static power. *Computer, 36*(12), 68–75. doi:10.1109/MC.2003.1250885

Kim, S., Mallipeddi, R., & Lee, M. (n.d.). Incremental Face Recognition: Hybrid Approach Using Short-Term Memory and Long-Term Memory. In T. Huang, Z. Zeng, C. Li, & C. Leung (Eds.), *Neural Information Processing* (Vol. 7663, pp. 194–201). Springer Berlin Heidelberg. doi:10.1007/978-3-642-34475-6_24

Kim, T., & Adali, T. (2002). Fully complex multi-layer perceptron network for nonlinear signal processing. *Journal of VLSI Signal Processing Systems for Signal, Image and Video Technology, 32*(1-2), 29–43.

Knuth, D. E. (1998). The Art of Computer Programming: Sorting and Searching (2nd ed.; vol. 3). Redwood City, CA: Addison Wesley Longman Publishing Co., Inc.

Kobla, V., Doermann, D., Lin, K-I., & Faloutsos, C. (1997). Compressed domain video indexing techniques using DCT and motion vector information in MPEG video. *Proc. Storage Retrieval Image video Databases(SPIE).*

Kohonen, T. (1982). Self-organized formation of topologically correct feature maps. *Biological Cybernetics, 43*(1), 59–69.

Koley, B., & Dey, D. (2012). An ensemble system for automatic sleep stage classification using single channel EEG signal. *Computers in Biology and Medicine, 42*(12), 1186–1195. doi:10.1016/j.compbiomed.2012.09.012 PMID:23102750

Kopparapu, S. K., & Ahmed, I. (2013). *Frugal method and system for creating speech corpus.* US Patent App. 13/533,174.

Ko, S. J., & Lee, Y. H. (1991). Center Weighted Median Filters and Their Applications to Image Enhancement. *IEEE Transactions on Circuits and Systems, 38*(9), 984–993. doi:10.1109/31.83870

Kristof, P., Yu, H., Li, Z., & Tian, X. (2012). Performance study of SIMD programming models on intel multicore processors. *Proc. Parallel and Distributed Processing Symposium Workshops PhD Forum* (IPDPSW). doi:10.1109/IPDPSW.2012.299

Kruppa, H., Bauer, M. A., & Schiele, B. (2002). Skin Patch Detection in Real-World Images. In *Annual Symposium for Pattern Recognition of the DAGM* (LNCS), (vol. 2449, pp. 109–117). Springer.

271

Kumar, R., Tullsen, D. M., Jouppi, N. P., & Ranganathan, P. (2005). Heterogeneous chip multi-processors. *Computer*, *38*(11), 32–38. doi:10.1109/MC.2005.379

Lee, K. Y., Kyung, G., Park, T. R., Kwak, J. C., & Koo, Y. S. (2015). A design of a GP-GPU based stream processor for an image processing. In *Telecommunications and Signal Processing (TSP), 2015 38th International Conference on* (pp. 535–539). http://doi.org/ doi:10.1109/TSP.2015.7296320

Leon-Santana, M., & Hernandez, J. M. (2008). Optimum management and environmental protection in the aquaculture industry. *Ecological Economics*, *64*(4), 849–857. doi:10.1016/j.ecolecon.2007.05.006

Leskelä, J., Nikula, J., & Salmela, M. (2009). Opencl embedded profile prototype in mobile device. *Proc. Signal Processing Systems*. IEEE.

Le, X., Chow, M., Timmis, J., & Leroy, S. (2007). Power Distribution Outage Cause Identification With Imbalanced Data Using Artificial Immune Recognition System (AIRS) Algorithm. *IEEE Transactions on Power Systems*, *22*(1), 198–204. doi:10.1109/TPWRS.2006.889040

Li & Xing. (2010). Parallel Decision Tree Algorithm Based on Combination. *International Forum on Information Technology and Applications*.

Li, W., & Xing, C. (2010). Parallel Decision Tree Algorithm Based on Combination. *International Forum on Information Technology and Applications*.

Lienhart, R. (1997). On the detection and recognition of television commercials.*Proc of IEEE Conf on Multimedia Computing and Systems*. doi:10.1109/MMCS.1997.609763

Likforman-Sulem, L., Zahour, A., & Taconet, B. (2007). Text line segmentation of historical documents: a survey. International Journal of Document Analysis and Recognition 9(2-4), 123–138.

Lines, J. A., Tillett, R. D., Ross, L. G., Chan, D., Hockaday, S., & McFarlane, N. J. B. (2001). An automatic image-based system for estimating the mass of free-swimming fish. *Computers and Electronics in Agriculture*, *31*(2), 151–168. doi:10.1016/S0168-1699(00)00181-2

Lin, T. C. (2007). A New Adaptive Center Weighted Median Filter for Suppressing Impulsive Noise in Images. *Information Sciences*, *177*(4), 1073–1087. doi:10.1016/j.ins.2006.07.030

Li, S. Z., & Jain, A. K. (2011). *Handbook of Face Recognition* (2nd ed.). Springer Publishing Company, Incorporated. doi:10.1007/978-0-85729-932-1

Liu, Y., & Gao, F. (2010). Parallel Implementations of Image Processing Algorithms on Multi-Core. In *Proceedings of Fourth International Conference on Genetic and Evolutionary Computing (ICGEC)*.

Lowe, D. G. (2004). Distinctive Image Features from Scale-Invariant Keypoints. *International Journal of Computer Vision*, *60*(2), 91–110. doi:10.1023/B:VISI.0000029664.99615.94

Compilation of References

Lu, C., & Tang, X. (2014). *Surpassing Human-Level Face Verification Performance on LFW with GaussianFace*. CoRR, abs/1404.3840

Lu, L., Ghoshal, A., & Renals, S. (2012). Maximum a posteriori adaptation of subspace gaussian mixture models for cross-lingual speech recognition. In Proceedings of ICASSP. doi:10.1109/ICASSP.2012.6289012

Luo, L., Sun, H., Zhou, W., & Luo, L. (2009, December). An efficient method of license plate location. In *Information Science and Engineering (ICISE), 2009 1st International Conference on* (pp. 770-773). IEEE.

Luo, M., Dementhon, D., Yu, X., & Doermann, D. (2006). *SoftCBIR: Object Searching in videos combining keypoint matching and graduated assignment*. Academic Press.

Luo, W. (2005). Efficient Removal of Impulse Noise from Digital Images. *IEEE Transactions on Consumer Electronics, 52*, 523–527.

Luo, W. (2006). An Efficient Detail-Preserving Approach for Removing Impulse Noise In Images. *IEEE Signal Processing Letters, 13*(7), 413–416. doi:10.1109/LSP.2006.873144

Ma, B., Su, Y., & Jurie, F. (2014). Covariance descriptor based on bio-inspired features for person re-identification and face verification. *Image and Vision Computing, 32*(6–7), 379–390. doi:10.1016/j.imavis.2014.04.002

Malacara, D. (2002). *Color vision and colorimetry: theory and application*. SPIE Press.

Malik, M. S., & Klette, R. (2014). *Automatic Detection and Segmentation of License Plates*. The University of Auckland.

Mantena, G.V., Bollepalli, B., & Prahallad, K. (2011). SWS task: Articulatory phonetic units and sliding DTW. *Mediaeval 2011*.

Martin, N., Perez, B. A., Aguilera, D. G., & Lahoz, J. G. (2004). *Applied Analysis of Camera Calibration Methods for Photometric Uses*. Paper presented at the VII National Conference of Topography and Cartography.

Matas, J., & Zimmermann, K. (2005, September). Unconstrained licence plate and text localization and recognition. In Intelligent Transportation Systems, 2005. Proceedings. 2005 IEEE (pp. 225-230). IEEE. doi:10.1109/ITSC.2005.1520111

Miao, Y., Metze, F., & Rawat, S. (2013). Deep Maxout Networks for Low-resource speech recognition. In *Proceedings ofIEEE Workshop on Automatic Speech Recognition and Understanding (ASRU)*. doi:10.1109/ASRU.2013.6707763

Miao, Y., Metze, F., & Waibel, A. (2013). Subspace mixture model for low-resource speech recognition in cross-lingual settings. In Proceedings of ICASSP. IEEE. doi:10.1109/ICASSP.2013.6639088

Miettinen, A. P., & Nurminen, J. K. (2010). Energy efficiency of mobile clients in cloud computing. *Proceedings of the 2nd USENIX conference on Hot topics in cloud computing*. USENIX Association.

Mishra, N., Patvardhan, C., Vasantha Lakshmi, C., & Singh, S. (2012). Shirorekha Chopping Integrated Tesseract OCR Engine for Enhanced Hindi Language Recognition. International Journal of Computer Applications, 39(6). doi:10.5120/4824-7076

Mitra, V., Wang, C.-J., & Banerjee, S. (2006). Lidar detection of underwater objects using a neuro-SVM-based architecture. *Neural Networks. IEEE Transactions on, 17*(3), 717–731.

Mitra, V., Wang, C.-J., & Banerjee, S. (2006). Lidar Detection of Underwater Objects Using a Neuro-SVM-Based Architecture. *IEEE Transactions on Neural Networks, 17*(3), 717–731. doi:10.1109/TNN.2006.873279 PMID:16722175

Monalisa, P., Bhattacharyya, S., Konar, A., & Tibarewala, D. N. (2015). An interval type-2 fuzzy approach for real-time EEG-based control of wrist and finger movement. *Biomedical Signal Processing and Control, 21*, 90–98. doi:10.1016/j.bspc.2015.05.004

Morais, E. F., Campos, M. F. M., Padua, F. L. C., & Carceroni, R. L. (2005). *Particle filter-based predictive tracking for robust fish count.* Paper presented at the Brazilian Symposium on Computer Graphics and Image Processing (SIBGRAPI). doi:10.1109/SIBGRAPI.2005.36

Morales, R. R., & Azuela, J. H. S. (2011). Procesamiento y análisis digital de imágenes (Ra-Ma Ed.). Ra-Ma.

Müller, M. (2007). *Information Retrieval for Music and Motion.* Secaucus, NJ: Springer-Verlag New York, Inc. doi:10.1007/978-3-540-74048-3_4

Munoz, A. R., Mompean, M. B., Olivas, E. S., Scarante, C., & Martinez, J. F. G. (2011). FPGA Implementation of an Adaptive Filter Robust to Impulse Noise: Two Approaches. *IEEE Transactions on Industrial Electronics, 58*(3), 860–870. doi:10.1109/TIE.2009.2023641

Murakami, H., Shinoda, K., & Furui, S. (2011). Designing text corpus using phone-error distribution for acoustic modeling. In *Proceedings of Automatic Speech Recognition and Understanding (ASRU), 2011 IEEE Workshop on.* doi:10.1109/ASRU.2011.6163929

Muralidharan, V., & Sugumaran, V. (2012). A comparative study of Naïve Bayes classifier and Bayes net classifier for fault diagnosis of mono-block centrifugal pump using wavelet analysis. *Journal of Applied Soft Computing, 12*(8), 2023–2029. doi:10.1016/j.asoc.2012.03.021

Nabaee, M., & Hossein-Zadeh, G. A. (2007, November). License Plate Detection in Complex Scenes based on Improved Gradient and Match Filtering. In *Signal Processing and Communications, 2007. ICSPC 2007. IEEE International Conference on* (pp. 564-567). IEEE. doi:10.1109/ICSPC.2007.4728381

Compilation of References

Naik, V. H., & Kusur, C. S. (2015). Analysis of performance enhancement on graphic processor based heterogeneous architecture: A CUDA and MATLAB experiment. In *Parallel Computing Technologies (PARCOMPTECH), 2015 National Conference on* (pp. 1–5). doi:10.1109/PAR-COMPTECH.2015.7084519

Nair, M. S., & Raju, G. (2012). A New Fuzzy-Based Decision Algorithm for High-Density Impulse Noise Removal. *Signal Image and Video Processing*, 6(4), 579–595. doi:10.1007/s11760-010-0186-4

Naruniec, J. (2010). A Survey on Facial Features Detection. *International Journal of Electronics and Telecommunications*, 56(3), 267–272. doi:10.2478/v10177-010-0035-y

Neuvo, Y. (2004). Cellular phones as embedded systems. *Proc. Solid-State Circuits Conference*. IEEE. doi:10.1109/ISSCC.2004.1332581

Ngan, S.-C., & Hu, X. (1999). Analysis of functional magnetic resonance imaging data using self-organizing mapping with spatial connectivity. *Magnetic Resonance in Medicine*, 41(5), 939–946. doi:10.1002/(SICI)1522-2594(199905)41:5<939::AID-MRM13>3.0.CO;2-Q PMID:10332877

Ng, P. E., & Ma, K. K. (2006). A Switching Median Filter with Boundary Discriminative Noise Detection for Extremely Corrupted Images. *IEEE Transactions on Image Processing*, 15(6), 1506–1516. doi:10.1109/TIP.2005.871129 PMID:16764275

Nilsson, J. (1999). *Introduction to Machine Learning*. Academic Press.

Nodes, T. A., & Gallagher, N. C. Jr. (1984). The Output Distribution Of Median Type Filters. *IEEE Transactions on Communications*, 32(5), 532–541. doi:10.1109/TCOM.1984.1096099

Nooshyar, M., & Momeny, M. (2013). Removal of High Density Impulse Noise Using A Novel Decision Based Adaptive Weighted and Trimmed Median Filter. *8th Iranian Conference on Machine Vision and Image Processing (MVIP)*. doi:10.1109/IranianMVIP.2013.6780016

Nuno, A., & Gama, J., & Silva, F. (2002). Parallel implementation of decision tree learning algorithm. *Chapters in Progress in Artificial Intelligence*, 2258, 6–13.

Ocak, H. (2008). Optimal Classification of epileptic seizures in EEG using wavelet analysis and genetic algorithm. *Signal Processing*, 88(7), 1858–1867. doi:10.1016/j.sigpro.2008.01.026

Ochoa Somuanom, J., Pérez Lara, C., Toscano Martínez, J. H., & Pereyra Ramos, C. G. (2013). *Clasificación de objetos rígidos a partir de imágenes digitales empleando los momentos invariantes de Hu*. Paper presented at the X Congreso Internacional sobre Innovación y Desarrollo Tecnológico, Cuernavaca Morelos, México. Retrieved from http://opencv.org

Own, C. M., & Huang, C. S. (2013). On the Design of Neighboring Fuzzy Median Filter for Removal of Impulse Noises. *Intelligent Information and Database Systems*, 7802, 99–107. doi:10.1007/978-3-642-36546-1_11

Ozawa, S., Toh, S. L., Abe, S., Pang, S., & Kasabov, N. (2005). Incremental learning for online face recognition. In *Neural Networks, 2005. IJCNN '05. Proceedings. 2005 IEEE International Joint Conference on* (Vol. 5, pp. 3174–3179). http://doi.org/ doi:10.1109/IJCNN.2005.1556435

Pajares Martinsanz, G., & De la Cruz García, J. (2007). Visión por computador imágenes digitales y aplicaciones (Ra-Ma Ed. 2ª ed.). Ra-Ma.

Pande, A., & Chen, S. (2013). Hardware Architecture for Video Authentication using Sensor Pattern Noise. *IEEE Transactions on Circuits and Systems, 24*, 157–167.

Parichit. (n.d.). Retrieved June 29, 2015 from https://code.google.com/p/parichit/

Park, I. K., Singhal, N., Lee, M. H., Cho, S., & Kim, C. W. (2011). Design and Performance Evaluation of Image Processing Algorithms on GPUs. *Parallel and Distributed Systems. IEEE Transactions on, 22*(1), 91–104. doi:10.1109/TPDS.2010.115

Pathak, A., Hu, Y. C., Zhang, M., Bahl, P., & Wang, Y. M. (2011). Fine-grained power modeling for smartphones using system call tracing.*Proceedings of the sixth conference on computer systems*. ACM. doi:10.1145/1966445.1966460

Petrell, R. J., Shi, X., Ward, R. K., Naiberg, A., & Savage, C. R. (1997). Determining fish size and swimming speed in cages and tanks using simple video techniques. *Aquacultural Engineering, 16*(1-2), 63–84. doi:10.1016/S0144-8609(96)01014-X

Petrou, M., & Bosdogianni, P. (2000). *Image Processing: The Fundamental*. John Wiley & Sons Ltd.

Peukert, W. (1897). Über die abhängigkeit der kapazität von der entladestromstärke bei bleiakkumulatoren. *Elektrotechnische Zeitschrift, 20*, 20–21.

Pickard, W. F., & Abbott, D. (2012). Addressing the intermittency challenge: Massive energy storage in a sustainable future. *Proceedings of the IEEE, 100*(2), 317–321. doi:10.1109/JPROC.2011.2174892

Pitas, I., & Venestsanopoulos, A. N. (1990). Nonlinear Digital Filters: Principles and Applications. Boston, MA: Kluwer.

Porikli, F., & Tuzel, O. (2006, October). Fast construction of covariance matrices for arbitrary size image windows. In *Image Processing, 2006 IEEE International Conference on* (pp. 1581-1584). IEEE.

Possa, P. R., Mahammoudi, S., & Valderrama, C. (2013). AS Multi-Resolution FPGA-Based Architecture for Real-Time Edge and Corner Detection. *IEEE Transactions on Computers, 63*(10), 2376–2388. doi:10.1109/TC.2013.130

Prahallad, K., & Black, A. W. (2011). Segmentation of monologues in audio books for building synthetic voices. IEEE Transactions on Audio, Speech, and Language Processing, 19(5), 1444–1449. doi:10.1109/TASL.2010.2081980

Compilation of References

Prinslow, G. (2011). *Overview of Performance Measurement and Analytical Modeling Techniques for Multi-Core Processors*. Retrieved from http://www.cse.wustl.edu/ jain/cse567-11/ftp/multcore/

Puertas, J., Cea, L., Bermudez, M., Pena, L., Rodriguez, A., Rabuñal, J., & Aramburu, E. et al. (2012). Computer application for the analysis and design of vertical slot fishways in accordance with the requirements of the target species. *Ecological Engineering*, *48*, 51–60. doi:10.1016/j. ecoleng.2011.05.009

Puertas, J., Pena, L., & Teijeiro, T. (2004). An Experimental Approach to the Hydraulics of Vertical Slot Fishways. *Journal of Hydraulic Engineering*, *130*(1), 10–23. doi:10.1061/(ASCE)0733-9429(2004)130:1(10)

Pulli, K., Baksheev, A., Kornyakov, K., & Eruhimov, V. (2012). Real-time Computer Vision with OpenCV. *Communications of the ACM*, *55*(6), 61–69. doi:10.1145/2184319.2184337

Qi, W., Gu, L., Jiang, H., Chen, H., & Zhang, H. J. (2000). Integrating visual, audio and text analysis for news video.*Proc. 7th IEEE Int.Conf.Image Process. (ICIP),520-523*. doi:10.1109/ICIP.2000.899482

Quinlan, J. R. (1986). Introduction of decision trees.*Machine Learning*, *1*(1), 81–106. doi:10.1007/BF00116251

Rajovic, N., Rico, A., Vipond, J., Gelado, I., Puzovic, N., & Ramirez, A. (2013) Experiences with mobile processors for energy efficient HPC.*Proceedings of the Conference on Design, Automation and Test in Europe*. doi:10.7873/DATE.2013.103

Rakhmatov, D., & Vrudhula, S. (2003). Energy management for battery-powered embedded systems. *ACM Transactions on Embedded Computing Systems*, *2*(3), 277–324. doi:10.1145/860176.860179

Raoui, Y., Bouyakhf, E. H., Devy, M., & Regragui, F. (2011). Global and Local Image Descriptors for Content Based Image Retrieval and Object Recognition. *Applied Mathematical Sciences*, *5*(42), 2109–2136.

Rath, T. M., & Manmatha, R. (2003). Features for word spotting in historical manuscripts. In *Proceedings of Seventh International Conference on Document Analysis and Recognition*. doi:10.1109/ICDAR.2003.1227662

Robson, D. (2008). From CPU to GPU. *High Performance Computing for Science*, (1), 8.

Rodriguez, A., Bermúdez, M., Rabuñal, J., & Puertas, J. (2014). Fish tracking in vertical slot fishways using computer vision techniques. *Journal of Hydroinformatics*. doi:0.2166/hydro.2014.034

Rodriguez, A., Bermudez, M., Rabuñal, J., & Puertas, J. (2015). Fish tracking in vertical slot fishways using computer vision techniques. *Journal of Hydroinformatics*, *17*(2), 275–292. doi:10.2166/hydro.2014.034

Rodriguez, A., Bermudez, M., Rabuñal, J., Puertas, J., Dorado, J., & Balairon, L. (2011). Optical Fish Trajectory Measurement in Fishways through Computer Vision and Artificial Neural Networks. *Journal of Computing in Civil Engineering, 25*(4), 291–301. doi:10.1061/(ASCE)CP.1943-5487.0000092

Ronkainen, S. (2010). *Camera based motion estimation and recognition for human computer interaction*. (Ph.D. thesis). Acta Univ Oul C 355.

Rublee, E., Rabaud, V., Konolige, K., & Bradski, G. (2011). ORB: An efficient alternative to SIFT or SURF. In *IEEE International Conference on Computer Vision* (pp. 2564 –2571). doi:10.1109/ICCV.2011.6126544

Ruff, B. P., Marchant, J. A., & Frost, A. R. (1995). Fish sizing and monitoring using a stereo image analysis system applied to fish farming. *Aquacultural Engineering, 14*(2), 155–173. doi:10.1016/0144-8609(94)P4433-C

Sadlier, D. A. (2000). Automatic TV advertisement detection fro MPEG bitstream. *Journal of the Pattern Recognition Society, 35*(12), 2–15.

Saeidi, M., Anzabi, L. C., & Khalegi, M. (2009). Image Sequences Filtering using A New Fuzzy Algorithm Based on Triangular Membership Function. *International Journal of Signal Processing. Image Processing and Pattern Recognition, 2*, 75–90.

Salembier, P., & Sikora, T. (2002). *Introduction to MPEG-7: Multimedia Content Description Interface* (B. S. Manjunath, Ed.). New York, NY: John Wiley & Sons, Inc.

Salvador, R., Otero, A., Mora, J., Torre, E. L., Riesgo, T., & Sekanina, L. (2013). Self-reconfigurable Evolvable Hardware system for Adaptive Image Processing. *IEEE Transactions on Computers, 62*(8), 1481–1493. doi:10.1109/TC.2013.78

Satyanarayanan, M. (2005). Avoiding dead batteries. *IEEE Pervasive Computing / IEEE Computer Society [and] IEEE Communications Society, 4*(1), 2–3.

Saxena, S., Sharma, N., & Sharma, S. (2013). Image Processing Tasks using Parallel Computing in Multi core Architecture and its Applications in Medical Imaging. International Journal of Advanced Research in Computer and Communication Engineering, 2(4).

Scheirer, W. J., Kumar, N., Iyer, V. N., Belhumeur, P. N., & Boult, T. E. (2013). How reliable are your visual attributes? In Proceedings of SPIE (Vol. 8712, pp. 87120Q–87120Q–12). http://doi.org/ doi:10.1117/12.2018974

Sezgin, M., & Sankur, B. (2004). Survey over image thresholding techniques and quantitative performance evaluation. *Journal of Electronic Imaging, 13*(1), 146–165. doi:10.1117/1.1631315

Sharif, M., Mohsin, S., & Javed, M. Y. (2012). A Survey: Face Recognition Techniques. *Research Journal of Applied Sciences. Engineering and Technology, 4*(23), 4979–4990.

Compilation of References

Sharma, P., Huang, C., & Nevatia, R. (2012). Efficient incremental learning of boosted classifiers for object detection. In *Pattern Recognition (ICPR), 2012 21st International Conference on* (pp. 3248–3251).

Shiliang, S., Changshui, Z., & Dan, Z. (2007). An experimental evaluation of ensemble methods for EEG signal classification. *Pattern Recognition Letters*, *28*(15), 2157–2163. doi:10.1016/j.patrec.2007.06.018

Shivakumara, P., Dutta, A., Phan, T., Tan, C., & Uma, P. (2011). A novel mutual nearest neighbor based symmetry for text frame classification in video. *Pattern Recognition*, *44*(8), 1671–1683. doi:10.1016/j.patcog.2011.02.008

Shye, A., Scholbrock, B., & Memik, G. (2009). Into the wild: Studying real user activity patterns to guide power optimizations formobile architectures.*Proceedings of the 42nd Annual IEEE/ACM International Symposium on Microarchitecture*. ACM. doi:10.1145/1669112.1669135

SIGMUR. (2003). *Filtering techniques. Geography degree. Tele detection*. Retrieved from http://www.um.es/geograf/sigmur/teledet/tema06.pdf

Silvén, O., & Rintaluoma, T. (2007). Energy efficiency of video decoder implementations. In *Mobile Phone Programming and its Applications to Wireless Networking*. Springer. doi:10.1007/978-1-4020-5969-8_23

Slabaugh, G. G., Boyes, R., & Yang, X. (2010). Multicore Image Processing with OpenMP. IEEE Signal Processing Magazine, 27(2), 134-138.

Soni, S., Ahmed, I., & Kopparapu, S. K. (2014). Automatic segmentation of broadcast news audio using self similarity matrix. In *Proceedings ofInternational Conference for Convergence of Technology (I2CT)*. doi:10.1109/I2CT.2014.7092245

Spampinato, C., Chen-Burger, Y.-H., Nadarajan, G., & Fisher, R. (2008). *Detecting, Tracking and Counting Fish in Low Quality Unconstrained Underwater Videos*. Paper presented at the Int. Conf. on Computer Vision Theory and Applications (VISAPP).

Srinivasan, K. S., & Ebenezer, D. (2007). A New Fast and Efficient Decision-Based Algorithm for Removal of High Density Impulse Noise. *IEEE Signal Processing Letters*, *14*(3), 189–192. doi:10.1109/LSP.2006.884018

Steig, T. W., & Iverson, T. K. (1998). Acoustic monitoring of salmonid density, target strength, and trajectories at two dams on the Columbia River, using a split-beam scaning system. *Fisheries Research*, *35*(1-2), 43–53. doi:10.1016/S0165-7836(98)00058-7

Stenger, B., Mendonca, P. R. S., & Cipolla, R. (2001). *Model-Based Hand Tracking Using an Unscented Kalman Filter*. Paper presented at the British Machine Vision Conference. doi:10.5244/C.15.8

Storbeck, F., & Daan, B. (2001). Fish species recognition using computer vision and a neural network. *Fisheries Research*, *51*(1), 11–15. doi:10.1016/S0165-7836(00)00254-X

Sugumaran, V., Muralidharan, V., & Ramachandran, K. I. (2007). Feature selection using Decision Tree and classification through Proximal Support Vector Machine for fault diagnostics of roller bearing. *Mechanical Systems and Signal Processing, 21*(2), 930-942.

Sugumaran, V., Muralidharan, V., & Ramachandran, K. I. (2007). Feature selection using Decision Tree and classification through Proximal Support Vector Machine for fault diagnostics of roller bearing. *Mechanical Systems and Signal Processing, 21*(2), 930–942. doi:10.1016/j.ymssp.2006.05.004

Sultana, M., Uddin, M. S., & Sabrina, F. (2013). High Density Impulse Denoising by A Novel Adaptive Fuzzy Filter. *International Conference on Informatics, Electronics & Vision (ICIEV).* doi:10.1109/ICIEV.2013.6572536

Sundaram, N. (2012, May). *Making computer vision computationally efficient.* EECS Department, University of California, Berkeley. Retrieved from http://www.eecs.berkeley.edu/Pubs/TechRpts/2012/EECS-2012-106.html

Sun, T., & Neuvo, Y. (1994). Detail-Preserving Median Based Filters in Image Processing. *Pattern Recognition Letters, 15*(4), 341–347. doi:10.1016/0167-8655(94)90082-5

Sutter, H. (2005). The free lunch is over: A fundamental turn toward concurrency in software. *Dr. Dobb's Journal, 30*(3), 202–210.

Szeliski, R. (2011). *Computer Vision: Algorithms and Applications.* Springer. doi:10.1007/978-1-84882-935-0

Taigman, Y., Yang, M., Ranzato, M. A., & Wolf, L. (2014). DeepFace: Closing the Gap to Human-Level Performance in Face Verification. In *Proceedings of the IEEE Computer Society Conference on Computer Vision and Pattern Recognition.* doi:10.1109/CVPR.2014.220

Tan, X., Chen, S., Zhou, Z.-H., & Zhang, F. (2006). Face recognition from a single image per person: A survey. *Pattern Recognition, 39*(9), 1725–1745. doi:10.1016/j.patcog.2006.03.013

Tarrade, L., Texier, A., David, L., & Larinier, M. (2008). Topologies and measurements of turbulent flow in vertical slot fishways. *Hydrobiologia, 609*(1), 177–188. doi:10.1007/s10750-008-9416-y

Tesseract. (n.d.). Retrieved June 29, 2015 from https://code.google.com/p/tesseract-ocr/

Texas-Instruments. (2011). *Omap3530 power estimation spreadsheet.* Technical Report. Author.

Thirilogasundari, V., babu, V. S., & Janet, S. A. (2012). Fuzzy Based Salt and Pepper Noise Removal Using Adaptive Switching Median Filter. *Procedia Engineering, 38*, 2858–2865. doi:10.1016/j.proeng.2012.06.334

Thoma, G., Antani, S., Gill, M., Pearson, G., & Neve, L. (2012). People Locator: A system for family reunification. *IT Professional, 14*(3), 13–21. doi:10.1109/MITP.2012.25

Timmis, J., Neal, M., & Hunt, J. (2000). An artificial immune system for data analysis. *Bio Systems, 55*(1-3), 143–150. doi:10.1016/S0303-2647(99)00092-1 PMID:10745118

Compilation of References

Tolia, N., Andersen, D. G., & Satyanarayanan, M. (2006). Quantifying interactive user experience on thin clients. *Computer, 39*(3), 46–52. doi:10.1109/MC.2006.101

Turcza, P., & Duplaga, M. (2013). Hardware-Efficient Low-Power Image Processing System For Wireless Capsule Endoscopt.*IEEE Conference on Biomedical and Health Informatics.*

Ubeyli, E. D. (2008). Analysis of EEG signals by combining eigenvector methods and multiclass support vector machines. *Computers in Biology and Medicine, 38*(1), 14–22. doi:10.1016/j.compbiomed.2007.06.002 PMID:17651716

Ubeyli, E. D. (2009). Statistics over features: EEG signals analysis. *Computers in Biology and Medicine, 39*(8), 733–741. doi:10.1016/j.compbiomed.2009.06.001 PMID:19555931

Übeyli, E. D. (2010). Least squares support vector machine employing model-based methods coefficients for analysis of EEG signals. *Expert Systems with Applications, 37*(1), 233–239. doi:10.1016/j.eswa.2009.05.012

Utaminingrum, F., Uchimura, K., & Koutaki, G. (2013). High Density Noise Removal based on Linear Mean-Median Filter.*19th Korea-Japan Joint Workshop on Frontiers of Computer Vision.* doi:10.1109/FCV.2013.6485451

Verikas, A., Malmqvist, K., & Bergman, L. (1997). Color image segmentation by modular neural networks. *Pattern Recognition Letters, 18*(2), 173–185. doi:10.1016/S0167-8655(97)00004-4

Vezhnevets, V., Sazonov, V., & Andreeva, A. (2003). *A Survey on Pixel-Based Skin Color Detection Techniques.* GRAPHICON.

Viola, P., & Jones, M. (2004). Robust real-time face detection. *International Journal of Computer Vision, 57*(2), 137–154. doi:10.1023/B:VISI.0000013087.49260.fb

Waldemark, J. (1997). An automated procedure for cluster analysis of multivariate satellite data. *International Journal of Neural Systems, 8*(1), 3–15. doi:10.1142/S0129065797000033 PMID:9228572

Wang, W., Jiang, Q., Zhou, X., & Wan, W. (2011, April). Car license plate detection based on MSER. In *Consumer Electronics, Communications and Networks (CECNet)*, 2011 International Conference on (pp. 3973-3976). IEEE.

Wang, Z. and Zhang, D. (1999). Progressive switching median filter for the removal of impulse noise from highly corrupted images. *IEEE Trans. on Circuits Syst. II, 46*, 78-80.

Wang, J. H., & Lin, L. (1997). Improved Median Filter using min-max algorithm for image processing. *Electronics Letters, 33*(16), 1362–1363. doi:10.1049/el:19970945

Watkins, A., & Timmis, J. (2002). Artificial immune recognition system(AIRS): revisions and refinements.*1st International Conference on Artificial Immune Systems (ICARIS2002).*

Watkins, A., Timmis, J., & Boggess, L. (2004). Artificial immune recognition system (AIRS): An immune-inspired supervised learning algorithm. *Genetic Programming and Evolvable Machines*, 5(3), 291–317. doi:10.1023/B:GENP.0000030197.83685.94

Welch, G., & Bishop, G. (2006). *An Introduction to the Kalman Filter*. Academic Press.

Weng, J., Cohen, P., & Herniou, M. (1992). Camera calibration with distortion models and accuracy evaluation. *IEEE Transactions on Pattern Analysis and Machine Intelligence*, 14(10), 965–980.

White, D., Svellingen, C., & Strachan, N. (2006). Automated measurement of species and length of fish by computer vision. *Fisheries Research*, 80(2), 203–210. doi:10.1016/j.fishres.2006.04.009

Wolf, W. (2004). The future of multiprocessor systems-on-chips. *Proc. Design Automation Conference*. IEEE. doi:10.1145/996566.996753

Wolf, W. (1996). Key frame selection by motion analysis. *Proc. IEEE Int. Conf. Acoust., Speech Signal Proc.*

Wu, S., Rajaratma, N., & Katopodis, C. (1999). Structure of flow in vertical slot fishways. *Journal of Hydraulic Engineering*, 125(4), 351–360. doi:10.1061/(ASCE)0733-9429(1999)125:4(351)

Xu, L. Q., & Li, Y. (2003). Video classification using spatial-temporal features and PCA. *Proc. Int. Conf. Multimedia Expo(ICME)*, 485-488.

Yadav, D., Sharma, A. K., & Gupta, J. P. (2007). Optical character recognition for printed Hindi text in Devanagari using soft-computing technique. In Proceedings of IASTED International Multi-Conference: Artificial Intelligence and Applications.

Yadav, D., S'anchez-Cuadrado, S., & Morato, J. (2013, March). Optical character recognition for Hindi language using a neural-network approach. *Journal of Information Processing Systems*, 9(1), 117–140. doi:10.3745/JIPS.2013.9.1.117

Yilmaz, A., Javed, O., & Shah, M. (2006). Object Tracking: A Survey. *ACM Computing Surveys*, 38(4), 13, es. doi:10.1145/1177352.1177355

Yu, M., & Kim, Y. D. (2000). An approach to Korean license plate recognition based on vertical edge matching. In *Systems, Man, and Cybernetics, 2000IEEE International Conference on* (Vol. 4, pp. 2975-2980). IEEE.

Yu, K. K. C., Watson, N. R., & Arrillaga, J. (2005). An adaptive Kalman filter for dynamic harmonic state estimation and harmonic injection tracking. *IEEE Transactions on Power Delivery*, 20(2), 1577–1584. doi:10.1109/TPWRD.2004.838643

Yun, X., & Bachmann, E. R. (2006). Design, Implementation, and Experimental Results of a Quaternion-Based Kalman Filter for Human Body Motion Tracking. *IEEE Transactions on Robotics*, 22(6), 1216–1227. doi:10.1109/TRO.2006.886270

Compilation of References

Zhang, L., Tiwana, B., Qian, Z., Wang, Z., Dick, R. P., Mao, Z. M., & Yang, L. (2010). Accurate online power estimation and automatic battery behavior based power model generation for smartphones. *Proceedings of the eighth IEEE/ACM/IFIP international conference on Hardware/software codesign and system synthesis.* ACM. doi:10.1145/1878961.1878982

Zhang, Z. (1999). *Flexible Camera Calibration By Viewing a Plane From Unknown Orientations.* Paper presented at the International Conference on Computer Vision (ICCV), Kerkyra, Greece. doi:10.1109/ICCV.1999.791289

Zhang, C., & Zhang, Z. (2010). *A Survey of Recent Advances in Face detection.* Microsoft.

Zhang, H. J., Wu, J., Zhong, D., & Smoliar, S. W. (1997). An integrated systemfor content-based video retrieval and browsing. *Pattern Recognition, 30*(4), 643–658. doi:10.1016/S0031-3203(96)00109-4

Zhang, S., & Karim, M. A. (2002). A New Impulse Detector for Switching Median Filter. *IEEE Transactions on Signal Processing, 9*(11), 360–363. doi:10.1109/LSP.2002.805310

Zhou, F., Duh, H. B. L., & Billinghurst, M. (2008). Trends in augmented reality tracking, interaction and display: A review of ten years of ismar. *Proceedings of the 7th IEEE/ACM International Symposium on Mixed and Augmented Reality.* IEEE Computer Society.

Zhou, H., Mian, A., Wei, L., Creighton, D., Hossny, M., & Nahavandi, S. (2014). Recent Advances on Singlemodal and Multimodal Face Recognition: A Survey. *Human-Machine Systems. IEEE Transactions on, 44*(6), 701–716. doi:10.1109/THMS.2014.2340578

Zhu, X., & Ramanan, D. (2012). Face Detection, Pose Estimation, and Landmark Localization in the Wild. In *Proceedings of the IEEE Computer Society Conference on Computer Vision and Pattern Recognition.*

Zion, B., Alchanatis, V., Ostrovsky, V., Barki, A., & Karplus, I. (2007). Real-time underwater sorting of edible fish species. *Computers and Electronics in Agriculture, 56*(1), 34–45. doi:10.1016/j.compag.2006.12.007

Zion, B., Shklyar, A., & Karplus, I. (1999). Sorting fish by computer vision. *Computers and Electronics in Agriculture, 23*(3), 175–187. doi:10.1016/S0168-1699(99)00030-7

Zion, B., Shklyar, A., & Karplus, I. (2000). In-vivo fish sorting by computer vision. *Aquacultural Engineering, 22*(3), 165–179. doi:10.1016/S0144-8609(99)00037-0

Zivkovic, Z. (2004). *Improved adaptive Gaussian mixture model for background subtraction.* Paper presented at the International Conference on Patern Recognition (ICPR 2004). doi:10.1109/ICPR.2004.1333992

About the Contributors

Mohan Sellappa Gounder is currently working as Associate Professor in CCIS, Al Yamamah University, KSA. He is the program coordinator for Computer Graphics and Multimedia concentration. His PhD was in 3D Computer Vision from University of Mysore, India in 2009. He served at various academic positions in universities like Amrita Vishwa Vidyapeetham, Anna University, Karunya in India. Before joining YU, he served as Head & Dean in colleges affiliated to Anna University, India. Dr. Mohan also served as Technical Trainer in Infosys Technologies Ltd, Mysore India. His major research interests include 3D computer vision, Multicore computer vision, Video Surveillance and Media Computing.

Vani Vasudevan holds Ph.D. in Computer Science and Engineering from Anna University and awarded doctorate in the year 2013. Her area of specialization includes Computer Graphics and Image Processing, Computational Intelligence and Software Engineering. She has more than 16 years of teaching and industry experience. To her credit, she has published 25 research papers in refereed International Journals and Conferences and presently working as Assistant Professor in College of Computer and Information Systems, Alyamamah University, Riyadh.

* * *

Maria Bermudez received her MSc and PhD in Civil Engineering from the University of A Coruña (Spain) in 2008 and 2013, respectively. Since 2008, she is a member of the Water and Environmental Engineering Research group of that University, where she conducts research in the field of environmental hydraulics. She currently holds a Postdoctoral Fellowship from the I2C program of the Xunta de Galicia (Regional Government) and is based at the School of Geographical Sciences at the University of Bristol (United Kingdom).

Chitralekha Bhat is a researcher in the Speech and NLP group of TCS Innovation Labs, Mumbai since 2011. She has worked at the Digital Audio Processing lab at IIT Bombay from 2010-2011. Completed her MSc in Signal Processing from NTU, Singapore in 2008. She is a music enthusiast and is training in Carnatic instrument, Veena.

Michael Bonifant is a graduate of the University of Maryland at College Park, with two bachelor degrees, one in computer science, the other in physics.

Miguel Bordallo López studied for a Bachelor's degree in Telecommunication Engineering at the Technical University of Madrid, Spain. He received his Master's and Doctoral degrees from the University of Oulu in 2010 and 2014 respectively. Already in 2005, he joined the Center for Machine Vision Research at the University of Oulu where he currently works as Post-Doctoral Research Scientist. Since 2007 he has been teaching the undergraduate course on DSP programming. His current research interests include image stitching, multi-frame reconstruction, multimodal mobile user interfaces, GP-GPU computing, energy efficient embedded computer vision and wearable devices. He has authored several scientific publications.

Eugene Borovikov is a computer vision and machine learning scientist at U. S. National Library of Medicine contributing to the R&D efforts of the Lost Person Finder (LPF) project family by researching and developing face detection and matching capabilities in unconstrained images, as well as in general content based image retrieval (CBIR) and efficient near-duplicate image detection/grouping/ removal. He received his Ph.D. degree from University of Maryland, College Park in 2003, with the dissertation titled "High-performance visual computing in multi-perspective environments", advised by professors Larry Davis and Alan Sussman. Eugene Borovikov received the degree of Master of Arts in Applied Mathematics from University of Maryland, College Park in 1998 with the thesis titled "Human Head Pose Estimation by Facial Features Location", advised by professors Larry Davis and David Harwood.

Marcos Gestal is an associate professor and member of the research laboratory Artificial Neural Networks and Adaptative Systems at the University of A Coruña (Spain). He has obtained his PhD in 2007, with a thesis about multimodal problem resolution using several approaches based on Genetic Algorithms. His actual research interests are focused on evolutionary computation (mainly genetic algorithms), artificial neural networks and their interaction to perform variable selection. Also he is interested in information processing and the efficient and secure develop in web applications.

Sunil Kumar Kopparapu (Senior Member, IEEE) obtained his doctoral degree in Electrical Engineering from the Indian Institute of Technology, Bombay, India in 1997. His thesis "Modular integration for low-level and high-level vision problems in a multi-resolution framework" provided a broad framework to enable reliable and fast vision processing. Between 1997-2000 he was with the Automation Group, Commonwealth Scientific and Industrial Research Organization (CSIRO), Brisbane, Australia working on practical image processing and 3D vision problems, mainly for the benefit of the Australian mining industry. Prior to joining the Cognitive Systems Research Laboratory (CSRL), Tata Infotech Limited, as a Senior Research Member, in 2001, he was associated with the R&D Group at Aquila Technologies Private Limited, India, as an expert for developing virtual self line of e-commerce products. In his current role as a senior scientist with the TCS Innovations Labs - Mumbai, he is actively working in the areas of speech, script, image and natural language processing with a focus on building usable systems for mass use in Indian conditions. He has coauthored a book titled Bayesian Approach to Image Interpretation and more recently a Springer Brief on Non-linguistic Analysis of Call Center Conversation apart from several patents, journal and conference publications.

Girish Lingappa works as a Software Architect for Medical Science and Computing. He has worked in various verticals of the software industry in areas such as big data, energy, forecasting, healthcare and industrial automation. He is a graduate of Mangalore University with bachelors degree in Electronics and Communications and received a Masters degree in computer science from George Mason University.

Mausumi Maitra is presently working as Associate Professor & HOD of the Dept. of Information Technology of Govt. College of Engg. and Ceramic Technology. She obtained her B.Tech., M.Tech. and Ph.D. degree from the Institute of Radiophysics and Electronics, C. U.. She has more than twenty years of research and teaching experiences in different institutes and has more than twenty publications in National / International Journals and Conferences. She has completed / pursuing four projects sponsored by AICTE and UGC. Her current research interest is in VLSI design and Image Processing.

Manali Mukherjee is working as a project fellow in the Department of Information Technology, Govt. College of Engineering & Ceramic Technology. She was born on the 15th day of August, 1986 at Kolkata. She obtained her B.Tech. degree from Saroj Mohan Institute of Technology and M. Tech. degree from West Bengal University of Technology(in house) in 2009 and 2011 respectively. She is now working under UGC sponsored project under the guidance of Dr. Mausumi Maitra, HOD in the Department of Information Technology.

Juan R. Rabuñal is an Associate Professor at the University of A Coruña, Spain, and Coordinator of the Research Centre of Technological Innovations in Construction and Civil Engineering (CITEEC). He finished his studies in computer engineering in 1996, and in 2002, he received the Doctor's degree in Computer Science with his thesis "Methodology for the development of knowledge extraction systems in ANNs." In 2008, he received the Doctor's degree in Civil Engineering with his thesis "Artificial intelligence techniques in civil engineering." He has worked on several Spanish and European projects, and he has published many books and papers on several international journals. He is currently working on the application of artificial intelligence techniques in civil engineering: artificial vision, evolutionary computation, artificial neural networks and knowledge extraction systems, construction, hydrology, ports, and coasts.

Angel Jose Rico-Diaz is a PhD Student (FPI grant ref. BES-2013-063444, from Spanish Ministry of Education) in University of A Coruña (Spain), Department of Information and Communication Technologies, RNASA.

Alvaro Rodriguez has achieved a PhD in Computer science in 2014, and he has been a researcher in the University of A Coruña, Spain, from 2008 to 2015. His expertise area is mainly focused in Computer Vision applications in practical fields such as biomedicine and Civil Engineering. He is currently working in the Physics Department of Umea University as a postdoc researcher.

Kamarujjaman Sk received the B.Tech degree in Computer Science and Engineering from West Bengal University of Technology, Kolkata, India, and M.Tech degree in Information Technology from Govt. College of Engineering and Ceramic Technology under Maulana Abul Kalam Azad University of Technology, Kolkata, India in 2012 and 2014 respectively. He is now working as a JRF (under MANF_UGC Fellowship 2014-15, Govt. of India) in Information Technology at Govt. College of Engineering and Ceramic Technology, Kolkata, India. His research interests include pattern recognition, image processing, VLSI design with the current focus on medical image processing and next generation sequencing for brain cancer detection and diagnosis.

Ramalingam V. V. received a Post graduate degree in Master of Computer Applications from Bharadhidasan University (2000), M.Phil Degree in Computer Science from Periyar University (2007) and M.Tech Degree in Computer Science and Engineering from S.R.M University (2012) and Pursuing Ph.D in Bharathiar University, Coimbatore. He also published seven papers in International Journals and Conferences. His research interest is in the area of Data Mining using Machine Learning Approach.

Rebecca Jeya Vadhanam received Post Graduate degree in Master of Computer Applications from Bharadhidasan University (2000), M.Phil Degree in Computer Science from Periyar University(2008) and pursuing Ph.D in Bharathiyar university, coimbatore. Currently, she is working as an Assistant Professor in the Department of Computer Applications in S.R.M university, Kattankulathur, Chennai. She also published eight papers in International Journals and conferences. Her research interest is in the area of computer vision, Image and video processing.

Index

A

Accessibility 136-137
acquisition system 78-79, 100
Adaptive Thresholding 243-245, 251, 253-255, 257
asymmetric multiprocessing 47-48, 59-61, 67
audio files 137, 147
audio segments 144-145, 149
Automatic Number Plate Recognition 257
Automatic Speech Recognition 136-137, 153

B

background subtraction 84, 196-197, 200-201, 208, 210
block intensity 108, 116-119, 122, 132, 134

C

classification accuracy 114, 122-130, 132, 167, 212-215, 219-231
clock frequency 4, 6, 32, 52, 59
comparison code 108, 116-117, 119, 122, 132, 134
computer vision 42, 46-48, 61-62, 69, 74, 84, 100, 103-106, 130, 133, 158, 183-193, 196, 198-199, 201-202, 205-210, 234-235, 239, 254, 257
Content Based Image Retrieval 155-156, 184, 187

D

data acquisition 78-79, 100, 171, 214
decision tree 114-115, 122-128, 131-134, 211, 213-214, 216, 219-221, 223, 225-226, 229-233
disparity 7, 190, 195-196, 198

E

editable text 136-137, 139-140, 150
EEG signals 211-214, 216-217, 222, 230-231, 233
embedded 6, 60, 67, 69-72, 105, 112
energy efficiency 47-48, 53-54, 56-58, 60, 66-67, 72

F

face detection 155, 158-159, 162-163, 166, 170-175, 182-185, 188-189
face matching 155, 157, 161, 163-164, 171, 175-176, 184-185
false positive 84, 91, 95, 130, 168, 202-203, 205
family reunification 155-157, 182, 184, 188
family tree 122, 132
Field programmable Gate Array (FPGA) 1
Finisterrae Aquarium 201-202
fish behavior 74-77, 91, 96, 100, 190-192
fish counter 101, 190-191, 201, 206-207
fish detection 190-192, 198, 206-207
fish size 96, 102, 190-192, 196, 198, 202-203, 205, 209

fishway model 74, 76, 91, 96, 100

fishways 74-75, 77, 100-104, 190-191, 198, 209-210

frame rate 109, 116, 119-122, 124, 126, 132

frequency ranges 225

G

Genesys Virtex5 20, 31-32, 41

gray scale 2-4, 12, 15, 23, 25, 41

H

hardware implementation 2-3, 6, 20-21, 24, 29, 31

heterogeneous computing 47-48, 58-60

high performance 3, 20, 31, 47-48, 64, 68, 152, 160, 187

high performance computing 68, 187

I

image descriptor 160, 163, 189

image processing 1-4, 7, 12, 41-46, 64, 66, 70, 101-102, 108, 137, 140, 145-147, 152-156, 158-160, 163-166, 171, 182-183, 186-187, 236, 239, 243, 254, 257

images corrupted 1, 7, 10, 42

impulse noise 1-5, 7-12, 14-20, 23, 25, 27-28, 32, 34-36, 41-46

India Radio 139, 141, 143, 147

Intelligent Transportation System 234-236, 241, 255, 257

intensity comparison 108, 116-117, 119, 122, 132, 134

interaction methods 47-48

interactivity 47-48, 54, 59-60, 67

ISE Design 1

K

K Star 211, 214, 223, 225, 228

L

Laser Detection 190, 204

laser sensor 192, 198, 202, 206

last processing value 19, 31

latency 6, 21, 23, 26, 29, 47-53, 60, 65, 67-68, 71

license plate 234-239, 241-242, 245, 247, 249-251, 254-257

License Plate Detection 234-235, 237-238, 241-242, 251, 255-257

lighting conditions 162, 164, 166, 238, 243

limb movements 211-214, 216-217, 219, 231

Line Elimination 245, 255

low power 47-48, 66, 68

M

median filter 1-6, 8-18, 20-21, 23-26, 28, 31-37, 41-46

missing children 181-182

mobile device 54-55, 59, 61, 63, 67, 71, 162

MOBILE PLATFORM 47-48, 63

multi-core CPUs 146, 152, 157-158, 164, 182, 186

mutliresolution 140

N

novel interaction 47-48

O

Object Classification 189

Object Clustering 189

object detection 173, 188-189, 198, 234-235, 239-241, 254, 256-257

Object Identification 189, 207

Object Recognition 187, 189, 234, 239-241, 256, 258

Object Verification 189

Optical character recognition 154, 250, 258

P

parallel computing 60, 100, 132, 147, 153, 155, 157, 162, 164, 187, 230

plate detection 234-235, 237-238, 241-242, 251, 255-257

power consumption. 47-48, 54, 57, 65, 68

programmable gate 1-2, 6-7
prosthetic limb 211-214, 217, 219, 230-231

R

real-world objects 235
region analysis 78-79, 100
resource-deficient languages 136, 150, 152
Retrieval Hit-Rate 189
river ecosystems 75

S

sound-glyph 136-138, 140, 144-151
sound model 145, 149
speech corpus 137-140, 151-152

T

template matching 236-237, 239-240
throughput 6-7, 39, 47-50, 60, 65-68, 71
tracking 50, 73-74, 78, 86, 91, 93-96, 100-104, 166, 205, 207-209, 240-241, 256

U

unconstrained images 156, 162-163, 171, 182
University of A Coruña 74, 190

V

vertical slot 74-77, 91, 96, 101, 103-104, 190-191, 198, 204, 209-210
vertical slot fishway 74-76, 91, 96, 190, 198, 204
vertical slot fishways 74-75, 77, 101, 103-104, 190-191, 209-210
video subtitling 136, 140, 150-151
Virtex5 board 20, 31-32, 41
Virtex V 1, 3
vision-based applications 47-48, 59, 65
vision techniques 74, 100, 103, 191-192, 198, 205-206, 209

W

water resources 75

X

Xilinx 1, 3, 20, 30-32

Printed in the United States
By Bookmasters